A HISTORY OF THE TWENTIETH CENTURY

BRYN O'CALLAGHAN

Longman
London and New York

British Library Cataloguing in Publication Data

O'Callaghan, Bryn
   A history of the Twentieth century.
   1. History, Modern — 20th century
   2. World politics — 20th century
   I. Title
   909.82   D443

   ISBN 0–582–33172–2

Library of Congress Cataloging in Publication Data

O'Callaghan, Bryn.
   A history of the twentieth century.

   Includes index.
   Summary: Traces the history of the world from the
beginning of the twentieth century to the present day
with emphasis on major events and their
consequences.
   1. History, Modern — 20th century — Juvenile
literature.
   [1. History, Modern — 20th century] I. Title. II. Title:
History of the 20th century.
   D421.025 1987   909.82   87–3858
   ISBN 0–582–33172–2

Acknowledgements

We are grateful to the following for permission to reproduce photographs: ANP Foto, page 225 centre; Associated Newspapers Group plc, pages 28, 29 above, 38, 47, 201 below, 206 above, 301; Atlas World Press Review, page 147; AP/Wide World Photos, pages 133, 134; B.T. Batsford Ltd, page 90; BBC Hulton Picture Library, pages 12, 32 left, 53 right, 206 below, 297, 308 (1), 310 (14, 15); The Bettman Archive, pages 308 (4), 310 (17); British Library, page 77 above; Camera Press, pages 39, 202 left (photo: Daniel Drooz), 220, 251 below, 307 below (photo: Edouard Boubat/Réalités), 309 (5, 8, 9 (photo: Ritchie), 10, 11 (photo: Ollie Atkins)), 310 (13, 18), 311 (20 (photo: Sana), 21 (photo: Marion Kaplan), 22, 23 (photo: Paul Conklin), 25 (photo: N.V. Edwards)); J. Allan Cash Ltd, page 307 above; Chicago Historical Society, page 105; Cormac/ Information on Ireland, page 196; *Daily Express*, page 196; *Daily Mirror*, page 190, 239 above, 261; Steef Davidson, page 17; Detroit Free Press, page 211; *The Economist*, page 283; Edimedia, pages 42 right, 201 above; Mary Evans Picture Library, page 269 right; from the Collections of Henry Ford Museum and Greenfield Village, page 100; Foreign Language Press, Peking, page 274; The Fotomas Index, pages 63, 82; The Gleaner Company Ltd, page 162; *The Guardian*, page 243; from *Herblock's Here and Now*, (Simon and Schuster, 1955) page 139; John Hillelson Agency Ltd, page 58 below, 288 (photo: Yosuhe Yamahata/Magnum); Imperial War Museum, pages 9, 185, 232; David King Collection, page 78; Library of Congress, page 120; Mail Newspapers plc, pages 28, 29 above, 38, 140, 189, 201 below, 206 above, 301; Mansell Collection, pages 25, 39; *The News Chronicle*, page 189; *New York News Inc.*, page 128; Novosti Press Agency, pages 62, 67, 72, 77 below, 87; Papas' Studio, page 215; Philadelphia Museum of Art: Lola Downin Peck Fund, page 108 right; The Photo Source, pages 29 below, 58 above, 303, 308 (2, 3, 16), 309 (6, 7), 310 (12), 311 (19); Popperfoto, pages 21, 279; *Punch*, pages 46, 171, 175, 257, 287, 311 (24); Donald Read: *Documents from Edwardian England 1901–1915*, Methuen and Co., page 167; Franklin D. Roosevelt Library, page 125; St Louis Post Dispatch, pages 37 (Fitzpatrick), 221 above (Engelhardt); School of Slavonic and East European Studies, University of London, page 50; Ronald Searle, page 251 above; *The Sunday Times*, page 226; Tennessee Valley Authority, page 121; *Time*, page 135; *The Times* page 239 below; Time-Life, page 116; Topham, pages 24, 101, 104, 108 left, 191, 210, 180; Ullstein Bilderdienst, page 32 right; Underwood and Underwood, page 112; United Nations, page 202 right; United Palestine Appeal, 1938, page 231; Universal Press Syndicate, pages 152, 153, 221 below; UPI/Bettman Newsphotos, page 113; US Army Archives, Washington DC, page 42 left; K.S. Wheelan, page 180; The Wiener Library, page 53 left.

We are unable to trace copyright holders of the following and would be grateful for any information that would enable us to do so: pages 117, 129, 181, 225 below, 269 left.

Table from *The Pilgrim Trust*, 'Men Without Work', Cambridge University Press, 1938; table from M. Kidron and R. Segal: *The New State of the World Atlas*, Pluto Projects, a division of Visionslide Ltd, 1984 and B.P. Price: *The Hamlyn World Atlas*, Hamlyn, 1980; diagrams and map from *Illustrated Reference Book of Modern History*, ed. James Mitchell, Windward, 1982; charts from S. Fothergill and J. Vincent: *The State of the Nation*, Pluto Projects, 1985.

CONTENTS

PART ONE
EUROPE

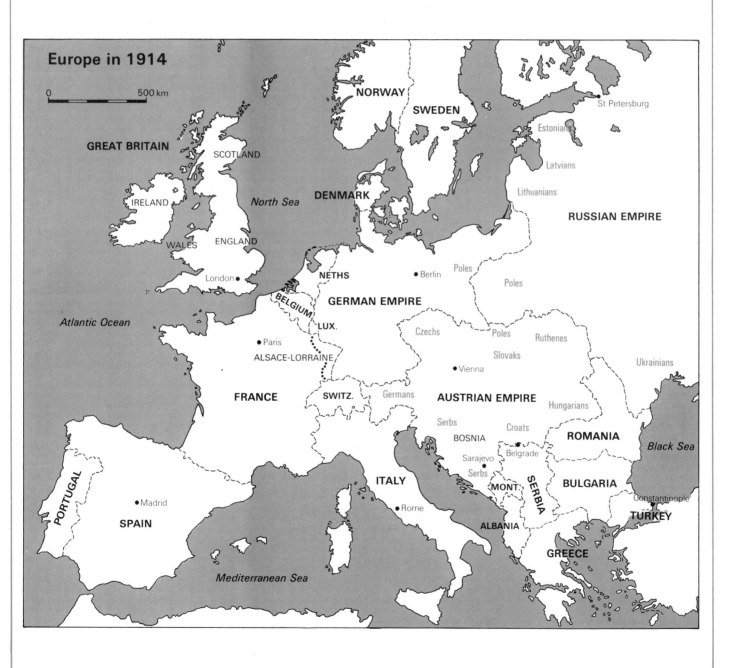

Europe in 1914

0   500 km

GREAT BRITAIN

SCOTLAND

IRELAND

WALES   ENGLAND

North Sea

London ●

Atlantic Ocean

NORWAY

SWEDEN

DENMARK

NETHS

BELGIUM

LUX.

● Paris

ALSACE-LORRAINE

FRANCE

SWITZ.   Germans

St Petersburg

Estonians

Latvians

Lithuanians

RUSSIAN EMPIRE

● Berlin   Poles

Poles

Czechs   Poles   Ruthenes

Slovaks

Ukrainians

● Vienna

AUSTRIAN EMPIRE   Hungarians

Serbs   Croats

BOSNIA

Sarajevo   Belgrade

●   Serbs

ROMANIA   Black Sea

PORTUGAL

● Madrid

SPAIN

ITALY

● Rome

MONT.

SERBIA

BULGARIA

ALBANIA

GREECE

Constantinople

TURKEY

Mediterranean Sea

Sarajevo, 28th June 1914

On the map on the previous page you will find, in the south-east of Europe, the town of Sarajevo. Today it is in Yugoslavia. In summer 1914 it was part of Bosnia, a district of the Austrian Empire.

On 28th June 1914, Sarajevo had an important visitor – Archduke Franz Ferdinand, the heir to the throne of the Austrian Empire. Crowds gathered to cheer the Archduke as he drove through the streets with his wife.

Among the crowds was a nineteen-year-old student, Gavrilo Princip. He was not in Sarajevo to cheer the Archduke. He was there to kill him.

Princip was a Serb, like most of the people of Bosnia. Many Serbs disliked being ruled by the Austrians. They wanted to be part of a nearby country called Serbia, where Serbs ruled themselves. A band of revolutionaries called the Young Bosnians was ready to fight for this. Princip was one of them.

Just before lunch Princip was standing where a side-street joined two main roads. A black open car swung round the corner into the side-street and stopped. The driver had taken a wrong turning.

Princip could hardly believe his eyes. On the rear seat sat the Archduke. Drawing an automatic pistol from his jacket, Princip stepped forward. From only four steps away, he shot the Archduke through the throat. A second bullet hit the Archduke's wife.

Spectators grabbed the gun and forced Princip to the ground. Too late. Within minutes both the Archduke and his wife were dead.

These two shots from Princip's automatic triggered off the bloodiest slaughter mankind had ever known. To understand why, you need to know about Europe's 'great powers' at this time.

Britain

Britain was one of these great powers. Most of its people worked in factories making goods for sale overseas. Britain was the world's richest trading nation and ruled an empire containing a quarter of the human race.

Merchant ships carried Britain's goods for export and brought back food and raw materials. To protect them, and Britain's many colonies, the Royal Navy's smoke-belching battleships patrolled the oceans. Command of the seas was vital to Britain. Without it, an enemy could starve its island people within a couple of months.

France

Britain's neighbour, France, had a strong army. But, in 1870, France had been defeated in war by Germany. Germany had taken two border areas called Alsace and Lorraine away from France. The French were constantly watching for a chance to win them back.

Germany

Germany had only become one country in 1870. Before then it had been divided into thirty-eight separate states, each with its own government. In 1870 the strongest state, called Prussia, had united them all under its leadership to form the German Empire. The Empire's ruler was Kaiser (Emperor) Wilhelm II.

Like France, Germany had a well trained army. It also had many modern steelworks and factories to make weapons. Germany was always on guard in case the French decided to attack to win back Alsace and Lorraine.

The Kaiser was jealous of Britain. He wanted an empire and a navy as strong as Britain's. So did other Germans. They believed that a big empire and a strong navy were the keys to more trade and power.

Austria

The Austrian Empire was headed by its eighty-four-year-old, bushy-whiskered Emperor, Franz Josef I. He ruled over people of many nationalities – Germans, Hungarians, Czechs, Poles, Serbs. Most of the Empire's power and wealth was in the hands of Germans and Hungarians. This was one reason its other peoples wanted to rule themselves.

Austria's rulers knew that once one group broke away, their whole patchwork empire would start to crumble. They were particularly afraid of the Serbs trying to join Serbia. To prevent this, they were looking for an excuse to crush Serbia.

Russia

The Russian Empire had more land and more people than any other power. Yet in many ways Russia was weak. Most of its people were poor and uneducated. It had few modern mines and factories. The government was badly run and only the Tsar (Emperor) Nicholas II had any real say in it.

Many Russians wanted changes. When Russia was badly beaten in war by Japan in 1904–5 (see Unit 65) they demanded an elected parliament. All they got was a powerless sham called the *Duma*. A growing number of Russians joined revolutionary groups. Their aim was to sweep away the Tsar's rule completely.

Fears and alliances

In the early years of the twentieth century the governments of the great powers grew more fearful. France and Germany each feared an attack by the other. Russia and Austria feared revolutions. All increased their armed forces to guard against such dangers.

They also looked for allies in case of war. By 1914 two groups had formed. Germany and Austria led one, France and Russia the other.

Britain belonged to neither group at first. But in the early 1900s Germany began to build a navy that looked like rivalling Britain's navy. Britain's leaders could only think that Germany intended to challenge their command of the seas. To meet the challenge they began building a powerful new kind of battleship, the Dreadnought.

They also looked for friends abroad. In 1902 they signed a naval treaty with Japan, so that in case of war Britain could bring back most of its own navy to the seas around Europe while Japan protected British possessions in the Far East. Then Britain signed agreements with France and Russia. The agreement with France was the Entente Cordiale (friendly understanding), signed in 1904. Britain's Entente with France's ally, Russia, was signed in 1907.

Germany's rulers started to feel that their country was gradually being surrounded by possible enemies.

The Schlieffen Plan

Europe goes to war, 28th July–4th August 1914

As the map on page 1 shows, the German Empire had frontiers with both France and Russia. If both attacked at the same time, the generals would have to weaken the German army by dividing it.

To deal with this danger a German general, Alfred von Schlieffen, worked out a plan in 1905. Schlieffen reckoned that it would take the Tsar's government several weeks to call up Russia's peasant soldiers from their scattered villages. So, as soon as a war began, most of the German army would attack France. It would march through neutral Belgium to bypass France's main defences, surround the French armies and force France to surrender. Then the German soldiers would turn east and beat the Russians.

The key to the Schlieffen Plan's success was surprise. To achieve this, Germany had to attack first. By 1914 the German generals were looking for the opportunity.

The opportunity came from the barrel of Gavrilo Princip's automatic. His deadly bullet gave the Austrian government the excuse it wanted to attack Serbia. It sent off telegrams to ask the Kaiser if Germany would stand by Austria if the Austrians taught Serbia a lesson. He replied that Germany would. Austria then blamed the government of Serbia for the Archduke's murder.

The Austrians knew that this was a lie. They had sent a special investigator to Sarajevo who had already reported that 'there is nothing to show the complicity (involvement) of the Serbian government'.

But the excuse to crush Serbia was too good to miss. On the evening of 28th July 1914 Austrian guns opened fire on Belgrade, Serbia's capital. They were the first shots in the First World War.

A mixture of fears, war plans and treaties turned Austria's quarrel with Serbia into a war between the great powers. This is how it happened.

Russia had promised to protect Serbia. Now, as a warning to Austria to leave the Serbs alone, she called up her armies. When Germany and Austria heard, they both declared war on Russia (1st August 1914).

But the German generals had no plan for war against Russia except the Schlieffen Plan – and that meant attacking France first. So, on 3rd August, Germany declared war on France as well.

The British government hesitated. Despite the Entente Cordiale of 1904, Britain had not made a firm promise to help France in war. But then, on 4th August 1914, German soldiers marched into Belgium, on the way to attack France.

Years before the British had promised to protect Belgium from attack. So the British government ordered Germany to leave the Belgians alone. It gave the Germans until 11.00 p.m. to reply.

On that warm summer evening of 4th August cheering crowds gathered in Trafalgar Square. The hours ticked by – 9 o'clock, 10 o'clock – no reply. At 11.00 p.m. Big Ben began to strike. When the last echoes died away, Britain was at war.

The great powers

1 Use the map on page 1 to help with the following:
   a) Make a list of Europe's great powers.
   b) Give one reason why: France was unfriendly towards Germany,
       Austria was unfriendly towards Serbia,
       Germany was envious of Britain,
       Britain was suspicious of Germany.
   c) Turn your answers to a) and b) into a diagram.
   d) Explain why Germany feared having to fight France and Russia at the same time.
   e) Explain how Germany's generals planned to deal with this problem.

Some important facts about Europe's great powers in 1914

	Population (millions)	Population of colonies overseas (millions)	Area of colonies overseas (million sq. km.)	Size of army (soldiers)	Size of navy (ships)	Coal produced each year (million tonnes)	Steel produced each year (million tonnes)
Britain	40.8	390.0	27.0	700,000	388	292.0	11.0
France	39.6	50.8	11.0	3,700,000	207	40.0	4.6
Germany	63.0	15.0	2.5	4,200,000	281	277.0	14.0
Austria	50.0	—	—	800,000	67	47.0	5.0
Russia	139.0	—	—	1,200,000	166	36.2	3.6

2 a) Which two countries had the biggest armies? Explain why.
   b) Which two countries had the biggest navies? Explain why.
   c) How were 1) population and 2) coal and steel industries important to a country's ability to make war?
   d) Using your answers to a), b) and c) to help you, suggest why both sides were confident they would win a quick victory.
   e) Use the same information to suggest why in fact neither side might win quickly.

Sarajevo, 28th June 1914

For many years historians believed that this photograph showed Princip being arrested after shooting Franz Ferdinand. Now they are not certain.

3 a) Can you think of any reasons why historians might have doubts?
   b) What do these doubts tell you about the way a historian should set about judging the value of *any* piece of historical evidence?

'It'll be over by Christmas.' That was what many people said when world war started in August 1914. Most of the leaders of the great powers were confident that their side was going to win quickly. The German generals certainly thought so.

The German advance, August 1914

The Schlieffen Plan nearly worked. In August 1914 German armies raced across the open countryside of Belgium and north France. By early September they had reached the River Marne. They were so close to Paris that they could see the Eiffel Tower.

The Battle of the Marne, 1914

The French armies had been retreating, but now they stood firm. Taxi-drivers worked day and night to rush out extra troops from Paris. A small but well trained British Expeditionary Force (BEF) lined up beside the French.

The Battle of the Marne went on for a week. The two sides moved to and fro, sparring like boxers looking for a chance to land a knock-out blow. Neither succeeded. But finally the Germans were forced to retreat 100 kilometres from Paris. The Schlieffen Plan had failed.

Up to the Battle of the Marne the armies had moved swiftly. Now a kind of siege warfare began. It was to go on for the next four years.

Britain, France and Russia were called the Allies, or the Allied powers. Germany and Austria were known as the Central powers.

The war world-wide

Armies fought in many parts of the world as well as in France and Belgium. There were fighting fronts along the borders of the Russian Empire and in Italy, Turkey, and Palestine. The war even spread to Africa and China.

The war on the Western Front

In this unit we shall be looking at the fighting on the 'Western Front', in France and Belgium. All along the Western Front the soldiers on both sides dug networks of trenches in the ground. By the end of 1914 the trenches stretched from the English Channel to the borders of the neutral country of Switzerland.

The trenches were protected in front by tangles of barbed wire. Chattering machine-guns cut down enemy soldiers every time they tried to advance. The land separating the trenches of the two sides was called 'no-man's-land'.

The generals on both sides – the British commander Haig, the French general Joffre and the German general Falkenhayn – tried to smash the enemy by sheer weight of numbers. They sent wave after wave of men charging at the enemy trenches.

Before an attack they plastered the enemy with thousands of high explosive shells. These massive artillery bombardments often went on for days. In winter they turned the heavy soil of no-man's-land into a huge swamp. The mud was so thick that the attacking soldiers could hardly struggle through it and were easy targets for the machine-guns. They were mown down in thousands.

Battles and casualties

The three best-remembered battles in which British soldiers took part were:

Loos (1915) – 50,000 British killed.
The Somme (1916) – 420,000 British killed.
Ypres (1917) – 324,000 British killed.

The bloodiest battle fought by French soldiers was at a fortress town called Verdun. 315,000 of them were killed there in 1916. So were 282,000 German soldiers.

By the time the war ended Germany and Russia had each lost about 1,750,000 men, France 1,350,000 and Britain 750,000. To this day the remains of soldiers killed on the Western Front are still found by French and Belgian farmers ploughing their fields.

In December 1916 David Lloyd George took over as British Prime Minister. People hoped that he would make a better job of organising the country's efforts to win the war.

But for month after month, year after year, the generals went on ordering their men forward to be slaughtered. Their idea was to kill so many of the enemy, no matter what the cost, that sooner or later he would no longer have the strength to fight. The name for a struggle of this kind is a 'war of attrition'.

Many soldiers' greatest ambition was to be wounded just badly enough to be sent on leave. British soldiers called this 'getting a Blighty' – 'Blighty' being their nickname for England.

As the wounded soldiers were carried off the trains bringing them from the Channel ports, they often noticed women doing jobs which before the war had been done by men. On the station women porters and ticket collectors hurried about. On the streets outside they worked as bus conductors and van drivers.

War on the Home Front

Before the war most people had thought that a woman's place was in the home. But so many men were killed on the Western Front that the British government grew desperate for more soldiers. At first it relied on volunteers, eager to take part in what they thought was a great adventure. But as the bodies piled up in the trenches, volunteers did not come forward so eagerly and the government had to start conscription. In 1916 Parliament passed the Military Service Acts. Hundreds of thousands of men between the ages of eighteen and fifty-one had to give up their peace-time jobs and join the army.

In Britain, and in all the fighting countries, women stepped into the gaps left by the men who went to war. Their war was fought on what people called the 'Home Front'.

Thousands of women worked long hours in munitions factories, filling shells with explosives. It was dangerous and unpleasant work. Apart from accidental explosions, the workers often caught diseases such as jaundice from the chemicals they worked with.

After the war European governments showed some appreciation of the women's efforts. Most gave them more legal rights. In Britain a law of 1918 allowed women over thirty to vote in electing Parliament, a right that women called suffragettes had struggled to obtain for years before the war.

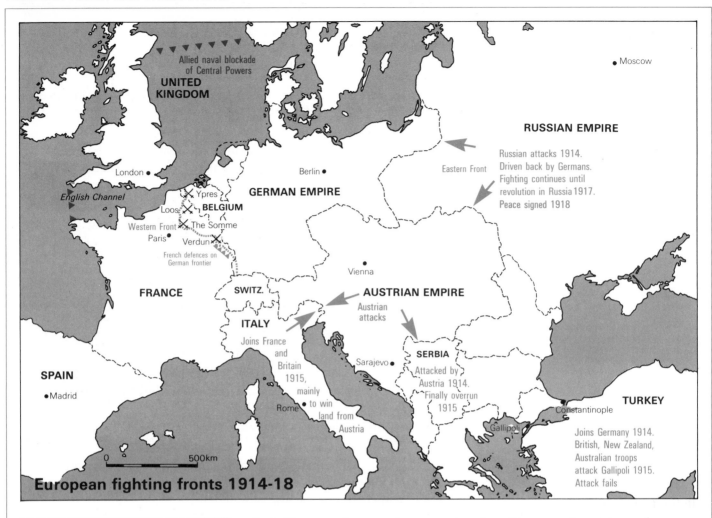

European fighting fronts 1914-18

Labels on map:
- Allied naval blockade of Central Powers
- UNITED KINGDOM
- Moscow
- RUSSIAN EMPIRE
- Berlin
- Eastern Front
- Russian attacks 1914. Driven back by Germans. Fighting continues until revolution in Russia 1917. Peace signed 1918
- GERMAN EMPIRE
- London
- English Channel
- Ypres
- Loos
- BELGIUM
- Western Front — The Somme
- Paris
- Verdun
- French defences on German frontier
- FRANCE
- SWITZ.
- Vienna
- AUSTRIAN EMPIRE
- Austrian attacks
- ITALY
- Joins France and Britain 1915, mainly to win land from Austria
- Sarajevo
- SERBIA
- Attacked by Austria 1914. Finally overrun 1915
- SPAIN
- Madrid
- Rome
- TURKEY
- Constantinople
- Gallipoli
- Joins Germany 1914. British, New Zealand, Australian troops attack Gallipoli 1915. Attack fails
- 0 ___ 500km

The fighting fronts 1914–18

1 a) How was Germany's geographical position an advantage *and* a disadvantage to the Germans?

b) Draw a sketch map to show how the Schlieffen Plan was carried out.

c) Suggest why Britain sent troops to try to land in Turkey in 1915.

d) What problems would Russia have in defending the Eastern Front?

War on the Home Front

On the Home Front, women were praised for their work in factories.

"The greatest honour seems due to those women who, knowing the risks, voluntarily undertake work in the danger houses of factories where high explosives (such as TNT) are handled . . .

TNT poison is absorbed through the skin . . . it is . . . through the hands . . . constantly in contact with the explosive, that the poison is most commonly absorbed.

Cases of death are very rare. More often, the result is skin eruption, short-lived but unpleasant . . . Most frequently the vulnerable part is the liver . . . some supervisors believe that young women who handle TNT are sometimes permanently sterilised by it."

' "W.M.", Women's Greater Sacrifice', *New Statesman*, 3rd February 1917

2 a) Does this work sound healthy/fairly dangerous/very dangerous? Explain your view.

b) Imagine a conversation between a woman who volunteers to do this work and her mother, who wants her to stay as a domestic servant.

Recruitment

This poster first appeared in the streets in 1914. The man in the centre is Lord Kitchener, a popular general the British government had made Minister of War.

3 a) Why did the Ministry of War need to put up posters such as this?
  b) Find two different ways in which the poster is trying to persuade men to join up.

In the trenches

A British officer describes a typical attack in the Battle of the Somme (1916) and fifteen years after the war a soldier remembers the trenches.

"I get up from the ground and whistle. The others rise. We move off at a steady pace. I see rows upon rows of British soldiers lying dead, dying or wounded in no-man's land . . . heaped up masses of British corpses suspended on the German wire, while live men rush forward . . . to swell . . . the numbers in the spider's web."

Unidentified officer in Purnell
History of the Twentieth Century, 1969

"Some men under heavy shell fire would cower down, holding their heads in their hands, moaning and trembling. For myself I wasn't worrying so much if a shell pitched clean amongst us: we would never know anything about it. It was the large flying pieces of a shell bursting a few yards off that I didn't like: they could take arms and legs off, or worst still, rip our bellies open and leave us still living."

Frank Richards, *Old Soldiers Never Die*, 1933

4 a) What did the officer mean by 'the spider's web'?
  b) How does the first passage help to explain why it was so difficult to win a First World War battle?
  c) If you had been with Frank Richards, what would you have wanted to say to a friend who had seen the recruiting poster and decided to join up?
  d) How did the government get recruits for the army after 1916?

War at sea

War in the air

The USA enters the war, 1917

Russia leaves the war, 1918

Attack and counter-attack

Tanks

By 1916 German submarines, or U-boats, were sinking many ships bringing Britain food from abroad. Food supplies were in serious danger.

To deal with the U-boat threat, Lloyd George set up the convoy system. He grouped merchant ships together and sent them to sea with escorts of warships. The convoys fought off the U-boat attacks so many more ships got through with their cargoes.

Aeroplanes also affected life on the home fronts. Both sides used aircraft to observe the enemy's movements and to bomb and machine-gun his trenches. But as the war went on they also used them to bomb civilian populations far away from the battle fronts.

The first air raids on Britain were made in 1915 by huge cigar-shaped German airships called Zeppelins. But the Zeppelins were slow-moving and easy to shoot down. In 1917 the Germans began to use aeroplanes instead. 1413 people died in these air-raids. The British retaliated by making bombing raids on German civilians.

In 1917 German U-boats began attacking American ships carrying supplies to Britain. It was a bad mistake. In April 1917 the American President, Woodrow Wilson, declared war on Germany.

The American declaration of war gave the British and French new hope. They knew now that they could beat Germany – if they could hang on until American soldiers reached Europe. The Germans' only hope was to win before the Americans landed.

Events in Russia gave the Germans their chance. In 1917 revolution broke out there. The Tsar's government was overthrown. A group of communist revolutionaries called Bolsheviks made peace with the Germans in February 1918 (see Unit 17).

The collapse of Russia gave the German generals 400,000 extra soldiers for the Western Front. In the spring of 1918 they flung them into a last huge attack.

The Allies were in great danger, but they hung on grimly. At last, fresh American troops started to reach the battle front. By early summer 250,000 of them a month were arriving. In August 1918 the Allied armies struck back.

Leading their attack was an important new weapon invented by the British – the tank. Hundreds of these armoured monsters crawled over the German trenches. Machine-gun bullets bounced off their sides like peas off a tin can.

On 8th August 1918, near Cambrai in north France, 456 tanks, backed up by Canadian and Australian infantry, advanced for 10 kilometres. The German commander, General Ludendorff, called it 'the black day of the German army'. In the Battle of the Somme it had taken more than four months to advance the same distance.

The German soldiers' will to fight crumbled away as the Allied armies pushed them back. The end came in the autumn.

Armistice, 11th November 1918

Sick of the endless slaughter and near starving, German workers rebelled. The Kaiser fled and a new government took over. The German generals told the new government that they could fight no longer, so it asked the Allies for an armistice – an agreement to stop fighting.

At 11.00 a.m. on 11th November 1918 the guns of the Western Front stopped firing. Austria had surrendered already, so the armistice marked the end of the First World War.

The Weimar Republic

After the armistice some of the rebel German workers tried to set up a communist-style government. But they were crushed by soldiers loyal to the new German government. The German people then voted for a new Parliament – a *Reichstag* – to run the country. Its members met in a town called Weimar. For this reason the new government was known as the Weimar Republic.

Peace negotiations

Early in 1919 the leaders of the countries which had beaten Germany met together in Paris. The three main leaders were Britain's Lloyd George, the Prime Minister of France, Georges Clemençeau, and the US President, Woodrow Wilson.

The Allied leaders agreed quite easily about letting new nations such as Czechoslovakia and Poland take the place of the old Austrian Empire. But they disagreed about how to treat Germany.

President Wilson wanted a treaty that would not leave the Germans with a lot of grudges which might one day tempt them to start a war of revenge. Clemençeau thought differently.

The war had been fought mainly on French soil. The damage was staggering – 750,000 homes destroyed, 23,000 factories, 5000 kilometres of railroad. Then there were France's dead soldiers – 1,350,000 of them. Clemençeau was sure that the only way to make peace last was to leave the Germans so weak that they would never fight again.

Nobody asked the Germans what they thought.

The Versailles Treaty, 1919

At long last the Allied leaders drew up a peace treaty. They called it the Versailles Treaty, after the Palace near Paris where it was signed in May 1919.

The Versailles Treaty took a lot of land off Germany. It also said that Germany could have only a tiny army and no air force or submarines. On top of this, the Germans had to take all the blame for the war and pay for all the damage it had caused. These 'reparation' payments were fixed at hundreds of millions of pounds.

Germans thought the Treaty was harsh and unfair. But they were too weak to start fighting again, so the Weimar government signed.

Many Germans never forgave the Weimar leaders for this. A lot of them joined new political parties which promised to get revenge.

One of these new parties was the National Socialist Party – Nazi for short. Its leader was an ex-soldier in the German army, who swore to destroy both the Weimar Republic and the Versailles Treaty. His name was Adolf Hitler.

The Versailles Treaty

"Germany accepts the responsibility of Germany and her allies for causing all the loss and damage which the Allied . . . Governments and their nationals have been subjected to as a consequence of the war imposed upon them by the aggression of Germany and her allies."

Article 231 of the Versailles Treaty

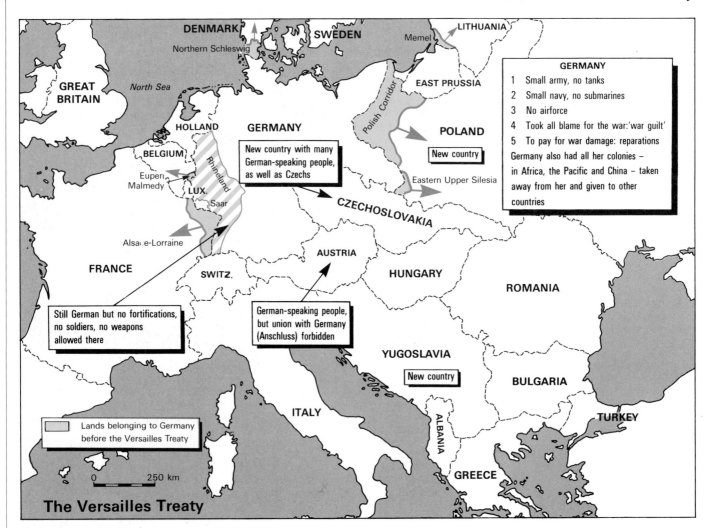

GERMANY
1 Small army, no tanks
2 Small navy, no submarines
3 No airforce
4 Took all blame for the war: 'war guilt'
5 To pay for war damage: reparations
Germany also had all her colonies – in Africa, the Pacific and China – taken away from her and given to other countries

New country with many German-speaking people, as well as Czechs

New country

Still German but no fortifications, no soldiers, no weapons allowed there

German-speaking people, but union with Germany (Anschluss) forbidden

New country

Lands belonging to Germany before the Versailles Treaty

0   250 km

The Versailles Treaty

1 a) List all the countries which gained land from Germany by the Treaty.

  b) What do you think were the Allies' aims in taking these lands?

  c) Suggest three ways in which the Treaty weakened German fighting power.

  d) The Allies also made a treaty with the Austrian Empire. Compare this map and that on page 1 to show what was done to the Austrian Empire.

  e) If you had been a French man or woman in the 1920s, which part of the Versailles Treaty would have pleased you most? Explain why.

  f) Read Article 231 of the Treaty very carefully. Can you explain why it was known in the 1920s as the 'war guilt clause'?

  g) Read Unit 1 again. Do you think it was fair to say that the war was caused by 'the aggression of Germany and her allies' (such as the Austrian Empire)? Why or why not?

  h) If you had been German in 1919 what do you think you would have felt about Article 231?

Germany and Versailles

German tanks being broken up in Berlin, 1919.

A German newspaper's opinion of the Versailles Treaty.

"Vengeance! German nation! Today in the Hall of Mirrors at Versailles a disgraceful treaty is being signed. Never forget it! On that spot . . . today German honour is dragged to the grave. Never forget it! The German people, with unceasing labour, will push forward to reconquer that place among the nations of the world to which they are entitled. There will be vengeance for the shame of 1919."

Deutsche Zeitung, 28th June 1919

2 a) Describe what is happening in the photograph.
  b) Explain why this had to be done.
  c) If you had been German in 1919 how would you have felt about this?
  d) Pick three words or short phrases from the *Deutsche Zeitung* extract which you think best sum up the feelings of its writer.
  e) Do you think the *Deutsche Zeitung* believed that it was Clemençeau or Wilson who most influenced the Treaty? Explain your answer.

3 Match the names on the left with the descriptions on the right. Write out the correct sentence and add to each one a sentence of your own.

Armistice	were payments for war damage.
Clemençeau	was the President of the USA in 1919.
Wilson	was the Prime Minister of France in 1919.
Weimar	is where the Treaty ending the war was signed.
Versailles	gave its name to the post-war German government.
Reparations	was an agreement to stop fighting.

Hitler speaks

The beer hall was crowded with people smoking and shouting for more beer. But the young man with the small moustache sat quietly, waiting for his moment. At last it came. Adolf Hitler climbed on to a chair and started to speak.

He began quietly. But soon he worked himself up into a shouting, spitting rage. Some listeners thought that he was crazy. Others were ready to believe anything he told them.

Hitler's message was one of hate. Hate for the Versailles Treaty, for the Weimar Republic, for communists. Hate, above all, for Jews.

Hitler and the Jews

Jews looked and spoke like other Germans, and lived like other Germans. Yet they were different. Many centuries before, their ancestors had come to Europe from Palestine. Modern Jews had kept alive their ancestors' customs and stuck faithfully to their religion.

Some Jews became successful businessmen, doctors, scientists, politicians. It may have been this that first made Hitler hate them. Before the war he had been a poor nobody in the city of Vienna. Plenty of Vienna's many Jews were poor, too. But Hitler envied the rich ones, and his twisted mind blamed them for his problems.

The 'stab in the back'

Now, years later, he blamed them for Germany's problems, too. He claimed that it was Jews and communists who had made Germany lose the war. They had stabbed the country in the back, he said, by persuading the soldiers to stop fighting.

This was a lie. But many Germans were ready to believe the lie. Hitler gave them something they needed – somebody to blame for their troubles.

Hitler's followers

Hitler's Nazi party grew quickly in the early 1920s. Many out of work ex-soldiers joined. It won support, too, from people with small businesses, such as shopkeepers. Many people like these had lost a lot of money due to the war. They thought the Nazis would stop the communists from taking the rest.

Hitler gathered a private army of brown-shirted thugs called the SA. These Nazi 'storm troopers' paraded the streets, beating up socialists and communists and supporters of other rival parties.

In 1923 the Weimar government said that Germany was too poor to pay the reparations demanded by the Allies in the Versailles Treaty. It stopped the payments. A chain of disasters started.

The Ruhr occupation, 1923

French troops marched into the Ruhr, Germany's richest industrial region. They took over its mines to collect the reparations in coal. The Ruhr workers went on strike and the Weimar government backed them by paying their wages. It printed millions of banknotes to do this.

Inflation, 1923

But Germany lacked the real wealth to back the notes. The result was massive inflation. Money lost its buying power. It became so worthless that bakers gave vouchers for loaves to their workers instead of wages. The inflation also wiped out people's savings. Some used bundles of worthless banknotes to light their fires.

The Munich Putsch, 1923

Hitler felt that the time was right to overthrow the Weimar government. His Nazis had a lot of support in Munich, the chief city of Bavaria in the south of Germany. Together with General Ludendorff, Hitler marched on the army headquarters there at the head of 3000 followers.

Armed police were waiting. Rifle fire scattered the Nazi marchers. They broke and ran away.

This attempted rebellion was called the Munich *Putsch* – a German word for an armed rising. Hitler and Ludendorff were put on trial. But they had powerful friends in the government of Bavaria and the army. The judges let Ludendorff go free. They sent Hitler to prison, but he was released nine months later.

Mein Kampf

Despite its failure, the Munich *Putsch* made Hitler's name known all over Germany. The time in prison also gave him the chance to write a book setting out his ideas. He called it *Mein Kampf* – My Struggle. For loyal Nazis *Mein Kampf* became a sort of bible.

Gustav Streseman

After 1924 life got better for the German people. A new Chancellor, or Prime Minister, had taken over the Weimar government. His name was Gustav Streseman. In 1924 he agreed to the Dawes Plan, a scheme to pay off the reparations by instalments. Then he brought in a new kind of money. Prices came down and wages were worth something again. Trade with other countries grew. Germans soon had more work and more food.

Hitler and the Reichstag

With Streseman in charge, people became more contented. Hitler found it more difficult to get them to support his plans to overthrow the government by force. So he changed his tactics. He set out to get more Nazis elected into the German Parliament, or *Reichstag*.

To do this he needed money to start newspapers to spread Nazi ideas and to set up party branches all over the country. He got the money from rich businessmen. They paid Hitler as a sort of insurance policy, to stop the communists from gaining power.

In 1929 Streseman died. The following year trade between the countries of the world started to fall sharply. All over Europe and America millions of workers lost their jobs (see Unit 26).

Germany and the Depression

This world depression, or slump, hit the German people very hard. By 1932 six million of them were out of work. Many felt that democratic government of the Weimar kind had failed.

Some turned to Communism. Even more turned to Hitler. They packed his meetings and cheered his speeches. Most important of all, they voted for him. In elections in 1930 and 1932 the number of Nazis in the *Reichstag* rose from 12 to 230. They had more seats than any other one party.

But votes for the communists were also rising. Hitler claimed that only the Nazis could prevent a communist takeover.

Hitler becomes Chancellor

Field Marshal Hindenburg, Germany's President, believed him. In January 1933 he made Hitler Chancellor of Germany.

Germany and the slump

Votes for the Nazis

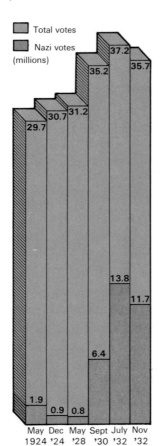

Total votes
Nazi votes
(millions)

29.7	30.7	31.2	35.2	37.2	35.7
1.9	0.9	0.8	6.4	13.8	11.7

May 1924   Dec '24   May '28   Sept '30   July '32   Nov '32

Unemployment in Germany

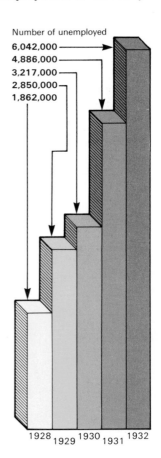

Number of unemployed

6,042,000
4,886,000
3,217,000
2,850,000
1,862,000

1928   1929   1930   1931   1932

A visitor to Germany in the early 1930s describes the effects of the world slump.

"Where two Englishmen will, in nine cases out of ten, begin by discussing sport, two Germans will ask each other why they and their families should go hungry in a world stuffed with food . . . [This] explains the avid interest which all classes in Germany are taking in politics . . .

When men and women in their tens of thousands, will sit for four hours listening to National Socialists, Centre Party men, Socialists, Communists . . . it means that politics have . . . become a matter of bread and butter.

On my last day in Hamburg . . . I ate lunch with some three hundred of the city's unemployed . . . all lucky enough to possess fourpence each – the price of the meal consisting of soup and potatoes . . . and one-fifth of a pound of sausage per person, with bread."

H. H. Tiltman, *Slump! A Study of Stricken Europe Today*, 1932

1 a) How many Germans voted for the Nazis in 1924?
   b) Give two reasons why this many voted for the Nazis at that time.
   c) Nazi support fell between 1924 and 1928. Give two reasons.
   d) How do the unemployment table and the H. H. Tiltman extract help to explain why support for the Nazis grew after 1930?
   e) Suggest two other reasons for the increase in Nazi support after 1930.
   f) Who made Hitler Chancellor of Germany? When and why?

The Nazis

This comic could be read in 1930. The title says 'Down with False Slogans and Knuckledusters'. The words below the open mouth read 'The truth is easily ignored in a mouthful of empty words'. The ones below the fist say 'He who isn't able to persuade with facts will try to persuade with brutal acts'.

Josef Goebbels, one of Hitler's chief supporters, wrote this in a Nazi newspaper.

"We will become Reichstag deputies in order to cripple . . . Weimar . . . with its own type of machinery. If democracy is so stupid as to provide us with free tickets . . . that is its own affair . . . We come as enemies! We come like the wolf which breaks into the sheepfold."

J. Goebbels in *Der Angriff* (The Attack), May 1928

In 1924, after the Munich Putsch *had failed, Hitler said this to a friend.*

"Instead of working to achieve power by armed *coup* we shall have to hold our noses and enter the Reichstag . . . Sooner or later we shall have a majority, and after that Germany."

Karl Ludecke, *I Knew Hitler*, 1938

2 a) How can you tell that the comic is about the Nazi party?

  b) Is it for or against the Nazis? Give reasons for your opinion.

  c) Write captions to explain what is happening in the pictures below the title.

  d) Can we trust this comic by itself as reliable evidence of how Nazis really behaved? Give reasons for your view.

  e) Do the extracts from Goebbels and Hitler support the views expressed by the comic? Explain your answer.

  f) What can we learn from Goebbels and Hitler of Nazi plans to win power?

  g) Explain why they decided on this way of gaining power.

Il Duce

People had been gathering for hours, streaming into the great square in the centre of the city. They had come to see and hear the man who liked them to call him simply '*Il Duce*' – The Leader.

At last he appeared, strutting out on to a balcony high above their heads. Thickset and balding, he was dressed in a showy uniform. His face was set in a stern, scowling expression.

Thrusting out his chin, Il Duce began a violent, bragging speech. As he spoke the carefully rehearsed crowd chanted the same word over and over again – '*Du-ce!*', '*Du-ce!*', '*Du-ce!*'

Il Duce's real name was Benito Mussolini. From 1922 to 1943 he was the ruler of Italy.

Italy and the First World War

In the First World War the Italians had fought on the side of the Allies. In return for this the British and French had secretly promised them lots of new land.

But the Versailles Treaty gave Italy next to nothing. Many Italians felt cheated and angry.

They had other problems after the war, too. Millions were out of work. Prices were rising and many people were short of food.

Strike broke out. In some places workers took over the factories and set up committees of workers called soviets to run them.

Better-off Italians grew worried. They feared a communist revolution like the one that had taken place in Russia (see Unit 16). Italy needed a strong leader, they said, to stop the disorder. They found their man in Benito Mussolini.

Mussolini and the Fascists

Mussolini ran a newspaper in Milan, a city in the north of Italy. He sneered at the idea of running a country by discussing things in parliament. What Italy needed, he said, was someone to give out orders and see that they were obeyed – a dictator.

In 1919 Mussolini started a new political party. He called it the Fascist Party. Mussolini took the name from an object called the '*fasces*', a bundle of sticks tied round an axe. In the ancient Roman Empire the *fasces* had been a sort of badge, to show the rulers' power. The sticks stood for unity and the axe for strength.

Mussolini's fascists were a mixed bunch. Some were ex-soldiers, angry because they couldn't get jobs. Others were students, on the look-out for excitement. Others were just bullies who wanted a chance to push other people around.

Mussolini kitted out his fascists in black shirts. They roamed the streets looking for trouble. Communists and trade unionists were their favourite targets. Mob battles became common. Between 1920 and 1923 nearly 3000 people were killed in fighting in the streets.

Many well-to-do Italians were pleased with Mussolini's fascists. Landowners gave him money. Factory owners gave him lorries. His Fascist Party grew as more people joined it.

In 1922 Mussolini decided that he was strong enough to grab

The March on Rome, 1922

The Matteotti affair, 1924

Mussolini the dictator

The Lateran Treaties, 1929

Mussolini's achievements

power by force. He ordered thousands of fascists from all over Italy to march on Rome, Italy's capital city. His idea was to scare the King into making him, Mussolini, the head of the government.

The army could easily have scattered the fascists. But the King decided it was either them or the communists. He didn't arrest Mussolini. He made him Prime Minister instead.

At first other political parties shared power with the fascists. Then came the Matteotti affair.

Giacomo Matteotti was a leading socialist member of Parliament. He was well known for speeches which attacked Mussolini and the fascists.

On 10th June 1924 Matteotti disappeared. Three days later his body was found in a shallow grave 20 kilometres from Rome. Fascist extremists had murdered him.

Anti-fascists made strong protests and demanded that the King should sack Mussolini. But the King refused and the murderers were let off.

Getting away with the Matteotti murder gave Mussolini confidence. He set out to make himself all-powerful.

He closed down newspapers which dared to criticise him. He told workers that they were no longer allowed to go on strike. He abolished other political parties. Their leaders were put in prison or forced to leave the country. Only the fascists and their wealthy backers had any say in how the country was run.

Mussolini's biggest triumph came in 1929. Practically all Italians were strong Roman Catholics. In 1929 Mussolini signed the Lateran Treaties with their religious leader, the Pope.

The deal was this. Mussolini recognised Roman Catholicism as Italy's official religion. He gave the Church full control over religious teaching in schools. He also accepted the Pope's right to rule his own independent state – the tiny Vatican City in Rome.

Mussolini got a lot in return. The Catholic Church now accepted his way of running Italy. If the Pope was ready to accept Mussolini, how could any ordinary Italian Catholic oppose him?

It was now that Mussolini stopped using his ordinary name and became simply 'Il Duce'. He taught the Italian people to see him as a kind of superman who would make Italy great and powerful. They were expected to admire his strength, his bravery, his cleverness.

It was all show. Mussolini the superman did not exist. The real Mussolini was clever, but he was also lazy and inefficient.

Yet Mussolini's Italy was not all empty bragging. Engineers built fine new roads between the main cities. They drained swamps to use as farmland. They built huge dams to produce electricity.

Seeing these improvements, many foreigners came to admire Mussolini. Here was a man who knew how to get things done.

One of these admirers was another would-be dictator – Adolf Hitler. Practically all the methods that Hitler later used to get power in Germany were copied from Mussolini.

Italy and the Depression

In the early 1930s Mussolini ran into problems. The world slump hit Italy. Unemployment grew. Most Italians were poor already. Now their lives became harder still.

Mussolini used an old trick to take people's minds off their troubles. He plunged Italy into warlike adventures overseas.

The Abyssinian War, 1935

In 1935 he sent Italian soldiers and airmen to attack a poor African country called Ethiopia, or Abyssinia. Italian bombs and poison gas slaughtered the badly armed Abyssinians in thousands.

The peaceful nations of the world protested. But they did nothing. Within six months the victorious Italians were riding in triumph into Abyssinia's capital, Addis Ababa.

The Rome-Berlin Axis, 1936

One of the few world leaders who did not condemn Mussolini for attacking Abyssinia was Hitler. This helped to draw Italy and Germany closer together. In 1936 the two men signed an agreement. They set up what they called the Rome-Berlin Axis (see Unit 7). In this Axis agreement they promised to support one another in quarrels with other nations.

The Spanish Civil War, 1936–9

In the same year a general named Franco started a civil war in Spain (see Unit 7). He wanted to set himself up as a dictator.

The League of Nations asked other countries not to interfere in the Spanish Civil War. But Mussolini sent Italian soldiers to fight for Franco. Hitler sent warplanes and airmen. Between them they made sure that when the Spanish Civil War ended in 1939, Franco was the winner.

Mussolini and the Second World War

A few months later Hitler attacked Poland and started the Second World War (see Unit 8). Despite the Axis agreement, Mussolini kept out of the war. He thought that Hitler would lose.

When Hitler smashed the French and British armies in 1940, Mussolini changed his mind. Believing now that Hitler was going to win, he joined in to get a share of the loot. He sent Italian soldiers to invade France from the south.

It was the worst mistake Mussolini ever made. He shared in Hitler's victories, all right. But he shared in his downfall, too.

In the next three years the Italian armed forces were beaten again and again. Thousands of soldiers were taken prisoner or killed, especially in the fighting in North Africa (see Unit 9).

Mussolini's fall, 1943

In 1943 American and British troops crossed from Africa and invaded Italy. The endless defeats turned the Italian people against Mussolini. In 1943 he was overthrown and put in prison.

Hitler sent paratroops who set Mussolini free. But Mussolini's end was only months away.

Mussolini's death, 1945

In April 1945 Mussolini was captured while trying to escape from the advancing American and British soldiers. He was shot and killed by anti-fascist Italian guerilla fighters, or partisans. They also killed his mistress.

The partisans took both bodies to Milan, the city where the dead dictator's rise to fame had started. There they hung them upside down in the main square for people to jeer and spit at.

Fascism

A collection of slogans which summed up what good fascists should believe.

"Believe! Obey! Fight!
He who has steel has bread!
Nothing has ever been won in history without bloodshed!
Better to live one day like a lion than a hundred years like a sheep!
A minute on the battlefield is worth a lifetime of peace!"

1 a) Choose two of the slogans and explain what they mean.
  b) Name two countries where Mussolini tried to put them into practice.
  c) Think up two slogans that might have been used *against* the fascists.

This extract comes from a book about Mussolini written in 1971 by the historian Richard Collier. The photograph was taken in 1943.

" 'Be proud to live in Mussolini's time', exhorted the posters, in letters as huge as a house. Who but Mussolini had set up 1,700 mountain and seaside summer camps for city children? Who gave the Italians the eight-hour working day and . . . insurance benefits for the old, the unemployed and the disabled? Only Mussolini, who proclaimed that his one ambition was to make the Italians 'strong, prosperous, great and free'.

. . . At morning prayers, pupils intoned [prayed] solemnly, 'I believe in the supreme Duce, creator of the Blackshirts and in Jesus Christ, the sole protector'.

. . . Pope Pius XI warned, 'Sooner or later the people end by throwing down idols'."

Richard Collier, *Duce*, 1971

The bodies of Mussolini and his mistress photographed in Milan in 1945.

2 a) List five reasons given by Richard Collier to explain why Mussolini was popular with the Italians. Turn your list into a picture diagram.
  b) What did Mussolini say was his one ambition?
  c) Do you think this was truly his one ambition? Give reasons for your opinion.
  d) Can we get any idea about what Richard Collier thought of Mussolini? Explain your answer.
  e) How did the Pope's warning to Mussolini come true?
  f) Look at the photograph. Why do you think that admiration for Mussolini had turned to such hatred?

The Reichstag fire, 1933

'Fire! Fire! The *Reichstag* is on fire!'

The news ran like fire itself through the snowy streets of Berlin. By half past nine on the cold, raw February night in 1933 an excited crowd had gathered on the snowy pavement outside the German Parliament building. They watched red and orange flames licking through the glowing metal girders of its great dome.

When Hitler heard the news he could hardly believe his luck. Hindenburg had made him Chancellor only a month before. Ever since he had been looking for an excuse to crush anyone who disagreed with Nazi policies. Now he had it.

The fire was the work of the communists, shouted Hitler's supporters. They were plotting a revolution! The only way to stop them was to give Hitler the power to do anything he thought was necessary.

The story about a communist plot was quite untrue. But most people believed it. Perhaps this isn't surprising. The police caught a communist called Van der Lubbe inside the *Reichstag* with matches and firelighters in his pockets.

What people didn't realise was that Van der Lubbe was mentally ill. Starting the fire was entirely his own idea.

Thousands of communists were arrested on the same night as the fire. So were many others the Nazis had grudges against.

The last election

With his rivals on the run, Hitler decided the time was right for a snap election. He called the election for just six days after the fire; hardly time for other parties to get organised, but enough for his storm troopers to beat up their followers. When the votes were counted, the Nazis were the biggest party in the *Reichstag*. But the German people had not all been fooled. Seventeen million voted for Hitler's men – but twenty million voted against.

That did not stop Hitler. Communist members were arrested or forced into hiding. When the other members came to the opening meeting of the *Reichstag* in its temporary home in an opera house, they found the corridors lined with SA troops.

The Enabling Act, 1933

Ninety-four socialist members stood up to Hitler. The rest of the *Reichstag* voted for a law which gave him the power to do what he liked: the Enabling Act. The Nazi rule of terror had begun.

Hitler banned all rival political parties and threw their leaders into prison. He closed down newspapers which had dared to criticise him, did away with trade unions and forbade workers to strike.

The Night of the Long Knives, 1934

Then he turned on some of his own men. The SA storm troopers had played a vital part in bringing Hitler to power. But he decided that they were getting too big for their boots.

Their leader, Ernst Roehm, wanted to form them into a new German army. But Hitler wanted the support of the old German army. He was afraid that Roehm's plan for an SA takeover of the army would turn its officers against him.

Hitler got rid of Roehm and many other leaders of the SA on the 'Night of the Long Knives' in June 1934. He had them dragged from their beds and murdered.

The Gestapo

The 'Night of the Long Knives' left nobody to challenge Hitler. His rivals were now dead or safely locked up. He set up a secret police force called the Gestapo to make sure things stayed like this.

The Gestapo had spies everywhere – in shops, in factories, in blocks of flats, even in schools. A word against Hitler or the Nazis meant instant arrest.

Thousands of people disappeared behind the barbed-wire fences of special prisons called concentration camps. Many were never heard of again.

The Jews and the Nuremberg Laws, 1935

The Jews suffered most. Just to be a Jew became a crime in Hitler's Germany. Their synagogues, or churches, were burned down. Their homes were smashed up by Nazi thugs. Customers were ordered away from their shops.

Finally Hitler took away all their rights. They could not hold government jobs or work as lawyers, doctors or teachers. These unjust 'laws' were called the Nuremberg Laws, after the city where Hitler announced them in 1935.

Thousands of Jews gave up everything and fled from Germany in fear of their lives. They were the lucky ones. Millions who stayed were finally herded into Nazi concentration camps. Here they were later murdered in cold blood – men, women, children, even babies.

Goebbels and propaganda

Despite Hitler's brutal treatment of Jews and other innocent people, most Germans supported his rule. A flood of clever publicity, or propaganda, organised by Josef Goebbels made sure of this.

Goebbels' job was to see that newspapers, magazines, films and the radio all hammered home the same simple message – that Adolf Hitler was Germany's saviour, a superman who could do no wrong.

Goebbels' propaganda was brilliantly convincing. Millions of Germans believed every word of it. Hitler, the ordinary man, became the *Fuehrer* – the Leader.

Why was Hitler popular?

A more solid reason for Hitler's popularity was that he found people jobs again. In less than four years he cut the number out of work from six million to under one million.

Hitler took many men into his growing army. He put thousands more to work in factories making tanks and aeroplanes. Others built a network of fine new roads, called *autobahns*, across Germany.

In return for steady jobs most Germans were ready to turn a blind eye to the concentration camps and other unpleasant sides of Hitler's rule.

The *Fuehrer* seemed to be building a strong and prosperous new Germany out of the ruins of the old one. What did freedom to vote for somebody different matter if you had a job and felt that your country was recovering at last from the shame of defeat in 1918?

The Reichstag fire

Communists arrested by Hitler's SA after the Reichstag *fire, 1933.*

1 Write two paragraphs:
   First, imagine that Hitler is speaking privately to a Nazi friend. Write what he might have said about how he intended to use the fire. For the second, imagine Hitler speaking over the radio to the German people. Now write what he might have told *them* about the fire.

The Jews

An American writer who lived in Germany in the 1930s describes how Jews were being treated in 1936. Later, things became much worse.

"Over the doors of the grocery and butchery shops, the bakeries and the dairies, were signs, 'Jews not admitted'. Pharmacies would not sell them drugs or medicine . . . Hotels would not give them a night's lodgings. And always, wherever they went, were the taunting signs 'Jews Enter This Place at Their Own Risk' . . . At a sharp bend in the road near Ludwigshafen was a sign, 'Drive Carefully! Sharp Curve! Jews 75 Miles an Hour!' "

W. L. Shirer, *The Rise and Fall of the Third Reich*, 1960

An English writer living in Berlin in 1933 describes his street.

"Uniformed Nazis strode hither and thither with serious set faces . . . The newspaper readers by the café turned their heads to watch them pass and smiled and seemed pleased.
   . . . They were pleased because . . . Hitler had promised to protect the small tradesmen, because their newspapers told them that the good times were coming. They were suddenly proud of being blond. And they thrilled . . . because the Jews, their business rivals, and the Marxists had been found guilty of the defeat and the inflation and were going to catch it.
   The town was full of whispers. They told of illegal midnight arrests, of prisoners tortured . . . They were drowned by the loud, angry voice of the Government, contradicting through its thousand mouths."

Christopher Isherwood, *Mr Norris Changes Trains*, 1935

2 a) From William Shirer's account, list the ways in which Jews were being treated badly in the middle of the 1930s.
   b) In what other ways did the Nazis persecute Jews?
   c) How does Christopher Isherwood's account explain why so few people protested about the ways Jews were treated?

Propaganda

Rallies were important in the Nazi propaganda effort. The picture shows a rally in Nuremberg in 1935. Below, an eyewitness describes another rally.

Extracts from Mein Kampf, *the book Hitler wrote in prison in 1923.*

"The masses of the people are a crowd of human children who are constantly wavering between one idea and another . . .

The chief purpose [of propaganda] is to convince the masses, whose understanding needs to be given time [to] absorb information; only constant repetition will finally succeed in imprinting an idea on the memory of a crowd."

A. Hitler, *Mein Kampf*, 1924

"Twelve huge SA bands played military marches with beautiful precision and terrifying power.

Behind the bands, on the field itself, solid squares of uniformed men were ranged in strict military order, thousands strong.

Suddenly, a wave surged over the crowd, it leaned forward, a word was tossed from man to man: Hitler is coming! Hitler is here!

A blare of trumpets rent the air and a hundred thousand people leaped to their feet. All eyes were turned towards the stand, awaiting the approach of the Fuehrer.

There was a low rumble of excitement and then the crowd burst into a tremendous ovation, the 'Heils' swelling until they were like the roar of a mighty cataract."

K. Ludecke, *I Knew Hitler*, 1938

3 a) What do you understand by the word 'propaganda'?
  b) Give examples which you think 1) support and 2) contradict what Hitler wrote about most people's intelligence in *Mein Kampf*.
  c) Read the second extract and then say how you can tell that the photograph was taken at a Nazi rally.
  d) Hitler is in the centre of the photograph, on the stand. Why do you think he is standing there?
  e) Can you see any connection between the extracts from *Mein Kampf* and the picture and description of the rally?

The League of Nations

Peace. In the years after the First World War millions of people everywhere wanted it more than anything. To keep the peace, the Versailles Treaty set up the League of Nations.

The idea of the League was to give leaders from all the countries of the world somewhere to talk over their differences. People hoped that this would make wars less likely, especially if the strongest countries agreed to cut back on weapons and fighting men.

Forty-two countries joined the League of Nations when it started in 1920 and others joined later. The League's headquarters were in Geneva, Switzerland. All member countries sent representatives to meetings there.

The League's weaknesses and strengths

The League's members promised to settle their quarrels without using arms. If any member broke this promise the League could call upon other members to stop trading with it. The idea was that these trade 'sanctions' would force it to stop making war.

What would happen if a country refused to obey? The answer was nothing. The League could only advise countries what to do. It had no power to make them. This was a fatal weakness.

Another difficulty for the League was that several important countries were not members. The United States did not join because it wanted to keep out of other countries' quarrels. Soviet Russia was kept out because the other members did not like Communism.

Germany, too, was kept out at first, although it joined later. But most Germans never like the League. To them it was just a disguise for the enemies who had beaten them in the war and still wanted to keep them down.

In the 1920s the League organised help for the many thousands of refugees left homeless by the war. It also worked to stamp out evils such as slavery and trading in dangerous drugs. But its main job of keeping the world at peace grew more and more difficult.

Japan attacks Manchuria, 1931

In 1931 the Japanese army attacked Manchuria (see Unit 65). Manchuria was part of China, Japan's huge but feeble neighbour. The Japanese wanted to grab its rich coal-mines and fertile farmlands.

The League told the Japanese to stop. But the Japanese went on with the attack, brought Manchuria under their rule and walked out of the League.

Disarmament fails, 1933

By now the League's hopes for disarmament were crumbling. It organised meeting after meeting to discuss the matter. All these disarmament conferences failed. Everybody was afraid to take the risk of disarming first.

The last big disarmament conference began in Geneva in February 1932. In October 1933 Hitler's spokesman there walked out. He said that the other nations were just trying to keep Germany weak.

The Geneva Conference broke up and its members never met again. From now on many countries started increasing their armed forces as fast as they could.

Italy attacks Abyssinia, 1935

In 1935 the League of Nations was tested again. The Italian dictator, Mussolini, attacked a poor, badly armed African country called Abyssinia (see Unit 5).

The League tried to stop Mussolini's attack by telling its members not to trade with Italy. But the trade sanctions did not work. Anyway, they did not include oil, the most vital supply of all for modern war.

Member countries went on trading with Italy and Mussolini went on with the war. In less than a year Abyssinia was under his rule.

Mussolini never forgave the League for trying to interfere in Abyssinia. In 1937 he followed the example of the Japanese and walked out.

Italy, Japan and Germany

Italy and Japan – and Germany, too – were alike in other ways at this time. The leaders of all three nations glorified war. They did this partly to take their people's minds off the fact that they were often poor and without jobs.

They all taught their people, too, to see themselves as members of super races, with the right to conquer and rule over other 'inferior' nations and races.

Finally, they all believed in 'totalitarian' types of government. This means governments which try to stamp out any rival views and look upon human beings as of no importance except as servants of the state.

The Rome-Berlin Axis, 1936

In 1936 Mussolini and Hitler signed an agreement setting up what they called the Rome-Berlin Axis. An axis is a line joining two points together. The two dictators used the word to tell the world that Germany and Italy would support one another in quarrels with other nations. In 1937 Japan joined the Axis.

The failure of the disarmament conferences, the wars in Manchuria and Abyssinia, the Axis agreements – all these made people realise that the League of Nations was not strong enough to keep the world at peace.

The Spanish Civil War, 1936–9

In 1936 a civil war broke out in Spain. General Franco led the Nationalists, who wanted to overthrow the elected government of the Spanish Republic. Franco was supported by the army, leaders of the Catholic Church and landowners. The Republic was backed by socialists, trade unionists and Spain's small communist party.

The League of Nations asked other countries not to interfere in the Spanish Civil War. But Mussolini sent soldiers to help Franco, while Hitler sent war planes. On the other side, volunteers from all over the world travelled to Spain to form an International Brigade to fight for the Republic. Stalin, too, sent help to the Republic's fighters.

But by 1939 Franco had won the Spanish Civil War. Another totalitarian leader was in power.

The League

1 The seven statements below are all about the League of Nations. Three of them are false.

a) Pick out these false statements and change them for true ones on the same subject.

b) Copy out all seven true statements, adding a sentence to each one to explain it more fully.

The League of Nations was set up by the Treaty of Versailles.

Some important countries were not members of the League.

To keep peace in the world, the League had its own army.

The League condemned the Japanese for attacking Manchuria.

The League supported Mussolini's attack on Abyssinia.

The League organised many successful disarmament conferences.

By the late 1930s the League had very little influence.

Disarmament

David Low was one of the most famous political cartoonists in the world in the 1930s. He drew this cartoon for the London Evening Standard *in May 1933 after the last big disarmament conference had broken down.*

THE CONFERENCE EXCUSES ITSELF

2 a) Who do the two groups of animals represent?

b) How does David Low show the relationship between them?

c) What reasons is the crocodile giving for the failure of the conference? Why does he seem to be crying as he speaks?

d) What do you think the cartoonist believed were the real reasons why disarmament failed? What evidence from these years could you use to support or contradict him?

e) Draw a picture diagram to show the main wars that broke out in various parts of the world in the 1930s.

f) Many people in the 1930s believed that the only way to make war less likely was for the countries of the world to disarm. Do you agree?

g) What are the main problems today which make it difficult to reach agreement about disarmament? Do you believe they could be overcome?

Italy, Japan and Germany

In this Evening Standard *cartoon in January 1936 David Low gave his view about the behaviour of Italy, Japan and Germany.*

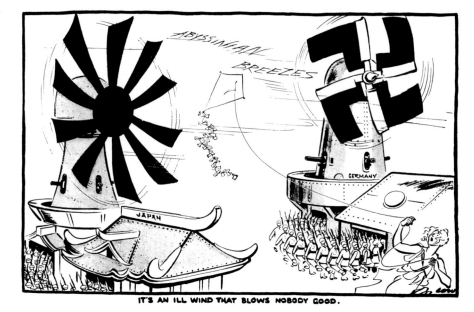

IT'S AN ILL WIND THAT BLOWS NOBODY GOOD.

3 a) How would you know that the windmills represented Germany and Japan, even if they had no names on them?

b) What military policy is David Low saying that Germany and Japan were following? What evidence was there to support this view?

c) In what other ways were Germany and Japan alike at this time?

d) Explain what David Low meant by the 'Abyssinian breezes'. Why are these breezes making the sails of the windmill turn so fast?

e) Look at the caption to the cartoon. What warning is it trying to give?

f) Is the cartoon biased in any way? Give reasons for your answer.

Spain

August 1936. The Spanish town of Barcelona during a pause in fighting in the Spanish Civil War.

4 a) What can you learn about the nature of the Civil War from this picture?

b) Do you think these women were on the side of the Republicans or Franco? Explain your answer.

c) Many people saw the Spanish Civil War as a sort of rehearsal for the Second World War. How does the photograph support that view?

Hitler's aims

The tall granite column stood on the German border with Poland. Chiselled deep into the hard stone were the words:

> 'Never forget, German, what blind hate stole from thee. Wait for the hour to avenge the crime of the bleeding frontier!'

The monument on the Polish frontier was a reminder of one of Adolf Hitler's most important promises to the German people – to win back the lands taken away from Germany by the Versailles Treaty (see map on page 12).

Hitler made other promises. One was to unite all of Europe's German- speaking people under his rule. Another was to gain lands – *lebensraum* or 'room to live' – for Germany in the east of Europe.

Hitler knew that keeping these promises meant risking war. The first meant taking land away from Poland. The second meant taking over Austria and parts of Czechoslovakia. The third was the most dangerous of all, for it meant taking land from the USSR.

Hitler rearms, 1935

In 1935 Hitler began to strengthen the German army. He gave orders that all young men had to serve for a time as soldiers. He started to build a strong air force.

These actions were forbidden by the Versailles Treaty, which had aimed above all to keep Germany too weak to make war. But a lot of people in other countries now thought that the Versailles Treaty had been unfair to Germany. So neither Britain nor France did anything to stop Hitler rearming.

Hitler occupies the Rhineland, 1936

Next to France is a part of Germany called the Rhineland. To make France safer from German attack the Treaty of Versailles had said that the Rhineland must be 'demilitarized' – Germany must never build fortifications or keep weapons or soldiers there.

In 1936 Hitler took a gamble. He ordered his new army to march into the Rhineland. He admitted later, 'The forty-eight hours after the march into the Rhineland were the most nerve-racking of my life'.

No wonder. His army was still weak. He ordered his generals to retreat if the French tried to stop them.

He need not have worried. The leaders of France and Britain protested, but that was all. Hitler won control of the Rhineland without firing a shot.

Hitler's easy success in the Rhineland gave him confidence. So did his Axis agreement with Italy and Japan (see Unit 7).

Anschluss with Austria, 1938

In March 1938, Hitler ordered his soldiers to march again. This time their destination was Austria, a country of German-speaking people. Hitler's excuse was that his army had to keep order there.

In April Austria was bullied into a union, or *Anschluss*, with Germany. The Treaty of Versailles had forbidden the *Anschluss*, but again nobody tried to stop Hitler. After all, most people argued, the people of both the Rhineland and Austria were Germans anyway. Why shouldn't Hitler rule them?

Czechoslovakia, 1938–9

Hitler's next target was Czechoslovakia, another neighbour of Germany's. He ordered the Czechs to hand over part of their country called the Sudetenland. Many Germans lived here. Hitler wanted it also because of its factories and coal-mines.

The Czechs said no and prepared to fight. Their country was only small, but they had a strong army. France had promised help, too, if ever the Germans attacked.

But France did not want a war. Nor did its ally, Britain. The British Prime Minister, Neville Chamberlain, thought there was no need for one anyway. He was sure that once Hitler had the Germans of the Sudetenland under his rule he would give no more trouble.

The Munich Agreement, 1938

In September 1938 Chamberlain and the French Prime Minister, Daladier, flew to Munich in Germany. Without asking the Czechs they told Hitler that he could have the Sudetenland – provided he left the rest of Czechoslovakia alone. Hitler accepted the offer. The three leaders – plus Mussolini – signed the Munich Agreement.

The Czechs knew that Britain and France had betrayed them. But they had to accept the Munich Agreement. 'We had no other choice', their leader said sadly. 'We were left alone.'

Hitler occupies Czechoslovakia, 1938 and 1939

Hitler's troops marched into the Sudetenland. A few months later he showed that his promises at Munich were worthless. In March 1939 he grabbed the rest of Czechoslovakia.

Up until now the British and French leaders had tried to buy off Hitler by giving him what he wanted. Now they saw that this idea of 'appeasement' had failed. They decided that if Hitler's armies marched again they would have to try to stop him.

Hitler and Poland

Soon after crushing Czechoslovakia Hitler started to threaten Poland. Britain and France quickly promised to help the Poles.

This did not worry Hitler. The British and French leaders were 'little worms', he told his generals. They would let Poland down just as they had done Czechoslovakia.

But Hitler had to take the USSR into account, too. Large parts of Poland had belonged to Russia up to the First World War. The Russians were not likely to stand by while Hitler took them.

The USSR's communist leader, Stalin, tried to get Britain and France to join him in an alliance against Germany. But their leaders disliked communism too much. They turned him down.

The Nazi-Soviet Pact, August 1939

Hitler grabbed his chance. To avoid having to fight the Russians when he attacked Poland, he offered Stalin a deal – to divide Poland between them. Hitler would get western Poland, Stalin the eastern part. Stalin accepted. The Nazi-Soviet Pact, as the deal was called, was signed on 24th August 1939.

Hitler invades Poland, September 1939

Hitler's way was clear. A week later, at dawn on 1st September, his tanks rumbled into Poland. Two days later, on 3rd September 1939, Britain and France declared war on Germany.

The Second World War had begun.

Munich and after

One of these newspaper photographs was taken in London in September 1938. The other was shot in Prague, the capital of Czechoslovakia, in March 1939.

1 a) How can you work out which photograph was taken in which city?

b) Explain as fully as you can what event links the two pictures.

c) How would you describe the mood of the crowd in each picture? Suggest reasons for the differences in their moods.

This extract from the Daily Express *describes the scene in London. (An earlier Prime Minister had talked about 'peace with honour' after signing an agreement with Germany in 1878.)*

"HUNDREDS OF THOUSANDS OF PEOPLE, IN THREE CHEERING CROWDS, WELCOMED HOME MR. NEVILLE CHAMBERLAIN, THE PRIME MINISTER OF PEACE, LAST NIGHT.

The first was at Hendon Airport, where he landed from Munich. The second was at Buckingham Palace, where the Premier and Mrs Chamberlain went on the balcony with the King and Queen. The third was at No. 10 Downing Street. There the Premier leaned out of a window and said:

'This is the second time in our history that there has come back from Germany to Downing Street peace with honour. I believe it is peace for our time. We thank you from the bottom of our hearts. And now I recommend you to go home and sleep quietly in your beds.' "

Daily Express, 1st October 1938

2 a) How does this account support the evidence in the picture of London?

b) Why did Neville Chamberlain believe the crowds could 'sleep quietly'?

c) Write out what Mr Chamberlain might have said if he had been asked to explain why the Munich agreement had given 'peace in our time'.

d) What name was given to the policy Chamberlain was following? How does the picture of Prague show that it had not worked?

Opinions of Hitler

The first opinion below was written by David Lloyd George, Britain's Prime Minister in the First World War. He wrote it after he visited Germany in 1936 and talked to Hitler. The second is from a letter by Thomas Mann, a great German writer who was also Jewish.

"As to his popularity, especially among the youth of Germany, there can be no manner of doubt. The old trust him; the young idolise him . . . It is the worship of a national hero who has saved his country . . . from all her oppressors.

The idea of a Germany intimidating Europe . . . that its army might march across frontiers forms no part of the new vision . . . The Germans . . . no longer have the desire . . . to invade any other land."

D. Lloyd George, *Daily Express*, 17th November 1936

"The sole possible aim and purpose of the National Socialist system can only be this: to prepare the German people for the 'coming war' . . . to make the German people into a widely obedient, uncritical instrument of war, blind and fanatic in its ignorance."

T. Mann, Letter to the Dean of the University of Bonn,
1st January 1937

3 a) What did   1) Lloyd George and   2) Thomas Mann believe Hitler's intentions were? Why do you think their opinions were so different?

b) If you had read both sets of opinions at the time they were written, which writer would you have thought was more likely to be right? (Remember that you would not have known what would happen after January 1937.)

Hitler's record

What did Hitler really intend? Anyone could have read the first extract below. The second was secret until German records were captured at the end of the Second World War. It is from a talk Hitler gave to German newspaper editors in October 1938.

"The soil on which we now live was not a gift bestowed by Heaven on our forefathers . . . they had to conquer it by risking their lives. So also in the future our people will not obtain territory, . . . as a favour from other people, but will have to win it by the power of a triumphant sword.

We National Socialists . . . turn our eyes towards the lands of the East . . . when we speak of new territory . . . we think of Russia."

A. Hitler, *Mein Kampf*, 1924

"Circumstances have obliged me to speak, for a decade or more, of almost nothing but peace . . . It has now, however, become necessary to submit the German people to a gradual change of its . . . state of mind and to make it plain that there are things which . . . *must* be achieved by means of force."

A. Hitler, secret speech, 10th November 1938

4 a) How much do you learn of Hitler's intentions towards other countries from the *Mein Kampf* extract?

b) Does it support Thomas Mann's or Lloyd George's view?

c) What do you think were the 'circumstances' which Hitler told the editors had obliged him to speak of peace for ten years or more?

d) What evidence can you find in this unit's text and sources that 'speaking of peace' had paid off for Hitler?

Blitzkrieg on Poland, September 1939

It took Hitler less than three weeks to conquer Poland. For one thing, his army was bigger. For another, it was more modern. Even more important, his generals used it in a completely new way.

Columns of tanks and armoured vehicles, supported by dive-bombers, smashed through key points in the Polish defences. The Polish soldiers found themselves cut off from their supplies and surrounded on all sides by Germans. They had to surrender.

The Germans called this new fast-moving way of fighting the 'lightning attack' or *blitzkrieg*.

Phoney War, 1939–40

For seven months after Hitler's conquest of Poland all was quiet. French and British troops gathered along Germany's western border, but they did not attack. Nor did the Germans.

The reason for this was that some leaders on both sides hoped that a peace might be arranged if no more fighting took place. These months of waiting were called the 'Phoney War'.

Dunkirk and the fall of France, 1940

But by May 1940 Hitler was tired of waiting. In another *blitzkrieg* his tanks smashed through the French and British defences.

In a few weeks German soldiers overran Holland, Belgium and France. The British army was forced back to the sea at a French port called Dunkirk. Hundreds of boats, large and small, crossed the sea from Britain on a rescue mission to the French coast.

On the Dunkirk beaches both the boats and the soldiers they had come to rescue were bombed and machine-gunned by Hitler's war planes. But the boats ferried over 300,000 soldiers across the English Channel to safety.

The Dunkirk evacuation saved the British army. But it could not save France. In June 1940 the French government surrendered. The Germany army moved in and took over most of the country.

Battle of Britain, 1940

Hitler now expected the British to make peace. But a new Prime Minister, Winston Churchill, said they would fight on. Hitler ordered his air force, the *Luftwaffe*, to attack. The air battle which followed became known as the Battle of Britain.

Hitler's idea was to soften Britain up for invasion by his army. His aim was to destroy the Royal Air Force to stop it from sinking his invasion ships as they crossed the English Channel.

The *Luftwaffe* began its attacks on 13th August 1940. Its main targets were RAF airfields in the south of England. By the end of August a thousand German bombers were attacking every day. The RAF was losing aircraft and pilots faster than it could replace them.

Then RAF planes bombed Berlin, Hitler's capital city. He was furious. To get his revenge he told his pilots to switch their attack from the RAF airfields to London.

The Blitz, 1940–1

The British called the big German air attacks on London the 'Blitz'. They killed many thousands of people. Thousands saw their homes blown to bits. The same thing happened to other British cities.

But the Blitz saved the RAF. With its airfields free from attack it grew stronger every day. Damaged aircraft were repaired or replaced. New pilots were trained. RAF fighters like the Spitfire and the Hurricane shot down more and more German aircraft every week.

By the end of September 1940 Hitler saw that he had lost the Battle of Britain. He had to call off his plans to invade.

For a time the Blitz on London and other cities went on. Then, in the summer of 1941, it stopped. Hitler needed his bombers for something else. On 22nd June 1941 he invaded the USSR.

Hitler attacks the USSR, June 1941

Do you remember Hitler's Pact with Stalin (see Unit 8)? Hitler had never intended this to last. Now that he had conquered Poland and France he no longer needed Stalin's friendship.

One reason Hitler attacked the USSR was to crush communism, which he hated. More important still, he wanted the living space or *lebensraum* in the east that he had promised the German people – the USSR's rich farmlands, coal-mines and oil wells. He intended to kill off the Russian people or turn them into slaves. In the parts of the USSR that his armies conquered he did exactly that.

Operation Barbarossa

The Germans code-named their attack Operation Barbarossa. Hitler hoped the name would be lucky. It came from a warlike German emperor who had been famous for conquering other lands eight hundred years earlier.

Operation Barbarossa took the Russians completely by surprise. The Germans drove them back everywhere. Millions of Russian soldiers were killed or captured. On 16th September alone more than half a million surrendered near the town of Kiev.

By the end of the year the German armies were only 30 kilometres from Moscow. Then a new enemy appeared to face them – the Russian winter.

First came heavy rain, turning the countryside into a sea of mud. Tanks, guns, everything on wheels was bogged down. Then came snow and icy cold. The Germans were not prepared for such weather. Their clothes could not keep out the Russian frost. Their guns froze. They had to light fires under their tanks to start them.

Then fresh Russian armies counter-attacked. At the end of 1941 the German advance ground to a halt.

The Battle of Stalingrad, 1942–3

In the spring of 1942 Hitler's armies attacked again. But now the Russians were ready for them. They fought back hard with well-equipped new armies.

Hitler's main target in 1942 was the Caucasus, an oil-rich area in the south of the USSR. Blocking his way was the city of Stalingrad. The German Sixth Army fought desperately to capture it.

But the Russians defended every street, every house, every room. The battle for Stalingrad went on without pause for five months. The city became a smoking graveyard with men fighting on top.

Then, in November 1942, two Russian armies closed around Stalingrad like a pair of huge pincers. 250,000 German soldiers were trapped in the city. Hitler was too conceited to let his soldiers try to fight their way out and retreat. They died in thousands. On 2nd February 1943 the last ragged survivors surrendered.

Hitler's defeat at Stalingrad marked the end of his dream of conquering the USSR. The Russians started to drive back his soldiers towards Germany.

By now things were going wrong for Hitler everywhere.

The Battle of El Alamein, 1942

A German army led by a general called Rommel was fighting the British in the deserts of North Africa. In October 1942 the two sides fought a fierce battle near a tiny village in Egypt called El Alamein. British and Commonwealth soldiers under General Montgomery forced Rommel to retreat. This was the beginning of the end for the Germans in North Africa.

In December 1941 Hitler had declared war on the USA to support his ally, Japan (see Unit 65). Now, in November 1942, an American army under General Eisenhower invaded North Africa to help Montgomery to finish off Rommel. In May 1943 the last German soldiers there surrendered. The desert war was over.

Invasion of Italy, 1943

In July 1943 the British and American armies moved on, across the Mediterranean Sea, to invade Italy. The angry Italian people turned on Mussolini, the man who had promised them victory, and overthrew him (see Unit 5). In September a new Italian government made peace with the invaders.

Hitler rushed German troops to Italy to plug the gap. By spring 1944 he was defending the approaches to his empire against the advancing Russians in the east, against the Allies in Italy, and waiting for another blow that he knew would come soon in the west.

Overlord and D Day, June 1944

All over the south of England that spring tanks rumbled through country lanes as General Eisenhower gathered massive forces to invade Normandy in German-occupied France. The invasion was code-named Operation Overlord.

Overlord began in the early hours of 6th June 1944 – D (for Deliverance) Day as it was called. Hundreds of landing-craft nosed onto the flat Normandy beaches to empty their loads of men and weapons.

The German soldiers fought hard to push the invaders back into the sea. But they failed. By the end of July 1944 Allied soldiers had broken out from the D Day beaches and were racing across France.

By now Hitler's armies were falling back everywhere.

Germany surrenders, 1945

The end came in the spring of 1945. Russian soldiers had fought their way across eastern Europe and were deep inside Germany. In April they met British and American troops advancing eastwards on the banks of the River Elbe in the middle of Germany.

In his bunker headquarters beneath the ruins of Berlin Hitler could hear the noise of battle as the Russians fought their way street by street towards him. On 30 April he shot himself.

German soldiers everywhere laid down their weapons. Hitler's war was over.

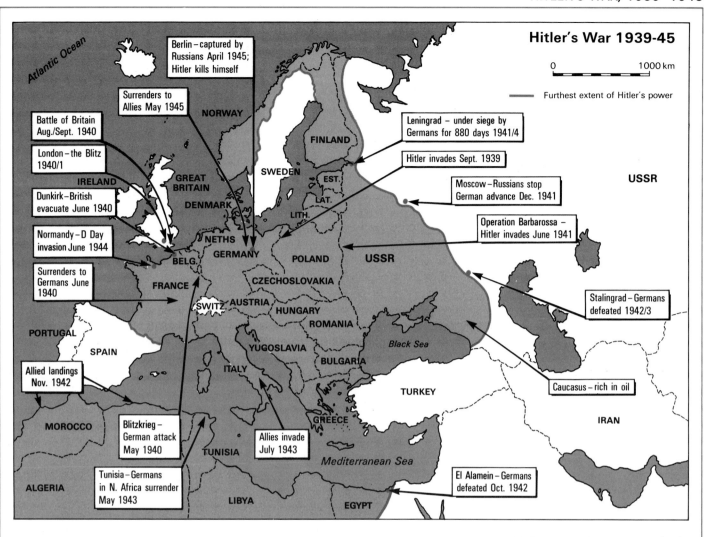

Hitler's War 1939-45

0   1000 km

—— Furthest extent of Hitler's power

Berlin – captured by Russians April 1945; Hitler kills himself

Surrenders to Allies May 1945

Battle of Britain Aug./Sept. 1940

London – the Blitz 1940/1

Dunkirk – British evacuate June 1940

Normandy – D Day invasion June 1944

Surrenders to Germans June 1940

Allied landings Nov. 1942

Blitzkrieg – German attack May 1940

Tunisia – Germans in N. Africa surrender May 1943

Allies invade July 1943

El Alamein – Germans defeated Oct. 1942

Leningrad – under siege by Germans for 880 days 1941/4

Hitler invades Sept. 1939

Moscow – Russians stop German advance Dec. 1941

Operation Barbarossa – Hitler invades June 1941

Stalingrad – Germans defeated 1942/3

Caucasus – rich in oil

Atlantic Ocean · NORWAY · FINLAND · SWEDEN · EST. · LAT. · LITH. · IRELAND · GREAT BRITAIN · DENMARK · NETHS · BELG. · GERMANY · POLAND · USSR · USSR · CZECHOSLOVAKIA · FRANCE · SWITZ · AUSTRIA · HUNGARY · ROMANIA · YUGOSLAVIA · *Black Sea* · BULGARIA · ITALY · TURKEY · GREECE · PORTUGAL · SPAIN · MOROCCO · TUNISIA · *Mediterranean Sea* · ALGERIA · LIBYA · EGYPT · IRAN

Hitler's war, 1939–45

1 Put these events of the Second World War into the correct order. Then write two sentences about each to show its importance.

The Normandy invasion	The Dunkirk evacuation
The Battle of El Alamein	Operation Barbarossa
The Battle of Stalingrad	The invasion of Poland
The *blitzkrieg* of 1940	The Battle of Britain
Hitler's suicide	The surrender of Italy

This cartoon by Daniel Fitzpatrick was printed in an American newspaper, the St Louis Post Dispatch, *on 24th August 1939.*

2 a) What is the cartoonist saying is about to happen?

b) In which ways was he right?

c) The artist called his cartoon 'Next'. Explain why.

d) Give the cartoon a new title of your own.

POLAND

The Battle of Stalingrad

A German soldier wrote this letter towards the end of the Battle of Stalingrad. It was confiscated by the German Army and not delivered.

"So now you know that I am not coming back. Break it gently to Mother and Father. It has given me a terrible shock and the worst possible doubts about everything . . . Once I was strong and believed; now I am small and unbelieving. Much of what is going on here I shall never know about; but even the little bit I am in on is too much to stomach. Nobody can tell me that comrades died with words like 'Germany' or 'Heil Hitler' on their lips . . . the last word a man speaks goes out to his mother or the person he loves most, or else it is merely a cry for help. I have already seen hundreds fall and die, and many, like myself, were in the Hitler Youth . . .

The Fuehrer has solemnly promised to get us out of here. This has been read out to us, and we all firmly believe it . . . If what we were promised is not true, then Germany will be lost, for no other promises can be kept after that."

Unknown German soldier, letter from Stalingrad, January 1943

3 Imagine you are a young German soldier trapped at Stalingrad. You have been brought up to believe that Hitler is a superman and that war is glamorous and exciting. You have just realised that Hitler has refused to let your army try to escape so you have only a few hours to live. What are your thoughts: about Hitler, the war, your own life?

   Either write them as if you are making the last entry in your diary; *or* work with a partner to write out or improvise your last conversation.

This cartoon by David Low appeared in a British newspaper, the Evening Standard, *in January 1943, just as the Battle of Stalingrad was coming to an end.*

4 a) What nationality are the soldiers shown in the cartoon?
   b) Which country does the hammer and sickle represent?
   c) What is Low suggesting will happen to the soldiers?
   d) Explain how the artist was proved right by events.
   e) Give the cartoon a new title of your own.

HAMMER AND SICKLE

Total war

Dead and injured in the Second World War.

	Military	**Civilian**
USSR	7,500,000	10,000,000
Germany	3,500,000	700,000
France	250,000	350,000
Great Britain	326,000	62,000
USA	300,000	Nil

Bomb damage in a London suburb, 1940.

A photograph taken in a Nazi concentration camp after it was entered by British troops in 1945. They were too late to save many of the prisoners. The Nazis had tortured and starved them to death. Millions died, especially Jews, in dozens of these camps. The British troops are making SS men load the starved corpses onto lorries to be taken away for burial. German civilians are being made to watch what is happening.

5 a) Use the table to draw a bar graph showing how many fighting men and women and how many civilians each country lost in the war.

b) Which country suffered more people killed or injured than any other? Can you suggest any reasons for this?

c) Which country had no civilian deaths? Can you explain why?

d) Use the photographs to suggest why more civilians were killed than in any previous war. What other reasons can you think of?

e) Who do you think was to blame for the terrible crimes in the concentration camps: 1) Hitler and the Nazi leaders, 2) the guards in the camps, 3) the German people as a whole? Give reasons for your view.

Ruin

Rivalry

The Iron Curtain

Containment and the Truman Doctrine

Divided Germany

How hungry would you have to be to cut your next meal from the body of a dead horse in the street? That is what the people in the photograph on page 42 are doing.

The photograph was taken in Germany in 1945. It shows one of the biggest problems facing people all over Europe at the end of the Second World War – hunger.

It was not the only one. Millions of people were without homes. Bombs and shells had blasted their houses or flats into rubble.

Millions more had fled from advancing enemy armies or had been driven out when their homelands were given to other countries. These 'refugees' grabbed what they could carry and took to the roads, searching for somewhere where they would be safe.

By 1947 the war had been over for two years. But times were little better. Food, homes, jobs – people were still desperately short of all of them. And that was not all. They were scared that at any moment another war might start.

The countries which had fought together to defeat Hitler's Germany had fallen out. The two strongest ones, the USA and the USSR, were now watching each other with suspicion. A 'Cold War' was starting between them (see Unit 48).

The Russian dictator, Stalin, knew that many Americans hated the USSR's communist way of life. He thought that the USA might attack the USSR at any moment with atomic bombs. The American President, Truman, was just as suspicious. He suspected that Stalin wanted to take Hitler's place as master of Europe.

The Russian soldiers who had driven Hitler's armies out of the east of Europe had helped communists to take over the governments in country after country there. Poland, Hungary, Romania, Bulgaria, Yugoslavia – all had communists in control by 1946. Britain's wartime leader, Winston Churchill, spoke of an 'Iron Curtain' across the continent, separating these communist-ruled lands of East Europe from those of the West.

President Truman decided to use American money and military power to stop communism from spreading further. He did this for the first time in 1947 when he helped the government of Greece to beat a communist army in a civil war.

From this time on the idea of 'containing' communism – that is, using American power to stop it from spreading – became the main aim of the USA in dealing with the rest of the world. Because Truman started containment it is sometimes called the Truman Doctrine.

Germany was the place where rivalry between the Americans and the Russians was fiercest (see Unit 12).

After the war the Allies had divided Germany into four parts called zones (see Unit 12). Each zone was run by one of the main countries which had beaten Germany – the USSR, the USA, Britain and France.

Deep inside the Russian zone lay Berlin, Germany's old capital. But Berlin did not all belong to the USSR. It, too, was divided into four parts, called sectors.

The Berlin Blockade and Airlift, 1948–9

To link the three western sectors of Berlin with the outside world, the Russians promised to let goods and people travel freely through their zone. But in 1948 they blocked all the land routes into the western sectors. Their aim was to make it impossible for the Western powers to feed the people of their sectors and provide them with fuel. They wanted to get the whole of Berlin under their control.

The Western powers decided they were not going to let this happen. American and British planes started to fly in supplies for the people of Berlin – an average of 13,000 tonnes a day. This 'Berlin Airlift' went on for a year. By May 1949 Stalin knew that his plan had failed. He called off the blockade.

Setting up NATO, 1949

The Berlin Blockade increased fears that Stalin was planning to attack Western Europe. To guard against this, in 1949 the United States persuaded most West European nations to join it in a military alliance called the North Atlantic Treaty Organisation (NATO). The idea was that if any member of NATO was attacked by the Russians, all the others would help it to fight back.

The Warsaw Pact, 1955

NATO soon had powerful combined land, sea and air forces equipped by the Americans. Six years later the Russians organised the communist nations of Eastern Europe into a similar military alliance called the Warsaw Pact. They did this in 1955, after West Germany became a NATO member (see Unit 12).

But President Truman knew that more than tanks and guns were needed to stop the spread of communism. People had to be given food, homes, jobs. Then, he believed, they would not be tempted to turn to the communist way of doing things to get a better life.

Marshall Aid, 1947–52

The United States had all the things that Europe needed – food, fuel, raw materials, machines. The Americans knew that the Europeans could not afford to buy these goods. So, in 1947, they offered to give them what they needed.

The scheme was announced by George Marshall, the American Secretary of State. It was named the Marshall Plan after him. The extracts on page 43 suggest why the Americans introduced it.

The Russians were offered help, too. But they claimed that the Marshall Plan was simply a plot to increase American power and refused to have anything to do with it. They made sure that none of the East European countries they controlled took part either.

But the countries of Western Europe jumped at Marshall's offer. For the next five years, from 1947 to 1952, a flood of American food, machinery and raw materials poured across the Atlantic Ocean.

It was like giving a dying man a blood transfusion. Marshall Aid brought food, shelter and jobs to millions of despairing people. By the start of the 1950s Western Europe was back on its feet again.

Ruin

*The photograph (below left) was taken in a German town in 1945.
The painting (below right) of 1946 shows how a Polish artist was affected
by the war's destruction of Warsaw.*

1 a) Imagine you had to survive in conditions like those in the
photograph. List the other problems you would have to face as well as
hunger and describe how you would tackle them.

b) What do you think the artist is trying to say about war? Do you think
he is successful in putting his message over?

c) Which of the two pictures do you feel tells you more about the effects
of war? Try to explain why.

Displaced persons

*A report describes a camp for DPs or Displaced Persons (refugees) which
Allied troops set up in a German town in the last month of the war.*

"The DP camp was in a five-floor block of the Siemens and Halcke
factory. All other parts of this factory had been bombed and were a heap of
debris. The town has just been taken and, of course, there is no light or
water. It is a dead town with no inhabitants – only ruins, stench of burned
things and dead . . .

We took over the place from another unit on the morning of April 5. The
situation was critical and nearly out of control. More than 3,000 people of
different nationalities were all mixed together. There were no
lavatories . . . too little food; looting on a universal scale."

Report to Supreme Headquarters, Allied Expeditionary Force, April 1945

2 a) Use the first paragraph to explain why camps for DPs were needed
when Allied soldiers occupied a town.

b) Use the second paragraph to explain the ways in which 'the situation
was critical'.

c) Imagine you are in charge of such a camp. What steps would you take
to deal with the situation?

Marshall Aid in Britain

A British writer explained the effect of the Marshall Plan on Britain.

"In 1948 the British Board of Trade estimated that, without Marshall Aid, the weekly rations of bacon, butter, cheese and sugar would have had to be cut by a third. Supplies of cotton goods in the shops would have dwindled to almost nothing; the shortage of timber would have reduced house building from 200,000 to 50,000 a year; the scarcity of other raw materials would have caused widespread unemployment."

Richard Mayne, *Post War*, 1983

3 a) Use the extract to list the benefits to Britain from the Marshall Plan.
  b) Turn your list into a picture diagram.

Marshall Aid and the Americans

In an interview in 1961 former American President Harry Truman explained why he decided to set up the Marshall Plan in 1947.

"The reports from Europe that I got in the winter and spring of 1946 and 47, I doubt if things in Europe had ever been worse, in the Middle Ages maybe but not in modern times. People are starving, and they were cold because there wasn't enough coal, and tuberculosis was breaking out. There had been food riots in France and Italy, everywhere . . .

And something had to be done. The United States had to do it, and the people and the Congress had to be persuaded that it was necessary.

I said, 'If we don't do it, Europe will have the worst depression in its history, and I don't know how many hundreds of thousands of people will starve to death, and we don't want to have a thing like that on our consciences . . .

And I said, 'If we let Europe go down the drain, then we're going to have a bad depression in this country'."

Merle Miller, *Plain Speaking*, 1976

An American historian gave this different view in 1980.

"The Marshall Plan of 1948, which gave $16 billion in economic aid to Western European countries in four years, had an economic aim: to build up markets for American exports.

The Marshall Plan also had a political motive. The Communist Parties of Italy and France were strong, and the United States decided to use pressure and money to keep Communists out of cabinets in those countries."

Howard Zinn, *A People's History of the United States*, 1980

4 a) List the reasons given in the two sources to explain why the Americans gave Marshall Aid to Europe.
  b) Pick out the ways in which the two accounts 1) agree and 2) disagree.
  c) Does either extract give a more favourable view of American actions than the other? If so, can you suggest reasons why?
  d) Explain which account you think is likely to be the more dependable.
  e) If you had been an American politician in 1948, which of the reasons given in the two extracts would have done most to persuade you to vote for the Marshall Plan? Explain your choice.

Steel

Think of a world without steel.

No cars. No bridges. No high-rise flats. No washing-machines. No tanks either. Or machine-guns. Or bombers.

Useful stuff, steel. Dangerous, though. After the Second World War nobody was more aware of this than the political leaders of Western Europe.

Europe's biggest steel works were in Germany. They had built the tanks and bombers for Hitler's *blitzkriegs*. Germany's neighbours did not want this to happen again. On the other hand, they all needed German-made steel to rebuild their industries.

Two main ingredients are needed to make steel – coal and iron-ore. You can see from the map (page 46) that in the Saar district of Germany there is plenty of coal. Just across the border, in France, there is lots of iron-ore.

The Schuman Plan, 1950

In 1950 Robert Schuman, who was the Foreign Minister of France, suggested a way to bring together the German coal and the French iron-ore without fuss about customs duties. So far as coal and steel were concerned, why not do away with frontiers?

France, Germany and any neighbouring country that wanted to join them would then be able to get their raw materials more easily. They would also have more customers to buy their coal and steel.

Schuman's plan had another attraction, too. The countries who joined in would become so dependent on one another that none of them, Germany included, would be able to use its industries to threaten its neighbours.

The ECSC, 1952

Six governments agreed to the Schuman Plan. In 1952 France, Western Germany, Belgium, Holland, Luxembourg and Italy set up an organisation called the European Coal and Steel Community (ECSC). The 'Six' agreed to run their separate coal and steel industries as one big concern. They asked Britain to join. But the British government thought that Britain could do better on its own.

The ECSC worked very well. The amount of the steel produced, and the trade of its members, both grew quickly. The Six began to plan other ways to work together.

The Treaty of Rome and the EEC, 1957

In 1957 their leaders signed the Treaty of Rome. Again they asked Britain to join, and again Britain refused.

The Treaty of Rome said that all the countries of the Six would be able to buy and sell goods freely inside each other's frontiers. They would become one huge 'Common Market' with more than 180 million customers. The official name of this Common Market was the European Economic Community, or EEC.

By the early 1970s the peoples of the Six were better off than ever before in their histories. Between 1960 and 1965 their countries' industrial outputs rose twice as fast as Britain's.

One reason for this was that factories in the EEC countries had lots more customers for their goods. An Italian factory, for example, could sell its goods just as freely in France or Germany as it could to customers in Italy.

Britain and the EEC

Because Britain was not a member of the EEC its factories could not do this. By the 1960s many people in Britain were starting to think that, for Britain to prosper, it too needed to join the EEC.

Britain applied to join the EEC twice in the 1960s, in 1961 and 1967. Each time the application was turned down. It was President de Gaulle, the French leader, who said no.

De Gaulle said that Britain had too many ties with the USA and the Commonwealth to be a loyal EEC member. But many people thought that his real reason for saying no was his fear that Britain might lessen France's influence in the EEC.

In 1969 de Gaulle resigned as President of France. Britain again applied to join the EEC and was accepted. It became a member in 1973. Denmark and the Republic of Ireland joined at the same time, Greece joined in 1981, and Spain and Portugal in 1986.

A united Europe?

From the very beginning some people have seen the EEC as much more than a trading arrangement. Men like Robert Schuman hoped that it would grow into a kind of United States of Europe, with one government for the people of all its nations.

A step towards this was taken in 1979 when voters in all the EEC countries went to the polls to elect members of a European Parliament.

But national rivalries between members of the EEC continued to be very strong. They often fell out, for example, about how much money each should put into the EEC's kitty and how much it should be able to draw out.

The CAP

The British government – and people – complained, too, about the vast amounts of money the EEC paid out every year on its Common Agricultural Policy (CAP). Most went to French and German farmers as extra payments called 'subsidies'. The British claimed that the CAP encouraged farmers to produce food that nobody wanted to buy. The result was so-called 'mountains' of unwanted butter and 'lakes' of unwanted wine and milk.

The EEC in the 1970s and 1980s

As the well-off 1960s gave way to the out-of-work 1970s and 1980s, more people criticised the EEC. What use was it, they complained, if it could not make sure that people had jobs?

This criticism was unfair. Many of the reasons for unemployment, such as the much higher cost of oil in the 1970s, were out of the control of the EEC. It did what it could to provide jobs. Many parts of Britain got new factories built with EEC money. Between 1975 and 1981 Britain received £650 million in grants.

In the middle of the 1980s the countries of Western Europe were more united than most people would have dreamed possible forty years earlier. But the goal of a United States of Europe was still a long way away.

Iron and steel

This cartoon 'Pont de la Concorde' (Bridge of Agreement) was printed in Punch *magazine in 1950.*

The map shows the main areas where coal and iron are mined in Western Europe.

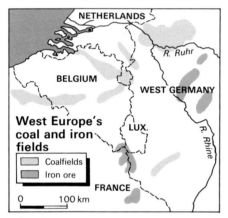

PONT DE LA CONCORDE

1 a) Who are the men in the cartoon? Which countries do they represent?

  b) Why are they shown with a gulf of suspicion between them?

  c) What does the girder represent? How did its supporters hope it would bridge the gulf?

  d) How does the map explain other ways in which members hoped to gain from the ECSC?

  e) Does the cartoonist think the Schuman Plan is   1) good, 2) bad,   3) a mixture of good and bad? Explain your answer.

  f) Do you think that what happened in later years showed that Schuman was right? Give reasons for your opinion.

Industrial output

Between 1954 and 1960 the total value of the goods turned out by Britain's factories, mines and other industries grew by 16 per cent. In the same years, France's 'industrial output', as this is called, grew by 30 per cent and West Germany's by 49 per cent.

2 a) Draw a bar graph for each country to show these figures.

  b) How much bigger was the increase in France's percentage output than Britain's? How much bigger was West Germany's than Britain's?

  c) Look at page 45. What did many people think was a reason for Britain's lower industrial output?

Britain and the EEC

This cartoon 'No entry' was printed in a British newspaper in 1963.

3 a) Which country is represented by the driver? What does he want, and why?

b) Who does the man with the long nose represent? What is he doing?

c) Give two reasons why the man with the big nose is acting like this.

d) In which year could the car be said to have reached its destination?

e) Think of an alternative title for the cartoon.

Steps to unity

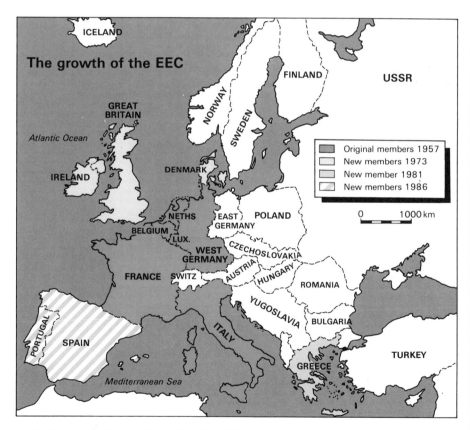

The growth of the EEC

Original members 1957
New members 1973
New member 1981
New members 1986

4 a) How would you describe the difference in geographical position between the EEC's first six members and the countries which joined later?

b) Suggest two kinds of reason why the later members wished to join.

c) Draw a diagram called 'The growth of European unity'. On it show the important stages towards unity from 1945 to the present day.

West Germany in 1945

In July 1945, Allied leaders met in a German town called Potsdam to decide Germany's future. The USA was represented by President Truman, the USSR by Stalin and Britain by Churchill.

The Allied leaders made various deals at Potsdam – about reparations, fixing Germany's frontiers, trying Nazi leaders. And about dividing Germany between them.

They had first decided to do this at the Yalta Conference in the USSR the previous February. The idea was that the division would be only temporary. One day the allies intended to put their separate occupation zones together and unite Germany under one government again.

There was a problem, though. Both the Western powers and the Russians wanted to be sure that this reunited Germany would be ruled by a government which was friendly towards them.

The Russians felt very strongly about this. They had suffered too much at the hands of the Germans already to take any risks.

The two sides argued and argued about Germany's future. At last the Western powers grew tired of trying to reach an agreement with the Russians. They decided to go ahead without them.

In 1949 they put their zones together to form the Federal German Republic – West Germany. In reply the Russians turned their zone into the German Democratic Republic – East Germany.

Konrad Adenauer

The West Germans elected Konrad Adenauer as their first Chancellor. This position is roughly the same as the British Prime Minister.

During the war Hitler's Nazis had put Adenauer in prison and threatened to shoot him. Now he was the leader of a political party called the Christian Democratic Union.

Adenauer was already over seventy when he became Chancellor. Unbelievably, the 'Old Man', as most West Germans called him, kept the job for another fourteen years.

Adenauer retired in 1963 at the age of eighty-seven. By then he had three main achievements to his credit.

Adenauer and the Western powers

First, he persuaded the Western powers to stop treating West Germany like a defeated enemy. He played on their fears of the Russians to get them to accept West Germany as an equal partner. By the middle 1950s the West Germans had their own army and air force again and their country was an important member of NATO (see Unit 10).

West Germany's economic miracle

Second, Adenauer's government brought in policies for industry and trade which resulted in what was called an 'economic miracle'. The man mainly responsible for these was Ludwig Erhard. Erhard held the important job of Minister of Economic Affairs in Adenauer's government from 1949 to 1963.

In these years builders and engineers rebuilt West Germany's war-ruined factories with American money. German businessmen sold more and more cars, televisions and other goods to other countries. Names of German firms like Volkswagen, Grundig and Telefunken became known all over the world.

In barely ten years West Germany changed from a country where people were homeless and close to starving, to one where they were amongst the best fed and best housed in the world.

Adenauer's third achievement was that he helped to end the long years of hatred and suspicion between Germany and France. He got on well with the French leader, President de Gaulle. Between them the two men encouraged a new spirit of friendship and co-operation between their countries.

But Adenauer's rule had a minus as well as a plus side.

He refused to accept that communist East Germany had the right to be a separate, independent country. He also said that the Poles should return to Germany large areas of land in the east which the Russians had forced the Germans to hand over to Poland at the end of the Second World War.

Both these policies caused a lot of suspicion and bad feeling between West Germany and her eastern neighbours.

Adenauer retired in 1963. But West Germany went on being ruled by men with similar ideas until 1969. Then a new Chancellor named Willy Brandt took over the government.

Brandt believed that Adenauer's ideas about one day swallowing up East Germany and about getting back the old German lands in the east of Europe were just dreams. Dangerous dreams, too. The sort that might one day lead to war.

So Brandt introduced his own policy towards the East – his *Ostpolitik*, as it was called in German.

In 1970 Brandt signed a treaty with Poland. In this treaty West Germany accepted that Germany's old lands in the East now rightly belonged to the Poles. Brandt also recognised East Germany. In 1972 he signed a treaty of friendship and co-operation with its rulers.

In ways like this, Brandt's *Ostpolitik* helped to reduce tension and suspicion between East and West Europe in the 1970s. For this reason some people called Brandt the 'Chancellor of Peace'.

Brandt resigned as Chancellor in 1974. But the men who followed him as West Germany's leaders went on with his *Ostpolitik*.

Brandt once summed up his aims as Chancellor by saying 'I would be happy if they [people in the future] found that I had done something to make my country a good neighbour in Europe.' If these words are anything to go by, he probably felt satisfied with the job he had done.

Adenauer and de Gaulle

Adenauer and East Europe

Brandt's Ostpolitik

The economic miracle

Ludwig Erhard was Minister for Economic Affairs in Adenauer's government. He describes what life was like in Germany in 1948.

"It was a time when it was calculated that for every German there would be one plate every five years; a pair of shoes every twelve years; a suit every fifty years; that only every fifth infant would lie in its own napkins; and that only every third German would have a chance of being buried in his own coffin."

Ludwig Erhard, in Richard Mayne, *Post War*, 1983

Theodore White, an American reporter, described the effects of West Germany's 'economic miracle' as he saw them in the early 1950s.

"People in the streets filled out visibly. Their clothes changed from rumpled rags to decent garments, to neat business suits, to silk stockings. Cigarettes disappeared as currency [a form of money], then became available everywhere, then, finally, were sold from slot machines on every corner. Food returned, food as Germans love it, with whipped cream beaten thick in the toffee, on cake, with fruit. The streets changed face as buildings rose, as neon signs festooned them, as their windows shone with goods."

Theodore White in Richard Mayne, *Post War*, 1983

1 a) If you had been a civil servant in Ludwig Erhard's ministry in 1948 what steps would you have recommended to improve the situation?
  b) What do you think had happened to German industry to bring about the changes described by Theodore White?
  c) Look again at Ludwig Erhard's account. Are there any grounds for thinking this might not be an accurate description of life in Germany before the 'economic miracle'?

Germany joins NATO

In the early 1950s the Russian magazine Krokodil *showed the USA and her allies building a German military monster.*

2 a) What does the cartoon tell you about Soviet fears about West Germany?
  b) Suggest reasons for these fears in the early 1950s.
  c) How has the cartoonist tried to make *Krokodil* readers share his view?
  d) Draw a cartoon in support of Willy Brandt's *Ostpolitik*, showing how it tried to deal with these fears.

De Gaulle and France

When the Germans conquered France in 1940 a general named Charles de Gaulle escaped to England. There he organised a Free French army to continue the fight against the Germans.

In 1944 de Gaulle was back at the head of Free French fighters who marched into Paris after the Germans fled. When the war ended he took charge of the country's government.

The French were deeply divided. Those who had fought against the occupying Germans hated the 'collaborators' who had helped the Nazis. Different groups who had stayed in France as resistance fighters quarrelled bitterly.

De Gaulle retires, 1946

De Gaulle became tired of all the arguing. In 1946 he gave up the job of Prime Minister and retired to a small country village. He was certain that one day the call would come to lead France again.

Rebuilding France

Under other governments France gradually recovered from the war. Wartime hatreds burned themselves out. Homes and factories were rebuilt. In the 1950s France took the lead in setting up the ECSC and the EEC (see Unit 11). Its factories, mines and farms were soon turning out goods in record amounts.

Yet France had problems. The worst of these concerned its colonies – foreign lands over which it still ruled. The most important of these were Indo-China and Algeria.

Indo-China and Algeria

The French were forced to give up their power in Indo-China in 1954 when they were beaten in war by the nationalist followers of Ho Chi Minh (see Unit 51). But the struggle in Algeria lasted longer.

Algeria is in North Africa. French soldiers had conquered its Arab people in the 1840s. Algeria was then ruled as part of France and many thousands of French people settled there.

The Algerian War begins, 1954

By the 1950s these French settlers, or *colons*, numbered 1.25 million. The other 8.25 million people of Algeria were Arabs. In 1954 the Arabs began fighting the French to win their independence.

The Algerian War cost both Arabs and French many young men's lives. Yet both sides fought on, the Arabs to win freedom, the colons because Algeria was their home. Other Frenchmen believed that giving up Algeria would show everyone that France no longer counted.

In June 1958 France was torn by riots. The riots started because a new French government seemed ready to make a deal with the Algerians.

In Algeria the *colons* and the generals of the French army prepared to take the law into their own hands to stop this.

Many people in France agreed with them. Others disagreed. But most were sure that France needed a strong man to lead it.

De Gaulle returns, 1958

The Algerian War ends, 1962

De Gaulle's foreign policy

The May riots, 1969

De Gaulle resigns, 1969

The call for which Charles de Gaulle had been waiting had come. In June 1958 he took over once more as France's leader.

A few months later de Gaulle put forward a new constitution, or set of rules for running France. The French people voted to accept it.

The new constitution set up the Fifth Republic. It gave most of the power to rule France to one man, the President – and de Gaulle was elected President.

Peace in Algeria came at last in 1962 when de Gaulle gave its people their independence. Most French people accepted his decision. But some accused him of betraying France. A group of generals set up a secret organisation called the OAS. Its aim was to keep Algeria for France by killing de Gaulle.

France came close to civil war. But the soldiers refused to follow the rebel generals. The OAS plot failed and its leaders fled or ended up in prison.

Another of de Gaulle's aims was to show the world that France was still a great nation. He disliked the way the United States expected the countries of Western Europe to follow its lead in dealings with the USSR, so he signed treaties of his own with the Russians. He also ordered French scientists to make nuclear bombs. Then he took France out of NATO and closed its bases in France.

De Gaulle knew that France was not strong enough to compete on its own with the superpowers. But he thought that a united Western Europe might be able to do so.

De Gaulle wanted France to lead this united Europe. To strengthen French influence in the EEC he twice stopped Britain from joining. He preferred to work with the West Germans. In 1963 he and Konrad Adenauer, the Chancellor of West Germany, signed a treaty of friendship.

De Gaulle gave the people of France more confidence and pride in their country. But not everybody was happy with his leadership. Some said he spent too much on weapons. Others complained of low wages. Many believed he had no respect for democracy.

In May 1968 the discontent boiled over. Students rioted and marched through the streets of Paris shouting for de Gaulle to resign. Millions of workers came out on strike.

De Gaulle used armed police to restore order. But the riots had hurt his pride. A year later he called on the French people to vote him still more power. When the vote went against him he resigned. In the following year, 1970, he died.

All through the 1970s Presidents who shared some of de Gaulle's ideas continued to rule France. But by the start of the 1980s rising prices and growing unemployment had made people ready for a change.

In 1981 the French people voted for a socialist named François Mitterand to become President of France's Fifth Republic.

A supporter of de Gaulle

Ginette Spanier is French, but she is also very fond of Britain. In a television interview in 1963 she explained why she supported de Gaulle when he said 'No' to Britain's attempt to join the EEC.

"It isn't a political issue for me. England saved me during the war but de Gaulle saved me twice. First of all during the war in France, and secondly, not so long ago, on 13th May, when we were on the edge of civil war and there were guns and troops all over Paris, and thanks to General de Gaulle, brother didn't kill brother and he kept France together and gave us peace."

Ginette Spanier, on *World in Action*, 1963.

1 a) Read this unit and work out what events took place on 13th May.
  b) What does Ginette Spanier see as de Gaulle's two biggest achievements?
  c) Having read this unit, what do you think were his two biggest achievements?
  d) Write a short paragraph to describe each achievement you chose.

Opponents of de Gaulle

Paris students ready for trouble in May 1968. One of their posters reads 'Be Young and Shut Up'.

2 a) Who is the man in black in the poster?
  b) What does the poster suggest about young people's objections to him?
  c) Why might older people in France be more likely to support him?
  d) In the photograph, why do you think some of the young men are
    1) wearing crash helmets,   2) wiping their eyes?
  e) As evidence of how French people felt about de Gaulle, how might a photograph like this be misleading?
  f) Explain which of the following might help you most to be more certain about what happened in Paris in 1968:   1) a student newspaper,   2) a newspaper which supported de Gaulle,   3) a diary of a student rioter,   4) a letter by a tourist in Paris,   5) a British television news report on the riots.

The USSR at war

In the Museum of History in the Russian city of Leningrad visitors can see a few pages torn from a notebook of the Russian alphabet.

Under the letters some entries are scrawled in a child's handwriting. The entries tell what happened to the family of Tanya Savicheva, an eleven-year-old schoolgirl, when Leningrad was under siege by Hitler's armies for thirty months during the Second World War.

One by one, she watched them starve to death.

Tanya herself was evacuated from Leningrad in the spring of 1942. But she was seriously ill with dysentry. In 1943 she died, too.

About twenty million other Russians died in ways like this in the Second World War. Nobody will ever know the exact number. There were so many that the government could not keep count.

The USSR's main aim in the years after the war was to make sure that this never happened again.

Stalin and Eastern Europe

In the last months of the war Russian armies poured like a flood over Eastern Europe. Everywhere they went they made sure that governments friendly towards the USSR were set up.

The Russian dictator, Stalin, let both communists and non-communists have jobs in these governments at first. But not for long. Anyone who would not obey his orders was soon thrown into prison or shot.

By 1948 most of the countries of Eastern Europe were under tight Russian control. The countries of this Soviet 'bloc' (group) had to follow the Russians in everything, as planets must circle the sun. Because of this, people in the west called them 'satellite' countries.

In 1949 the Russians set up the German Democratic Republic in the parts of Germany they had occupied at the end of the war. East Germany became a full member of the Soviet bloc.

In all of Eastern Europe only Yugoslavia now stood outside the Soviet bloc. Her President, Marshal Tito, was a loyal communist. But in 1948 Tito quarrelled with Stalin as the USSR tried to tighten its grip over Yugoslavia's government and economic life. Yugoslavia became an important oddity – the only independent communist state in Eastern Europe.

Stalin forced the other satellites to become mini-Soviet Russias. Their communist leaders banned all other political parties. The governments took over factories, farms and businesses. Government planners told workers and farmers what to produce.

A lot of the goods the satellite countries turned out went to help Stalin to rebuild the USSR. He fixed the price. The Poles, for example, had to sell coal to the Russians at only a tenth of the price they could have got from other countries.

Discontent in Eastern Europe

The people of Eastern Europe hated being under Stalin's thumb. But there was little they could do about it. Three million Russian soldiers occupying their countries made sure of that.

Everyday life was hard in the satellite countries. Working hours were long and wages were low. Peasants were forced to work as labourers on collective farms instead of looking after their own fields. Food, clothing, everything was hard to get.

In March 1953 Stalin died. Factory workers in East Germany marched through the streets demanding better living conditions. But their communist rulers called in Russian tanks to restore order. It seemed that Stalin's death had made no difference.

Demonstrations in Poland, 1956

In 1956 workers in Poland organised similar demonstrations. This time the demonstrators had more success. No Russian tanks rolled in to stop them. They were able to make the government listen to their complaints.

The Russian leader was now Nikita Khrushchev. He told Poland's communist rulers that they could make changes – provided Poland stayed communist and friendly towards Russia.

A new leader called Wladislaw Gomulka took over in Poland. Gomulka ordered the secret police not to pry into people's lives so much. He told the country's farmers that they could keep their own land instead of having to join government-run collective farms.

The Hungarian rising, 1956

The Poles' success encouraged the people of Hungary to try to get improvements. In October 1956 they, too, rebelled.

The people of Budapest, Hungary's capital city, drove out the old communist bosses. They hunted down and killed members of the hated secret police. They broke open the gaols and set free political prisoners.

Some of Hungary's top communists were better liked than others. One of these, a man called Imre Nagy, took over the government. Nagy announced that from now on Hungary would run its affairs without interference from the USSR.

This was too much for the Russians. They knew that if Hungary broke loose from their grip, other satellites would soon try to do the same. Khrushchev gave orders for tanks to move in. They rumbled into the streets of Budapest to crush the Hungarians.

Hungarian soldiers, workers and students fought back bravely. But their rifles and home-made petrol bombs were no match for the Russian tanks.

When the fighting ended thousands of Hungarians were dead. Hundreds of thousands more were arrested or fled abroad to safety.

But the Hungarian rebellion did not fail completely. It warned other communist governments not to drive people too hard.

Changes in Eastern Europe

After 1956 they tried to give their people easier lives. By the 1960s life in Eastern Europe had become more comfortable and enjoyable. Many peasants got their small farms back. The Roman Catholic church, to which most belonged, was not persecuted so harshly.

As things grew calmer the Russians relaxed their grip. They took many of their soldiers back to Russia. They let the people of Eastern

Czechoslovakia: the Prague Spring, 1968

Europe have more freedom to run their own affairs.

In 1968, however, the Russians showed the world that they were still Eastern Europe's masters.

In January the communist rulers of Czechoslovakia chose a new leader. His name was Alexander Dubcek.

Dubcek wanted to make communist rule more tolerant – to give it a 'human face'. Amongst other things he gave people more freedom of speech.

The result was what came to be called the 'Prague Spring' of 1968. Television, radio and newspapers were soon filled with lively discussion – including criticism of communist ideas.

The Russians became afraid that other communist-ruled peoples – their own included – might want the same rights that Dubcek was giving the Czechs. They believed that this would weaken the USSR's hold on Eastern Europe and undermine communist rule everywhere.

So, once more, Russian tanks rolled forward. The Czechs woke up on the morning of 21st August 1968 to find that their country had been taken over. The Prague Spring was over. Dubcek was sacked and his reforms done away with. The Russians saw to it that leaders they could trust took over in Czechoslovakia.

The Brezhnev Doctrine

The Russian leader, Brezhnev, defended his actions. He said that a threat to communist rule in any country in Eastern Europe gave other communist countries the right to step in to crush the threat.

This 'Brezhnev Doctrine' was a clear warning to other countries in Eastern Europe. This is our patch, the Russians were saying. We will have the final say about any changes that are made here.

The Brezhnev Doctrine was a fact of life that the peoples of Eastern Europe had to accept. But it did not stop them going on trying to get more control over their lives.

Poland and Solidarity

One sign of this was the growth in Poland of an independent trade union called Solidarity.

In 1980 shipyard workers in the Polish port of Gdansk went on strike when the government put up food prices. Soon workers all over the country joined in the strike. This was the start of Solidarity.

Solidarity's leader was an electrician named Lech Walesa. Walesa forced the Polish government to give the workers a better deal. It agreed to freeze food prices. It also said that workers could have their own trade unions, free from government control. Solidarity soon had thousands of members all over Poland.

The Russians became worried. They thought about invading Poland as they had done Czechoslovakia in 1968. But instead they ordered the Polish government to clamp down on Solidarity.

Solidarity had its meetings banned. Its offices were closed down. Walesa and its other leaders were put in prison.

Despite this, Solidarity lived on underground. It went on speaking for the rights of the Polish people.

The effects of war

A post-war visitor describes what the Second World War did to the USSR.

"For hundreds of miles, for thousands, there was not a standing or living object to be seen . . . Every town was flat, every city. There were no barns. There was no machinery. There were no stations, no water-towers. There was not a solitary telegraph pole left standing and all along the line lay the twisted rails pulled up by the Germans who had worked with special trains fitted with great draghooks as they moved west. In the fields nobody but women, children and very old men could be seen – and these worked only with hand tools."

In Joan Hasler, *The Making of Russia*, 1969

1 a) Suggest why there was so much destruction in huge parts of the USSR.

b) How would you explain the fact that only women, children and the very old were to be seen in the fields?

c) Do you think the extract and the map help to explain why the Russians were determined to control Eastern Europe? Give reasons.

Eastern Europe after 1945

Use the map and what you have read in the text to answer the questions.

2 a) Why was it in the east rather than the west of Europe that communist power became strong?

b) Which countries did the USSR take land from or swallow up completely?

c) Which country lost most land to the USSR? What compensation was it given?

d) In which other ways did the USSR strengthen its power in Eastern Europe?

e) Jan Masaryk was the non-communist Foreign Minister of Czechoslovakia until 1948. He told a reporter, 'Russia is like a big fat cow with its head grazing in Prague and its udders in Moscow'. What did he mean?

f) Use the map to suggest one reason why Yugoslavia was able to break away from Soviet control while Hungary in 1956 could not.

Eastern Europe after the Second World War

Hungary, 1956

A photograph taken in Budapest, the capital of Hungary, in 1956.

3 a) Whose head has been pulled off the statue?

b) What does the picture show you of the feelings of the people of Hungary towards the Russians?

c) Explain why they felt like this.

d) How else did Hungarians show these feelings in 1956?

e) What did the Russians do about these events in Hungary? Why?

The Prague Spring, 1968

Part of a statement the Soviet government put out on 21st August 1968, the morning after it sent troops into Czechoslovakia.

"Leaders of the Czechoslovak Socialist Republic have asked the Soviet Union and other allied states to render the Czechoslovak people urgent assistance, including assistance with armed forces.

This request was brought about by the threat which had arisen to the socialist system in Czechoslovakia . . .

Nobody will ever be allowed to wrest [pull away] a single link from the community of socialist states."

A cartoon stuck up on a street in Prague in August 1968.

4 a) According to the statement, who wanted the troops to enter Prague?

b) What does it say was the reason for troops being needed there?

c) In the cartoon, which countries do the figures represent?

d) Put the cartoon's message into your own words.

e) Does the cartoon support or cast doubt on the Soviet statement? Explain your answer.

f) Imagine you are the Czechoslovak who drew the cartoon and that you are speaking to a Russian soldier. How would you try to convince him that the Soviet government was doing wrong? What might he reply?

PART TWO
THE USSR

The Russian Empire in 1914

The Russian Empire

Big and backward. That was Russia at the start of this century.

Just how big you can see from the map on page 59. Russia was more than a country. It was an Empire.

This Russian Empire stretched halfway round the world, from the middle of Europe across all of Asia. 130 million people lived in its vast lands. Half were Russians. The rest were conquered people. In the west many were Europeans, such as Poles. In the south and across the vast stretches of Siberia were Asian people.

The peasants

The backwardness of Russia showed in the people's lives. Only one in four had any schooling. Four out of five were poor farmers.

Only forty years earlier these peasants had been serfs. Rich landowners had owned them, just like cattle. Now most scratched a living from small plots of land hardly big enough to feed their families.

The peasants were usually hungry. Sometimes they starved. Their dearest dream was to get hold of more land.

A few peasants were better off than others. They were called *kulaks*. *Kulaks* owned more land and cattle, and had the money to pay other people to work for them. Their farms and those of the rich landowners grew most of the food that fed the people of the towns.

The workers in industry

By the beginning of the twentieth century Russia's towns were growing quickly. Businessmen were setting up factories. Hungry peasants moved in from the countryside to look for jobs.

In 1900 Russia had about 2.5 million of these industrial workers. Some laboured in the factories and workshops of cities like Moscow and St Petersburg. Others worked in mines and steelworks on the coalfields in the south of Russia.

Hours were long – often thirteen or fourteen a day. Wages were barely enough to buy food and pay the rent on a single room – or just part of a room – for the family.

A factory inspector described how 'workers, all in greasy, soot-covered rags, covered with a thick layer of grime and dust, swarm like bees in dirty and over-crowded quarters'.

But the factory and mine-workers had one advantage over the peasants in the villages. Crowded together in their factories and slums, they could unite to set up trade unions. They organised strikes to try for a better deal. The strikes were usually put down by the government, often with bloodshed.

The rule of the Tsar

Only one man mattered in everything to do with government in Russia. He was the Emperor, or Tsar, Nicholas II.

In 1905 Russia lost a war against Japan. The Tsar's government was blamed. There were riots and protests.

After this the Tsar allowed better-off people to vote for a sort of parliament called the *Duma*. But the *Duma* had no real power. The Tsar still chose the men who ran the government, and the law was what he said it was.

The Tsar had an army of officials to run his vast empire and collect the taxes. A hated secret police force called the *Okhrana* could arrest anyone it suspected of being against the Tsar.

People hated the Cossacks of south Russia also. The government sent these mounted soldiers galloping in when disturbances broke out – if workers went on strike or starving peasants tried to take corn from the store of some rich landowner.

The workers and peasants were obviously discontented under the Tsar. But others, too, wanted to improve things.

Reformers

Businessmen were fed up with having to bribe crooked officials. Educated people generally wanted to see Russia run in a more honest and efficient way.

People like these wanted to reform the Tsarist system. They wanted Russia to be governed like Britain, where an elected Parliament had gradually taken over the power to rule.

Revolutionaries

Other Russians thought that the Tsarist system was too rotten to be reformed. They wanted to sweep it away completely. There were many of these revolutionary groups. Each had plans for destroying the old system and its own ideas about what to put in its place.

One revolutionary group called themselves the Bolsheviks. The Bolsheviks took their ideas from a German writer called Karl Marx.

The ideas of Karl Marx

Marx believed that all human history was a story of struggles for power between different classes. Marx called the ruling class in the modern industrial world 'capitalists'. These capitalists had plenty of money (capital) and owned the factories, mines and land.

The capitalist way of life was supported by a middle class of people who did well out of capitalism. Marx called this group the 'bourgeoisie'. The bourgeoisie consisted of people such as shopkeepers, bank clerks and office workers.

The proletariat

The capitalists and the bourgeoisie were doomed, said Marx. Their power would one day be destroyed by the workers in their factories and mines – the 'proletariat', as Marx called them.

He claimed that all mankind's wealth came from the hard work of the proletariat. Yet everywhere the capitalists and the bourgeoisie were cheating them of their reward.

But not for much longer. As more factories were built the proletariat was becoming bigger and stronger. One day it would rebel and overthrow its capitalist masters by force. Then everything would be run in a new way. Marx called it 'communism'.

Communism

Under communism the workers would own the factories, the mines, the farms – all the ways of producing wealth. Profits would be shared out fairly, so that everyone could have a happier life.

Marx first wrote down his ideas in 1848, in a short book called *The Communist Manifesto*. He explained them in more detail in a later book called *Capital*.

Those books probably brought more changes to people's lives than anything else written in the last 200 years.

The changes began in Russia. You can read how in the next unit.

Peasants and poverty

An official Russian government report of about 1900 describes what life was like for peasants living in one of the Russian Empire's richest farming areas.

"The dwelling . . . is usually a cottage of eighteen by twenty-one feet and about seven feet high . . . Cottages having no chimneys are still very common, the smoke being let out through a hole in the roof . . . Almost all cottages have thatched roofs which often leak, and in the winter the walls are generally covered with dung to keep the place warm . . . Earth floors are the rule because in cold weather lambs, calves, pigs and even cows are brought in to the cottage. The terrible overcrowding makes the air heavy and unhealthy . . . In localities which have no forests the peasants use straw for fuel . . . The peasants wash in their cottages, spreading the dirt on their bodies with very little hot water. They almost never use soap. . . . Skin diseases progress at a terrible rate . . . the anti-sanitary conditions in the villages are such that the prevention of epidemics is almost impossible . . . An important factor is the weakened physical condition of the peasants due to under-nourishment . . . The normal fare consists of bread . . . and often cabbage and onions, to which fresh vegetables may be added in the autumn."

In M. Florinsky, *The End of the Russian Empire*, 1976

A photograph of peasant homes, taken in Novgorod at about the time of the report.

1 a) From the report, pick out facts which show the peasants' poverty.
  b) Pick two features in the photograph which suggest that the family living in the house was poor.
  c) How do these two sources help to explain 1) why most peasants were desperate to get more land; 2) why they were not very good farmers?
  d) Do the extract and picture support the first sentence of this unit?
  e) Could a similar statement be made about Britain in 1900? (See Unit 40.)

Bloody Sunday, 1905

22nd January 1905 came to be called 'Bloody Sunday'. A young priest, Father Gapon, led a workers' procession to the Tsar's palace in St Petersburg, carrying a petition for something to be done about the food shortages and rocketing prices caused by the war with Japan. Soldiers blocked the way. Father Gapon wrote this account of what happened next.

" . . . infantry barred the road, and in front of them a company of cavalry was drawn up with their swords shining in the sun. Would they dare to touch us? For a moment we trembled and then started forward again.

Suddenly the company of Cossacks galloped rapidly towards us with drawn swords . . . striking on both sides. I saw the swords lifting and falling, the men, women and children dropping to the earth like logs . . .

Again we started forward, with . . . rising rage in our hearts. The Cossacks turned their horses and began to cut their way through . . .

We were not more than thirty yards from the soldiers when suddenly, without any warning, . . . was heard the dry crack of many rifle-shots . . .

At last the firing ceased. I stood up with a few others who remained uninjured and looked down at the bodies that lay prostrate around me. I cried to them. 'Stand up!' But they lay still. Why did they lie there? I looked again and saw the scarlet stain of blood on the snow . . . .

The thought flashed through my mind, 'and this is the work of our Little Father, the Tsar' . . . now I knew in very truth that a new chapter was opened in the book of the history of our people."

Father Gapon, *The Story of My Life*, 1905

2 a) Imagine you are a marcher on Bloody Sunday. You start off as a reformer but end the day as a revolutionary. Write to a friend describing the effect of the day on your ideas about Russia's future.

Russia under the Tsars

This cartoon of 1901 shows an artists' view of society under the Tsars.

3 a) Who do the figures on each level represent?
  b) Who are the figures with the flag and what are they supposed to be doing?
  c) Is the artist in favour of Tsarist rule or against?
  d) Who would have been most likely to agree with the cartoon: 1) the Tsar, 2) a capitalist, 3) a Bolshevik? Explain your answer.
  e) Give the cartoon a title.

Russia goes to war

In August 1914 the first shots were fired in the First World War. Russia found itself as an ally of Britain and France fighting Germany. Most Russians didn't understand why they were at war. But a wave of patriotism swept the country.

The capital, St Petersburg, was renamed Petrograd, because the old name was too German-sounding.

All the criticisms of the Tsar's government suddenly seemed unimportant. Germany had declared war on Russia. Russia must be defended. It was that simple.

Russia's army at war

Russian soldiers marched into eastern Germany. But the German army was better armed and better led. It soon defeated them at the Battle of Tannenberg.

By the middle of September 1914 the Russians had been driven back across their own frontiers. They left behind thousands of dead and still more thousands of prisoners.

It was the first of many disasters. In 1915 German armies advanced deep into Russia. The spirit of the Russian soldiers sank lower and lower. Whole fighting units simply surrendered.

Supply shortages

The Russian soldiers were short of just about everything – ammunition, food, clothing, medical supplies, even rifles. Many had to rely on picking up a gun dropped by a dead or wounded comrade.

One reason for the shortages was that Russia still did not have enough factories to make the things the army needed. Another was the poor state of the railways and transport system. Even when shells and food were available, they often failed to get through to the men who needed them.

Supplies sent to Russia by Britain and France piled up at the ports because there were no trains. 'We go about in ragged uniforms and without boots', wrote one soldier in a letter home. 'I have to go practically barefoot, just in my socks.'

On top of the shortages the Russian soldiers were badly led. The Tsar's minister in charge of the war boasted that he had not read a book on army affairs for twenty-five years.

As the months passed the soldiers got more angry and less inclined to fight. By 1917 most of them had had enough. They deserted in thousands and started to make their way home.

The war at home

Things were bad there, too. The towns were short of food. So many men had been taken into the army – fifteen million by 1917 – that not enough were left to do the work on the farms. The towns were short of coal, too, so people were cold as well as hungry.

On top of this there were endless price rises. Between 1914 and 1916 wages doubled – but the price of food and other goods rose between three and five times.

The Tsar and the Tsarina

Most people blamed the Tsar for the mess the country was in. Despite the fact that he had no military training, in 1915 he made himself Commander in Chief of the army. This was a bad mistake. It meant that everyone now blamed him for all the things that were going wrong with the army.

The Tsar made another mistake. He left his wife, the Tsarina, in charge of the government.

Rasputin

The Tsarina was deeply under the influence of a supposedly holy man called Rasputin. Rasputin was an ignorant, dirty drunkard. But he had mysterious powers of healing.

The Tsar's only son was ill with a dangerous blood disease called haemophilia. Only Rasputin seemed able to relieve his suffering. The grateful Tsarina would hear nothing bad about him.

The Tsarina came to rely on Rasputin's advice. Soon he was practically running the government. Any ministers he did not like got the sack and the Tsarina put his friends in their place.

As things went from bad to worse, the Tsarina and Rasputin came to be more and more hated. In December 1916, a group of noblemen decided that there was only one way to save Russia from Rasputin's evil influence. They murdered him.

Killing Rasputin was not easy. First the nobles gave him poisoned sweets. Then poisoned wine. When neither the sweets nor the wine seemed to have any effect, they shot him. To make quite sure that he was dead, they threw his body into an icy river.

The last winter

Bad weather finally ended the Tsar's rule.

The winter of 1916–17 was bitterly cold. Heavy snowfalls brought the railways to a standstill. In Petrograd and other cities people queued for hours outside empty bakers' shops for bread that never came. There was hardly any coal or firewood in the city.

By February 1917 thousands of workers were on strike. The Tsar was blamed for everything. Revolutionaries gave out leaflets in factories and on street corners calling on the people to overthrow him.

At the end of February queuing women in Petrograd were told yet again that there was no bread. They refused to believe it and started looting bakeries and foodshops.

The government called out troops to restore order. But the soldiers joined the hungry rioters.

The February* Revolution, 1917

*After the revolutions one of the changes made by Russia's new government was to bring their calendar into line with the one used by the rest of Europe. This was about a fortnight ahead, so in some history books and records the February and October revolutions are said to be the March and November revolutions.

Without the army's support the government was powerless. Within days it collapsed. The Tsar gave up his throne and was arrested. The February Revolution of 1917 had begun.

For a while nobody knew quite what was happening. In the countryside peasants burned and looted the houses of landowners. Armed groups of workers and soldiers set up soviets (a Russian word meaning councils) to run the factories and towns.

The Provisional Government

In Petrograd politicians in the *Duma* – the middle-class Parliament which Nicholas had always ignored – decided they must give a lead. They declared that Russia was now a Republic. To run the Republic they set up a 'Provisional Government'. It would rule Russia provisionally – that is, for the time being – until elections could be held later in 1917.

Kerensky

But no one could run Russia without the support of the soviet in Petrograd. It put itself at the head of the other soviets around the country. This meant that the Petrograd Soviet controlled the railways, food supplies and other vital services.

The most important member of the Provisional Government was a young socialist lawyer named Alexander Kerensky. Kerensky was a member of the Petrograd Soviet, too. He tried hard to get the two organisations to work together.

But the job of putting Russia back on its feet was beyond Kerensky. The Provisional Government was out of touch with what the people wanted. It planned to move gradually towards an elected government. Everything else it wanted to leave more or less as it was. For example, it refused to give peasants the go-ahead to take over landlords' lands.

But Kerensky's worst mistake was to try to go on with the hated war. Soldiers still wanted to go home. Townspeople wanted more food. Everybody wanted peace.

Lenin and the Bolsheviks

On 16th April 1917 a small, bald, middle-aged man got off a train at Petrograd's main railway station. His name was Lenin. He was the most important leader of the Bolsheviks, the revolutionary group who believed in the ideas of Karl Marx (see Unit 15).

Ten years before, the secret police had driven Lenin abroad for plotting against the Tsar. He was in Switzerland when the February Revolution began.

The Germans saw their chance to make trouble for the Provisional Government, which wanted to go on fighting them. They laid on a special sealed train – one that nobody was allowed to get off – to hurry Lenin back to Russia to organise a Bolshevik take-over.

'Peace! Bread! Land!'

Lenin promised the Russian people 'Peace! Bread! Land!' – an end to the war, food for everyone and land for the peasants.

The way to 'Peace! Bread! Land!' was summed up by Lenin in another slogan – 'All power to the soviets!'. The Petrograd Soviet started to back his every move.

Lenin ordered his supporters to get control of all means of spreading news and information, such as newspapers and post-offices. Bolshevik newspapers were soon being read all over Russia.

Support for the Bolsheviks grew and grew. By the summer their influence had spread to other parts of Russia.

In Petrograd Lenin set up his own fighting force of workers armed with rifles. By July he had 10,000 of these 'Red Guards'. Their leader was Leon Trotsky, one of Lenin's chief supporters.

The October Revolution, 1917

The final Bolshevik take-over came in the autumn. On the night of 24th October 1917 Trotsky's Red Guards took over all key buildings in Petrograd – railway stations, telephone exchanges, banks. By morning the rule of the Provisional Government was over. Kerensky and its other ministers fled abroad or were arrested.

Within a week Bolsheviks had taken over most of Russia's main cities. Lenin was in control. The big question was – for how long?

Discontented soldiers

From a police report sent to the Tsar's government in October 1916.

"The high cost of living and the shortage of foodstuffs, from which soldiers' wives are the first to suffer, have been made known to the army by the soldiers returned from leave . . . The rumours of famine in Petrograd which circulate at the front are perfectly monstrous and have already soared into the realm of pure imagination. According to statements by the soldiers themselves, the army believe that in the capital . . . 'meat is sold only to the nobles and landlords', that a new cemetery has been opened for those who have died of starvation, and so on . . . The anxiety of soldiers about their families is perfectly . . . understandable, but it . . . grows from day to day and offers a fertile ground for the spreading of both German and revolutionary propaganda . . . Letters . . . speak of the 'day of reckoning' when the War is over, or even before."

In M. Florinsky, *The End of the Russian Empire*, 1976

Mutinying soldiers mix with the crowds in Moscow, February 1917

1 a) How do you think the agent who wrote this report got his information?
   b) Why do you think rumours like those mentioned in the report would spread quickly?
   c) What danger is the report warning about in the last two sentences?
   d) How does the photograph suggest that there was unrest in Moscow as well as Petrograd?
   e) What evidence in the photograph suggests that the soldiers were mutineers?
   f) How does the photograph suggest that other classes as well as soldiers and the poor were protesting against the Tsar's government?

The Petrograd Soviet

In March 1917 the Petrograd Soviet issued 'Order No. 1'

"The Soviet of Workers' and Soldiers' Deputies has resolved:

1. In all . . . regiments . . . and the vessels of the navy, committees of elected representatives from the lower ranks . . . shall be chosen immediately . . .

4. The orders of the . . . Duma shall be executed [carried out] only in such cases as they do not conflict with the orders . . . of the Soviet of Workers' and Soldiers' Deputies.

5. All kinds of arms, such as rifles, machine-guns, armoured automobiles and others, must be kept . . . under the control of the . . . committees and must in no case be turned over to officers . . .

6. In the ranks . . . soldiers must observe the strictest military discipline, but . . . standing at attention and compulsory saluting, when not on duty, are abolished.

7. Also, the addressing of officers with the titles 'Your Excellency', 'Your Honour' and the like is abolished, and these titles are replaced by . . . 'Mr General', 'Mr Colonel', and so forth. Rudeness towards soldiers of any rank . . . is prohibited, and soldiers are required to bring to the attention of the company committees . . . all misunderstandings occurring between officers and men.

The present order is to be read to all . . . regiments, ships' crews . . . and other commands.

The Petrograd Soviet of Workers' and Soldiers' Deputies."

In G. Vernadsky, *A Source Book of Russian History Vol. 3*, 1972

2 a) What was a soviet? Where were they set up?

   b) Why was the Petrograd Soviet in a particularly strong position at this time?

   c) What effect would Order No. 1 have on the power of the *Duma*?

   d) Which of Kerensky's policies would run into difficulties because of Order No. 1?

   e) Why did this Order make it important for the Bolsheviks to get the support of the soviets?

   f) Two officers are reading the order. One is the son of a landowner and still loyal to the imprisoned Tsar. The other, the son of a member of the *Duma*, wants Russia to remain a Republic but believes in carrying on with the war. Write, or act out, a conversation in which they discuss Russia's future.

3 Write one or two sentences about each of the following. Try to show the part each played in helping Lenin and the Bolsheviks to win control of the revolution in Russia.

   a) Lenin's sealed train.

   b) 'Peace! Bread! Land!'

   c) 'All power to the Soviets!'

   d) Red Guards.

Autumn 1917

John Reed, a young American reporter, lived in Petrograd at the time when the Bolsheviks were getting ready to overthrow Kerensky.

"September and October are the worst months of the Russian year – especially the Petrograd year. Under dull grey skies, in the shortening days, the rain fell drenching, incessant [not ceasing]. The mud underfoot was deep, slippery and clinging . . . Bitter damp winds rushed in from the Gulf of Finland, and the chill fog rolled through the streets . . .

Week by week food became scarcer. The daily allowance of bread fell from a pound and a half to a pound, then three-quarters, half and a quarter-pound . . . Towards the end there was a week without any bread at all. Sugar one was entitled to at a rate of two pounds a month – if one could get it at all, which was seldom . . . There was milk for about half the babies in the city; most hotels and private houses never saw it for months . . .

For milk and bread and sugar and tobacco one had to stand in queue for long hours in the chill rain. Coming home from all-night meetings I have seen the *kvost* [tail] beginning to form before dawn, mostly women, some with babies in their arms . . . Think of the poorly clad people standing on the iron-white streets of Petrograd whole days in the Russian winter! I have listened in the bread-lines, hearing the bitter . . . note of discontent which from time to time burst up through the miraculous good nature of the Russian crowd."

John Reed, *Ten Days That Shook the World*, 1919

People were short of food in other cities, as well as Petrograd. This is a bread queue in Moscow in autumn 1917.

4 a) List the ways in which John Reed and the photographer agree about conditions in the autumn of 1917.

b) Explain why there was a food shortage in the cities.

c) Imagine you are in the queue in the photograph. Write down some of the comments you overhear which show the 'bitter note of discontent' that John Reed mentions at the end of his account.

The Constituent Assembly

The Council of People's Commissars

Peace with Germany

The Treaty of Brest Litovsk, 1918

Lenin's opponents

Before the October Revolution of 1917, Kerensky's Provisional Government had promised the Russian people the right to elect a Parliament – a Constituent Assembly.

The elections took place soon after Lenin seized power. His Bolsheviks got only a quarter of the votes. But Lenin had no intention of handing over power. He sent Red Guards to close the Constituent Assembly and pack its members off home.

Lenin set up a new Bolshevik government to run Russia. He called it the Council of People's Commissars. A Commissar was someone with special responsibility for a government department.

The Council was soon pouring out a flood of orders, or decrees. It abolished all titles and ranks. From now on people were to simply call one another 'Comrade'. It made the Church stop teaching religion. It closed down newspapers which criticised the Bolsheviks. It took over the banks, all big privately-owned houses and palaces.

Most important of all, one decree from the Commissars said, 'All private ownership of land is abolished immediately without compensation'. It gave no orders about how the land should be shared out. In most villages, committees of peasants simply divided it among themselves.

But the most urgent question was how to end the war with Germany. Lenin knew that any Russian government that failed to bring peace would be too unpopular to go on running the country. In December 1917 he sent Trotsky to a town called Brest Litovsk to start peace talks with the Germans.

The Germans knew that the Russians were desperate for peace. Their terms were hard. By the Treaty of Brest Litovsk in March 1918 Russia had to hand over one quarter of its land and one third of its people.

The lands Russia gave up included its richest farming areas and most of its factories and mines. But Lenin argued that peace was vital to give the Bolsheviks a chance to tighten their grip on Russia.

One big danger to Bolshevik rule was that many of the people of the old Russian Empire were not Russians at all (see Unit 15). These 'minority peoples' had suffered under the Russian Tsars. They were determined not to suffer again under Russian Bolsheviks. People such as the Ukrainians in the south of the country formed governments and armies of their own to fight for independence.

Other groups got ready to fight, too. There were supporters of rival political parties banned by the Bolsheviks, rich peasants who wanted to keep their land, Tsarist officials and officers who had lost their jobs and pensions.

In the north of Russia anti-Bolshevik politicians set up a rival government. To the east, in the part of the Empire called Siberia, an army led by a Tsarist Admiral named Kolchak took control.

Civil War in Russia

By the end of 1918 Lenin's Council of Commissars was just one Russian government amongst many. A civil war began to decide which should rule Russia.

The Bolsheviks' opponents in the Civil War called themselves the Whites. The Whites received a lot of help from Russia's wartime allies, the British and the French.

After the Treaty of Brest Litovsk the Germans were able to send many more soldiers to fight in France. This made the French and British eager to bring Lenin down. They wanted Russia to have a government that would start fighting the Germans again. They poured guns, money and men into Russia to help the White armies. So did their allies, the Japanese.

Trotsky's Red Army

Lenin put Trotsky in charge of trying to beat the Whites. Trotsky's first job was to organise a Bolshevik army – the Red Army.

Getting ordinary soldiers was easy. All Trotsky had to do was to put workers and peasants into uniforms and send them off to fight.

Finding officers to turn these recruits into skilled soldiers was more of a problem. The only officers with any experience were those who had fought for the Tsar. Could Trotsky trust them?

To solve the problem Trotsky warned the officers that if they went over to the Whites he would arrest their families. He also appointed special Commissars to watch their every move. He soon had 20,000 ex-Tsarist officers leading his Red Army.

The Red and White Terrors

The Civil War between the Reds and the Whites raged across Russia for over two years. Both sides behaved with great cruelty.

Lenin set up a secret police force. He called it the *Cheka*. The *Cheka's* job was to root out anyone Lenin suspected might plot against him. Whole families were wiped out simply because they had once been rich.

The Whites' reply to the *Cheka's* 'Red Terror' was their anti-Bolshevik 'White Terror'. Between them the two sides tortured and killed thousands of people.

Death at Ekaterinburg

The best-known victims died in a town called Ekaterinburg. The Reds were holding the Tsar and his family prisoners there. On the night of 16th July 1918 the *Cheka* shot them dead to prevent a rescue by the Whites.

The Red Victory

The Bolsheviks came very close to defeat. At one time four separate White armies advanced into the area they held.

Yet finally the Bolsheviks won. How did they do it?

One of the reasons was that in Trotsky the Bolsheviks had the Civil War's most skilled leader. Under him they fought as a single force. Their enemies, on the other hand, fought separately.

The Bolsheviks also controlled most of Russia's best land. By seizing food from the peasants they kept the Red Army well fed.

The peasants did not like the Bolsheviks for this. But they liked the Whites even less. If the Bolsheviks won the peasants had more chance of hanging on to the land they had grabbed off the landowners – or so they thought.

Brest Litovsk

The Treaty of Brest Litovsk, 1918

Legend:
— Russian frontier in 1914
— Russian frontier after the Treaty of Brest Litovsk

0   500km

Part of what Lenin told the Bolshevik Central Committee in January 1918.

"The Army is extremely exhausted by the war, the . . . position of the Germans . . . is so favourable that if they attack they will be able to take . . . Petrograd with their bare hands . . .

Undoubtedly the peace we are obliged to sign now is a foul peace, but, if war begins, our Government will be swept away and peace will be signed by another Government. At present we are supported not only by the proletariat, but also by the poorest peasants, who will abandon us if the war continues."

In A. Rothstein,
History of the USSR,
1950

1 a) Use the map to explain why Lenin thought the peace was 'foul'.
  b) Explain who Lenin meant by the 'proletariat'.
  c) Why were the proletariat and poor peasants supporting the Bolsheviks?
  d) What did Lenin think would turn them against the Bolsheviks?
  e) Write a newspaper headline to show what British or French leaders would have thought about the Treaty of Brest Litovsk.

The Red Army

A recruiting poster for the new Red Army.

2 a) Which side in the Civil War does the artist suggest that working people supported?
  b) How does he do this?
  c) Do you think this poster or Trotsky's proclamation on the next page gives the more reliable picture of how workers and peasants felt about the Civil War? Explain your answer.

Red Terror

A proclamation by Trotsky to the people of Kazan Province, or 'Guberniya'.

"To the Peasants and Workers of Kazan Guberniya

The enemies of the working people . . . are attempting to mobilise the working population of Kazan Guberniya to fight against workers and peasants.

. . . I declare the following so that in the future no one may plead ignorance of the revolutionary laws . . . of Soviet power:

1. Any one who . . . joins the army of the enemies of the people, commits a most serious state crime.
2. All workers and peasants who have joined, under duress [force], the ranks of the hostile army must immediately go over to the side of the Soviet troops . . . they will be guaranteed a full pardon.
3. Those peasants and workers who have sold themselves to the White Guards and who do not voluntarily lay down their arms will be shot . . . All their property will be handed over to the wounded . . . Red Army men and the families of fallen soldiers . . .

WORKERS AND PEASANTS OF KAZAN GUBERNIYA! The word of the Soviet power is firm. Its punishment is severe. Do not give a single soldier to the corrupt Guards. Give everything to the defence of Soviet power!"

In M. McCauley, *The Russian Revolution and the Soviet State 1917–21, Documents*, 1975

3 a) Who does Trotsky mean by 'enemies of the working people'?
 b) Which side in the Civil War do you think the working people of Kazan were supporting before the proclamation appeared? Explain your answer.

The Civil War

4 a) Does Kazan's location suggest anything about reasons for Trotsky's proclamation?
 b) How does information on the map suggest that
  1) the Reds might lose the war,
  2) they might win it?
 c) What do you think was the main reason for the Red victory in the end?

Russia at the height of the Civil War, early 1919

➤ Attacks by White armies and their allies

Land still held by Bolsheviks at the height of White success

╂ Main railway lines

0   300km

Even before the Civil War ended, Lenin set about reorganising Russian life.

To keep the Red Army supplied during the fighting he brought in a way of running things called 'War Communism'.

War Communism

Under War Communism factories were taken over by the government. Workers were ordered into whatever jobs the government wanted doing. Nobody was allowed to make or sell goods for their own profit.

The scarce supplies of food were strictly rationed. 7 kilos of bread, 450 grammes of sugar and 225 grammes of imitation butter had to last a worker in a heavy job for a month – and many people got less!

To keep the army and the workers fed, the government sent soldiers into the countryside. The soldiers forced the peasants to hand over any grain they had stored away. Often they beat and even killed them.

But the peasants hit back. One Bolshevik observer described how 'savage peasants would slit open a commissar's belly, pack it with grain and leave him by the roadside as a lesson to all'.

War Communism kept the Red Army going through the Civil War. But in every other way it was a disaster.

The peasants knew that any surplus grain they produced would be taken by the government. So they only grew what they needed to feed their own families

In industry things were even worse. The years of war had left mines flooded, machines smashed, factories and railways in ruins. Industrial output dropped to only one seventh of its pre-war level.

In 1920 and 1921 famine and epidemic diseases swept Russia. Millions died – 3.5 million of typhoid alone.

The Kronstadt Rebellion, 1921

Early in March 1921 sailors at the navy base of Kronstadt rebelled against Lenin's rule. They said that he should allow more freedom and give other people more say in running the country.

Trotsky quickly crushed the Kronstadt rebels. But the rising made Lenin change his plans. It was, he said, 'the flash which lit up reality'.

The sailors at Kronstadt had demanded out loud what most Russians wanted – an end to the hardships of War Communism. Lenin's answer was the New Economic Policy – the NEP.

The NEP

The NEP allowed the peasants to sell part of what they produced for their own profit. It also let the better-off peasants, or *kulaks*, rent extra land and hire other peasants to work for them. Lenin hoped that these changes would encourage the peasants to work harder and grow more food.

The NEP worked. In 1922 the peasants gathered in a grain harvest of 22 million tonnes. In 1925 they gathered in 72.5 million tonnes. The danger of more famines disappeared.

The NEP brought big changes to the towns, too. Lenin let people set up their own small factories and shops. This again was to encourage them to work harder and produce more goods – goods which the peasants could buy with the money they received for growing more food.

The NEP put more food on people's tables and more goods in the shops. Life in Russia slowly became more comfortable.

Opposition to the NEP

But many Bolsheviks – or communists as they now called themselves – disliked the NEP. To them it seemed to be the start of a return to capitalism, to a system based upon selfishness, where the rich made profits out of the poor.

Something else about NEP worried them, too. It was giving people more consumer goods like shoes and clothing, all right. But it was doing nothing to give Russia more heavy industries – steel works, power stations, engineering factories.

How could a communist Russia ever grow into a strong, modern country without these things, they asked? How could she hope to survive in a world where every other country seemed to be her enemy?

Lenin's death

Lenin was not there to answer these questions. In January 1924 he suffered a stroke and died. His body was preserved and placed in a glass coffin inside a great stone tomb in Moscow's Red Square. To this day, thousands of Russians file past it every year to gaze on the dead face of the man who founded modern Russia.

By the time Lenin died the Russian Empire had a new name. It was called the Union of Soviet Socialist Republics – the USSR, or Soviet Union for short. Its new capital was Moscow.

Trotsky versus Stalin

Two men struggled to take the dead Lenin's place as the USSR's leader. One was Trotsky. You have read a lot about him already. The other was another leading communist called Stalin.

Trotsky and Stalin had very different ideas about the USSR's next step forward.

Trotsky was keen to spread communism to other countries. He wanted the Russians to encourage communist revolutions all over the world. This, he said, was the only way to make the USSR safe.

Stalin disagreed. He thought that the Russians should make the USSR itself much stronger before bothering about world revolution.

Trotsky was famous all over Russia. All through the years of revolution he had been Lenin's right-hand man.

He had organised the Red Guards who had seized power for the Bolsheviks in 1917. He had led the Red Army to victory in the Civil War. Now he held the important job of Commissar for War.

Trotsky and world revolution

In speech after speech in the early 1920s Trotsky hammered home his message. Yes, Russia must make itself strong, he said. It must build up its industries and armies. But anyone who thought that this was enough was a fool, he claimed.

The rich capitalist countries – Britain, France, the United States – would never let the USSR travel in peace along the path to communism. Sooner or later they would attack again, as they had done in the Civil War. They would try to smash communism to stop its ideas from spreading to their own working people.

There was only one way to prevent this, thundered Trotsky. The USSR must help the workers of the capitalist countries to rise in revolution so that their countries, too, became communist. Only then would communism in the USSR be safe.

Many people were convinced by Trotsky's arguments. But they were not ready to make him their leader.

Trotsky had only joined the Bolsheviks just before the Revolution. Despite his work since then, many of the other top Bolsheviks still did not really trust him. Nor did most of them like him. He could be sharp and sarcastic, and was full of his own importance.

Stalin, the General Secretary

Stalin was not particularly well-liked either. Lenin had left a will warning his fellow communists about Stalin's lack of consideration for other people. He suggested that they should think about sacking him as one of the leaders of the party. Luckily for Stalin, Lenin's advice was not taken.

Compared with Trotsky, Stalin seemed dull and boring – a hard-working plodder. Someone who knew him in the early years of the Revolution described him as a 'grey blur'. But Stalin outwitted Trotsky in the struggle to succeed Lenin.

Stalin had two great talents which helped him to win power. He knew how to organise and he knew how to use people.

Working away behind the scenes, Stalin held one important organising job after another. In 1922 he landed the most important one of all. He became General Secretary of the Communist Party.

While Trotsky was busy speechmaking, Stalin quietly put his own followers into key jobs in the Communist Party, which ran the government in Moscow and in every town and village. These loyal yes-men would back him in his struggle for power. Soon he was confident enough of his position to go on to the attack.

Socialism in one country

Stalin spoke out particularly against Trotsky's ideas about world revolution. He put forward instead a policy of 'socialism in one country'. The 'one country' he meant was the USSR.

For communism to survive, said Stalin, the Russians had to be prepared to go it alone. This meant strengthening the USSR's ability to defend itself against attack. And this meant two things.

First, building up the USSR's military power. Second, constructing the factories, steel works and power stations to produce the tanks, the aircraft and the munitions to give her that power.

Stalin's victory

Stalin's arguments worked. So did his moves against Trotsky.

In vote after vote at vital Communist Party meetings Stalin's followers whittled away Trotsky's influence.

Trotsky was sacked first from the government, then from the Communist Party. In 1928 he was banished to a distant part of the country. In 1929 he was kicked out of the USSR altogether.

Stalin was in the saddle. He soon started to give the Russian people a rough ride.

Famine in the villages

A picture drawn by an anti-Bolshevik artist at the time of War Communism.

A peasant family in the Volga region in 1921.

1 a) What do you think   1) is happening in the picture,   2) the artist wants you to feel about what is happening?

  b) The picture was drawn by an anti-Bolshevik. Does that mean we cannot trust it as evidence of what the Bolsheviks did?

  c) Either in words or by making a sketch, show how a pro-Bolshevik picture or cartoon might justify these same actions.

  d) In what ways did the Bolsheviks   1) gain and   2) lose by such actions?

  e) Is there any connection between the scenes in the drawing and the photograph? If so, what is it?

  f) Do you think that photographs give better evidence about events than drawings? Use these two pictures to explain your answer.

Trotsky versus Stalin

The cover of Communist International, *October 1919, urging communists throughout the world to start revolutions.*

2 a) What would Trotsky's attitude to this cover have been?

b) What arguments might Stalin have put for or against the cover?

3 Three of these statements apply to Trotsky and three to Stalin. Copy the three which are about Trotsky in the correct order and add to each a sentence of your own to explain the statement. Do the same with the statements about Stalin.

. . . . . was the chief organiser of the Communist Party in the USSR.

. . . . . believed that the USSR should concentrate on encouraging communist revolutions in other countries.

. . . . . was expelled from the USSR by his main rival in 1929.

. . . . believed that the USSR should concentrate on becoming stronger.

. . . . . was in charge of the Red Army during and after the Civil War.

. . . . . had more power than anyone in the USSR by the end of the 1920s.

Lenin and the NEP

In May 1921, Lenin wrote this about his government's policies towards industry under his New Economic Plan (NEP).

"Want and destruction have gone so far that we cannot at once restore large-scale factory, state, socialist production . . . that means it is indispensable in a certain measure to help the restoration of small industry which does not require machines, does not require either state-owned or large stocks of raw material, food and fuel and can immediately give some aid to the peasant economy and raise its productive powers."

4 a) In your own words, explain what Lenin means by 'large-scale factory, state, socialist production'.

b) Why did he believe this kind of production was not possible in 1921?

c) Give two reasons why he thought that it would be easier to start small privately-owned industries working again.

d) How did he think the country would benefit from this?

The peasants and the NEP

Food production during the NEP.

	1922	1925
Grain harvest (millions of tonnes)	22.0	72.5
Number of cattle (in millions)	45.8	62.1
Number of pigs (in millions)	12.0	21.8
Number of horses (in millions)	21.7	27.1

This description of life in the 1920s in the village where he grew up was written by Fedor Belov, who later went to live in the United States.

"No one knew whom to believe, whose leadership to follow. One government followed another, and the peasants hung on grimly and waited for the end of the confusion.

It was a long time before the peasants felt safe in relinquishing [giving up] their guns, for it was not until 1923 that the village was free from the raids of armed bands, whether Communists, anti-Communists or ordinary brigands.

Following the Civil War, with all its anxieties and confusion, the village began gradually to revive. After the famine of 1921 (I should mention that no one in the village died of hunger during this time), the village lands were re-partitioned according to the new regulations. At that time the village numbered more than three thousand inhabitants, with total holdings of 4,380 hectares. This total included the . . . individual garden plots, which averaged 6 to 7 hectares per household.

Our land produced good crops . . . Every household had large surpluses of grain which it could dispose of as it saw fit; for the most part, the grain went to market for sale.

. . . the majority of the peasants were able to increase and improve their holdings. They built houses, barns and sheds, and bought agricultural implements. By 1926 the village had more than 500 cows, 300 horses, 600 swarms of bees, 2 watermills, 13 windmills, and 6 stores. More than 100 houses were fitted out with sheet-iron roofs, a sure sign of peasant prosperity. A villager who did not kill one or two pigs a year (for Christmas and Easter) was a rarity. As a rule, lard and eggs could be found in every home. These were the golden days of the NEP, which the peasants still look upon with longing . . ."

Fedor Belov, *The History of a Soviet Collective Farm*, 1956

5 a) Choose a suitable scale (such as 1 cm = 1 million) and turn the figures in the table into a bar graph.

b) Which product shows the biggest percentage increase?

c) Using Fedor Belov's account to help you, suggest reasons for the increases shown in the table.

d) Why do you think the peasants looked back on the NEP as 'the golden days'?

e) How might a communist who was against the NEP have commented on Belov's account?

f) In which ways might he feel that the table did not give the most important figures about the state of the USSR in the 1920s?

The need for more food

More food. Stalin knew that the USSR's farms had to grow more food to make a success of his plans to strengthen industry.

For one thing, he would have to feed a growing number of industrial workers. For another, the USSR needed lots of machines from abroad – coal cutters, dynamos, drills. It could only buy these by selling foodstuffs like butter and wheat to other countries. Food was all that the USSR had to sell.

Stalin thought he would never get the extra food without drastic changes in the way Russian agriculture was organised. A lot of people think that he was wrong about this. See what you think.

Lenin had let the peasants keep the land they had taken during the Revolution. Under the NEP many of them made a good living selling grain, meat, butter and eggs to the people of the towns.

Collective farms

But in 1929 Stalin started to force the peasants to give up their separate farms. He made them pool all their land and animals and work together in groups on big new farms called collectives.

Stalin believed that on collective farms the peasants would make a much better job of farming the land. His idea was that bigger farms with bigger fields would make it worthwhile to use expensive machines like tractors and combine harvesters. More crops would be grown – and by fewer workers. The spare peasants could become factory workers and so speed the growth of industry.

Collective farming appealed to Stalin for another reason, too. He saw the better-off peasants – the *kulaks* – as a threat to his plans for a truly communist USSR.

A peasant who owned land would never become a good communist. His main concerns would always be his own land, his own animals, his own profits. Doing away with land-owning peasants would mean a big step forward for communist ideas, Stalin believed.

Many peasants were bitter and angry about collectivisation. This was especially true of the *kulaks*. Many killed their animals rather than hand them over to the collectives. They slaughtered so many cattle, pigs and sheep that the USSR lost over half its livestock.

Crushing the peasants

Stalin replied by practically declaring war on the peasants. Anybody who opposed collectivisation was a *kulak* to him. And that was as good as a death sentence.

Nobody was safe. Thousands of peasants were shot and their land handed over to the collective farms. Stalin's soldiers marched off hundreds of thousands more to faraway prison camps. In these *gulags* they made them work as slave labourers – cutting timber, mining, digging canals.

Stalin's first collective farms were a disaster. The peasants he had marched off to the prison camps included many of the best farmers. Those left were often lazy and poor at their jobs. On top of this, Stalin did not have enough tractors or other new machines to go round. The result was that the output of important crops like wheat fell sharply. In some years the farms failed to grow enough to feed the people.

Yet Stalin went on taking food away from the villages to feed the towns and to sell abroad. In 1932 and 1933 famine swept across the USSR's countryside. Over five million peasants starved to death on some of the richest farmland in the world.

Stalin realised that his plans had gone badly wrong. He pushed the blame on to local officials and sent out fresh orders.

Stalin thinks again

He allowed many of the deported peasants to return from the prison camps to the villages. To encourage them to work harder he gave them little private plots of land of their own and allowed them to keep a few poultry and pigs.

Factories built under the Five Year Plans for industry (see Unit 20) helped to improve things, too. They turned out more and more tractors, combine harvesters and other farm machines.

Before 1930 less than 25,000 tractors and under 1000 combine harvesters were at work on Russian farms. By 1940 525,000 tractors and 182,000 combines were chugging across the fields.

The new machines slowly helped Russian farming to get back on its feet. Supplies moved steadily into the towns and famine looked like becoming a thing of the past.

Collectivisation: success or failure?

Yet, had collectivisation been a success? If we judge it by the amounts produced on the farms, the answer is no.

It was not until 1954 that farming output again reached the levels of 1928 – the year *before* Stalin started to force the peasants to join his collectives. And by 1954 the USSR had millions more people. No one needed to starve in the 1950s, but food was often rationed and every town had long queues of people hoping for the chance to buy a few extra eggs or apples.

So had all the suffering and all the waste caused by collectivisation been necessary?

Stalin would have answered 'Yes'. Collectivisation had fed his factory workers. It had crushed the *kulaks*. To him that was enough.

In the 1930s many peasants saw things differently. To them the price of collectivisation was starvation, broken families, imprisonment. Most farm work ended up being done by women and old men at wages far below those of factory workers.

And what about the schools, clinics and community centres that Stalin had promised? They did go up – in the handful of collective farms that foreign visitors or parties of young communists from the towns were shown around. Everywhere else village buildings and peasant homes were often as bad as in the days of the Tsar.

All the peasants could do was joke about the bad deal that Stalin had given them. One story went like this.

Stalin had lice in his hair. He asked a friend what he could do about it. 'Simple', replied the friend. 'Collectivise one louse and the rest will run away.'

Collectives: the dream

This strip cartoon in favour of collective farming appeared around 1920.

Ни достатка, ни порядка;
Ходит сам не свой Касьян:
У Касьяна есть лошадка,
Нету плуга и семян.

У Емели дует в щели,
С горя, бедный, будто пьян:
Плуг есть старый у Емели,
Нет лошадки и семян.

Злая грусть берет Нефеда,
Дед клянет весь белый свет:
Семена нашлись у деда,
Нет лошадки, плуга нет.

Повстречал Касьян Нефеда,
Подошел к ним Емельян.
Слово за слово—беседа
Завязалась у крестьян.

— Ох-ти, брат, не жизнь, а горе.
— Я вот стал совсем мощá.
Все на том сошлися вскоре:
С горем биться сообща.

Что у всех имелось втуне,
То теперь слилось в одно:
Есть коммуна, а в коммуне—
Плуг, лошадка и зерно.

Дед с Касьяном поле пашет,
С ними спаянный трудом,
Молотком Емеля машет,
Подновляя общий дом.

Труд не в труд, одна утеха,
Стал милее Божий мир.
— Братцы, счастья и успеха!
Демьян Бедный «Камунир».

Part of an interview that an old Russian peasant gave to an American reporter in 1964. He is praising a young Communist Party official, Nikita Sergeivitch Khrushchev. About twenty-five years after the events of the peasant's story, Khrushchev became ruler of the USSR.

"There were thirteen of us, the poorest peasants of the region, trying to start a collective farm . . . We had pooled all we had, a few cattle, a few plough oxen and some old and broken ploughs. Nikita Sergeivitch came and saw what we had done and congratulated us that we wished to start a collective . . .

'But you must all now forget the old ways', he said. 'You must now do new things in a new way. I will help you.'

Not long after that a marvellous machine called a Fordson arrived at our farm. It pulled great ploughs and had the strength of many oxen. All the peasants came to watch it work . . . They walked behind it, and marvelled at its strength, but it gave off a peculiar smell. The peasants shook their heads. 'Grain will never grow again', they said. 'The machine is poisoning the land.'

Nikita Sergeivitch was angry at such stupid talk . . . 'Old ways will never build a new society', he told them."

In *The Sunday Times Magazine*, 13th December 1964

1 a) In your own words describe what is happening in the cartoon.

b) Who do you think the cartoon was meant for? What was it meant to do?

c) Can you find any ways in which the cartoon and the peasant's story agree about the benefits of collective farming?

d) What impression of the work of the Communist Party does the peasant give? Would you have any reasons to distrust his account?

Collectives: the reality

A Russian novelist, Mikhail Sholokhov, describes what often happened when a village was about to be collectivised.

"Animals were slaughtered every night. Hardly had dusk fallen than the muffled bleats of sheep, the death squeals of pigs or the lowing of calves could be heard. Both those who had joined the collective farms and individual farmers slaughtered their stock. 'Slaughter, they'll take it for meat anyway . . . Slaughter, you won't get meat on the collective farm . . .', crept the . . . rumours. And they slaughtered. They ate until they could eat no more. Young and old suffered from indigestion. At dinner time tables groaned under boiled and roasted meat."

Mikhail Sholokhov, *Virgin Soil Upturned*, 1931

Malcolm Muggeridge, an English journalist, visited the USSR in 1933.

"A little market town in the Kuban district of the North Caucasus suggested a military occupation . . . the civilian population was obviously starving . . . there had been no bread at all in the place for three months, and such food as there was I saw for myself . . . black cooked meat . . . fragments of cheese and some cooked potatoes, half rotten . . .

'How are things with you?' I asked one man. He looked round anxiously to see that no soldiers were about. 'We have nothing, absolutely nothing. They have taken everything away,' he said and hurried on . . . It was true. They had nothing. It was also true that everything had been taken away. The famine is an organised one. Some of the food that has been taken away from them – and the peasants know this quite well – is being exported . . .

The little villages round about were even more depressing . . . Only smoke coming from some of the chimneys told that they were populated. It is literally true that whole villages had been exiled . . . I saw myself a group of some twenty peasants being marched off under escort."

The Manchester Guardian, 25th March 1933

Agricultural production 1928–35

	1928	1929	1930	1931	1932	1933	1934	1935
Grain (million tonnes)	73.3	71.7	83.5	69.5	69.6	68.4	57.6	75.0
Cattle (millions)	70.5	67.1	52.5	47.9	40.7	38.4	42.4	49.3
Pigs (millions)	26.0	20.4	13.6	14.4	11.6	12.1	17.4	22.6
Sheep and goats (millions)	146.7	147.0	108.8	77.7	52.1	50.2	51.9	61.6

2 a) Turn the figures in the table into two bar graphs, one for the grain harvest each year and one for the number of cattle.

b) What reason is suggested by Sholokhov for the fall in animal numbers?

c) Suggest one reason for, and one against, believing that Sholokhov is a reliable source of evidence for what happened.

d) What evidence did Malcolm Muggeridge have for stating that people were starving?

e) Who, or what, did he blame for this?

f) What evidence does he give to support this opinion?

g) How does the table help to explain Malcolm Muggeridge's account?

The problem

'We are fifty to a hundred years behind the advanced countries. We must make good this lag in ten years. Either we do it, or they crush us.'

These words were spoken by Stalin in 1929. They give us the key to what was to happen in the USSR under his rule. The country had to be made strong before its enemies could destroy it – no matter what the cost.

'We must make good this lag in ten years.' Easy to say, less easy to do. Steel works, power stations and factories could not be built and equipped without money. And the USSR did not have the money.

One way to get it was to borrow from abroad, from the capitalist countries.

Stalin did not want to do this. In return for their money the foreign capitalists would want a big share of industry's profits. And a big say in how it was run. Stalin was not prepared to give them either.

Another choice was to wait for improvements to come gradually. They had already started under the NEP.

But Stalin did not think that the USSR had the time to let things happen gradually. It had too many enemies, eager to attack while it was still weak.

Anyway, as a good communist follower of Karl Marx, Stalin wanted to destroy the last traces of capitalism in the USSR – the private businessmen and rich peasants who were thriving again under NEP.

If foreign money and gradual improvement were both ruled out, how could he make the USSR strong?

Stalin's solution

There was only one answer, Stalin decided. He would pay workers starvation wages, or less. He would force peasants to hand over crops at rock bottom prices. The USSR would be hauled into the modern world by the sweat and the blood of the Russian people.

Gosplan

All this needed careful planning, the job of experts in the State Planning Commission, or Gosplan. The planners' job was to match up the goods the country needed – tractors, say – with the resources it had to make them. They were supposed to make sure that every one of these resources – raw materials, machines, workers, power – was used to the best advantage.

The plans for each industry were finally gathered together in a thick book. This giant collection of information and production targets was called the Five Year Plan. The Plan's targets were government orders. Every manager had to make sure that his factory produced its share – or else!

The first Five Year Plan, 1928–32

Stalin's first Five Year Plan ran from 1928 to 1932. Its aim was to bring about a massive increase in the USSR's 'means of production'.

'Means of production' meant coal, electricity, steel, cement, machinery – things that would be useful in factories and workplaces, rather than for making people's lives more comfortable.

Amongst the first Five Year Plan's projects were the biggest hydro-electric station in Europe, on the River Dnieper; a giant new tractor factory in the town of Stalingrad; and new coal-mines and iron and steel works.

Many of the new industries were set up deep inside the USSR, to the east of the Ural mountains. For one thing these eastern lands contained vast amounts of coal and other raw materials. Just as important, Stalin knew that any attack on the USSR was most likely to come across her western borders. So it made good sense to build most of the new factories in the east, away from danger.

The second Five Year Plan, 1933–7

In the five years of the First Plan the output of electricity, coal and steel rocketed. The second Five Year Plan (1933–7) pushed production higher still. A great new steel works was built at a new town called Magnitogorsk. Thousands of workers laboured to build a new railway line linking Moscow with the industrial regions of the southern USSR. Tens of thousands more sweated to dig canals between the Baltic and White Seas and from Moscow to the River Volga, giving the USSR a network of waterways to carry goods across vast distances.

The result of the Five Year Plans was that the USSR's heavy industries, such as coal and steel, were amongst the strongest in the world by the late 1930s.

What the Plans cost

For the Russian people the years of the Five Year Plans were years of suffering. Men and women worked harder and longer for less and less pay. They were short of food, of clothing, of housing.

A popular riddle at the time went as follows.
Question: Why were Adam and Eve like Soviet citizens?
Answer: Because they lived in Paradise and had nothing to wear.

At first most workers accepted the hardships. They believed that they were building a better future. But as production targets went up, and wages came down, the workers became resentful.

There was little they could do, though. Their trade unions were just branches of the Communist Party, there to pass on government orders. Any worker who dared to object could be sacked. Worse still, he might be arrested for sabotage. That could mean years of slave labour in one of the dreaded forced labour camps, or *gulags*. You can read about these in Unit 21.

Success or failure?

Did the Five Year Plans succeed? Were the sufferings necessary? Stalin's answer to both questions would have been 'Yes'.

His Plans turned the USSR into an industrial giant. In 1941, when Hitler's armies made the attack Stalin had forecast, the USSR survived. Without the industrial strength that Stalin had given it, it would have been crushed.

Stalin's critics still wonder, though. Yes, his new steel works, power stations and factories saved the USSR. But need the Russian people have suffered so much to build them?

Soviet industry

Changes in industrial production 1913–37

	1913	1927/8	1932	1937
Coal (millions of tonnes)	29.8	36.1	65.6	138.6
Steel (millions of tonnes)	4.4	4.1	6.0	18.1
Oil (millions of tonnes)	10.5	11.9	22.7	29.1

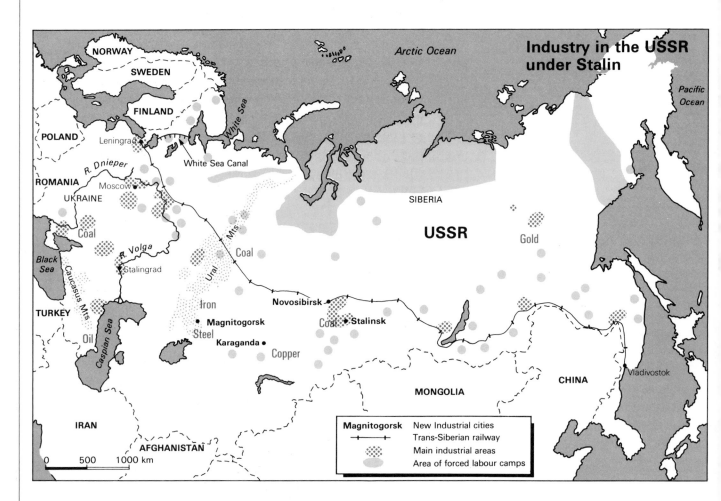

Industry in the USSR under Stalin

1 **a)** Turn the figures in the table into three bar graphs, one each for coal, steel and iron.

b) Why was increased production in these industries so important?

c) Which product had the greatest percentage increase between
1) 1927 and 1932,   2) 1932 and 1937?

d) How do you explain the increases in output shown on the table?

e) Do these statistics prove that Stalin's Five Year Plans succeeded?

f) Why does the map show so little industrial development west of Moscow?

g) What is the connection between the areas of labour camps and the changes in Soviet industry?

h) The towns named in heavy type were either villages or did not exist at all in the 1920s. Imagine you work in Gosplan in 1931. Make a list of all that you would need to arrange before new factories or steelworks could be opened in one of these places.

Soviet workers

In 1932 a twenty-year-old American welder, John Scott, arrived in the USSR. For five years he helped to build the giant new steel works at Magnitogorsk. Here he describes a conversation between some fellow workers.

"At about six o'clock a dozen or so young workers, men and women, gathered . . . Work was finished for the day, supper was on the stove, it was time for a song . . . Workers' revolutionary songs, folk tunes, and the old Russian romantic lyrics . . .

Then a discussion sprang up. 'Why don't we get more sugar? We've received only two hundred grams . . . per person this month. Tea without sugar doesn't get you anywhere.' Almost everybody had something to say. One young fellow explained that the sugar crop was bad this year . . . Somebody else pointed out that the USSR exported a great deal of candy, which meant sugar.

'We still have to export a lot to get the money to buy rolling mills and other such things that we can't make ourselves yet.' . . .

There was nearly always someone to explain the official position and the majority was usually satisfied.

'Just wait five or ten years and we won't need a single thing from the capitalist world', said Anya, a young woman welder, 'then we won't have to export food. We'll eat it all ourselves.'

'In five or ten years there won't be any capitalist world', said a young rigger, waving his hand . . . 'What do you think the workers in the capitalist world are doing? Do you think they are going to starve through another ten years of crisis, even supposing there is no war during that time? They won't stand for it.' "

John Scott, *Behind the Urals*, 1942

2 Imagine you are one of the people taking part in this conversation. Decide whether you would speak for or against Stalin's way of industrialising Russia. Then write down what you would say.

Stakhanov

In 1935 Alexei Stakhanov cut over a hundred tonnes of coal in six hours. It was a publicity stunt arranged with help from other workers.

The government made him into a hero through pictures like this one showing Stakhanov explaining his methods.

3 a) Why do you think the Soviet government made a hero of Stakhanov?

b) Would Soviet miners be pleased or worried by Stakhanov's achievement?

The purges

Discontent in the early 1930s

Purging the old Bolsheviks

The murder of Trotsky

Purging the Red Army

'I demand that the mad dogs be shot – every one of them!'

The time was August 1936. In a court room in Moscow the Soviet Supreme Court was meeting to try sixteen men for treason. All the prisoners had confessed to plotting with the exiled Trotsky to murder Stalin and other Soviet leaders.

The judges found them guilty. They sentenced them to be shot.

This trial in Moscow was part of Stalin's 'purges'. A purge means a drastic clean-out. The aim of these purges was to get rid of anyone Stalin did not trust. Between 1936 and 1939 the purges brought death or imprisonment to fifteen million people.

The purges took place on Stalin's personal orders. To understand why we need to look at the USSR in the early 1930s.

Many people disliked the way that Stalin was running things. Not just peasants and workers, but leading communists. They were suspicious about the way Stalin was gathering power into his own hands. They criticised him for the suffering and problems that collectivisation was causing.

Some of these top communists became convinced that it was time to get rid of Stalin. But Stalin struck first.

The murder of another top communist named Kirov in December 1934 gave Stalin his excuse. He began a campaign of terror against anyone he thought might oppose him.

The first men Stalin wiped out were the other surviving leaders of the 1917 Revolution. These 'Old Bolsheviks' were Stalin's most dangerous rivals. They had enough support in the Communist Party to set up a new government if they could get rid of Stalin.

Stalin had practically all the Old Bolsheviks arrested and executed. Some were persuaded – nobody is quite sure how – to confess their guilt in big public show trials before they were shot.

The most dangerous Old Bolshevik, Trotsky, was out of Stalin's reach at first. But on an August day in 1940 a visitor from the USSR called to see Trotsky in a hide-out in far away Mexico. Trotsky thought the visitor was a friend. In fact he was a member of Stalin's secret police. As Trotsky sat working at his desk, the visitor smashed an ice-pick into Trotsky's skull.

Once Stalin had got rid of the Old Bolsheviks he turned on the Red Army. He suspected – perhaps rightly – that its generals might try to overthrow him.

Stalin arrested the Commander in Chief, Marshal Tukhachevsky, and fourteen of the Red Army's sixteen generals. He accused them of plotting with the Germans and had them shot. In the months which followed he had a quarter of the army's officers, 20,000 of them, shot or imprisoned.

Millions of ordinary Russians suffered in Stalin's purges, too.

They were grabbed by the secret police and shot or packed off without trial to distant prison camps. In these camps, or *gulags*, thousands died from overwork and ill treatment.

Why the purges?

Why did Stalin order the purges?

The basic reason was simple – to destroy all possible opposition to his own absolute power. Stalin claimed that he had to do this for the good of the USSR.

By the time of the purges Adolf Hitler had become ruler of Germany. Stalin knew how much Hitler hated Russian communism. An attack on the USSR seemed dangerously close. The USSR could not afford disagreements at a time like this, decided Stalin. To him, that meant everybody doing what he said.

Stalin's critics claim that this sort of reasoning was just an excuse. In fact, they say, Stalin's purges weakened the USSR. His purge of the army, in particular, nearly gave Hitler victory on a plate when the Nazis did attack the USSR in 1941.

The real reason for Stalin's purges, his critics claim, was that he was a cruel and suspicious monster. He was so addicted to power that he was ready to kill without mercy to hang on to it.

The 1936 Constitution

In 1936 Stalin gave the people of Russia a new set of rules for governing the country. This Constitution promised them all sorts of rights. For example, it said that 'no person can be arrested except by decision of a court'. In fact, the only rights any Russians had in these years were what Stalin decided they could have. And that included the right to go on breathing.

After the Second World War

In the years after the end of the Second World War in 1945 Stalin's grip on the USSR grew even tighter. People were taught to look upon him as the heroic war leader as well as the great builder of communism.

Stalin now feared an attack on the USSR by the USA and her allies (see Unit 10). He went on spending vast amounts of money on the armed forces and on heavy industry.

Because of this, and even more because of the immense destruction caused by the war (see Unit 14), the Russian people were short of food, clothing and housing. On top of this, every year the dreaded secret police sent thousands more of them to the *gulags*.

Yet, despite the hardships and the fear, the adoration of Stalin got louder. People thought the more they shouted his praises, the better their chance of escaping the attention of the secret police.

If anything good happened, Stalin got the credit. If things went wrong, the blame was put on people who were supposed to have done things that he did not know about.

The death of Stalin

But even Stalin the superman could not live for ever. In 1953 he suffered a stroke and died.

When they heard the news the people of the USSR felt confused and fearful. They had suffered and slaved under Stalin. Yet without him the USSR would have perished – or so they had been taught. What lay ahead now?

Victims of the purges

This mock travel poster was issued in the 1930s by anti-communists who had fled from the USSR. The words in French say 'Visit the USSR's pyramids'.

Eleanor Lipper was a prisoner in Stalin's gulags for eleven years.

"The quantity of bread in all Soviet camps is governed by the amount of work the prisoner performs . . . a person unaccustomed to physical labour . . . quickly falls into a vicious circle. Since he cannot do his full quota of work, he does not receive the full bread ration: his under-nourished body . . . gets less and less bread, and in the end is so weakened that only clubbings can force him to drag himself from camp to gold mine.

Once he reaches the shaft . . . he is too weak to defend himself when a criminal punches him in the face and takes away his day's ration of bread. He employs his last remaining strength to creep off to an out-of-the-way corner where neither the curse of the guards nor their eternal cry of 'Davai, Davai!' (Get going) can reach him. Only the fearful cold finds him out and mercifully gives him his sole desire: peace, sleep, death."

Eleanor Lipper, *Eleven Years in Soviet Prison Camps*, 1951

1 a) In the poster, what are the pyramids made of?
  b) What is the artist saying about life in the USSR?
  c) What was the value of labour camps like this to the USSR?
  d) Write a conversation between two guards, one of whom is happy with the system in the camp and another who feels that it is run wrongly.
  e) Lipper's account was written years after the events she describes. Do you think that this makes it any less valuable as evidence?

Assessing Stalin

Nikita Khrushchev became ruler of the USSR in the 1950s. Three years after Stalin died he attacked Stalin's record in a speech to the Communist Party Congress in 1956.

"It was during this period (1935–1937–1938) that the practice of mass repression . . . was born, first against the enemies of Leninism . . . and subsequently against many honest Communists . . . Stalin originated the concept [idea] 'enemy of the people'. This term . . . made possible the . . . most cruel repression . . . against anyone who in any way disagreed with Stalin . . .

It was determined that of the 139 members of the Party's Central Committee who were elected at the Seventeenth Congress, ninety-eight persons, i.e. 70 per cent, were arrested and shot . . . The same fate met not only the Central Committee members, but also the majority of delegates to the . . . Party Congress. Of 1966 delegates . . . 1108 persons were arrested on charges of anti-revolutionary crimes . . .

Stalin was a very distrustful man, sickly suspicious; we knew this from our work with him. He could look at a man and say: 'Why are your eyes so shifty today?' or 'Why are you turning so much today and avoiding to look me directly in the eyes?' . . .

When Stalin said that one or another would be arrested, it was necessary to accept on faith that he was an 'enemy of the people'."

Fourteen years after Stalin's death the manager of a collective farm describes how he felt about him to a reporter.

"I was in love with that man, and I love him still. The day he died, I wept like a baby . . .

I loved him for his mind, his logic, his manliness and especially his courage. He was the one person who was great enough to keep the Soviet Union together and make us a great nation after Lenin died. When he was old, of course, he made some serious mistakes; democracy in this country suffered and innocent people died. But without him *everything* would have been lost. He was the only leader who could have saved us from the Trotskys and Bukharins [an old Bolshevik] and then from the Nazis. It was for him that we worked and sacrificed and died. He was the genius of his time."

In *The Sunday Times Magazine*, 21st May 1967

2 a) In your own words, describe Khrushchev's main criticisms of Stalin.

b) What evidence does Khrushchev give that many victims of the purges were active Communist Party members? Can you suggest why Stalin had them purged?

c) Imagine you are a Communist Party member who has been coming to Congresses for twenty years. What would you think about Khrushchev's speech? How would it affect your opinion of Stalin?

d) In which ways does the farm manager accept Khrushchev's criticisms of Stalin?

e) List the points the farm manager makes in defence of Stalin's reputation.

f) Considering Stalin's complete record, would *you* describe him as 'the genius of his time'? Explain why or why not.

Khrushchev

Relief. That was what leading men in Stalin's government felt when he died. Relief that they would not be the next to be purged.

To make sure, they arrested Beria, the feared chief of the secret police. They had him shot to stop him from becoming a new Stalin.

The new leaders said that the USSR would now be led by a group of them working together. They called this 'collective leadership'.

The members of the new collective leadership were supposed to be equal. But by 1954 one man had come out on top. He was a stout, bald-headed, one-time coal-miner named Nikita Khrushchev.

Khrushchev was very different from Stalin. He seemed much more human. He loved to travel about the country, cracking jokes and beaming happily as he mingled with the crowds.

The Twentieth Congress, 1956

In 1956 Khrushchev spoke to members of the Communist Party from all over the USSR when they met in Moscow for their Twentieth Congress, or Conference. At a secret meeting he told them some of the real truth about Stalin (see page 91).

The Russian people knew already about the suffering and killing under Stalin. Most of them had suffered themselves. But they had always believed that the prison camps and the purges had been necessary to save their country from its enemies.

Now Khrushchev told them this was only partly true. They gasped in horror and amazement as he gave them examples of the dictator's greed for power, his suspicious nature, his pitiless cruelty. Khrushchev promised that from now on things would be different.

De-Stalinisation

Khrushchev's speech to the Twentieth Congress marked the start of his attempt to 'de-Stalinise' the USSR. Stalin's statues and pictures were taken down from public places. History books which did nothing but praise him were rewritten. A few years later his body was taken out of its glass coffin beside Lenin and quietly buried.

Khrushchev reduced the powers of the secret police. He also closed down the worst of Stalin's prison camps and set free many thousands of prisoners. The prisoners were 'rehabilitated'. That is, the government admitted they had been innocent all along.

For the first time in years people started to feel free to speak their minds. Writers and artists began to express their true feelings instead of just turning out propaganda in support of communism.

One of the best known writers was Alexander Solzhenitsyn. Solzhenitsyn had spent years as a *zek*, or prisoner, in a labour camp. Now he turned his experiences into a true-to-life novel called *One Day in the Life of Ivan Denisovich*.

Solzhenitsyn's book was the first Soviet novel to tell the truth about life in Stalin's labour camps, the *gulags*. It supported what Khrushchev had said about Stalin. Because of this Khrushchev allowed it to be put on sale.

Khrushchev and living standards

Khrushchev also set out to improve everyday living standards. 'We must help people to eat well, dress well and live well', he said. 'If after forty years of communism a person cannot have a glass of milk or a pair of shoes, he will not believe that communism is a good thing, no matter what you tell him.'

Khrushchev began by increasing wages. Then he saw to it that there was more to buy. Not only food, but clothes, furniture and household goods. To provide more of these 'consumer goods' he ordered changes in Soviet industry. More money went into building factories to turn out products such as artificial fibres and plastics, the raw materials for clothing and other consumer goods.

Khrushchev built new blocks of flats in cities all over the USSR. Between 1959 and 1965 fifty million people were rehoused. Even so, there were not enough new homes to go round.

Khrushchev and farming

Food was still in short supply, too. In the middle 1950s Russian farmers were producing barely enough to feed the people. Khrushchev tried various schemes to remedy this. He paid the peasants more for what they produced on the collective farms. In 1958 he also told them that they could keep all the produce from their private plots. After feeding their families they could sell what was left and pocket the money.

The peasants' private plots totalled only 3 per cent of the USSR's total area of farmland. But by the early 1960s that 3 per cent was producing 25 per cent of the nation's supply of food, including most of its vegetables, fruit and milk.

But Khrushchev's biggest farming plan failed badly. This was his 'virgin lands' scheme.

The virgin lands scheme

These virgin lands lay in the east of the USSR – millions of hectares of rolling grasslands that had never been used to grow crops. Khrushchev decided to plough them up and plant wheat.

The virgin lands produced a bumper harvest in 1958. But it proved difficult to get the crops to market because of the poor roads and a shortage of lorries.

Later years brought weather problems. Some years the winter snows came early, burying the unharvested crops in the fields. Other years there was very little rain and the land turned to dust and was blown away by the wind.

The sacking of Khrushchev

In 1964 the harvest failed yet again and the USSR had to buy wheat from its great rival, the USA. This was too much for the other Soviet leaders. In October they banded together and made Khrushchev resign.

The failure of Khrushchev's farming policies was only one reason for his downfall. Other leaders felt that his de-Stalinisation campaign was undermining the Soviet people's belief in the communist way of life. They were unhappy, too, about his foreign policies – his handling of the Cuban Crisis of 1962 (see Unit 50) and his quarrel with the Chinese communist leader, Mao Zedong (Unit 52).

Khrushchev retired to a house outside Moscow and lived there

Brezhnev and Kosygin

until his death in 1971. The fact that he was allowed to do this instead of being shot showed how much he had changed the USSR.

Two men called Brezhnev and Kosygin took over as the Soviet Union's main leaders. Brezhnev and Kosygin were amongst those who felt that Khrushchev had let people criticise the communist way of life too much. They set out to stop this.

In 1966 two writers named Daniel and Sinyavsky were thrown into prison for letting books which criticised the USSR appear abroad. In 1974 Alexander Solzhenitsyn was kicked out of the USSR for the same offence.

Others who dared to criticise government policies – 'dissidents', as they were called – disappeared into mental hospitals. Brezhnev and Kosygin used mental hospitals in the same way that Stalin had used prison camps – to get rid of critics of their government.

In agriculture Brezhnev and Kosygin faced the same problems that had troubled Lenin, Stalin and Khrushchev – how to ensure that the Soviet countryside produced enough food to feed the towns.

All through the 1970s a mixture of bad weather, poor organisation and shortages of equipment meant that the countryside was still failing to do this. The USSR had to go on buying vast amounts of foreign grain, especially from the USA.

The Brezhnev years

By the early 1970s Brezhnev had pushed Kosygin into the background. From then until his death in 1982 he was the unchallenged leader of the country.

Brezhnev wanted to make the USSR the strongest military power on earth. Under his leadership the country spent more on weapons than any other nation. By the end of the 1970s the USSR had more, and bigger, nuclear missiles than the USA. In the 1980s one out of every six of the world's soldiers was in the USSR's Red Army.

At home Brezhnev was not an experimenter like Khrushchev. In all important matters he was conservative – that is, he liked to keep to old ways of doing things. He changed nothing unless he had to.

This suited the thousands of government officials who ran the USSR. They had disliked Khrushchev's constant experiments. With Brezhnev they knew where they stood.

Millions of ordinary Russians accepted Brezhnev for the same reason. In place of Stalin's terror and Khrushchev's experiments he gave them almost twenty years of calm and growing prosperity.

When Brezhnev died in 1982, an engineer summed up the feelings of many other Russians. 'We used to complain and tell jokes about the old man', he said. 'But now that Brezhnev is dead I feel sad, because he conveyed a sense of security and stability.'

But some of the top people in the government felt that it was now time for change – in ways of running the government, in dealings with the outside world, in organising industry and farming.

In 1985 a new younger leader took over. His name was Mikhail Gorbachev. The people of the USSR, and of the world, waited to see what changes the Gorbachev years would bring.

Khrushchev and agriculture

The boss of a collective farm talks to a reporter about Khrushchev, a few years after he fell from power.

"Nikita was a good man with a good heart, and he tried hard – but that wasn't enough to be leader of a great country. He had too much wild enthusiasm and not enough brains, and the silly schemes that resulted from that combination caused a lot of unnecessary waste.

He tried to tell everyone everything – where to plant what, for example – on the basis of his personal whims instead of scientific evidence and practical experience. No man can know everything, but he thought his instincts were infallible."

In *The Sunday Times Magazine*, 21st May 1967

This diagram from The Illustrated Reference Book of Modern History *shows farm production figures from the last years of Stalin until just after Khrushchev was dismissed.*

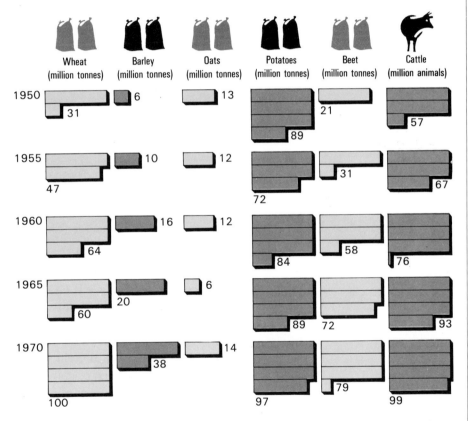

1 **a)** Give examples of Khrushchev's policies which you think justify the farm manager's view that he was 'a good man with a good heart'.

b) What does the diagram tell you about the amount of food produced in Khrushchev's time as ruler? Suggest reasons for the change.

c) Suggest a 'silly scheme' of Khrushchev's that the manager might have had in mind.

d) What might Khrushchev have said to defend his farming policies against accusations such as this?

e) How far do the statistics for wheat production in 1960 and 1965 support the farm manager's view that Khrushchev followed some silly schemes?

f) Why have all Soviet leaders had difficulties with agriculture?

Soviet life in the 1950s

Wright Miller is an English writer who has visited the USSR many times. This is his impression of how Soviet people felt about their country and their lives at the end of the 1950s.

"To ask the ordinary person what he thinks of . . . 'Communism' is too general a question . . . He may approve of the new school his children attend, or the new goods in the shops; he may speak of sputniks [satellites] or recall that Soviet power defeated the Germans . . . he may recall the . . . price cuts since the war, or if he is old enough he may recall the village where peasants used to eat with their fingers from a common bowl and now, though living in the same huts, most of them have TV sets.

On the other hand he may . . . recall half a dozen friends who were hauled off to Siberia and died there, or the brutal questioning he had himself to endure from Soviet security police.

In 1959 and 1960 my own general impression was that people were simply happy at being able to relax . . .

. . . one can change one's job easily if one wants . . . People have . . . much more chance of acquiring the clothing or footwear they want, or a refrigerator or other consumer goods . . .

In 1959 a . . . friend put the new situation to me: 'For forty years', he said, 'we have been asked to work for the future, for posterity, for our grandchildren, and now at last we are being asked to work for something we can have in our hands now.' "

Wright Miller, *Russians as People*, 1960

2 a) Make a list of all the ways in which life was better for Russians in the 1950s than in the 1930s. Try turning it into a diagram or cartoon.

b) Imagine you are a Soviet leader in 1964 who has helped to overthrow Khrushchev. You have to write a television news bulletin to explain to ordinary Russians why Khrushchev has been dismissed. What would you say?

Khrushchev

3 The following statements are all about Khrushchev. Two are false. Pick these out and replace them with true statements. Copy out all six statements and add a sentence to each to explain it more fully.

a) He made himself leader of the USSR by killing off all his rivals.

b) He set out to 'de-Stalinise' the Soviet Union.

c) He tried to improve the living standards of the Russian people.

d) He made the secret police more powerful.

e) He ordered millions of hectares of virgin land to be planted with crops.

f) He was sacked by other Soviet leaders who disagreed with his policies.

Brezhnev

When Brezhnev died in 1982 an English magazine wrote about him:

"The most appropriate monument to him would be a multi-warhead nuclear missile with a stopped clock."

The Economist, 12th November 1982

4 What do you think that *The Economist* meant by this?

PART THREE
THE USA

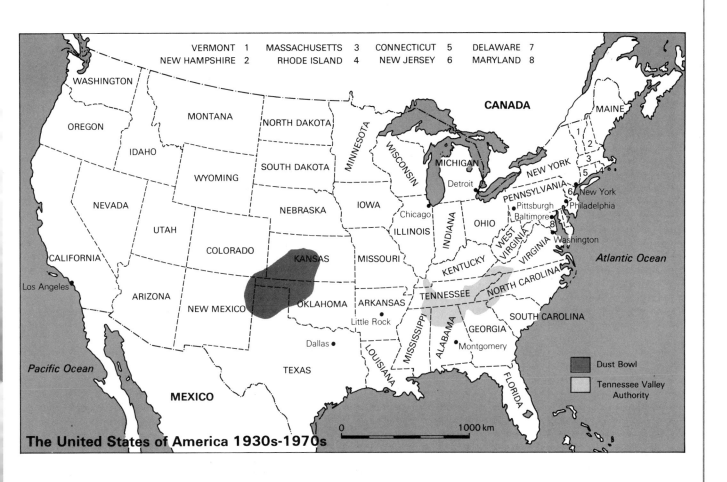

VERMONT 1 MASSACHUSETTS 3 CONNECTICUT 5 DELAWARE 7
NEW HAMPSHIRE 2 RHODE ISLAND 4 NEW JERSEY 6 MARYLAND 8

The United States of America 1930s–1970s

Dust Bowl

Tennessee Valley Authority

0   1000 km

Gangsters blazing away with machine-guns. Rowdy parties. Girls dancing the Charleston. These are the pictures that come into many people's minds when they think of the USA in the 1920s. The 'roaring twenties'. Wild times. Good times.

The United States was the richest nation on earth in these years. Its national income – the total earnings of its citizens – was higher than Britain's, Germany's, Japan's and those of nineteen other countries put together. The American people enjoyed the highest living standards the world had ever seen.

The rich Americans

One reason Americans were so well off was their country's great natural riches. The USA had vast areas of fertile land. Its stock of vital raw materials such as coal, iron ore and oil seemed unlimited.

By the 1920s the hard work and drive of the American people had put these resources to work. American oil was powering engines and lubricating machines. American coal was generating electricity and smelting iron ore. The iron ore became steel, which went into a vast range of products from safety pins to skyscrapers.

Mass production

The USA became the first nation to build its way of life on selling vast quantities of goods to give ordinary people easier lives. These 'consumer goods' – cars, refrigerators, radios, electric cleaners – poured off mass-production assembly lines in huge new factories. Between 1919 and 1929 such factories doubled their output.

Even ten years earlier, many of their products had been luxuries. Some had hardly been invented. Now millions of Americans came to look upon them as everyday necessities.

The most famous factories belonged to the car-maker, Henry Ford. One of the secrets of Ford's success was that he made all his Model T automobiles exactly alike. 'The customer can have any colour he likes', he once said, 'so long as it's black.'

The sales boom

Year by year car, radio and other consumer goods sales rose to new heights. Bigger sales meant busier factories. Busier factories meant good profits and wages for more factory workers. The extra money in people's pockets was one reason sales went on rising.

There were others, such as radio and newspaper advertising campaigns, and easy ways of paying through 'instalment plan' (hire purchase) schemes. Live now, pay tomorrow – a tomorrow which most Americans were convinced would be like today only better, with even more money bulging in their wallets.

'The man who builds a factory builds a temple', said Calvin Coolidge, the President from 1923 to 1928. 'The man who works there, worships there.'

In 1928 the new President, Herbert Hoover, told the American people, 'We shall soon be in sight of the day when poverty will be banished from this nation.' Most Americans believed him. They could see it happening in their own lives.

The government and industry

The words of Hoover and Coolidge explain the policies of American governments in the 1920s.

These governments were controlled by the Republican Party. The Republicans had one main belief. If the government looked after the well-being of the businessman, everybody would become better off.

Businessmen whose firms were doing well, the Republicans claimed, would take on more workers and pay more wages. Their growing wealth would trickle down and benefit everybody.

The majority of representatives in Congress (the American parliament) were Republicans. Congress placed high tariffs, or import taxes, on goods from abroad. The aim was to make them more expensive, so that American manufacturers would have less competition from foreign rivals. At the same time Congress reduced taxes on high incomes and company profits. Rich men had more money to invest.

The poor Americans

Yet, despite all the prosperity, there were still lots of poor Americans. In the great industrial cities of the north, such as Chicago and Pittsburgh, immigrants from other lands laboured long hours for low wages in steel mills, sweat shops and slaughter houses. In the south thousands of poor farmers, some black and some white, worked from sunrise to sunset to scrape a bare living.

The wealth that the Republicans said would trickle down to everybody never reached people like these. A survey in 1929 showed that half the American people had barely enough money to buy sufficient food and clothing.

Factory workers

The main reason for poverty among workers was low wages. Owners could get away with giving low pay because there were usually plenty of unemployed immigrant workers looking for jobs.

Many workers had no trade union to stand up for them either. Skilled workers were earning good wages and felt that they did not need unions. If unskilled workers tried to join one, employers would threaten them with the sack or have them beaten up.

Farmers

Farmers and farm workers had a hard time for different reasons. In the south many farmers did not own the land they farmed. They were share-croppers. For rent a share-cropper gave the landowner part of what he grew – often so much that he was left with hardly enough to feed his family.

In the west most farmers did own their land. But they, too, faced hard times. During the First World War they had been able to sell their wheat to Europe for high prices. By 1921 the countries of Europe no longer needed as much American food.

By then farmers were finding it more difficult to sell their produce at home, too. Immigration had fallen, so the number of people needing food was growing more slowly. All the new cars didn't help either. Cars ran on petrol, not on corn and hay like horses.

American farmers found themselves growing products they could not sell. By 1924 600,000 of them were bankrupt.

The automobile

Cars in a small town in farming country, Texas, in the mid 1920s.

An American historian wrote this about the mid 1920s motor industry:

" . . . the motor vehicle was now consuming annually 90 per cent of the country's petroleum products, 80 per cent of the rubber, 20 per cent of the steel, 75 per cent of the plate glass and 24 per cent of the machine tools."

John B. Rae, *The American Automobile*, 1966

1 a) What would you have seen on this street instead of cars, twenty or so years before the photograph was taken?

  b) Suggest ways in which the car's arrival would have changed the lives and work of the families who lived on the farms around this town.

  c) Think about this scene from the point of view of the people of this town and the district around. What new jobs would it mean for them?

  d) Explain how each of the products mentioned by John Rae was used in the motor industry.

  e) What might happen to jobs in industries making these products if   1) more and   2) fewer motor vehicles were sold?

2 The list below gives reasons for the USA being prosperous in the 1920s. Write them out in what you think is their order of importance. Then write two or three sentences about each of your top *three* choices to explain why you have put them there.

Plenty of raw materials	Mass-produced consumer goods
Advertising	Instalment plan buying
Government policies	High profits and wages

Prosperity and poverty

Changes in American life in the 1920s.

	1920	1929
Kilometres of surfaced roads	620,000	1,000,000
Motor cars on roads	9,000,000	26,000,000
Telephones in homes and offices	13,000,000	20,000,000
Radios in homes	60,000	10,000,000

3 a) Do you think the figures show that life in the 1920s was
    1) changing fast, 2) not changing much, 3) not changing at all?
    Use the figures to explain your choice.

b) How might the changes have benefited each of the following
    groups: 1) factory workers, 2) shopkeepers, 3) farmers,
    4) shareholders in companies?

c) One of these groups might have been harmed. Which one do you
    think that it was? Explain how its members might have suffered.

*A cartoon in an American magazine at Christmas, 1928. The little boy is
asking his father, 'D'ya think yuh'll be workin' by next year, Papa?'*

4 a) How does this cartoon show that many Americans were well off?

b) What does this cartoon tell you about poverty in the USA?

c) Imagine what the small boy's father was thinking and feeling. Write
    what he might have told his wife later about the incident.

d) Make a list of those groups of Americans who did not share in the
    prosperity of the 1920s.

e) In your own words, say how each of the following helped to stop
    people from becoming better off:

        Powerful employers   Surplus workers
        Weak unions and lack of unions   Lack of skill
        Share-cropping   Peace

The seven men faced the white-washed garage wall with their hands in the air. The machine-guns chattered, mowing them down in a hail of bullets. All seven were killed.

This was the 'St Valentine's Day Massacre'. It happened in Chicago on 14th February 1929. It was ordered by the gangster chief Al Capone. The St Valentine's Day Massacre was Capone's way of protecting his business against rivals. Capone's business was making and selling booze – alcoholic drinks like beer, wine, whisky and gin. Doing this was against the law in the 1920s.

Prohibition

In 1919 the American people had voted to alter, or amend, their country's Constitution – the set of rules by which the USA is governed. This Eighteenth Amendment said that no one in the USA could make or sell alcoholic drinks of any kind.

Shortly afterwards Congress passed a law called the Volstead Act. This was to make sure that people obeyed the new 'prohibition' amendment.

People who supported the Eighteenth Amendment were nicknamed 'dries'. They claimed that prohibition would stop drunkenness and make the USA a happier, healthier country.

People who were against prohibition ('wets') did not accept such arguments. They looked upon the dries as narrow-minded killjoys.

Speakeasies and bootleggers

So many Americans were 'wets' that by the middle of the 1920s breaking the prohibition law became accepted and respectable. Some people concocted booze in bathrooms and kitchens. Others became customers of illegal drinking places called 'speakeasies'.

Speakeasies sprang up in basements and back rooms all over the country. The city of Chicago alone had 10,000. New York had 32,000 – twice the number of legal saloons before prohibition!

The speakeasies got their drink from gangsters such as Capone. You could get rich quickly by supplying alcoholic drinks illegally – 'bootlegging', as it was called.

Bootlegging was a dangerous business. In cities like Chicago competition between rival gangs of bootleggers exploded into street wars, fought out with armour-plated cars and machine-guns.

The winners of the gangster wars became rich and powerful. They used their wealth to bribe the police and other public officials to turn a blind eye to what they were doing.

Al Capone

Al Capone became the real ruler of Chicago. He had a private army of nearly a thousand machine-gun-equipped thugs. His income was over 100 million dollars a year. With it he bribed policemen, politicians and newspaper reporters.

By the end of the 1920s most Americans regarded the prohibition laws as half-scandal, half-joke. The dishonesty and corruption which grew with prohibition made them lose their respect both for the law and for the people who were supposed to enforce it.

The end of prohibition

Immigrants

Ku Klux Klan

Immigration laws

Prohibition was finally given up in 1933. But it had done the USA lasting harm. Gangsters remained powerful. They used the money they had made from bootlegging to set up other criminal businesses.

Worse still, prohibition had made law breaking a habit for many otherwise respectable Americans. Once people get used to breaking one law, what are the rest worth?

Like millions of other Americans in the 1920s, Al Capone was an immigrant. In the first fifteen years of the twentieth century over thirteen million such people from other lands moved into the USA.

Unlike Capone, most immigrants were honest and hard-working. Many came from countries in the south and east of Europe, such as Italy, Russia and Poland. These new arrivals were usually very poor, unskilled and unable to speak English.

The immigrants found work in booming cities like Chicago and Pittsburgh – feeding the furnaces, labouring on factory assembly lines, hacking out coal. They worked hard, often for low wages, because they wanted to make a success of their new lives.

Some Americans were glad to have the immigrants at first. But by the 1920s many had turned against them. 'America is a garbage can', warned the leader of an organisation called the Ku Klux Klan.

Members of the Ku Klux Klan paraded about in long, white gowns and hid their faces with pointed hoods. They beat up anyone they did not like, burned down their homes, even murdered them.

The Ku Klux Klan was not just against immigrants. Most Klan members were American-born, white and Protestant. They felt threatened by anyone with a different language, colour or religion. All these things were 'un-American', they said. Being 'un-American' was their excuse for violence against blacks, Jews and Catholics, as well as new immigrants.

Other Americans did not use violence against the newcomers. But they attacked them in other ways. Immigrants, they said, took jobs from American workers; they lowered standards of health and education; they threatened the country's way of life by bringing in 'un-American' ideas like communism.

By the early 1920s such feelings were so strong that Congress passed laws to limit the number of immigrants. The one which had most effect was the Immigration Quota Law of 1924.

The Immigration Quota Law said that no more than 150,000 immigrants a year would be let in to the USA. Each country which sent immigrants was given a 'quota'. The quota was based upon the number of its people living in the USA. The more already there, the more new immigrants it would be allowed to send.

The quota favoured immigrants from Britain and north Europe – and it was meant to. These were the countries from which the ancestors of most 1920s Americans had originally come.

The 1924 Immigration Law marked the end of one of the most important population movements in world history. The rules that it laid down did not really change for the next forty years.

Bootleggers

Al Capone in 1930 on the cover of Time, *one of the most read American magazines.*

TIME

The Weekly Newsmagazine

ALPHONSE ("SCARFACE") CAPONE
A pink apron, a pan of spaghetti.
(See NATIONAL AFFAIRS)

Volume XV   Number 12

Al Capone said this to a man who was writing a book about him.

"They call Al Capone a bootlegger. Yes, its bootleg while it's on the trucks, but when your host . . . hands it to you on a silver tray, its hospitality. What's Al Capone done, then? He's supplied a . . . demand. Some call it bootlegging. Some call it racketeering. I call it a business. They say I violate the prohibition law. Who doesn't?"

F. D. Pasley, *Al Capone. The Biography of a Self Made Man*, 1931

1 a) Does the fact that a national magazine had Capone's picture on its cover mean he was 1) famous, 2) admired, 3) disliked, 4) despised? Give reasons for your choice.

b) How does Al Capone's statement help to explain how he became so rich?

c) Explain how it helps you to understand why prohibition failed.

d) Which of these statements do you think is most likely to be correct? 1) The lack of respect for law in the 1920s led to there being gangsters like Al Capone. 2) Gangsters like Al Capone led to there being a lack of respect for law in the 1920s. Explain your choice.

2 Match up the names below with the descriptions. Write out each sentence and to each one add a sentence of your own to explain it more fully.

A wet	was an illegal drinking place.
A speakeasy	was a person who supported prohibition.
A dry	was a person who was against prohibition.
A bootlegger	was a law forbidding making or selling alcohol.
Prohibition	was a person who illegally made and sold alcohol.

Immigrants

The son of a Jewish immigrant from Poland describes his father's experiences of life in the USA in the early years of the twentieth century.

" . . . the exploitation of labour was fearful and my father was having a terrible time. He was just getting by, making a living working twelve to fourteen hours a day. And he was suffering like a coal miner suffers, because in the sweat-shops, at that time, instead of coal dust what you got was lint. . . . Lint got down the throat and into the lungs and caused the same coughing, the same diseases, the same sickness as dust. And in the end it killed you. And in the end it probably was what killed him. . . .

But he still wanted to live in America. He never became rich, he never became successful – and he never became bitter . . . even though he took the worst the country had to hand him, he knew he was better off than he would have been in Poland. Remember, he had come from a place where, if you were Jewish, you didn't count as a human being and you had no rights at all. In America they gave my father the vote, they allowed him a place to live, and they let his children grow up as Americans. Because of that he could never feel bitter or disillusioned."

Leon Stein, in D. Wilcox, *Americans*, 1978

An Italian mother and her family in the bedroom of their home in a New York tenement, about 1910.

3 a) What sort of work do you think Leon Stein's father did?
  b) Imagine you are either Stein's father or the father of the family in the photograph. Write what you might tell your children about your feelings about being an immigrant worker in the USA.
  c) What problem would you have as a Polish or Italian immigrant that a British immigrant to the USA would not have?
  d) How do the extract and the photograph help to explain anti-immigrant feelings in the USA?
  e) How might Stein's father have answered people who criticised immigrants?

In the heart of New York city lies a narrow street enclosed by the walls of high office buildings. Its name is Wall Street.

One Thursday afternoon in October 1929 a workman outside an upper floor window of a Wall Street office found himself staring into the eyes of four policemen. They reached out to grab him. 'Don't jump', shouted one of the policemen. 'It's not that bad.' 'Who's going to jump?' asked the startled worker. 'I'm just washing windows!'

To understand this incident we need to look at what had been going on in Wall Street in the months and years before that October afternoon in 1929.

Stockbrokers and shares

Wall Street is the home of the New York Stock Exchange. Here dealers called stockbrokers buy and sell important bits of paper. The bits of paper are share certificates. Each certificate represents so much money invested in a business company.

Owning shares in a business gives you the right to a share of its profits. But you can make money from shares in another way. You can buy them at one price, then, if the company does well, sell them later at a higher one.

In the spring of 1929 the stockbrokers of Wall Street were happy. A new President, the Republican Party's Herbert Hoover, took office.

Hoover's 'chicken in every pot'

Hoover was a strong supporter of American businessmen. He believed that it was their hard work and know-how that had made the USA so prosperous.

Hoover claimed that American prosperity would go on growing. The poverty in which some Americans still lived would become a thing of the past. He said that there would soon be 'a chicken in every pot and two cars in every garage'.

Looking at the way their standard of living had risen during the 1920s, many other Americans thought the same.

To share owners, especially, the future looked bright. Every year the sales of cars, radios and other consumer goods were rising. This meant bigger profits for the firms which made them. This in turn sent up the value of shares in such firms.

'Playing the market'

More and more people were eager to get some of this easy money. By 1929 'playing the market' – buying and selling shares – had become almost a national hobby.

You could see this from the rise in the number of shares bought and sold. In 1923 the number changing hands was 236 million; by 1928 it had grown to 1125 million.

Like most other things in the USA in the 1920s, you could buy shares on credit. A hundred dollars cash would 'buy' a thousand dollars' worth of shares from any stockbroker. Many people borrowed large amounts of money from the banks to buy shares in this way – 'on the margin', as it was called.

Most of these 'on the margin' share buyers were really gamblers. Their idea was to spot shares that would quickly rise in value. The trick was to buy at one price then resell at a higher one a few weeks later, and so make a quick profit. You could then pay back the bank and still have dollars to spare.

By the autumn of 1929 the urge to buy shares had become a sort of fever. Prices rocketed. One visitor to Wall Street was reminded of a street fight, as stockbrokers pushed and scrambled to buy shares for their customers.

Yet some people began to have doubts.

The true value of shares in a business firm depends upon its profits. By the autumn of 1929 the profits being made by many American firms had been falling for some time.

If profits were falling, thought more cautious investors, then share prices, too, would soon fall. Slowly, such people began to sell their shares before this happened.

Day by day their numbers grew. Soon so many people were selling shares that prices *did* start to fall.

At first many investors held on to their shares, hoping that prices would rise again. But the fall gathered speed. A panic began.

The Wall Street Crash

On Thursday 24th October 1929 – Black Thursday – 13 million shares were sold. On the following Tuesday, 29th October – Terrifying Tuesday – 16.5 million were sold.

By the end of the year the value of all shares had dropped by a staggering $40,000 million.

Thousands of people, especially those who had borrowed to buy on margin, found themselves facing debt and ruin. Some committed suicide. This was what the policemen thought that the window cleaner was planning.

This collapse of American share prices was known as the Wall Street Crash. It marked the end of the prosperity of the 1920s.

In the next three years American industry sank deeper and deeper into depression. By 1933 over 100,000 companies had closed. Industrial production had fallen by half and about fifteen million workers – 25 per cent of the total labour force – had lost their jobs.

What had gone wrong? people asked.

The reasons for the Crash

Some blamed the blindness of politicians, others the greed of investors and stockbrokers.

Without doubt the actions of all these people helped to bring about the Wall Street Crash. But it had a more important underlying cause.

The simple fact was that by the end of the 1920s not enough people were buying the products of America's expanded industries.

Why? Because too little of the USA's increased wealth had been finding its way into the hands of the workers and the farmers.

The most important cause of the Wall Street Crash was simply this – that too many Americans were not earning enough money to buy the goods they themselves were producing.

The Wall Street Crash

(Left) Wall Street on Black Thursday, 24th October 1929. (Right) A drawing by James Rosenberg of Terrifying Tuesday, 29th October 1929.

1 a) What events are the two illustrations recording?

b) Why do you think there are so many people in the street photograph?

c) What is James Rosenberg trying to show about the Wall Street Crash?

d) In which ways do the two pictures give   1) similar,   2) different impressions?

e) For each picture, say what you think about its value as historical evidence.

2 The list below suggests various reasons for the Wall Street Crash.

  1) American factories were producing more goods than they could sell.
  2) Gambling on shares had pushed their prices above their real value.
  3) American workers did not have enough money to spend.
  4) Too many people were buying shares on the margin.
  5) People panicked when their shares started to fall in price.
  6) Too many people tried to sell their shares at the same time.

a) Place the six items in what you think is their order of importance.

b) Explain how your top *two* factors played an important part in the Crash.

Share prices tumble

Changes in the price of shares in some leading US companies in 1929.

Company	3 Sept. $	13 Nov. $
Anaconda Copper	131.5	70
General Electric	396	168
General Motors	72	36
Radio	101	28
United States Steel	261	150
Woolworth	100	52
Electric Bond & Share	186	50

3 a) If you had bought $1010 worth of Radio shares on 3rd September, what would they have been worth on 13th November?

b) How much money would you have lost?

c) Choose any three of the shares and suggest why they were popular with buyers in September.

d) Suggest why their value had fallen by November.

Effects of the Crash

In 1980 an American historian described some effects of the Crash.

"After the Crash, the economy was stunned, barely moving. Over five thousand banks closed and huge numbers of businesses, unable to get money, closed too. Those that continued laid off employees and cut the wages of those who remained, again and again. Industrial production fell by 50 per cent, and by 1933 perhaps fifteen million (no one knew exactly) – one-fourth or one-third of the labor force – were out of work. The Ford Motor Company, which in the spring of 1929 had employed 128,000 workers, was down to 37,000 by August of 1931. By the end of 1930, almost half the 280,000 textile mill workers in New England were out of work."

H. Zinn, *A People's History of the United States*, 1980

In 1931 the actor Will Rogers gave his views on the Crash.

"There is not an unemployed man in the country that hasn't contributed to the wealth of every millionaire in America. The working classes didn't bring this on, it was the big boys that thought the financial drunk was going to last forever. . .

We got more wheat, more corn, more food, more cotton, more money in the banks, more everything in the world than any nation that ever lived ever had, yet we are starving to death. We are the first nation in the history of the world to go to the poorhouse in an automobile."

Will Rogers in S. Winslow, *Brother Can You Spare a Dime?* 1976

4 a) From H. Zinn's account make a list of five different ways in which the Crash affected the American economy.

b) Explain how the fall in share prices in the Crash affected jobs.

c) Who does Will Rogers blame for the Depression which followed the Crash?

d) What sort of people does he mean by 'the big boys'?

e) What do you think he means by 'the financial drunk'?

f) In what different ways are the extracts from   1) Will Rogers,
2) H. Zinn useful for understanding the Crash and the Depression?

Still and silent factories. Shabbily dressed men standing on street corners. Queues of hungry people waiting to be fed.

Sights like these could be seen all over the USA in the years of hardship that came to be called the Great Depression.

The Depression begins

The Wall Street Crash started the trouble. It made people nervous and uncertain about the future. Many decided to save any money they had instead of spending it on such things as new cars and radios.

American factories were already making more goods than they could sell. Now they became even more short of customers.

The Crash affected their sales to foreign countries, too. In the 1920s American goods had sold well in overseas countries, especially in Europe. But countries such as Britain and Germany had not boomed after the war as the USA had. Import companies had often paid for their purchases with money borrowed from banks.

The banks had often borrowed that money from American lenders. After the Wall Street Crash the American lenders wanted their money back.

The countries which used to buy US goods became short of cash. American overseas sales dried up almost completely.

Goods piled up unsold in factory warehouses. The wheels of industry turned more and more slowly. Factory owners laid off workers and cut back production.

Unemployment

By 1931 nearly eight million Americans were out of work. They received no unemployment pay from the government. Many were soon without homes or food and had to live on charity.

Millions spent hours shuffling slowly forward in queues called 'breadlines'. Here they got free pieces of bread or bowls of soup paid for by collections from the better-off.

By 1932 things were worse still. The number of people out of work had gone up to twelve million.

The city of Chicago alone had almost three-quarters of a million workers without jobs. This was four out of ten of the normal working population. The position was just as bad in other places.

Farmers and the Depression

The Depression was easiest to see in the towns. But it brought ruin to the farmlands, too.

Farmers just could not sell their produce. It did not matter whether the produce was wheat or oranges, butter or beef. With the number of people out of work rising day by day, the farmers' customers in the cities could no longer afford to buy. If they did buy, it was at rock-bottom prices. The same was true of the farmers' overseas customers.

Many farmers grew desperate. They got out shotguns and banded together to drive away the men who came to throw them off their farms for not paying their mortgages and other debts.

How can we pay, the farmers asked, when nobody will give us a fair price for our crops? They paraded through the streets in angry processions. They waved placards with slogans such as 'In Hoover we trusted, now we are busted'.

By 1932 people from every walk of life were calling on President Hoover to take stronger action to deal with the Depression.

The bonus army

That spring thousands of out-of-work ex-servicemen poured into Washington, the capital of the USA. They wanted the government to hand over some bonus payments that it owed them. The newspapers called them the 'bonus army'.

The men of the bonus army were determined to stay in Washington until the President did something to help them. They set up a camp of ramshackle shacks and huts on the edge of the city.

Similar camps could be found on rubbish dumps outside every large American city by this time. The homeless people who lived in them named their camps 'Hoovervilles', after the President.

This gathering of desperate men alarmed President Hoover. He ordered soldiers and the police to drive them out of Washington.

The soldiers carried out his orders without great difficulty. But as the smoke billowed up from the burning shacks of the bonus army, many people were deeply worried. The USA was in a mess – and nobody seemed to know the way out.

Then, Franklin D. Roosevelt came on the scene.

Franklin D. Roosevelt

Roosevelt was the Governor of the big and important state of New York. In 1932 the Democratic Party chose him to run against President Hoover in that year's election for a new President.

Years earlier Roosevelt had been crippled by a polio attack. But this didn't stop him from setting off to tour the United States.

Roosevelt travelled by train. The train made 'whistle-stops' at hundreds of towns and villages. The train pulled up with its whistle shrieking and Roosevelt hauled himself along on his crippled legs to the open platform at the end. He spoke for a few moments to the people who had gathered to meet him. Then, with a cheery wave, he disappeared into the train and off it went to the next whistle-stop.

Roosevelt convinced worried people all over the country that here at last was a man who understood their problems. He made them believe that he would do something to help them.

Roosevelt's New Deal

Roosevelt promised the American people a 'New Deal'. His main point was that it was up to the nation's government to help people against the Depression.

President Hoover condemned Roosevelt's New Deal idea. He said that it would 'destroy the very foundations of the American system'. He claimed that giving people government help would make them lose their ability to stand on their own feet.

Roosevelt elected President, 1932

Most of the American people ignored Hoover's gloomy warnings. In November 1932 they flocked to the voting booths and elected Franklin D. Roosevelt to take over as the next President of the United States.

The Depression

*'Brother Can You Spare a Dime?',
written in 1932, was a very popular
song at the time.*

1 a) What does the lyric tell you
about the jobs done by Al?
  b) Suggest what sort of dream Al
had believed he was building.
  c) Why do you think the song
was so popular?

*A bonus soldier's way of protesting
in Washington in 1932 (or '02').*

2 a) Why does the notice refer to
1917–18?
  b) Why does it claim that these
years 'has been forgotten'?
  c) Why did the marchers come to
Washington?
  d) How did President Hoover
deal with them?

"They used to tell me I was building a dream
And so I followed the mob –
When there was earth to plow or guns to bear
I was always there – right on the job.

They used to tell me I was building a dream
With peace and glory ahead –
Why should I be standing in line
Just waiting for bread?

Say, don't you remember, they called me Al
It was Al all the time.
Say, don't you remember, I'm your Pal –
Buddy can you spare a dime?"

E. Y. Harburg, 'Brother Can You Spare a Dime?', 1932

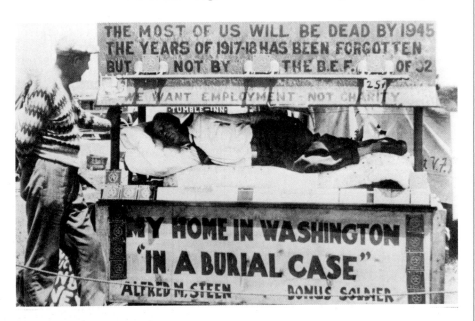

An American writer of the time describes some signs of the Depression.

"First, the bread lines in the poorer districts. Second, those bleak
settlements ironically known as 'Hoovervilles' on the outskirts of the cities
and on vacant lots – groups of makeshift shacks constructed out of
packing-cases, scrap iron . . . in which men and sometimes whole families
of evicted people were sleeping on automobile seats carried from auto-
grave yards, warming themselves before fires of rubbish in grease drums.
Third, the homeless people sleeping in doorways or on park benches, and
going the rounds of the restaurants for left-over half-eaten biscuits, pie-
crusts, anything . . . Fourth, the vastly increased numbers of thumbers on
the highways, and particularly of freight car transients on the railroads: a
huge army of drifters ever on the move, searching half-aimlessly for a
place where there might be a job."

F. L. Allen, *Since Yesterday*, 1940

3 a) List the four main signs of the Depression noted by F. L. Allen.
  b) Explain in your own words the meaning of 'bread line', 'Hoovervilles'
and 'freight car transients'.

Desperation

An American historian describes one effect of the Depression.

"Eleven hundred men standing in a Salvation Army bread line on March 19, 1930, near the Bowery Hotel in Manhattan, descended upon two trucks delivering baked goods to the hotel . . . cookies, rolls and bread were flung into the street with the hungry jobless chasing after them.

Joseph Drusin of Indiana Township, Pennsylvania, in November 1930, stole a loaf of bread from a neighbour for his four starving children. When caught, Drusin went to the cellar and hung himself.

. . . By 1932 organised looting of food was . . . nation-wide . . . Helen Hall, a Philadelphia social worker, told a Senate committee that many families sent their children out to steal from wholesale markets, to snatch milk for their babies, to lift articles from pushcarts to exchange for food."

Irving Bernstein, *The Lean Years*, 1960

4 a) Imagine you are one of the men in the breadline described in the first paragraph. Write out or improvise what a small group of you say as you decide whether or not to grab food from the delivery trucks.

b) Suggest what the neighbour might have told a newspaper reporter writing a story on Joseph Drusin's death.

Franklin D. Roosevelt campaigning in Indianapolis in October 1932.

5 a) What job was Roosevelt campaigning for? How did he plan to carry out the promise on the placard? Design a Republican slogan to answer it.

b) Suggest what Roosevelt meant when he said in 1932, 'I have looked into the faces of thousands of Americans. They have the frightened look of lost children.'

On a cold, grey Saturday in March 1933 Franklin D. Roosevelt was sworn in as President of the United States. He started straightaway on the New Deal that he had promised the American people.

Roosevelt believed that the most urgent need was to set people to work. He was particularly concerned about jobless teenagers.

Young men – and sometimes girls – were stealing rides on freight trains to travel round the country searching for jobs. To help them Roosevelt set up an organisation called the Civilian Conservation Corps – CCC for short.

By August 1933 thousands were already at work all over the country. By the time the scheme ended in the early 1940s, 2.5 million young men had served in the CCC.

The CCC workers cut fire-lanes through forests, strengthened river banks against flooding, planted trees to stop the wind blowing away fertile soil. In four years they planted 1500 million trees. If that many trees were planted 3 metres apart in a line, they would circle the earth *three* times!

The CCC workers lived in special camps. They received food and shelter and a wage of a dollar a day from the government. Many sent most of their wages home to help their families.

Roosevelt quickly followed the CCC with other organisations to make work for the unemployed. The American people knew these New Deal organisations, or agencies, by their initials. They called them 'alphabet agencies'.

In 1935 Roosevelt set up the Works Progress Administration (WPA). Like the CCC, the WPA aimed to set people to work on jobs that would be useful to the community.

By 1937 WPA workers had put up thousands of schools and other public buildings. They also built tens of thousands of kilometres of new roads.

The WPA even found work for out-of-work artists and writers. The artists painted pictures on the walls of post-offices and schools. The writers produced guide books to states and cities.

Another important alphabet agency was the Public Works Administration. The PWA concentrated on heavy construction work, like building dams and bridges. It also cleared large areas of city slums and put up modern houses and flats in their place.

The alphabet agencies put millions of people to work. From the summer of 1935 to its end in 1942, the WPA alone provided jobs for eight million men and women.

The money these workers earned helped to bring trade back to life. Shops had customers again. Factories became busy once more. Farmers had someone to buy their produce.

This was what Roosevelt had hoped for. He had spent millions of dollars of public money on the unemployed to 'prime the pump'. He

CCC

Alphabet agencies

WPA

PWA

believed that putting money into people's pockets was like pouring petrol into an engine to get it started again. The engine drove the machinery which earned the country its living.

Roosevelt also helped workers in other ways. Take trade unions – labor unions, as Americans called them – for instance.

Trade unions

Many American workers now believed that they needed stronger unions to get them decent wages and working conditions.

A look at some 1932 wage levels helps to show why they believed this. Shop assistants were getting about $5 (i.e. £3) a week. Dressmakers got less than half this. New York hat makers were even worse off. They crocheted hats for 40 cents a dozen – and to make two dozen took a worker a week!

In 1935 Roosevelt persuaded Congress to pass a New Deal law which gave workers the right to form unions.

But big employers such as Henry Ford hated the unions. They sacked any worker who joined one. When workers tried to win recognition for their unions, strikes and fighting broke out in factories all over the country.

The Wagner Act, 1935

To stop the trouble another union law was passed. It was called the Wagner Act, after the man who guided it through Congress.

The Wagner Act gave every worker the right to join a union. This time the government set up a body called the National Labor Board to help the workers to get their rights. One result was that trade union membership grew quickly in the later 1930s.

The Social Security Act, 1935

But despite the New Deal reforms like these, millions of Americans still lived in fear. What if their jobs disappeared again? Would they be left once more with only a breadline between them and starvation?

'No', Roosevelt told them. To show that he meant business, in 1935 he brought in a law called the Social Security Act.

The Social Security Act was several laws in one. One part gave government pensions to people unable to provide for themselves – old people, widows and the blind, for example. Another part gave the USA its first system of unemployment insurance.

The money to pay for the Social Security benefits came from special taxes paid by both workers and employers. The new scheme did not cover all workers at first. But in later years more and more were protected by it.

The Fair Labor Standards Act, 1938

In 1938 Roosevelt improved life for workers yet again. He brought in a law called the Fair Labor Standards Act, which set out maximum hours of work and minimum wages for many jobs.

This law meant pay rises and shorter hours of work for hundreds of thousands of people.

Which of these many laws meant most to Roosevelt?

A close helper said that the President's favourite was the Social Security Act. This was probably because, to Roosevelt, it summed up best what his New Deal was all about – helping people to live full and useful lives.

New President and New Deal

In May 1932, before he was elected President, F.D. Roosevelt said:

"The country needs . . . the country demands bold, persistent experimentation . . . It is common sense to take a method and try it: if it fails, admit it frankly and try another. But above all, try something. The millions who are in want will not stand by silently for long . . ."

The Public Papers and Addresses of Franklin D. Roosevelt, 1938

In 1933 when Roosevelt became President, the actor, Will Rogers, said

"America hasn't been as happy in three years as it is today. No money . . . no work, no nothing, but they know they got a man in there who is wise to Congress and wise to our so-called big men. The whole country is with him, just so he does something. Even if what he does is wrong they are with him. Just so he does something. If he burned down the Capitol, we would cheer and say, 'Well, we at least got a fire started anyhow'."

In S. Winslow, *Brother Can You Spare a Dime?* 1976

1 a) What did Roosevelt mean by 'the country demands experimentation'?
 b) Why did he believe that experimentation was so necessary in 1932?
 c) How does Will Rogers explain the big advantage Roosevelt had when he started work as President?

A poster from the Roosevelt years.

When You
BUY an AUTOMOBILE
You GIVE
3 Months' Work
to Someone

Which Allows Him to **BUY OTHER PRODUCTS**

BUY A CAR NOW—HELP BRING BACK PROSPERITY

2 a) What is the poster trying to persuade readers to do?
 b) In which ways is the advertiser making use of Roosevelt's ideas for recovery?
 c) Explain how the motor industry and the CCC were each important to efforts to end the Depression.

The CCC

In 1939 a black teenager told reporters about his life in the CCC.

"I git plenty to eat here. I didn't always at home, not the same kind of stuff, anyhow . . . I git to go more, git to see more. I'm learning, too. I watch the others, and, then, I have more clothes and can keep cleaner . . . Ain't never been sick to speak of. Ain't never had nothing but measles and 'pendicitis and had them both in Camp and got my bills paid. If I'd been at home, I wouldn't have had no operation, couldn't have paid for it . . .

I git up about five in the morning, eat breakfast, go to morning classes, then go to the field. I don't work nearly so hard in this as I do in the field at home. I git to be with lots of boys that I wouldn't at home. They help me lots, show me how to do things I wouldn't have never knowed about."

In N. G. Toler and J. R. Aswell, *These Are Our Lives*, 1939

This account of the CCC by an American historian was written years later.

"They . . . planted trees, made reservoirs and fish ponds, built check dams, dug diversion ditches, raised bridges and fire towers . . . cleared beaches and camping grounds, and in a multitude of ways protected and improved parks, forests . . . and recreational areas.

They reclaimed and developed themselves. They came from large cities, from small towns, from slum street corners . . . from the road and the rails and from nowhere . . . Their muscles hardened, their bodies filled out, their self-respect returned. They learned trades; more important, they learned about America, and they learned about other Americans."

Arthur Schlesinger, *The Coming of the New Deal*, 1959

3 a) Which two points made by the teenager would matter most to you?
  b) Make two columns, 'primary source' and 'secondary source'. In the first, list the points the teenager makes about the CCC. In the other, note statements by Arthur Schlesinger which match the teenager's.

Unions

A union leaflet given out in a strike in 1933 by the United Automobile Workers of America.

4 a) What does 'Unionism not Fordism' mean?
  b) Explain what 'The Wagner Bill is behind you' means.
  c) Put the strike's aims in the order which might have been most important to a worker at Ford's.
  d) Is the leaflet a piece of primary or secondary evidence?

Ford Workers

UNIONISM NOT FORDISM

Now is the time to Organize!
The Wagner Bill is behind you!
Now get behind yourselves!

General Motors Workers, Chrysler Workers, Briggs Workers have won higher wages and better working conditions. 300,000 automobile workers are marching forward under the banner of the United Automobile Workers Union.

JOIN NOW IN THE MARCH AND WIN:
Higher Wages and Better Working Conditions
Stop Speed-up by Union Supervision
6 Hour Day, 8 Dollars Minimum Pay
Job Security thru Seniority Rights
End the Ford Service System
Union Recognition

Organize and be Recognized - JOIN NOW!

The farmers' problems

Helping the farmers

The Dust Bowl

The Okies

You know about gas fires . . . electric fires . . . coal fires. Have you ever heard of *corn* fires?

In the early 1930s some farmers in the USA were burning corn to heat their homes. Corn prices were so low that it made more sense to burn the stuff than to sell it and buy coal.

A wagon-load of oats fetched less than the price of a pair of shoes. The price of many other crops was too low to cover even the costs of harvesting them. Farmers just left them to rot in the fields.

By 1933 many farmers' incomes were less than one third of what they had been in 1929 – and they had been badly off then (see Unit 26). To help them Roosevelt set up another alphabet agency. This one was the Agricultural Adjustment Agency (AAA).

The AAA decided to try to persuade farmers to produce less meat, corn, cotton and other main crops. The idea was to make such products scarcer, so that selling prices would rise and farmers would be better off. Farmers who agreed to grow less were given money by the government to make up for having less to sell.

To many people this seemed wicked. With millions of people hungry, the government was paying farmers *not* to grow food!

But for the farmers this crop limitation scheme, as it was called, did its job. By 1936 they were earning half as much again as they had in 1933. By 1939 they were earning twice as much.

But cutting back production was only a short-term answer to the farming problem. Roosevelt hoped that once the American people became better off, they would have enough money to buy all that the farmers could produce.

To prepare for this day the government spent money to keep the land in good condition. The money was given to farmers to buy machinery and fertilisers and to insure crops against disasters like hurricanes and droughts.

But Roosevelt's schemes came too late to help farmers in the 'Dust Bowl'.

The Dust Bowl was a vast area in the south and west of the USA. From 1933 onwards it suffered year after year of drought. Over thousands of square kilometres the rains never fell.

The glaring sun turned the soil into light, powdery dust. Then the winds swirled the dust away in great choking clouds.

On top of the dust storms, many farmers faced another problem. They were tenants, paying rent on land owned by other people. Many lost both their homes and their living when the owners decided to work the land themselves using tractors.

The dust storms and the tractors often left the farmer with only one option – to pack what he could carry on to a battered old car and move out. Many of these Dust Bowl refugees came from the state of Oklahoma. Because of this they were nicknamed 'Okies'.

Most Okies headed west, to California. Here they hoped to find some way to make a living.

But the Californians were afraid of these hungry and ragged strangers who came pouring into their towns and villages. 'Okies go home', said posters on the California border. 'No relief available in California.'

The only jobs the Okies could find were poorly paid and short lasting, like fruit and vegetable picking. Conditions improved for them only when the Second World War began and Californian factories started to take on more workers.

Far away on the eastern side of the country, meanwhile, life was getting better for another group of farmers.

The Tennessee Valley

These farmers lived in the valley of the Tennessee, one of the great rivers of America. It drains an area as large as the whole of England and Scotland put together.

The Tennessee Valley had once been a country of timber covered slopes. But generations of farmers had cut down the trees and ploughed the slopes to grow corn, tobacco and cotton.

All these crops were planted in the spring and harvested in the autumn. In the winter the land lay bare. Its top soil was washed away by the heavy winter rains. The same rains often caused floods, which drove people from their homes.

By 1933 the Tennessee Valley's land was exhausted. It was producing poorer crops every year. The very names that the farmers gave to the countryside – Hard Labor Creek, Long Hungry Creek, Poorland Valley – showed how hopeless they were.

Roosevelt's TVA

Roosevelt set up a special body to organise help for the Tennessee Valley's millions of people, the Tennessee Valley Authority (TVA).

The TVA had three main aims – to stop floods, to make electricity and to make the land fertile again. It achieved all of them.

The key to TVA's success was its dams. From 1933 onwards the valley of the Tennessee echoed to the roar of heavy machinery. Huge new steel and concrete dams rose up.

When heavy rains fell the dams held back the flood water in great man-made lakes. By guiding the same water through turbines, they also made electricity.

The TVA sold the electricity cheaply to farmers. It also used it to power new factories making paper, aluminium, chemicals and cheap fertilisers for the farmers. These factories meant new jobs and a better life for the Tennessee Valley's people.

TVA also stopped soil erosion. It planted millions of trees and persuaded farmers to plant more crops like grass and clover. These covered the ground all year round and prevented the soil from being washed away. As the scars of erosion healed, the fields and hills of the Tennessee Valley became green again.

Roosevelt believed that TVA showed how great changes could be made in people's lives without taking away their freedom. It was, he said, 'a demonstration of what a democracy at work can do'.

The Dust Bowl

A visiting reporter describes the Dust Bowl in 1934.

"Temperature above 100 in shade for forty-three successive days. Missouri Pacific Railway hauling tankcars of water for use of livestock . . . Sam Nance, farmer near Ardmore, Oklahoma, shoots 143 head of cattle to save them from starving. Cotton crop one half normal. Apples, peaches, small fruits 30 per cent normal. Livestock congesting packing centres. Beef selling on foot as low as $.01 a pound. Pasturage exhausted."

C. M. Wilson, *Commonweal* magazine, 14th September 1934

An Oklahoma farmer who had moved to California speaks to a reporter, 1939

"You see, back in Oklahoma we had a farm. There's me and the three kids and the old lady and my mother. We got along, yea, and then things started to happen. First came the Depression and we couldn't get nothin' for our crops. Make maybe two hundred dollars a year. Course the farm started to go downhill – to dry up . . . . There were a couple of years when we tried mighty hard. Didn't eat much those years.

Well, come '35 it weren't no use trying any longer so we just packed up and pulled out. Came here cause we hear you could make fair money harvesting crops."

In D. Congdon (ed.), *The Thirties*, 1962

An Okie stranded in southern California with his stalled car and no money. March, 1937.

'End o' my line', a song by the folk singer Woody Guthrie.

" 'Long about Nineteen thirty-one,
My field burnt up in the boiling sun.

'Long about Nineteen thirty-two,
Dust did rise and the dust it blew.

'Long about Nineteen thirty-three,
Living in the dust was killing me,

'Long about Nineteen thirty-four
Dangburn dust it blew some more.

'Long about Nineteen thirty-five,
Blowed my crops about nine miles high.

End o' my line, end o' my line,
I reckon I come to the end o' my line."

1 a) Using all the sources, imagine you are a Dust Bowl farmer in about 1936. Make a list of the problems you are facing.

b) You decide to move out. Write a letter to a friend to explain 1) why you are leaving, 2) where you are going, 3) how you hope to be better off.

The TVA

A hillside in the Tennessee Valley. Before 1933 both sides were eroded. Then the land on the left was ploughed across the slope instead of up and down, fertilised and planted with grass to hold the soil.

2 a) Use the photograph and information in the unit to write a description of life in the Tennessee Valley in the early 1930s. Work in these points: floods, erosion, electricity, dams, trees, fertilisers.

b) Write a description of the Valley in the late 1930s saying 1) what is the same, 2) what is different, 3) how things have improved since the early 1930s.

Roosevelt and the farmers

Percentage changes in the prices farmers were paid for selling their products between 1932 and 1942. The price they had been getting between 1900 and 1914 is reckoned at 100.

Year	Price
1932	065
1934	090
1936	114
1938	097
1940	100
1942	150

3 a) A farmer gets $260 from selling his produce in 1932. How much would he get for selling the same amount of produce in 1936?

b) Suggest three possible reasons for the improvement.

c) How much would the farmer get for the same amount of produce in 1942?

d) Suggest a reason for this further change.

e) Design an election poster which aims to persuade farmers to vote for Roosevelt by reminding them of what he has done for them.

One day during the New Deal, President Roosevelt received this personal letter:

'Dear Mr President,

This is just to tell you everything is all right now. The man you sent found our House all right and we went down to the bank with him and the mortgage can go on for a while longer. You remember I wrote you about losing the furniture too. Well, your man got it back for us. I never heard of a President like you, Mr Roosevelt.'

Support for the New Deal

That letter, written by a shaky hand on a scrap of yellow paper, shows how millions of ordinary Americans felt about Roosevelt in the 1930s.

Thirty years later their feelings were summed up by a New York taxi-driver in a television interview. 'Roosevelt?', he said. 'He was God in this country.'

Opposition to the New Deal

But not to everybody. Many people feared and hated everything that Roosevelt stood for.

Some of them were alarmed at the vast sums of money the President was spending on jobs for the unemployed. The country could not afford this, they cried.

Others claimed that much of the money was being wasted anyway. They feared that Roosevelt's policies would make people idle and stop them standing on their own feet.

'You can't make the world all planned and soft', complained one businessman. 'The strongest and best survive – that's the law of nature after all.'

Even people who generally supported Roosevelt were worried by some of his actions.

Roosevelt and the Supreme Court

In the USA a group of judges called the Supreme Court has the power to say whether a law is legal or not. In 1936 these judges declared that one of Roosevelt's New Deal laws was illegal.

Roosevelt's reply was to try to 'fix' the Supreme Court by giving positions on it to judges he could trust to back his policies.

Members of Congress condemned Roosevelt for this. They pointed out that Hitler had recently destroyed democracy in Germany by tampering with the law courts and the rules of the government (see Unit 6). Some accused Roosevelt of wanting to become a dictator himself. Faced with this storm of protest, he had to drop his attempt to pack the Supreme Court with his supporters.

Roosevelt's re-election, 1936

But the criticisms made little difference to Roosevelt's popularity with the voters. To millions of Americans he was the man who had given them jobs and saved their homes and farms. In 1936 they re-elected him President by the largest majority of votes in American history.

As one wit put it, 'Everyone was against the New Deal but the voters'.

The Second World War

Yet it was not the New Deal that finally ended unemployment in the United States. The German dictator, Adolf Hitler, did that.

By 1939, despite the New Deal, ten million workers again had no jobs – one American worker out of four. 'This country cannot continue as a democracy with ten million or twelve million unemployed', Roosevelt was warned by one of his closest advisers. 'It just can't be done.'

Then, in September 1939, Hitler's armies marched into Poland. The Second World War began.

The USA quickly became the main supplier of weapons to the countries fighting Hitler. American factories began working round the clock. The number of people without jobs fell. In 1941 the USA joined the war itself and unemployment disappeared.

President Roosevelt was now too busy to give attention to reforms at home. 'Old Dr New Deal has to be replaced by Dr Win-the-War', he said. His New Deal was over.

Roosevelt's efforts as 'Dr win the War' wore him out. By 1945 he was a sick man.

A few weeks before the end of the war, on the morning of 12 April, he suffered a stroke. Within hours he was dead. His Vice President, Harry Truman, took over as President of the United States.

The New Deal's importance

By this time Americans from almost every walk of life were better off than they had been in the dark days of the Depression.

Some argued that this was due mainly to the coming of war. But most gave a lot of the credit to the New Deal.

People still argue about this. But there is no argument about the importance of the New Deal in other ways.

The most long-lasting change was that the New Deal altered Americans' ideas about the rightful work of the government.

Before the New Deal most Americans thought of the government as a kind of policeman. It was there just to keep order, while factory owners and businessmen got on with making the country better off.

The Depression weakened this belief. Roosevelt taught Americans to look to the government to see that everyone got a fair share of what he called 'the good things of life'.

Presidents after the war dealt with the USA's problems in the same basic way that Roosevelt had tackled the Depression – by using the powers of the Federal Government.

They gave help to farmers. They brought more people under the protection of the Social Security laws. After a delay, they passed laws to try to ensure fairer treatment for American blacks.

So, in a way, the New Deal never ended. In 1984 a reporter asked a historian, who had worked in Roosevelt's CCC as a boy, what was left of the New Deal.

'In a sense', replied the historian, 'what remains of the New Deal is the United States.'

Attitudes to the New Deal

Frances Perkins, who wrote this opinion, was Secretary of Labor in Roosevelt's New Deal government in the 1930s.

"As Roosevelt described it, the 'new deal' meant that the forgotten man, the little man, the man nobody knew much about, was going to be dealt better cards to play with.

. . . Roosevelt understood that the suffering of the depression had fallen with terrific impact upon people least able to bear it. He knew that the rich had been hit hard too, but at least they had something left. But the little merchant, the small householder and home owner, the farmer who worked the soil by himself, the man who worked for wages – these people were desperate . . .

. . . The idea was that all the . . . forces of the community should . . . be directed to making life better for ordinary people."

Frances Perkins, *The Roosevelt I Knew*, 1947

The view of S. B. Fuller, a self-made black businessman in Chicago.

"The New Deal of Franklin Roosevelt hurt us. He was a rich man's son. All he received was given to him. So he thinks it's right to give. He didn't understand, when you give people, you hurt them. We had soup lines and the depression because men lost confidence in themselves . . .

Welfare kills a man's spirit. It may give his body the vitamins that make him big and fat, and he may be happy. But he doesn't have the spirit of initiative. A dog you feed will not hunt. If you want a dog that hunts, you have to let him get hungry. If you want a man to search, man needs to face the recesses [setbacks] of life. You're free to eat if you can pay for your food, and you're free to starve if you don't pay for it."

S. B. Fuller, in S. Terkel, *American Dreams Lost and Found*, 1980

View in a magazine article to commemorate the 100th anniversary of Roosevelt's birth.

"Alexander Heard, 64, who is retiring soon as chancellor of Vanderbilt University, remembers working in the CCC as a youth; remembers it as a time when a new president 'restored a sense of confidence, morale and hope – hope being the greatest of all'."

Time, 1st February 1982.

1 a) Explain in your own words what Frances Perkins believed the New Deal did for ordinary Americans.

b) Explain in your own words how S. B. Fuller disagreed with her.

c) Which of the previous sources do you think Alexander Heard would be most likely to agree with?

d) From what you know about the writers, in which ways would you expect each of the sources to be biased?

e) If you had used *only* the Frances Perkins extract, what conclusion would you have come to about the New Deal?

f) If you had used *only* the S. B. Fuller extract, what conclusion would you have come to?

g) What does this tell you about how historians should use evidence?

The war boom

Part of a historian's summary of the effects of the Second World War on the USA.

"During Franklin Roosevelt's first term, the New Deal did not cure the underlying economic problems. It was the war that did that.

. . . . Within a matter of months, six million workers found new jobs. Within a couple of years, mass unemployment had virtually disappeared. Soon the Great Depression itself was becoming an unhappy memory. The Great Boom had begun.

. . . The war boom brought record . . . profits, with one third of all war orders to ten giant corporations. The war . . . also meant an end to hard times for most . . . of the population. Even allowing for inflation, real wages jumped by 44 per cent in the four years of war. The proportion of families living on incomes of less than two thousand dollars a year fell from three quarters to one quarter of the population."

Geoffrey Hodgson, *In Our Time*, 1976

2 a) Explain, with your own examples, what Geoffrey Hodgson means by 'underlying economic problems'.

b) Use this source to explain in your own words how the war helped cure the pre-war problems of: 1) unemployment, 2) low profits, 3) low earnings.

A war-time propaganda poster issued by the US government.

3 a) What idea is the poster trying to put across?

b) How does it help you to understand why there was a wartime boom?

4 Some historians claim that the New Deal was a success. Others argue that it was really a failure.

a) Look over the evidence in this unit and in Units 27 and 28. Decide whether *you* think the New Deal was a success or failure. Choose the evidence which you think supports your view.

b) Why do you think that people still argue about whether the New Deal was good or bad, a success or a failure?

Isolationism and the First World War

Thousands of kilometres of sea separate North America from the world's other continents. This is one reason why for many years the people of the USA kept themselves to themselves – 'isolated' themselves.

Early in the twentieth century it looked as if this 'mind your own business', or 'isolationist', attitude might be changing.

In 1914 quarrels between nations in Europe exploded into war – the First World War. Most Americans wanted to stay out of it.

But then German submarines started to sink American ships carrying supplies to Britain. In 1917 the United States declared war (see Unit 3). By 1918 over a million American soldiers were fighting in Europe.

Wilson and the League of Nations

In 1919 President Woodrow Wilson took a leading part in working out the Versailles Treaty (see Unit 3). The most important part of the Treaty to Wilson was an idea of his own. It was to set up a new international organisation called the League of Nations.

Wilson wanted the League of Nations to be a sort of parliament of mankind, where representatives of the world's nations would meet to settle their differences by peaceful discussion. He persuaded European leaders to accept his plan. Then he returned to the USA to win the backing of Congress and the American people.

But many Americans were suspicious. Wouldn't joining the League mean that the USA might be dragged into quarrels, perhaps even wars, that were none of its business?

Wilson tried to calm such fears. But in 1920 Congress voted against joining. The USA went back to minding its own business.

Isolationism in the 1920s and 1930s

In the 1920s Americans were busy making money and having a good time. In the 1930s they were busy trying to struggle out of the Depression. With so much on their own plate, most were not much interested in what was going on in the rest of the world.

But in the 1930s every year brought a new war, or a threat of war, somewhere. Nations built more tanks and warships and trained more soldiers. Leaders like Hitler threatened and bullied.

President Roosevelt saw the dangers. In 1937 he warned the American people about the wars in Spain and China (see Units 7 and 62). 'If these things come to pass in other parts of the world, let no one imagine that America will escape.'

But Spain and China seemed very far away. Most Americans took no notice of Roosevelt. They went on believing that the best thing was to let foreigners sort out their problems amongst themselves.

These isolationist ideas were very strong in Congress. They were seen in a series of 1930s laws called Neutrality Acts.

The Neutrality Acts said that American citizens would not be allowed to sell military equipment, or lend money, to any nations at war. Even non-military supplies such as foodstuffs would be sold to such countries only if they paid for them on the spot and collected them in their own ships.

Then American public opinion started to change. By the summer of 1940 Hitler's armies had overrun all Western Europe (see Unit 9). Only Britain – exhausted and short of weapons – still defied them.

With Hitler the master of Europe, and Hitler's ally, Japan, becoming ever stronger in Asia, Americans saw at last the dangerous position of the USA, sandwiched between the two.

Roosevelt had already persuaded Congress to suspend the Neutrality Acts. Now he turned over to Britain every scrap of military equipment that the USA could spare – rifles, guns, ships. When the British ran out of money, Roosevelt persuaded Congress to accept his Lend Lease Plan.

The Second World War

Lend Lease

Lend Lease gave Roosevelt the right to 'transfer or lend' military equipment and other goods to Britain without payment. He could do the same for any country whose defence he considered necessary to the safety of the USA.

American guns, food and aircraft flooded across the Atlantic Ocean. They played a vital part in helping Britain to continue to fight against Hitler. When Hitler attacked the USSR in June 1941 Roosevelt used the Lend Lease scheme to send aid to the Russians, too.

Pearl Harbor

Congress passed the Lend Lease Act in March 1941. By this time isolationism was really dead. But it was only finally buried on 7th December 1941, when waves of Japanese aircraft attacked the American naval base at Pearl Harbor (see Unit 65). With only one vote against, the American Congress declared war on Japan. A few days later Germany declared war on the USA.

The USA went on to play a leading part in winning the Second World War.

The USA's forces did most of the fighting against the Japanese in the Pacific (see Unit 65). Its soldiers also helped to win the war against the Germans in Europe (see Unit 9). American industries helped to keep the USA's allies supplied with war materials of every kind. The United States became what Roosevelt called 'the arsenal of democracy'.

The end of isolationism

Before the war ended in 1945 most Americans had decided that isolationism had been a mistake. Some felt that it had actually helped to cause the Second World War by encouraging dictators like Hitler to follow warlike policies.

But it was the explosion of an atomic bomb over the Japanese city of Hiroshima which really settled the matter. This one bomb from an American plane destroyed the city and killed almost 100,000 people (see Unit 65).

The atomic bomb made it clear that no nation could find safety by trying to cut itself off from the rest of the world.

Far from isolating itself, most Americans believed that the USA now had to play a leading part in international affairs.

The USA and the League

Part of a speech that President Wilson made in 1919 when he was trying to persuade Americans that the USA should join the League of Nations.

"What of our pledges to the men that lie dead in France? We said that they went over there . . . to see to it that there was never such a war again. My clients are the children . . . the next generation. They shall not be sent upon a similar errand.

There seems to me to stand between us and the rejection . . . of this treaty the . . . ranks of those boys in khaki, not only those who came home, but those dear ghosts . . . upon the fields of France."

In R. D. Heffner, *A Documentary History of the United States*, 1952

In 1931 a historian suggested why the USA did not join the League.

" . . . There were a vast number who saw in the League . . . obligations with which they were not willing to have the nation saddled . . .

. . . there was another factor to be reckoned with: the growing apathy of millions of Americans towards anything which reminded them of the war . . . They were fast becoming sick and tired of the whole European mess. They wanted to be done with it. They didn't want to be told of new sacrifices to be made – they had made plenty."

F. L. Allen, *Only Yesterday*, 1931

1 a) Who does Wilson mean by the 'boys in khaki' and the 'dear ghosts'?
  b) How does he use them as an argument in favour of the League?
  c) How might other Americans have used them to argue *against* it?
  d) Does F. L. Allen believe that most Americans were for or against joining the League? What reasons does he give for his belief?
  e) Does the fact that the USA did not join prove that he was right?
  f) One of these two extracts is from a 'primary source' and the other is from a 'secondary source'. Which is which? Explain your answer.

The USA and the Second World War

A cartoon in the New York Daily News *just after the Second World War started in 1939.*

2 a) Which part of the world is represented by the foreground of the picture?
  b) Who or what does the woman shown there represent?
  c) Which of the background figures represents isolationism?
  d) Which of these figures would have supported Lend Lease?
  e) Is the cartoonist for or against isolationism? Explain your answer.

To fight or not to fight?

Views of Americans in 1939 and 1940 about the USA and the Second World War.

A politician, Senator Ludden, 1939.

" . . . not a dollar should be wasted nor a drop of American blood nor a single American soldier should be sacrificed over the boundary disputes of the Old World."

A famous aviator, Charles Lindbergh, September 1939.

"We must not be misguided by foreign propaganda to the effect that our frontiers lie in Europe . . . What more could we ask than the Atlantic Ocean on the East and the Pacific Ocean on the West? . . . An ocean is a formidable barrier, even for modern aircraft."

President Roosevelt in a private letter, December 1939.

" . . . my problem is to get the American people to think of consequences without scaring the American people into thinking that they are going to be dragged into the war."

The American ambassador to France, William C. Bullitt, 1940.

"Why are we sleeping, Americans? When are we going to wake up? When are we going to tell our government that we want to defend our homes and our children and our liberties whatever the cost in money or blood?"

In S. Winslow, *Brother Can You Spare a Dime?* 1976

A cartoon in the Chicago Daily News, *28th November 1940.*

PATH OF APPEASEMENT

NAZISM

LET ME ALONE, IT IS SO PEACEFUL

3 a) Which of these sources put forward isolationist views? Explain your choices.

b) Charles Lindbergh had made the first solo transatlantic flight in 1927. Why would this make him a valuable spokesman for or against isolationism?

c) Do you think a private letter such as the one from Roosevelt is more or less reliable as historical evidence than a public document? Why?

d) What message is the cartoonist trying to get across?

e) Which of the other sources would you expect the cartoonist to agree with?

'How should we punish Hitler?', a reporter asked an American black girl towards the end of the Second World War.

'Paint him black and bring him over here', she replied.

Her reply showed how many black Americans felt about the way they were treated at that time.

In 1900 most blacks had lived in the south of the USA. Here they scraped a poor living working the land.

White southerners treated the blacks as inferiors. Any who tried to improve their positions risked being beaten up and even killed. Every year 100 or more were murdered without trial – lynched.

The black migration

Some blacks moved out in search of better lives before the First World War. 'I don't care where, so long as I go where a man is a man', wrote one. The Second World War turned this trickle of migrants into a flood. Between 1940 and 1970 4.5 million southern blacks headed for the northern cities and California.

In the 1940s the booming wartime factories of cities like Chicago and Los Angeles had plenty of jobs for the often unskilled migrants. But by the end of the 1950s the jobs had dried up. Many of the people of the crowded black neighbourhoods – the ghettos – of cities all over the country had no work.

The Watts riots, 1965

In the sweltering summer of 1965 the streets of Watts, the black ghetto in Los Angeles, became a battlefield.

Police and rioters fought among burning cars and buildings. An area of 2.5 square kilometres was burned out. Thirty-four people were killed and over a thousand were injured.

The Watts riot was followed by others – in Chicago, Detroit, New York and even Washington. A government enquiry blamed lack of work for the riots. But the causes went deeper.

The people of Watts, like most American blacks, knew that they were getting a raw deal generally. And they were sick of waiting for things to get better.

The Civil Rights movement

For years blacks had been trying to improve their position in peaceful and legal ways through the Civil Rights movement.

The aim of the Civil Rights movement was to change the regulations which denied blacks the same rights as other Americans.

This sort of thing was called 'segregation'. The laws that enforced segregation were nicknamed 'Jim Crow' laws, from a character in an old song who had to jump whenever his boss told him to.

In 1954 Civil Rights supporters persuaded the Supreme Court to declare that black children should be allowed to attend the same schools as white pupils.

Little Rock, 1957

On the morning of 23rd September 1957 a group of black students set out to enrol at the all-white High School in the southern town of Little Rock. An angry mob of whites gathered to scare them off.

President Eisenhower sent soldiers to enforce the Supreme

Court's decision. The black girls and boys were admitted.

So began a long struggle for equal rights in education. It was still going on thirty years later.

Another landmark in the black struggle for Civil Rights came in a strictly segregated southern city called Montgomery.

Montgomery, 1955

In 1955 a black woman named Rosa Parks refused to give up her seat on a crowded bus to a white man. Under Montgomery's Jim Crow laws this was an offence. She was arrested.

Other blacks rallied to support Mrs Parks. Led by a young Baptist minister named Martin Luther King, they refused to use Montgomery's buses.

De-segregation

The boycott went on for a year. The money the city authorities lost in fares forced them to de-segregate Montgomery's buses.

This success in Montgomery encouraged blacks in other places to act against segregation.

They stopped buying from shops which refused to give jobs to black workers. They held 'sit ins' at eating places which would not serve black customers. All over the USA they brought about the de-segregation of shops, restaurants and work-places.

The march on Washington, 1963

The climax to the Civil Rights campaigning came in August 1963. Led by Martin Luther King, 200,000 people, black and white, took part in a mass march to Washington to demand full racial equality.

The march was seen on television and won American blacks a lot of sympathy at home and abroad.

The Civil Rights Act, 1964

In 1964 President Johnson persuaded Congress to pass a Civil Rights Act. It was intended to make sure that all Americans, black and white, received fair and equal treatment from the laws.

But the problems faced by black Americans were too complicated and deep rooted to be cured just by a new law.

Black Power

Most blacks were still worse paid, worse fed, worse housed and worse educated than other Americans.

Some decided that Martin Luther King's idea that blacks and whites could live together in equality was a hopeless dream.

When King was shot dead by a white gunman in 1968, many blacks turned to the Black Power movement. Black Power taught that the way for blacks to get justice was to fight for it.

Power through voting

But in the 1970s and 1980s other blacks decided that there was a more effective way – through the ballot box.

Their idea was to vote fellow blacks into positions of power – as local councillors, as mayors of cities, and as members of Congress.

In many places the policy worked. By the 1980s cities such as Washington, Los Angeles and Chicago all had black mayors.

Jesse Jackson became the chief spokesman for this idea. He travelled the country telling blacks to claim their right to vote.

Jackson's goal was the same as Martin Luther King's – an equal place for black Americans in the life of the United States.

By the 1980s blacks had made progress towards this. But they still had a long way to go.

Black voices

1 a) What colour is the boy telling the story? How does he feel before the incident?

b) What colour is the other boy? How do you know?

c) Why does the writer remember this childhood event?

d) What is the poem saying about being black in America in the 1920s?

e) Could the poem have been written in the 1960s – or today?

A poem written by Countee Cullen in 1925. He describes an incident in Baltimore, a town in Maryland – one of the southern states of the USA.

"Once riding in old Baltimore,
Heart-filled, head-filled with glee,
I saw a Baltimorean
Keep looking straight at me.

Now I was eight and very small,
And he was no whit bigger,
And so I smiled, but he poked out
His tongue, and called me, 'Nigger'.

I saw the whole of Baltimore
From May until December;
Of all the things that happened there
That's all that I remember."

In A. Chapman (ed.), *Black Voices*,
Mentor 1968

Dick Gregory is a black American entertainer who grew up in the Chicago ghetto. In the 1960s he became active in the Civil Rights movement and used his comedy act to make serious points about the disadvantages suffered by black Americans.

"About a year ago in Chicago I was walking down the street . . . about ten o'clock in the evening. A white cat [man] walking down the sidewalk, he see me coming, he jump all the way off the sidewalk and get in the gutter. Scared to death. He say, 'Mister, you're not going to bother me, are you?'

I said, 'No, my man. I'm Dick Gregory. I'm dedicated and committed to non-violence.' 'You mean you are *the* Dick Gregory? You don't carry no gun or no knife?' I said, 'No'. He said, 'You don't do no shooting or cutting?' I said 'No'. He said, 'Well stick 'em up, nigger'."

Dick Gregory, in P. Jacobs and S. Landau, *To Serve the Devil*, 1971

2 a) Do you think that this incident really happened?

b) What do you think Dick Gregory intends the moral of his story to be?

c) Is the story directed against Gregory himself, the white man or both? Explain your answer.

d) Is the story racist?

From a book by a famous black American writer, James Baldwin.

"The only thing that white people have that black people need, or should want, is power . . ."

James Baldwin, *The Fire Next Time*, 1963

3 Why do you think James Baldwin picked power as the only thing worth having from white people?

Little Rock

23rd September 1957; morning. Fifteen-year-old Elizabeth Eckford on her way to enrol at the all-white Central High School in Little Rock, Arkansas.

23rd September 1957; afternoon. A statement by President Eisenhower.

"I want to make several things clear in connexion with the disgraceful occurrences of today at Central High School in the City of Little Rock . . .
1. The Federal Law . . . cannot be flouted . . . by any individual or any mob of extremists.
2. I will use the full power of the United States, including whatever force may be necessary, to prevent any obstruction of the law and to carry out the orders of the Federal Court.
3. . . . every right-thinking citizen will hope that the American sense of justice and fair play will prevail in this case. It will be a sad day for this country – both at home and abroad – if schoolchildren can safely attend their classes only under the protection of armed guards."

In Keesing's Research Report, *Race Relations in the USA*, 1970

24th September 1957. President Eisenhower in a television broadcast.

"At a time when we face grave situations abroad . . . it would be difficult to exaggerate the harm that is being done to the prestige and influence of our nation . . . Our enemies are gloating over this incident and using it everywhere to misrepresent our whole nation."

In *Race Relations in the USA*, Keesing's Research Report, 1970

4 a) Explain the background to these three sources as fully as you can.
b) What actions did Eisenhower take to deal with the situation?
c) From all the sources, find three reasons for Eisenhower's concern.
d) Which of the following words best fit   1) the white woman on the left of the photograph,   2) the black girl on the right? Anger, sympathy, fear, pride, hatred, determination, courage. Explain your choices.
e) What would your reaction have been if you as   1) a black American,   2) a white American, had seen the scene shown in the photograph on television?

Views on black power

Martin Luther King and Malcolm X were the best known black American leaders of the 1960s. Both wanted their people to win freedom and equality. But they held different ideas about how they should do this.

Martin Luther King

"Non-violent resistance has a way of disarming an opponent; it weakens his morale and at the same time it works on his conscience . . . violent resistance will mislead Negroes . . . and place them as a minority in a position where they confront a far larger adversary than it is possible to defeat."

"We have come to the day when a piece of freedom is not enough for us . . . Freedom is like life. You cannot be given life in instalments. You cannot be given breath but no body, nor a heart but no blood vessels. Freedom is one thing – you have it all, or you are not free."

In P. Jacobs and S. Landau, *To Serve the Devil*, 1971

Malcolm X

"Being born here in America doesn't make you an American . . . I'm not an American. I'm one of the twenty-two million black people who are the victims of Americanism . . . And I see America through the eyes of the victim. I don't see any American dream; I see an American nightmare."

In P. Jacobs and S. Landau, *To Serve the Devil*, 1971

"You'll get freedom by letting your enemy know that you'll do anything to get your freedom . . . It's the only way you'll get it . . . they'll call you an extremist or a . . . red or a radical. But if you stay radical long enough and get enough people to be like you, you'll get your freedom."

In H. Zinn, *A People's History of the United States*, 1980

The Civil Rights march on Washington, August 1963.

5 a) What does Martin Luther King mean by 'non-violent resistance'?

b) Give two reasons why he is in favour of it.

c) In which ways do Malcolm X's views   1) agree with, 2) differ from, Martin Luther King's?

d) In their second extracts each leader speaks of 'freedom'. Give examples to show what they had in mind.

e) How does the photograph support the views of Martin Luther King in his first extract?

f) Use the photograph to identify three grievances of black Americans in 1963.

Black voters

A diagram from the American weekly Time *in August 1983, showing the rise in the numbers of blacks who had their names on the registers of Americans allowed to vote.*

ON THE ROLLS

Number of registered black voters, in millions

10

9

8

7

'66 '68 '70 '72 '74 '76 '78 '80 '82

From the 1959 report of a government enquiry into electoral registers in the southern states of the USA.

" . . . in 16 of the 158 Southern counties where Negroes formed a majority of the population there was not one Negro voter, and in 49 others fewer than 5 per cent of eligible Negroes were registered. This was partly due to the Negroes' . . . poverty, lack of education and historically submerged status, but other causes included intimidation, economic coercion [force] and the use of legal subterfuges [tricks]. Negro businessmen who tried to vote had been refused deliveries by wholesalers or had lost their customers. . . . Registrars . . . had kept Negro applicants waiting all day. The literacy [reading and writing] tests imposed in nineteen States were applied much more stringently [strictly] to Negroes than to whites, and Negroes were often disqualified for errors in spelling or pronunciation."

Report of the Civil Rights Commission, 1959

From a magazine report of speeches by Jesse Jackson in 1983.

"For the past few months, Jackson has been criss-crossing the country conducting voter-registration revival meetings . . .

He will cry: 'We need 10,000 blacks running for office from Virginia round to Texas . . . Just run! Run! Run! . . .

'When you run, the masses register and vote . . . If you run, you might lose. If you don't run, you're guaranteed to lose'."

Time, 22nd August 1983

6 a) Explain in your own words what you can learn from the sources   1) about American election rules,   2) about changes in black attitudes to voting.
  b) How does the Civil Rights Commission's report help you to understand the chart's figures for 1966?
  c) From the *Time* report, what do you think were the two main aims of Jackson's speeches?

Americans and the Second World War

'The war?', the former Red Cross worker said to the interviewer. 'The war was fun for America.'

A strange thing to say, you may think. But the Americans were the only people in the world that the Second World War made better off. Their homes had not been bombed or their land fought over. Busy wartime factories had given them good wages.

In the years that followed the war Americans became better off still. Between 1947 and 1971 the value of their wages in buying power – their 'real incomes' as this is called – more than doubled. Americans could buy more of everything – houses, cars, television sets, consumer goods of every kind. They became better off than any people the world had ever seen.

Yet these were worrying years for them. They were haunted by fears of war with the USSR.

Americans and communism

Both President Truman (1945–53) and President Eisenhower (1953–61) believed that the Russians' communist way of running a country was cruel and wrong. They made up their minds to stop it from spreading to other countries – to 'contain' it (see Unit 10).

But this 'containment' policy was not enough for some Americans. They saw communism as a dangerous disease. They wanted to wipe it off the face of the earth, not just contain it.

In 1949 such people got two bad shocks.

The first was when communist rulers took over in China. The second was when the Russians exploded an atomic bomb. Only the Americans had possessed atomic bombs until then.

A wave of fear swept across the USA. Many Americans started to see communist plots everywhere. Some even claimed that the government itself was riddled with traitors plotting to betray the USA to the Russians.

McCarthyism

A drunken and dishonest politician named Joseph McCarthy used such fears to get fame and power for himself. He started what came to be called a 'witch hunt' – a search for people he could blame for the supposed threats to the USA.

In the early 1950s McCarthy accused all kinds of people – government officials, scientists, famous entertainers – of secretly working for the USSR. He never gave proof, but Americans were so full of fears about communism that many still believed him.

McCarthy ruined hundreds of innocent people. People grew afraid to give jobs or even to show friendship to anyone he accused. If they did, they risked being named as traitors themselves.

Then people began to doubt McCarthy. They watched him questioning 'suspects' on television. They saw that he was a bully and a liar. By the mid 1950s McCarthy had lost his power. He went on making wild accusations, but nobody listened.

In 1957 McCarthy died. But 'McCarthyism' had done serious

President Kennedy, 1961–3

President Johnson, 1963–9

President Nixon, 1969–74

damage to the USA's reputation for justice and fair play.

In 1961 a new President called John F. Kennedy (1961–3) took over from Eisenhower. He told the American people that they were facing a 'new frontier'.

You can read about Kennedy's dealings with the USSR and other foreign lands in Unit 50.

At home, one of the USA's most worrying problems was poverty. Despite the fact that most Americans were well off, millions of others were too poor to lead decent lives.

Some of these poor Americans were crowded together in city slums. Others lived off the beaten track in places like old coal mining districts where the pits had closed down.

Kennedy was a Democrat, as Roosevelt had been. He tried to help these people with government money and food. He also wanted to help other groups who were not getting a fair deal, like the blacks.

But Kennedy was shot and killed by a fanatic while he was driving through the streets of Dallas in Texas in November 1963.

Lyndon Johnson (1963–9) took over from Kennedy as President.

Johnson had spent years as a member of Congress, making political friends and winning influence there. He used this influence to speed up Kennedy's plans for reform.

One of Johnson's first actions was to persuade Congress to pass Kennedy's plan to improve the position of American blacks. In 1964 this became law as the Civil Rights Act (see Unit 31).

Johnson also promised the American people a 'war on poverty'. He said that he wanted to turn the USA into 'the great society' – a country where everyone received fair and decent treatment.

Johnson doomed his own plans to failure. In the later 1960s he involved the USA more and more deeply in the war in Vietnam (see Unit 51).

The huge cost of the Vietnam war forced Johnson to give up many of his plans for improvements. Riots and protests flared up all over the country – against the war, against continuing racial injustice.

By 1968 the American people were bitterly divided. Many blamed Johnson for the country's problems. He became so unpopular that he decided it was hopeless to try to get re-elected. In 1969 he gave up the Presidency and retired.

Richard Nixon (1969–74) took Johnson's place as President.

Nixon was much less interested than Kennedy and Johnson in helping the poor. The government was giving out more than enough money on welfare schemes already, Nixon claimed. He believed that people should overcome hardship by their own efforts.

In November 1972 the American people re-elected Nixon. The main reason for this was that by then he was close to getting the USA out of the hated war in Vietnam.

A cease-fire was finally signed in January 1973. Arrangements were made for all American fighting men to come home. The American people felt a huge sense of relief.

The Watergate affair

It was Nixon's moment of greatest triumph. But trouble was brewing.

Nixon was a Republican. Six months earlier a group of men had been arrested while breaking into the rival Democratic Party's headquarters in the Watergate office block in Washington.

Journalists on the *Washington Post* newspaper started to look into the burglary. They revealed that the burglars had been paid to steal information to discredit Nixon's Democratic opponents. The aim had been to make sure that Nixon was re-elected.

The Senate (the senior part of Congress) set up a committee to look into the Watergate affair. Its meetings were televised.

Day by day viewers watched the committee uncover a network of lies and dishonesty at the very heart of the nation's government.

Nixon vowed time and time again that he had known nothing about the Watergate break-in. But as the investigations went on, fewer people believed him. Many began to demand that he should be put on trial – impeached – for misusing his powers as President.

The end came in August 1974. A tape recording made in Nixon's office proved that he had known all about the Watergate affair.

Impeachment and even imprisonment now seemed certain for Nixon. To avoid it he resigned as President of the USA – the first man ever to do so.

Nixon was followed as President first by Gerald Ford (1974–7) and then by Jimmy Carter (1977–81). Neither Ford nor Carter won much success or popularity as President.

President Reagan, 1981–

In 1980 the Americans voted for a man they hoped would make a better job of running the country. He was a former film actor named Ronald Reagan. Like Nixon, Reagan was a Republican.

At home, Reagan showed little sympathy for the poor. He said that he aimed to make Americans depend less on government help and more on self help.

Abroad, Reagan was determined to make the USA stronger than its old rival, the USSR. He spent many millions of dollars on developing powerful new missiles and on research into 'star wars' weapons to knock out enemy missiles from space (see Unit 52).

Many people at home and abroad criticised Reagan. Some said that he was unfeeling. Others called him a dangerous warmonger.

But his policies – including the spending on weapons – helped more Americans to find jobs. Businessmen made bigger profits. Most Americans – all except the poorest of them – became better off.

This helped to make Reagan popular. So did his relaxed manner, which came over well on television.

But he was popular for another reason, too. After the shame of Vietnam and Watergate, Reagan's simple 'stand on your own feet and act tough' policies made many Americans feel proud of their country again.

In 1984 they re-elected Reagan as President by one of the biggest majorities in American history.

McCarthyism

An American newspaper
cartoon showing Senator
McCarthy, May 1954.
('I have here in my hand',
from Herblock's Here and
Now, Simon and Schuster 1955)

"I Have Here In My Hand —"

President Eisenhower, June 1954:

"Have you heard the latest? McCarthyism is McCarthywasm."

1 a) What was McCarthyism?
  b) Why was it so powerful in the early 1950s?
  c) Why did 'McCarthyism' turn into 'McCarthywasm'?

Part of what ex-President Truman said years later in a television interview about McCarthy.

" . . . he was just a no-good son of a bitch. And he was a coward . . .
   And of course, it wasn't just McCarthy. A fella like that couldn't have got anywhere if he'd been fought from the very beginning. They didn't do it, though. A man like that – it's like a sickness. It isn't going to disappear if you just ignore it . . .
   And the others, the people who know a man like that is up to no good but who encourage him . . . Now that's where the real danger comes . . . the ones who encourage them, who'll do anything in the world to win an election. They're just as bad."

   Harry Truman, 1962; in Merle Miller, *Plain Speaking*, 1976

2 a) Is the cartoonist for or against McCarthy? Explain your answer.
  b) Is President Truman for or against McCarthy? Explain your answer.
  c) Apart from McCarthy himself, who does Truman blame for McCarthyism?
  d) Explain which of the following might help you to decide whether what the sources on this page are saying about McCarthy is true or untrue: 1) A photograph of McCarthy talking to reporters.   2) The results of a public opinion poll asking whether people agreed with McCarthy.   3) A recording of one of McCarthy's speeches.   4) McCarthy's private diary.   5) A list of American Communist Party members.
  e) 'The sources on this page prove that McCarthy was "a cheat and a liar".' Do you agree with this statement? Explain your answer.

Watergate

A cartoon in a British newspaper at the time of Richard Nixon's resignation in August 1974.

From a book by an expert on the American presidency, written a year later. The words in italics are taken from a tape recording of a conversation between Nixon and his close advisers. Nixon himself had arranged for everything said in his office to be recorded secretly.

"The true crime of Richard Nixon was that he broke the faith that binds America together, and for that he was driven from power.

The faith he broke was . . . that somewhere in American life there is at least one man who stands for law.

From mid-April, 1973, to the end the President lied and continued to lie; and his lying not only fuelled the anger of those on his trail, but slowly corroded [ate away] the faith of Americans in that president's honour.

'We'll survive', said Nixon. *'Despite all the polls and all the rest, I think there's still a hell of a lot of people out there, and . . . they want to believe, that's the point isn't it?'*

That was the point. They did want to believe, and they could not."

T. H. White, *Breach of Faith: The Fall of Richard Nixon*, 1975

3 a) In the cartoon, what is the *Washington Post* and who is the man?

b) Why is the *Washington Post* shown as a pen pinning the man to the wall?

c) Is the cartoonist for or against the man? Explain your opinion.

d) What reason is T. H. White suggesting for the fall of Nixon?

e) Does what T. H. White says contradict or support what the cartoon is saying?

f) Does the fact that Nixon had the recordings made make what he says in the extract more, or less, likely to be true?

g) The recordings finally forced Nixon to resign. Explain why they were such important evidence against him.

h) You are an American in the summer of 1974. You argue with a friend over Watergate. Your friend thinks that the affair proves that the way your country is run is rotten. You think that it shows that nobody is too important to get away with lawbreaking. Write out or improvise the conversation.

PART FOUR
LATIN AMERICA AND THE CARIBBEAN

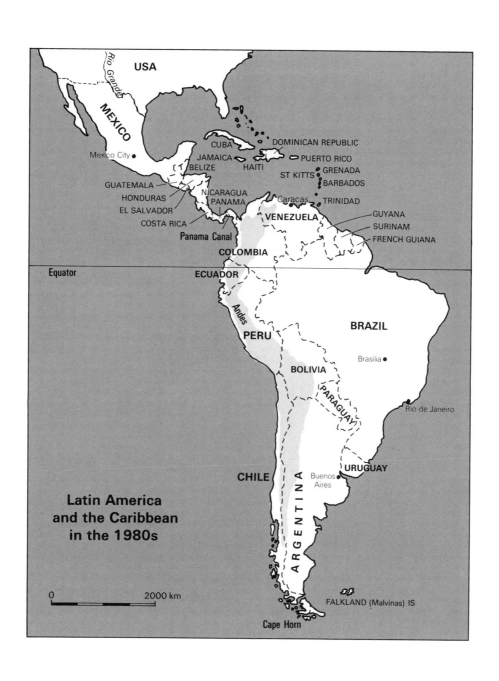

Latin America
and the Caribbean
in the 1980s

Latin America begins at a river, the Rio Grande, which separates the people of the USA from their Spanish-speaking neighbours in Mexico. It ends more than 11,000 km to the south, where the tip of Cape Horn curves out like a beak into the South Atlantic Ocean.

The people

These central and south American lands are called 'Latin' because nearly all their people – 333 million of them in the early 1980s – speak either Spanish or Portuguese. Both of these derive from Latin, the language of the ancient Roman Empire.

Treasure-seeking explorers from Spain and Portugal brought them to America 500 years ago when they sailed small wooden ships across the Atlantic Ocean to reach the islands of the Caribbean Sea and the shores of central and south America. In Brazil, the biggest country in Latin America, the usual language is Portuguese. In other countries it is Spanish.

The early European newcomers wiped out or conquered the original Indian inhabitants and settled on the Indians' land themselves. In Mexico and Peru most of the people today are descended, at least in part, from the Indians who lived there before the coming of the Spanish conquerors.

In Brazil the story has been different. The early Portuguese settlers found too few native Indians to work for them. They shipped in black slaves from Africa to labour on the land, so today many Brazilians are black.

In Argentina the story has been different again. In the nineteenth century many thousands of immigrants from Europe settled there. Today a walk along a street in Argentina's capital city, Buenos Aires, will show hardly any black or brown faces.

The land

The land of Latin America is rich. In the north much of it is warm and fertile, good for growing tropical farm crops like coffee, sugar cane and bananas. In the far south some of the largest herds of beef cattle in the world graze on the vast *pampas* (grasslands) of Argentina. The Andes mountain chain, stretching like a spine down the west coast of South America, is rich in valuable minerals such as tin and copper.

The poor

Yet most of Latin America's people have not so far benefited from this natural wealth. In the countryside the peasants are usually Indian or *mestizo* (part Indian, part European). Few own the land they work upon. The wealthy landowners are almost always *criollos* (people of European descent). They take a large share of the peasant produce every year. It is not surprising that the peasants have often been ready to support revolutionary leaders who have promised to give them land.

Today many peasants leave the land and move to the big cities in search of jobs and better lives. Often they simply exchange one kind of poverty for another, for the cities have too few jobs to go round.

The cities

Alongside this drift from the countryside, Latin America has the fastest rate of population increase in the world. By the 1980s nine of its cities had more than a million people.

One of the best known cities is Rio de Janeiro in Brazil. In Rio miles of luxury apartment blocks line the beaches of a beautiful bay. Yet thousands of Rio's people live in *favelas*, clusters of tin-roofed shacks clinging crazily to steep hillsides above the city.

Similar dirty and diseased shanty towns without water, drainage or electricity, can be found on the edge of all of Latin America's big cities. In Chile people call them *callampas* (mushrooms) because of the way in which they often seem to spring up overnight.

Earning a living

Latin America lives by selling its products abroad. Eighty per cent of these exports is farm produce – bananas from the steamy lowlands of Costa Rica, coffee from Brazil and Colombia, beef and wheat from the *pampas* of Argentina. The remaining 20 per cent consists of raw materials for industry – oil from Venezuela, copper from Peru, tin from Bolivia.

Much of the money to develop these resources came originally from overseas. British and American companies put up the cash to drill for oil and mine for tin, to plant coffee and banana plantations and to stock the *haciendas* (ranches) of the grasslands with cattle.

Their investments made huge profits for them. Some Latin Americans profited, too – especially landowners, businessmen and the politicians who made deals with the foreign companies.

But most of the profits went abroad. The peasants who laboured to cut the sugar cane, pick the coffee beans and mine the tin benefited little. The main features of their lives continued to be backbreaking labour and near starvation.

Economic difficulties

During the world depression of the 1930s Latin Americans could find few buyers for their raw materials. They started to use more and more of them in their own countries.

Manufacturing industries grew again when the Second World War cut off Latin America from its usual suppliers of manufactured goods in the United States and Europe.

Even so, Latin America today has far fewer factories than the USA or Europe to provide its people with jobs and earn them money. Almost all of its countries still live by exporting one or two main food or raw material products.

This almost guarantees that they will stay poor. The prices for these 'primary' products often rise and fall. This makes it very difficult to plan for the future. From year to year individuals and governments do not know how much money they will have.

To get round this difficulty, Latin American governments have borrowed huge sums of money from abroad in recent years. In the 1980s most of them were heavily in debt. Add this to their other problems – the desperate poverty of so many people, a rapidly increasing population needing jobs and food, and rocketing prices – and you have plenty of ingredients for political troubles.

Winning independence

Mention Latin American and many people will think of revolutions and governments being overthrown by force. Unit 33 may have given you some ideas about why this is so. A look at the region's political history may give you some more.

At the beginning of the nineteenth century Latin America was still ruled by Spain. The exception was Brazil, which Portugal ruled. In the early 1800s, however, the white settlers in Latin America – the *criollos* – threw off Spanish rule.

The most admired revolutionary leader was Simon Bolivar. Bolivar wanted the *criollos* to unite in one independent state. He dreamed of a sort of United States of Latin America which would one day become as strong and prosperous as its northern neighbour.

But the breakaway settlers were cut off from one another by countless kilometres of jungles and mountains. Instead of uniting they formed a string of separate states, each with its own rulers.

According to legend the disappointed Bolivar's last words, as he lay dying in December 1830, were 'We who have served the revolution have ploughed the sea'.

The Caudillos

For over a century the history of politics and government in Latin America was the story of endless fights for personal power between rival dictators called *caudillos*. In Bolivia, for example, in the hundred years from 1852 to 1952 there were 100 *coups d'état* – overthrows of governments by force.

The *caudillos* were often generals. Usually they came from land-owning families, so they had the support of the people who controlled the countries' wealth. With soldiers to back them, they had the power to force the rest of the people – the Indians and *mestizos* who worked the land – to obey them.

Zapata and Mexico

But in 1910 in Mexico a revolution took place that was more than just a change of *caudillos*. Its leader was a peasant, turned bandit, turned revolutionary, named Emiliano Zapata.

Zapata's aim was to help the poor by sharing out the land more fairly. He was killed by enemies in 1919, but his ideas lived on.

In the 1930s Mexico's revolutionary government broke up many of the country's privately owned *haciendas*, or great estates. It gave their land to the peasants, who worked it together on a co-operative basis as their Indian ancestors had done. By 1950 Mexico had 17,579 of these *ejidos*, or co-operative farms, occupying almost half (44 per cent) of the country's cultivated land.

Perón and Argentina

Thirty years after Zapata another revolutionary leader who claimed to be acting in the interests of the poor appeared, this time in Argentina. He was an army officer named Juan Perón.

By the 1940s Argentina was Latin America's leading industrial nation. It had more people employed in factories than in all kinds of farming put together.

This gave Perón the idea of setting himself up as a new kind of *caudillo*. Borrowing an idea from the Italian dictator Mussolini, he decided to base his power on support from Argentina's industrial workers instead of from its landowners.

In 1943 Perón was Argentina's Secretary of Labour, one of a team of army officers running the country's government. He used his position to win the support of the country's industrial workers – 'the shirtless ones', as he called them – by improving their working and living conditions. He brought in holidays with pay, old age pensions and unemployment insurance.

Perón's reforms made him so popular with the workers that when elections for a new government were held in 1946 he won easily. He became President and his supporters won two thirds of the seats in Argentina's parliament.

Eva Perón

The new President was encouraged by his wife, Eva. Many people believed that she was the real brains of the partnership.

Perón set out to modernise Argentina's economy and free it from foreign control. He nationalised key industries, including the British-owned railway system. He placed the export of beef and wheat, Argentina's main products, under government control. He tried to develop new industries.

To try to make sure that he kept his power Perón closed down newspapers which dared to criticise him, banned rival political parties and threw their leaders into prison. He also provided still more benefits for 'the shirtless ones', building flats, schools and hospitals, and introducing shorter working hours and minimum wages schemes.

But by the 1950s Perón was in trouble. Eva died in 1952. Heavy taxes to pay for his social reforms, especially on the middle classes, forced up prices and turned people against him. Droughts and poor harvests caused hardship in the countryside.

The last straw for Perón's opponents came in 1955. Rumours spread that he was planning to arm 'the shirtless ones'. The generals of the army turned against him and drove him from the country. He went to live in exile in Spain.

Argentina after Perón

For most of the next twenty years the generals ran Argentina. But 'Perónista' ideas remained strong. Perón himself continued to be so popular with the workers that in 1973 public opinion forced the generals to let him return with his new wife, Isabel.

But Perón was now a sick old man and in 1974 he died. Isabel tried to carry on in his place, but the job was beyond her. In 1976 the generals again took over the government.

The generals continued to run Argentina until 1982, when they led the country to a disastrous defeat by Britain in a war to decide who should rule the nearby Falkland Islands – the Malvinas, as the Argentinians called them. The Falklands defeat made the generals so unpopular, even with their own soldiers, that they handed over power to an elected government once more.

Country	Area (sq. km.)	Population 1981 (millions)	Income per head 1974, in US dollars	Mean annual percentage increase in population 1974	Chief exports	Chief trading partners 1980s
Argentina	2,776,889	28.2	1,922	1.3	Beef, wheat	USA, Brazil, Europe
Bolivia	1,098,581	5.7	299	2.6	Tin	USA, Argentina
Brazil	8,511,965	120.5	975	2.8	Sugar, coffee, cotton	USA, Japan, Europe
Chile	756,945	11.3	661	1.7	Copper	USA, Europe
Colombia	1,138,914	26.4	479	3.2	Coffee, cotton	USA
Costa Rica	50,900	2.3	795	2.7	Coffee, bananas	USA
Cuba	114,524	9.7	n.a.	1.8	Sugar, tobacco	USSR
Dominican Republic	48,734	5.6	505	2.9	Sugar, coffee	USA
Ecuador	283,561	8.6	482	3.4	Bananas	USA
El Salvador	21,393	4.7	382	3.0	Coffee	USA
Guatemala	108,889	7.5	470	2.5	Coffee	USA
Honduras	112,088	3.8	306	4.0	Bananas	USA
Mexico	1,972,546	71.2	1,051	3.5	Oil, coffee	USA, Europe, Japan
Nicaragua	130,000	2.8	n.a.	3.3	Coffee	USA (pre 1980s)
Panama	75,651	1.9	n.a.	3.3	Bananas	USA
Paraguay	406,752	3.1	n.a.	3.0	Meat, timber	USA
Peru	1,285,216	17.0	468	3.2	Copper, lead	USA
Uruguay	177,508	2.9	1,158	1.2	Meat, wool	Brazil
Venezuela	912,000	15.4	2,046	3.1	Oil, iron-ore	USA
United Kingdom	244,013	55.9	3,106	0.3	Manufactured goods	Many
USA	9,363,125	217.2	5,923	0.8	Manufactured goods	Many

From M. Kidron and R. Segal, *The New State of the World Atlas*, Pan 1984, and B. P. Price, *The Hamlyn World Atlas*, Hamlyn 1980

Latin America: economics

The table opposite gives information about the countries of Latin America.

1 a) Name the *three* countries which have the highest incomes per head.

b) Choose *one* of these countries and use the table and the text to suggest reasons for its high income.

c) What terms would you use to describe the types of exports from Latin America? What problems are met by countries which depend heavily on such exports?

d) What difference does the table show between the trading arrangements of Latin American countries and those of the USA or the UK? Do you think that such arrangements are an advantage or a disadvantage to Latin America? Explain why.

e) Give *two* ways in which you think the table helps to explain why living standards in Latin America are lower than in the USA or the UK.

Latin America: politics

A cartoon from a Mexican magazine in the 1970s.

RIUS IN SIEMPRE! (MEXICO CITY)

2 a) Which social groups are represented by   1) the man on the left and   2) the group on the right?

b) What information about the group on the right can you gather from the drawing?

c) What reason is the artist suggesting for discontent in Latin America?

d) What is he suggesting that the discontent is leading to?

e) Imagine the man on the left is a political leader. What might he say to a television interviewer who asked about his attitude to doing more to help the poor of his country?

f) From what you have read in the text about conditions in Latin America, do you think that the artist is giving a fair picture? Explain your answer.

'Death to Nixon!'

'Muera Nixon, Muera Nixon.' Death to Nixon!

A barricade blocked the road. The car rocked wildly as the chanting mob tried to overturn it. Rocks and iron bars thudded against its roof and shattered its windows. Inside the car Richard Nixon, Vice-President of the United States, was inches away from death.

It was 13th May 1958 in Caracas, the capital of Venezuela. Nixon was visiting the city as part of a goodwill tour of Latin America. But he found only hatred on the streets of Caracas.

Nixon's life was saved when a truck forced a way through the barricade and his car was able to accelerate away.

When news of the attack reached the United States, the American people were shocked and angry. But it made them realise how much some Latin Americans hated their country.

Ever since the countries of Latin America won their independence the USA has taken a special interest in them. They are its closest neighbours and it is important to the USA's safety to make sure that no foreign enemies gain influence there. Much of Latin American agriculture and industry is owned by the USA. This gives the Americans another reason for trying to control events there.

The Monroe Doctrine, 1823

As early as 1823 President Monroe of the USA had warned the great powers of Europe not to interfere in Latin America's affairs. In later years the USA enforced this 'Monroe Doctrine' to make sure that its influence was what counted in Latin America.

By the end of the nineteenth century American businessmen had invested millions of dollars there. They were making fortunes from banana plantations, sugar estates and mines. Most Americans came to see Latin America as little more than a huge private estate to supply the USA with food, raw materials and customers.

The USA and Cuba, 1898–1902

American soldiers made sure that the region stayed that way. Take Cuba, for example. In 1895 its people rebelled against their Spanish rulers. To protect American investments, the USA declared war on Spain in 1898 and sent troops to help Cuba's people to win their independence.

But Cuba's independence was little more than a sham. Before the Americans took away their troops in 1902 they forced the new Cuban government to agree to a condition called the Platt Amendment. This said that the USA could send troops to take over in Cuba any time it felt that American interests were in danger – in other words, whenever it wanted to.

Roosevelt's Corollary, 1904

In 1904 President Theodore Roosevelt claimed even wider rights of interference in Latin America. His motto, he once said, was to 'speak softly and carry a big stick'. In Roosevelt's Corollary (addition) to the Monroe Doctrine he now said that the USA would interfere in the affairs of *any* Latin American country whenever necessary – and whether the Latin Americans liked it or not.

Roosevelt had shown what this could mean the year before. The Americans wanted to build a canal across the isthmus of Panama, the neck of land separating the Caribbean Sea from the Pacific Ocean. Building it would mean that their ships could travel quickly between the east and west coasts of the USA instead of having to make the long sea journey round South America.

The problem was that the United States did not own the isthmus of Panama; Colombia did. When the Colombian government was slow to give the Americans permission to build the canal, Roosevelt sent warships. The warships helped a small group of Panamanian businessmen to rebel against the Colombian government and set up an independent state of Panama.

Within days Panama's new rulers handed over to the Americans a 17-kilometre-wide strip of land across their country to build the canal.

Most Latin Americans thought that Roosevelt had set up the whole affair. They thought so even more when he openly boasted 'I took Panama'.

'I took Panama', 1903

Another side to the USA's dealings with Latin America in the early twentieth century was 'dollar diplomacy'. The term was used by President Taft, who followed Theodore Roosevelt. Dollar diplomacy meant encouraging American businessmen to invest still more money in Latin America so that its governments would have to go on doing as the Americans wished.

After the First World War American governments became worried about how unpopular their 'big stick' and 'dollar diplomacy' policies were making the USA in Latin America. They decided to do more 'speaking softly'.

In the 1920s President Coolidge said that his government no longer supported Roosevelt's Corollary. In future, he said, it would respect the right of Latin American countries to run their own affairs.

Dollar diplomacy

The good neighbor policy

The best known statement of this new approach was the 'good neighbor' policy, set out a few years later by another Roosevelt, President Franklin D. Roosevelt. 'I would dedicate this nation to the policy of the good neighbor', said Roosevelt in 1933, 'the neighbor who . . . respects the rights of others.'

Roosevelt ordered home the American troops and officials who, off and on, had been running the affairs of Latin American countries such as Nicaragua (occupied by American troops from 1912 to 1933) for the past thirty years. He also gave up the USA's claim to interfere in Panama and Cuba whenever it wanted.

But many Latin Americans were not convinced by Roosevelt's talk about being a good neighbor. True, the American troops had gone home. But the *caudillos* who took over when they left – the Somoza family, who held power in Nicaragua from 1937 to 1979, for example – were often seen as little more than American puppets.

The Second World War brought better times for Latin America. All the raw materials that it could produce – copper, tin, oil and countless others – were swallowed up by the wartime factories of the USA. The result was more money and more jobs for the Latin American people – but also even more American control.

As soon as the war ended fresh calls of 'Yankee go home' were heard. To try to reduce anti-American feeling, in 1945 the United States took the lead in setting up the Organisation of American States (OAS).

The Organisation of American States (OAS)

The idea of the OAS was to encourage the countries of Latin American to co-operate with one another, and with the USA, as partners. One of its aims was to improve living standards.

Population

But hardship and hunger continued to be widespread. One reason for this was the rapid growth in the region's population. Brazil, for example, had a population of 52 million in 1950. By 1978 it had 116 million. The need to feed, house and find jobs for all these extra people cancelled out any benefits brought by improvements in farming and industry.

Inflation and the generals

Another problem was inflation – prices rising so fast that people's incomes and savings lose their value. In the 1960s and 1970s inflation was one reason why generals seized power in country after country – Brazil in 1964, Chile in 1974, Argentina in 1976.

The generals claimed they were acting to stop revolutionary groups from winning power by gaining the support of the workers, who were angry at the fall in the buying power of their wages. The generals often used torture and murder to crush opposition.

Reformers accused the USA of helping to put these undemocratic governments in power. There was some truth in this.

In the years after the Second World War the USA became deeply involved in Cold War rivalry with the USSR (see Unit 48). One result was that USA governments often seemed more concerned with stamping out communism in Latin America than with improving conditions of life there.

The CIA and Honduras, 1954

What happened in Guatemala in 1954 was an example of this. Jacobo Arbenz, Guatemala's President, formed a government that included some communists. He announced that his government was taking over thousands of hectares of unused farming land to share out among landless peasants – including 80,954 hectares belonging to the American-owned United Fruit Company.

The American government of President Eisenhower was not prepared to stand for this. Its secret service branch (the Central Intelligence Agency, or CIA) gave money and weapons to enemies of the Arbenz government so that they could invade Guatemala from neighbouring Nicaragua and Honduras.

With this CIA aid the rebels overthrew Arbenz in July 1954.

When he asked the United Nations to look into the affair, the Americans used their Security Council veto (see Unit 47) to prevent an investigation.

The CIA and Cuba, 1959–61

The CIA's plots did not always succeed. When Fidel Castro won power in Cuba in 1959 he started to take over American businesses there (see Unit 50). The CIA persuaded President John F. Kennedy to let it help Cubans who were opposed to Castro to organise an invasion to overthrow him.

This Bay of Pigs invasion in 1961 was a disastrous failure (see Unit 50). But fearing more American attempts to get rid of him, Castro turned for help to the USSR. The Americans were alarmed, but they reluctantly decided to accept the situation after coming close to war with the Russians over Cuba in 1962 (see Unit 50).

Che Guevara

In 1965 one of the men who had helped Castro in Cuba, Ernesto 'Che' Guevara, went to Bolivia to try to organise a revolution. Bolivian government troops hunted down and killed Guevara in 1967, but he became a legend for years to come.

American interventions

American governments were determined to prevent any more Cubas appearing on their doorstep. In 1965 President Johnson sent 22,000 American marines to the Dominican Republic to stop a reforming president named Juan Bosch from regaining power. In 1973 CIA agents helped Chile's generals to overthrow President Allende, who had nationalised some American-owned mining companies. In 1983 American marines overthrew a pro-communist government on the tiny Caribbean island of Grenada.

In the middle of the 1980s the American President Reagan gave money and weapons to rebels called *contras* who were fighting to overthrow the Sandinista government of Nicaragua.

The Sandinistas had come to power in 1979, overthrowing the Somoza family. President Reagan claimed that, since 1979, the Sandinistas had allowed communists to take over their government.

American aid

But there was a more humanitarian side to American dealings with Latin America. During their earlier occupations of countries such as Cuba the Americans had built hospitals, laid on water supplies and wiped out killer diseases like malaria and yellow fever. In the early 1960s President Kennedy continued this tradition.

The Alliance for Progress, 1961

In 1961 Kennedy set up an organisation called the Alliance for Progress. This aimed to provide American money to improve the lives of Latin America's millions of poor. Kennedy hoped that pouring aid into Latin America would make it possible for governments there to make enough improvements to stop people from turning to communism.

But the Alliance for Progress never came near to achieving Kennedy's goals. The generals running much of Latin America continued to rely more on guns to keep power than on reforms.

In the 1970s and 1980s the struggle for political power was fought with bullets and bombs as much as with votes. And meanwhile Latin America's poor stayed poor.

The Alliance for Progress

The Prime Minister of Trinidad's view of the Alliance for Progress.

"The Alliance for Progress ought to promote internal social revolution by non-violent means. By 1964–5 it had already failed, partly because, when the chips were down, the US Government became afraid of genuine social revolution, fearing that all such revolution would be contaminated by 'communism', and also partly because any thorough-going social revolution had to affect adversely the interests of the large American corporations operating in Latin America."

Eric Williams, *From Columbus to Castro*, 1970

An American cartoonist's view of American policy in Latin America, 1983.

1 **a)** In your own words describe what Eric Williams believes the Alliance for Progress should be trying to do.

   b) Do you think the cartoonist would agree with him? Explain your answer.

   c) How does Eric Williams explain the failure of the Alliance to achieve its aims?

   d) How does the cartoonist give a similar explanation?

   e) Can you think of other reasons for the Alliance's failure?

2 Test your knowledge of the USA's dealings with Latin America.

   a) Write two or three sentences about each of: The Monroe Doctrine, Roosevelt's Corollary, the Platt Amendment, the good neighbor policy, the OAS, the Alliance for Progress.

   b) Imagine yourself in the position of one of the following in the 1970s: 1) a peasant farmer in Costa Rica, 2) an army officer in Chile, 3) the manager of a hotel in Brazil, 4) a meat canning factory worker in Argentina. Write a letter to a friend saying whether you think the influence of the USA is good or bad for your country and explaining why.

Nicaragua

President Reagan explains his support for the contras in Nicaragua.

"We have a right to help the people of Nicaragua . . . determine their own government.

What happened there was a hijacking. The people of Nicaragua set out to get rid of an authoritarian government: the Somoza dictatorship. The revolutionaries appealed to the Organisation of American States and said, 'Would you ask Somoza to step down, so we can end the killings?' The OAS asked them, 'What are your revolutionary goals?' They told them democracy, pluralistic society, . . . freedom of religion. But . . . the Sandinistas . . . ousted their other allies in the revolution and then they established a totalitarian Communist regime, the same process that Castro employed in taking over Cuba.

All of this talk that I am nursing an ambition to send in troops – no. To send in troops would lose us every friend in Latin America. They want us to help the contras, but not with troops. The only thing I've uttered is a warning that if this . . . Sandinista group is allowed to solidify their base, they intend to spread . . . revolution to other countries."

Time, 31st March 1986

An American cartoonist's view of President Reagan's policy in Nicaragua, 9th May 1985.

3 **a)** What do you understand by   1) the Somoza dictatorship,
   2) Sandinistas?
   b) Give two reasons why President Reagan believes the USA has a right to interfere in Nicaragua.
   c) In the cartoon which lands lie   1) above and   2) below the Rio Grande?
   d) How does the cartoonist think that Ronald Reagan sees
   1) Nicaragua,   2) Cuba,   3) the USSR?
   e) What is the link between your answer to d) and the man in a top hat?
   f) Does the cartoon give a fair or unfair picture of Reagan's views?

The early years

The story of the modern West Indies begins in 1492. In that year the explorer Christopher Columbus became the first European to reach these islands, which curve like a necklace round the rim of the Caribbean Sea. Columbus claimed the islands for his employer, the King of Spain. They became outposts of the vast Spanish Empire, which covered much of central and south America.

The islands soon began to attract other Europeans. First came pirates and buccaneers. They used the islands as bases to attack Spanish ships sailing back to Europe with cargoes of gold and silver from the mines of Mexico and Peru. Then came settlers – French, Dutch, British.

The first British settlers landed on a small island they called St Kitts in 1624. Other British settlers colonised Barbados in 1625 and Nevis, Antigua and Montserrat in 1632. In later years the British captured the larger islands of Jamaica (1655) and Trinidad (1802) from the Spaniards.

Sugar and slaves

The fertile soils and hot tropical climate of the islands provided ideal growing conditions for sugar. This could be sold for high prices in Europe, so the settlers set up large and profitable sugar farms, called plantations.

Growing sugar cane was back-breaking work. The plantation owners imported slaves from Africa to do most of it.

The Africans were shipped across the Atlantic Ocean in terrible conditions, chained and packed together on stinking slave ships. Many died on the way. But enough survived to create a large black population in the Caribbean. By the eighteenth century most Caribbean islands had more black people than white.

Freeing the slaves

In 1834 the British Parliament abolished slavery everywhere in the British Empire. In Britain's Caribbean colonies 668,000 black slaves were set free. Many of them left the sugar plantations to farm small plots of land of their own.

To replace the freed slaves some plantation owners shipped in workers from India. By 1917, when the British Parliament passed a law to stop this trade, more than 416,000 Indians had been sent to the West Indies, most of them to British Guiana (Guyana), Trinidad and Jamaica.

Protection and free trade

Up until the middle years of the nineteenth century the sugar growers of the West Indies prospered. They were able to sell their sugar in Britain at a good profit, because the British government placed heavy import duties on sugar from anywhere else.

But in the 1840s the British government started to follow policies of free trade. It abolished all import duties, including those on sugar. Foreign sugar, including large amounts produced from sugar-beet grown on farms in Europe, flooded Britain's shops.

For the West Indians this was a disaster. Sugar prices fell

sharply. Many plantations went out of business. Those which struggled on cut their workers' already low wages.

The Morant Bay Rising, 1865

In 1865 a riot broke out at Morant Bay in Jamaica, Britain's biggest Caribbean colony. The riot was rooted in the hardships of sugar depression. Black farmers needed more land to make a living and felt that the British government was treating them unfairly.

The British governor, Edward Eyre, declared that the riot was a rebellion. He hunted down the protestors and executed their main leader, Paul Bogle, and hundreds of others.

A government enquiry decided that Eyre had been harsh and unjust, and he was sacked. But the Morant Bay Rising had important effects on the way Britain governed its Caribbean colonies.

Up until this time the affairs of Jamaica and most of Britain's other West Indian islands had been run by local parliaments elected by white property owners. But the Morant Bay Rising frightened the whites so much that they gave up these rights of self-government and agreed to more control – and more protection – from the British government in London.

Crown Colony government

By the later years of the nineteenth century most of Britain's West Indian islands had become what were called Crown Colonies. Crown Colonies had no elected assemblies or parliaments. Instead their affairs were run by a governor appointed by the British government in London, helped by advisers he chose.

The years which followed brought some improvements to life in the West Indies. Reforming governors like Sir John Peter Grant of Jamaica built roads, bridges and railways. Island farmers began to earn money from new crops such as bananas and cocoa, which they exported in ship-loads to the outside world.

Hard times

Yet in most ways the West Indies continued to be poor and backward. In the 1920s and 1930s the increase in population meant that every year more mouths had to be fed. But the depression in trade which hit the whole world at this time brought sugar prices crashing down again and put many people out of work. On top of this, disease ruined many small farmers' banana crops.

The people of the West Indies grew discontented and angry. Under leaders like Arthur Cipriani in Trinidad and Alexander Bustamante and Norman Manley in Jamaica, workers joined together in trade unions to demand improvements.

Trade unions and political parties

At first the new trade unions concentrated on pressing for increased wages and better working conditions. But their leaders soon saw that political changes – changes, that is, in the way their islands were governed – were also needed to improve people's lives.

So, out of the trade unions grew political parties. In Trinidad, Cipriani's Trinidad Working Men's Association (1919) became the Trinidad Labour Party (1932). In Jamaica, both Manley's People's National Party (PNP – 1938) and Bustamante's Jamaica Labour Party (JLP – 1943) grew out of the earlier Jamaica Workers' and Tradesmen's Union (1935).

1938 was the year the West Indies boiled over. Strikes and riots broke out in Trinidad, Barbados and Jamaica. Dozens of people were killed and hundreds wounded.

The British government sent warships and soldiers to help the governors of the colonies to put down the riots. But it also sent out a Royal Commission, headed by Lord Moyne, to discover the reasons for them.

The Moyne Commission, 1938–9

The ten members of the Moyne Commission spent fourteen months in the West Indies, from August 1938 to November 1939. They visited nearly every one of the colonies, listening to the views of people from many walks of life. They asked questions about anything and everything – jobs, wages, housing, education, health.

The Moyne Commission handed its report to the British government in 1940. By that time Britain was at war with Germany. Only part of the report was published in 1940. The full details were not made public until 1944, when the war was almost won.

There was a good reason for the secrecy. The Moyne Commission's report painted a shocking picture of widespread hunger, disease and unemployment in the West Indies – and it placed a lot of the blame for this on neglect by the British authorities.

This is part of what the Moyne Commission wrote about housing:

' . . . in the poorest parts of most towns and in many of the country districts, a majority of the houses are largely made of rusty corrugated iron and unsound boarding . . .; sanitation in any form and water supply are unknown in such premises . . . Such is the pressure of poverty that when a second room is available, it will often be sub-let for the sake of a few shillings.'

Not surprisingly, disease was widespread. In Barbados, for example, the Commission found that out of every 1000 babies born alive, 217 died before their first birthday. In England at this same time the infant mortality (death) rate was less than 58 per 1000.

After the Moyne Report

The British government was afraid that making public details like these would cause anti-British feeling in the colonies. It could not afford to risk this in 1940, when it was locked in a life or death struggle against Hitler. It needed to keep the colonies quiet and producing food and raw materials to help to win the war.

To make sure that the colonies went on supporting its war effort the British government acted quickly to carry out Lord Moyne's main recommendations.

The first of these was that the British government should give all the help it could to bring about a quick improvement in living and working conditions in the West Indies. The second was that the people of the West Indies should be given more power to run their own affairs, including full self-government as quickly as possible.

In 1940 the British Parliament passed a law called the Colonial Development and Welfare Act. This provided money to improve living standards in all the poor colonies of the British Empire. The West Indian share was £1 million a year.

Colonial Development and Welfare Acts

The money was shared out from the Caribbean headquarters of the Colonial Development and Welfare Organisation (CDWO) in Barbados. The CDWO became the first important organisation to treat all of the English speaking colonies of the Caribbean as one unit with common problems. It provided money to build roads, schools and medical centres. It set up training schemes to provide more nurses and other specialist workers. It organised agricultural research to find better crops and farming methods. Although such CDWO measures came nowhere near to solving the problems of the West Indies, they were important steps forward.

After the end of the Second World War the British government passed another Colonial Development and Welfare Act (1945) which gave the CDWO another £15.5 million to continue its work.

Political changes

Changes also began on the political scene. In 1943 the British government greatly increased the number of people allowed to vote for the Barbados House of Assembly, or Parliament. In 1944 Jamaica was given an elected House of Representatives, for which all Jamaicans were allowed to vote.

Similar reforms were soon introduced elsewhere in the West Indies. By the 1950s most of Britain's West Indian colonies had assemblies elected by universal suffrage (a vote for all adults) helping to run their affairs.

But 'helping' was all they did at first. Important government powers, such as control of the police and armed forces, were still in the hands of the governor and other officials appointed by the British. Just how important this could be was shown in the mainland West Indian colony of British Guiana.

British Guiana, 1953

At an election in 1953 the People's Progressive Party (PPP), led by Dr Cheddi Jagan, won a majority of the places in British Guiana's National Assembly. The British government claimed that Jagan intended to set up a communist-style dictatorship. With backing from the USA it sent in troops, dismissed the National Assembly, and appointed British officials to run British Guiana.

But fear of communism was not the main reason the British government was slow to let West Indians run their own affairs. It doubted whether the colonies were strong enough to stand on their own feet as independent nations. It thought that they were too poor to provide their people with a comfortable standard of living, too small to defend themselves against outside enemies.

The answer to these problems was federation, the British decided. They planned to join the scattered British colonies of the Caribbean region together as one West Indian nation, with the same government ruling all of them.

Social conditions

A list of the subjects which could be studied by pupils in government elementary schools on St Kitts in 1917. Only 46.2 per cent of St Kitts children attended school at this time.

"Obligatory [compulsory] subjects: Reading, Writing, Needlework for girls. Moral Instruction and Tropical Hygiene.

Optional subjects: Elementary science, Geography, Singing and Dancing. Only two optional subjects may be taught, and on condition that the work in the compulsory subject is sufficiently good."

In W. Claypole and J. Robottom, *Caribbean Story Book 2*, 1981

An extract from a government report on schools in British Guiana in 1925.

"The sanitary conditions of the majority of schools are rightly condemned by medical . . . opinion. There is no systematic physical training, and a large number of schools have not sufficient space, either indoors or outdoors, to carry out this branch of education. No serious attempt is made to provide any manual instruction at any stage of the child's school life. Very few schools have furniture suitable for infant handwork; and at the other end of the scale there is neither accommodation, staff nor apparatus provided for the purpose of introducing the elder boys to woodwork or any other craft, or the elder girls to cookery, mothercraft, or any of the necessary duties of women in the home."

In *Report of the Commissioner of Education*, British Guiana, 1925

1 a) Do these sources suggest that West Indian governments were
  1) very concerned,   2) concerned,   3) a little concerned,
  4) unconcerned, about economic and social problems at this time? Explain your answer.
  b) Suggest reasons for the governments' attitude.
  c) Which subject in St Kitts would pupils have found most useful?
  d) If you had been in charge of schools in a West Indian colony at this time, what new subjects would you have tried to introduce and why?

A historian put together from newspaper reports this account of a cane-cutters' strike in British Guiana in 1905.

"One man told the Doctor that he and his two grown-up sons, after working hard all week, getting up at 4.00 o'clock in the mornings and working until six in the afternoons, could earn no more than 10 to 15 shillings [50–75p] during the grinding season. Another said he only earned from 4 to 7 shillings [20–35p] per week . . . Dorothy Rice assisted by her two daughters as 'fetchers' said she earned 6 to 7 shillings [30–35p) per week. She marked out the work on Monday, started cutting on Tuesday and worked up to mid-day on Saturday. Her normal knock-off time was 7 p.m."

A. Chase, *A History of Trade Unionism in Guyana*, 1967

2 a) What does this source tell you about conditions for sugar-cane workers?
  b) Suggest two reasons for these conditions.

The Moyne Commission

Evidence given to the Moyne Commissioners when they visited Nevis.

"We find that the minimum requirements for a labourer amount to one shilling and three pence per diem [day], as shown below:

Breakfast – Bread 2d., sugar 1d.

Dinner   – Meal or flour 2d., potatoes 1d., meat or fish 2d., lard or butter 1d.

Supper   – Rice 2d., peas 1d., meat or fish 2d., lard or butter 1d.

In the above estimate there is no provision made for house repair, clothes or for protective nourishing foods such as milk or eggs. Nor is allowance made for household necessities such as oil, matches, soap, starch etc., or for church and society dues, provision for sickness, medical fees . . . .

The chief industry that gives employment for a period of a few days per week for two or three months in the year, is cotton. Sugar-cane cultivation provides very little employment under the present system. Men who are fortunate in getting employment earn one shilling, the women, sixpence per diem. It is therefore evident that even in the case of the employed, income falls far short of bare, minimum subsistence."

Memorandum of Nevis Agricultural and Commercial Society, 1938

Part of a summary of the Commission's Report that was published in 1940.

"Rightly or wrongly, a substantial body of public opinion in the West Indies is convinced that far-reaching measures of social reconstruction . . . depend upon greater participation of the people in the business of government. . . . An examination of the social and economic problems of the West Indies which . . . took no account of this point of view would therefore be regarded by some sections of public opinion in the Caribbean area as having failed . . . . Moreover, we are satisfied that the claim . . . that the people should have a larger voice in the management of their affairs . . . is sufficiently widespread to make it doubtful whether any schemes of social reform . . . would be completely successful unless they were accompanied by the largest measure of constitutional development which is thought to be judicious [wise] in existing circumstances."

West Indian Royal Commission 1938–9, 1940

3 a) From the first extract pick out four different problems facing the people of Nevis.

  b) Explain which you think would be the worst of these problems.

  c) Do you think that such problems would be common to all the West Indian colonies or to Nevis alone? Give reasons for your answer.

  d) If you had been a West Indian trade union leader in 1938, what actions would you have wanted the government to take to deal with these problems?

  e) How could the Moyne Commission claim to know what a 'substantial body of opinion in the West Indies' thought?

  f) In your own words say what change the Report is advising.

  g) Why does it think this change is necessary?

  h) Describe what steps were taken in the 1940s and 1950s to bring about the changes recommended by the Moyne Commission.

The idea of federation

Arthur Cipriani, the Trinidadian trade union leader, had favoured federation as early as the 1920s. After the Second World War so did West Indian leaders such as Grantley Adams of Barbados and Eric Williams of Trinidad. They claimed that federation would benefit all the people of the English-speaking West Indies. For example, it would give them the opportunity to sell their products at higher prices, by bargaining together with foreign buyers.

But there were problems. The biggest was simply that most of the people of the West Indies thought of themselves as Jamaicans, Trinidadians or Barbadians first, and as West Indians only second. This was partly a matter of history, partly of distance.

It is more than 1700 kilometres from Barbados to Jamaica – further than the distance from London to Warsaw in Poland. Also, most of the islands produced similar goods, such as sugar and bananas, so they traded very little with one another. This meant that it was often easier for a West Indian to get a plane or a boat to Britain or the USA than to another part of the West Indies.

The Montego Bay Conference, 1947

The supporters of federation believed that its benefits would be so great that it was worth trying to overcome these difficulties. So in 1947 representatives of all Britain's West Indian colonies met at Montego Bay in Jamaica to discuss the idea.

The representatives at the Montego Bay Conference agreed to set up a group called the Standing Closer Association Committee (SCAC). SCAC's job was to work out detailed arrangements for setting up a federation.

For the next ten years the members of the SCAC discussed and argued. Finally they came up with a plan which most of the colonies agreed to try. Only the mainland colonies of British Guiana (Guyana) and British Honduras (Belize) refused. They believed that they could work out a better future on their own.

The Federation of the West Indies, 1958

The Federation of the West Indies eventually came into being in 1958. A Federal Parliament of forty-five members was elected, with the seats divided between the ten separate islands roughly according to the size of their populations. The Federation's first Prime Minister was Sir Grantley Adams of Barbados.

From the beginning the Federation government ran into trouble. One weakness was that it had no power to raise money from taxes; instead it had to rely on fixed payments from the various members. An even more serious weakness was that many of the people of the larger islands were not convinced that they needed the Federation.

Jamaica and the Federation

This was especially true of Jamaica, whose people made up half of the Federation's total population. Jamaicans felt that the money they were handing over to the Federation was being spent more for the benefit of the smaller islands than of Jamaica.

Jamaicans also disliked some of the future plans for the

Federation. If workers were allowed to move freely from one of its members to another, for example, they feared that Jamaica might attract large numbers of immigrants from smaller, poorer islands. And if freedom of trade were introduced, they feared that the growth of new industries in Jamaica might be held back.

In 1961 Alexander Bustamante, the leader of the opposition in the Jamaican Parliament, started a campaign to take Jamaica out of the Federation. This forced his old rival, Norman Manley, Jamaica's Prime Minister, to call a referendum – that is, a vote in which Jamaicans could say whether or not they wanted their island to remain in the Federation. When the votes were counted 54.1 per cent of them had said 'no' and only 45.9 per cent 'yes'.

Federation ends, independence begins

It was the end of the road for the Federation. 'Ten minus one equals nothing', said Trinidad's leader, Eric Williams, and announced that if Jamaica was leaving, so was Trinidad. In August 1962 both Jamaica and Trinidad became independent states in their own right. They were no longer British colonies.

Barbados followed Jamaica and Trinidad to independence in 1966. British Guiana, which had never joined the Federation, also became independent in 1966 under the new name of Guyana.

Britain's smaller West Indian colonies followed suit in the 1970s – Grenada in 1974, Dominica in 1978, St Lucia in 1979. They were joined by Belize in 1981. By then all except the very tiniest of Britain's former West Indian colonies were independent.

CARIFTA, 1968

But the end of federation was not the end of co-operation between the now independent West Indian states. By 1968 they had organised themselves into the Caribbean Free Trade Area (CARIFTA). By abolishing import duties on many of the goods that its members sold to one another, CARIFTA encouraged trade between them.

CARICOM, 1973

Out of CARIFTA there emerged in 1973 an even more ambitious organisation called the Caribbean Common Market (CARICOM). CARICOM's aims went further than free trade between members. It hoped, for example, to encourage them to work together on joint development plans in farming and industry.

One such scheme aimed to use natural gas from Trinidad to smelt alumina (the main ingredient in aluminium) in Guyana and Jamaica. Another planned to have workers on the smaller islands manufacture Jamaican-made cloth into garments.

Schemes such as these were badly needed. Most West Indians continued to be very poor. Finding work was still a problem. In Jamaica in the 1970s, for example, the government estimated that one worker in five was without a regular job.

Finding solutions to problems like this would decide what sort of future the people of the independent West Indies were able to build for themselves. Experts believed that an important part of the answer was to persuade industrial countries to buy more products from the Caribbean and pay enough for them to give West Indian countries the money to invest in development.

For Federation

A declaration passed at a meeting of Caribbean Trade Unions in 1947.

"This Conference declares in favour of the establishment of a Federation of the British Caribbean Territories . . .

The Conference is convinced that the . . . orderly and vigorous development of our resources in human material and in land, the achievement of the individual and collective aspirations [hopes] of our people and the creation of civilised standards of life whereby each and all may hope to enjoy life, liberty and the pursuit of happiness, can best and most fully be secured by the Federation of the territories concerned."

In F. R. Augier and S. C. Gordon, *Sources of West Indian History*, 1965

1 a) How were the British Caribbean Territories governed at this time?
  b) What change did the Trade Union Conference favour?
  c) What benefits did the Conference believe the change would bring?
  d) Suggest a reason why this trade union meeting itself might have been seen as an important step towards federating the British West Indies.

Against Federation

The Daily Gleaner in September 1961 with the results of Jamaica's referendum. The pictures show the Federation flag, Alexander Bustamante and Norman Manley (bottom).

A speech by Alexander Bustamante in the referendum campaign.

"Rather this kind of federation be smashed to nothing than for thousands of my people to be thrown out of work through a customs union, by Trinidad dumping its manufactures here."

2 Imagine you are a Jamaican in September 1961, about to vote on whether your country should stay in the Federation. Write a letter to *The Daily Gleaner* saying how you intend to vote and why.

PART FIVE
BRITAIN

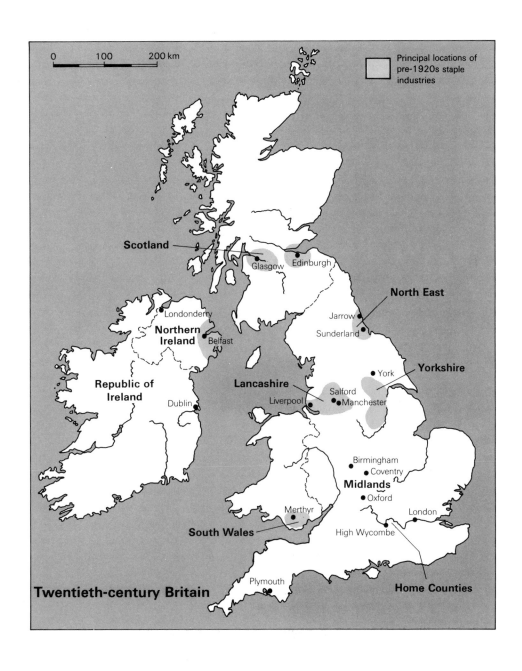

Principal locations of pre-1920s staple industries

Twentieth-century Britain

In 1917 the British government ordered all young men in Britain to have a medical examination to see if they were fit to serve in the army. The doctors found that only three in ten were reasonably fit. One in ten were 'totally unfit', four had 'marked disabilities' and two 'partial disabilities'.

These results were no surprise to some people. The reasons for them had been made clear almost thirty years earlier by a Liverpool ship-owner, Charles Booth.

Poverty: the Booth and Rowntree surveys

Booth had spent seventeen years gathering information about the lives of working people in London. In 1889 he began publishing the results in his book, *The Life and Labour of the People of London*.

Seebohm Rowntree carried out a similar survey based on a house to house enquiry in York. He published his results in 1901 in *Poverty: A Study of Town Life*.

Booth and Rowntree agreed that a family of father, mother and three children needed a minimum income of about £1 a week to buy just enough food, clothing and housing to stay in good health.

They found that about a third of the people of London and York scraped by on less than this – underfed, badly clothed, poorly housed. Booth and Rowntree showed that the main causes of this poverty were low wages, unemployment, illness and old age.

Reformers

These facts gave useful ammunition to people who wanted to improve working people's lives. Many such reformers believed that the key to improvement was for working people to have more say in Parliament.

This was possible from 1884, when a Parliamentary Reform Act gave all male householders the right to vote. After this almost half of Britain's voters were working class.

Keir Hardie

The main parties, the Liberals and the Conservatives, tried to win their support. But working class leaders like Keir Hardie believed the workers needed a political party of their own. 'Politics is but a football game between the rich Tories and the rich Liberals,' he warned, 'and you working men are the ball which they kick vigorously and with grim delight between their goalposts.'

Keir Hardie had started work in Scottish coal mines when he was ten, and had gone on to become a trade union leader and a journalist. In 1892 the people of West Ham in London elected him their MP.

The ILP, 1893

In 1893 Hardie took the lead in forming the Independent Labour Party (ILP). The ILP's policies were based on socialism; the idea that the country's wealth in land, mines and factories should be owned by the government, on behalf of the people as a whole.

The Fabians, 1884

In 1884 a group called the Fabian Society had been founded to write articles and books to help to spread such ideas. One of its best known members was the playwright George Bernard Shaw. Shaw tried to put over socialist ideas by working them into his plays.

The Labour Representation Committee, 1900

The Taff Vale Dispute, 1901

Support for the LRC

General election, 1906

The Osborne Judgement, 1909

Political funds

In the 1895 general election the ILP put up twenty-eight candidates. All were defeated, including Hardie himself.

ILP leaders realised that success would come only if they had much more support from the trade unions. In 1900 they joined with such other socialist groups as the Fabians to set up the Labour Representation Committee (LRC). The LRC's aim was to build a strong working class party in Parliament.

In its first year the LRC got little backing from the unions. Then, in 1901, the Taff Vale Railway Company in South Wales claimed damages from a railwaymen's union – the Amalgamated Society of Railway Servants – for money that it had lost because of a union-backed strike. It won the case. In the Taff Vale decision, the judges ordered the union to pay £23,000 in damages.

The Taff Vale decision was a serious blow to all unions. It meant that if they went on strike in future the employers would be able to ruin them by claiming damages.

To get the law changed, many unions now agreed to give money to the LRC. The money was to cover its election expenses and pay a salary to any working-class MPs who were elected. This was important, for MPs were not paid at this time.

In 1903 the LRC's Secretary, James Ramsay MacDonald, made a secret deal with the Liberals. In thirty constituencies (voting districts) the Liberals agreed not to put up candidates against the LRC at the next election. In return, MacDonald agreed that the LRC would support the Liberals in other constituencies.

The deal paid off in the 1906 general election, when twenty-nine Labour MPs were elected. The day the new Parliament met they decided on a simpler name for their group – the Labour Party.

The Liberals were the biggest party in the new Parliament, so they formed the government. This new government brought in the Trade Disputes Act (1906). The Act gave unions the right to strike again, by saying that employers could not claim damages if they did.

Not all union members outside Parliament supported the Labour Party. Some were Liberals or Conservatives and they objected to their unions giving money to a rival party.

One union member who backed the Liberals was W. V. Osborne. Osborne took his union to court to stop it handing over money from members' subscriptions to the Labour Party. He won his case. In the Osborne Judgment in 1909 the judges forbade the unions to give money to political parties.

The Osborne Judgment meant that the Labour Party would be starved of funds to pay its MPs and its election bills. The Liberal government solved the problem, in return for Labour backing in a quarrel with the Conservatives over the powers of the House of Lords (see Unit 41). First, in 1911, Parliament voted all MPs a salary of £400 a year. Then, in 1913, the Trade Union Act said that unions could give money to political parties, provided that any member who objected was allowed to 'contract out' of paying.

The poverty line

Seebohm Rowntree reckoned that about a £1 a week was the least a family could manage on in the early 1900s. Here he reminds readers what it was really like to live on that much.

"A family living on the scale allowed for in this estimate must never spend a penny on railway fare or omnibus. They must never go into the country unless they walk. They must never purchase a halfpenny newspaper or spend a penny to buy a ticket for a popular concert. They must write no letters to absent children, for they cannot afford to pay the postage. They must never contribute anything to their church or chapel, or give any help to a neighbour which costs them money. They cannot save, nor can they join a sick club or Trade Union, because they cannot pay the necessary subscriptions. The children must have no pocket money for dolls, marbles or sweets. The father must smoke no tobacco, and must drink no beer. The mother must never buy any pretty clothes for herself or for her children . . . Finally the wage-earner must never be absent from his work for a single day."

S. Rowntree, *Poverty: A Study of Town Life*, 1901

Mrs Pember Reeves made a study of working-class life in parts of London, using a similar method to Seebohm Rowntree's.

"In the poorer budgets items for clothes appear at extraordinarily distant intervals, when, it is supposed, they can no longer be done without. 'Boots mended' in the weekly budget means less food for that week, while any clothes which are bought seem to be not only second-hand, but in many instances fourth- or fifth-hand.

The women seldom get new clothes; boots they are often entirely without. The men go to work and must be supplied, the children must be decent at school, but the mother has no need to appear in the light of the day. If very badly equipped, she can shop in the evening . . . and no one will notice under her jacket and a rather long skirt what she is wearing on her feet. Most of them have a hat, a jacket and 'best' skirt to wear in the street. In the house a blouse and patched skirt under a sacking apron is the universal wear."

Mrs Pember Reeves, *Round About A Pound a Week*, 1913

1 a) From Seebohm Rowntree's statement, can you explain why he described an income of around a £1 a week as the 'poverty line'?

b) Do you think he chose examples which would make readers of his book sympathetic to the poor? Explain your answer.

c) Look at the title of Mrs Reeves's book. Why do you think she chose it?

d) In which ways do her facts support Rowntree's claims about the poor?

e) Which of the following were most likely to be the wage-earners in the families Seebohm Rowntree and Mrs Reeves were writing about:
1) skilled craftsmen, 2) unemployed workers, 3) unskilled workers and labourers in regular jobs, 4) old people,
5) teenagers? Explain your answer.

f) Imagine you are the mother of one of the families described by Mrs Reeves. You have to choose between going without shoes or not eating for several days. Which would you choose and why?

25

Class in Edwardian Britain

Two ways of looking at class differences in the early 1900s. Stella Davies remembers her childhood in Manchester at that time.

"A street of working class houses ran the length of our garden and we were not allowed to speak, much less play, with the children in this street. On the other side of the house the son of . . . a wealthy Manchester merchant . . . lived with his family. They had a nursemaid in cap and apron to look after the three children. *They* were not allowed to play with *us*. We used to stand . . . and look at both lots of children and say how daft it was that we could not all make up a game of rounders."

C. Stella Davies, *North Country Bred*, 1963

The front page of the book Riches and Poverty *by Chiozza Money, 1905.*

BRITISH INCOMES IN 1904

RICH 1,250,000 persons £585,000,000	COMFORTABLE 3,750,000 persons £245,000,000

POOR

38,000,000 PERSONS

£880.000,000

2 a) What other terms might Money have used on his diagram instead of 'rich', 'comfortable' and 'poor'?

  b) What differences between Money's three groups does Stella Davies's childhood memory show?

  c) If you were making a chart dividing people by incomes today, would you divide it into three like Chiozza Money, or use more groups? If so, what would your groups be?

An American visitor to London in 1908 described some of Britain's poor.

"Look at the people who swarm the streets to see the Lord Mayor's Show, and where will you see a more pitiable sight? . . . Poor, stunted, bad-complexioned, shabbily dressed, . . . are these denizens [inhabitants] of the East End [of London]. Crowds I have seen in America . . . and in most of the great cities of Europe . . . Nowhere is there . . . such pinching poverty, . . . so much human rottenness as here . . ."

P. Collier, *England and the English from an American Point of View*, 1909

3 a) From what you have read in the text and sources, 1) suggest reasons for the poverty Collier found in London; 2) decide whether the other sources in this unit tend to support or contradict his opinions.

  b) Do you think Collier's view is a fair and complete one of the lives of people of this time? Explain your answer.

Liberal governments ruled Britain from 1906 to 1916. Two forces encouraged them to carry out changes to help Britain's poor. One was pressure from the Labour Party in Parliament. The other was the determination of a group of Liberal ministers that their party should be seen as the party of reform.

The Minister for Trade, Winston Churchill, put it like this: 'The cause of Liberalism is the cause of the left out millions. We want to draw a line, below which we will not allow people to live and labour.'

In 1906 Parliament passed the Education (Provision of Meals) Act. This said that local authorities could spend money to provide meals for school children who were too hungry to concentrate on their lessons. By 1914 150,000 pupils were eating daily school meals. In 1907 the government told local authorities to arrange to have their school pupils medically examined.

The government then turned to helping the old. In 1908 Parliament passed an Old Age Pension Act. This copied an idea introduced in Germany twenty years earlier. It gave a weekly pension of up to 5s. (25p), or 7s. 6d. (37½p) for a married couple, to old people over the age of seventy. To get the pension they had to have incomes of less than 10s. (50p) a week.

The money wasn't much, but it took away the threat of old people having to end their days living on the charity of relatives or in the dreaded 'workhouses'. Workhouses were prison-like buildings where the poor had previously had to live if they wanted help.

The first old age pensions were not very generous. But the scheme was an important landmark.

Its real importance was that the pensions were paid entirely out of money raised by the government from taxes. For the first time the national government was taxing the better off in order to help the poor.

The government was also planning other schemes. One was a national system of Labour Exchanges to help the unemployed find work. The first eighty-three Exchanges were opened in 1910.

The pensions, the Labour Exchanges and other government schemes such as new battleships for the navy (see Unit 1), had to be paid for. The Chancellor of the Exchequer, Lloyd George, worked out that he needed to raise an extra £16 million in taxes. He set out plans to do this in his budget for 1909.

Lloyd George's 1909 budget was soon nicknamed the 'People's Budget'. He raised some of the money by increasing taxes on drink and tobacco and putting up the rate of income tax. From now on anyone with an income of £3000 a year would have to pay 1s. 2d. (6p) in the pound in tax.

Two other measures made his Conservative opponents furious – an increase in death duties (a tax on property left by rich people

School meals and medicals, 1906 and 1907

Old age pensions, 1908

Labour Exchanges, 1910

Lloyd George and the People's Budget, 1909.

when they died) and a tax on profits gained from selling land that had increased in value.

To become law the budget had to be passed by majority votes in Parliament: first in the House of Commons, whose members were elected by the voters, and then in the House of Lords, whose members inherited their positions from their fathers.

The House of Lords and the People's Budget

Lloyd George had no problems in getting his budget passed in the Commons. There the Liberals had the big majority they had won in the 1906 general election. But most members of the House of Lords were rich Conservative landowners. They objected strongly to Lloyd George's proposal to tax their land and threatened to throw out his budget.

'Let them realise what they are doing', Lloyd George warned. 'They are forcing a revolution and they will get it . . .'

The House of Lords ignored Lloyd George's warning and refused to pass his budget. The government decided it was time to show who really ruled Britain.

To prove that the voters supported the budget, the government called a general election. It just won it. In January 1910 the House of Lords reluctantly passed the budget.

The Parliament Act, 1911

But the government decided to make sure that the House of Lords would never again stop a government which had the backing of the voters from carrying out its policies. It announced plans for a law to cut the Lords' powers.

Naturally, the Lords refused to accept the plan. So the Prime Minister, H. H. Asquith, called another election.

The Liberals won again. The Lords still stood out, though. Then Asquith persuaded the King to agree to make hundreds of new Liberal lords to see that the law went through. The threat was enough and the Lords agreed to the Parliament Act of 1911.

The 1911 Parliament Act said that from now on the House of Lords was not allowed to stop any laws concerning money, such as the budget, from passing. So far as other laws were concerned, it could do no more than delay them for two years (reduced to one year in 1949).

These changes gave the House of Commons – and the voters who elected its members – much more power. To make sure that MPs did not misuse this power, the Parliament Act reduced the maximum life of any one Parliament from seven to five years. MPs would now have to answer to the voters more often.

The National Insurance Act, 1911

After the Parliament Act the Liberals brought in their last important scheme to help the poor. This was Lloyd George's National Insurance Act of 1911.

The Act said that all workers earning less than about £3 a week (£160 a year) had to join an insurance scheme organised by the government. To pay for the scheme, the government took 4d. a week (just over 1½p) from workers' wages, made their employers pay in another 3d. a week and put in 2d. itself from taxation.

To win workers' support for the plan, Lloyd George told them they would be getting '9d. for 4d.'. Workers' payments were shown by sticking stamps on a card. In return, they received free medical attention when they were ill and 10s. (50p) a week, for a maximum of twenty-six weeks, when they were too sick to work.

The 1911 National Insurance Act also gave some workers – but only some – protection against unemployment.

In trades such as building and shipbuilding workers never knew how long a particular job would last. These workers now had to pay in 2½d. (1p) a week, whilst their employers and the government each paid in another 2½d. In return the workers could claim 7s. (35p) a week for up to fifteen weeks in any one year when they were out of a job. The money was paid out at the Labour Exchanges.

By later standards, neither the Old Age Pension Act nor the National Insurance Act went very far. But they were essential foundations for the Welfare State that grew up later (see Unit 45).

Trade union unrest, 1910–14

At the time, though, many people thought that the Liberal reforms came nowhere near giving the workers a fair deal. The years between 1910 and 1914 were marked by bitter quarrelling between workers on one side, and their employers and the government on the other.

Growing unemployment was one cause of trouble. On top of this, prices were rising faster than wages. More and more groups of workers – miners, railwaymen, dockers – demanded more money to make ends meet.

Some influential trade unionists – a dockers' leader named Tom Mann and a miners' leader named A. J. Cook, for instance – thought that money alone was not the answer.

The way for workers to get a better deal, Mann and Cook said, was to follow the direct action policies of 'syndicalism'. Syndicalism taught that workers should use strikes to bring industry to a standstill and take over the government of the country.

In 1910 the government sent troops to stop riots in the South Wales coalfield. In the summer of 1911 dockers, seamen and railway workers came out on strike. Again the government sent in troops and this time they shot and killed several of the strikers. 1912 was worse still. Forty million days' work were lost through strikes, the highest number ever until then.

The Triple Alliance, 1914

In 1914 the National Union of Railwaymen came together with the transport workers' and miners' unions to form a group called the Triple Alliance. The idea was for these three big unions to help one another in an all-out struggle for better wages and conditions.

In the summer of 1914 the leaders of the Triple Alliance were planning a big combined strike. But it never began.

On 4th August Britain declared war on Germany (see Unit 1). On 24th August the Trades Union Congress called on all unions to drop plans for strikes until the war was won.

Edwardian people and politics

A cartoon which appeared in the humorous magazine Punch *in 1908.*

1 a) Who do you think is the man in the cartoon?

b) What government position did he hold at this time?

c) Explain why the cartoonist has drawn him as a highwayman and say who he is waiting to 'rob'.

d) Explain as fully as you can who would be paid out of the box.

e) In which way was this pension fund an important 'first time' in British history?

2 From your reading of Units 40 and 41, match each name with a description to make a complete sentence. Then add a sentence of your own to each.

Seebohm Rowntree	was a leader of the mineworkers' union.
Keir Hardie	was Secretary of the Labour Representation Committee.
Ramsay MacDonald	objected to paying money to the Labour Party.
David Lloyd George	became MP for West Ham in 1892.
A.J. Cook	introduced the People's Budget in 1909.
W.V. Osborne	made a survey of poverty in York.

A year to the day after the First World War ended, on Armistice Day, 1919, an ex-soldier wrote to *The Times*.

"I have today given two minutes praying for our dead and two hours regretting I am not one of them", he wrote. "They 'live' in a world where no bread is needed; I am condemned to exist in a land that threatens to starve me."

What was going wrong?

Post-war depression

The problem was lack of jobs. The main reason for the shortage was that Britain was finding it difficult to sell her products abroad.

Faced with massive bills for the war, many countries were buying fewer foreign goods in the years which followed. The result was a big drop, or depression, in world trade.

More than any other nation, Britain's living depended on trading with other countries. And the goods which foreign countries no longer wanted were exactly the ones that had made up most of her exports before the war – ships, coal, cotton, iron and steel.

Less trade between countries meant that fewer new ships were needed. Oil taking over as fuel for factories and ships meant that less coal was needed. The man-made fibre rayon being used to make clothing meant less cotton was needed.

Some of Britain's best pre-war customers no longer turned to her for the products they did still need. Some, like India, now had factories of their own. During the war, others had started to buy from the USA and Japan.

Unemployment

Fewer goods sold abroad meant fewer jobs in the cotton mills of Lancashire, the shipyards along the Tyne and Clyde rivers, the coal mines of South Wales. By June 1921 more than two million workers, most of them in these 'staple' industries, were unemployed.

A twenty-year trade depression, or 'slump', had started. Every year between 1921 and 1940 at least one British worker in ten was out of work. In the early 1930s the figure rose to one in five.

In places where most jobs were in one of the staple industries the figures could be even higher. In the north-eastern shipbuilding town of Jarrow, eight out of ten workers had no jobs in 1933. In the South Wales coal and steel town of Merthyr Tydfil in 1934 the figure was seven out of ten.

Coal mining in the 1920s

Coal mining was hit particularly hard. In 1913 Britain's mines had provided jobs for 1,105,000 men. By 1932 only 819,000 men were needed. The world had too much coal chasing too few customers.

To try to win more customers the mine-owners cut their prices. In 1920 British coal merchants were selling coal at £4 a ton. By 1923 their price was £2.50 a ton. Export prices for coal dropped even more, from £5 a ton in 1920 to just over £1 a ton a year later.

Miners' jobs and wages depended on these prices. The cheaper the coal, the fewer the jobs and the lower the wages.

The miners' strike, 1921

As early as 1921 disputes over wages were causing trouble in the pits. In March the mine-owners said that the miners would have to work for less money. The miners refused and went on strike.

The miners asked their partners in the Triple Alliance (see Unit 41) for help. But the railwaymen and transport workers turned them down. The bitterly disappointed miners called this day, 15th April 1921, 'Black Friday'. They were forced to go back to work on the owners' conditions.

The government and coal mining

To avoid more trouble in the mines, the government agreed to pay the coal industry a 'subsidy' – money out of taxes – of £10 million a year until 1925. It hoped that this would help to prevent any more wage cuts or job losses until sales and prices rose again.

But neither did rise. In 1925 the owners told the miners that when the subsidy ran out they would have to work an extra hour a day for less pay. 'Nowt doin', replied Herbert Smith, the President of the Miners' Federation.

The miners began to prepare for another strike. This time it looked as if the railwaymen and other big unions would also strike to help them.

The Prime Minister, Stanley Baldwin, gave another subsidy for just nine months, until 1st May 1926. Meanwhile, a Royal Commission, headed by Sir Herbert Samuel, would look into the coal industry. The nine months also gave Baldwin's Conservative government time to make preparations in case there *was* a strike.

The Samuel Commission, 1926

In March 1926 the Samuel Commission brought out its report. Amongst other things, it said that the subsidy should not carry on after 1st May and that miners' wages should be reduced.

On 13th April 1926 the owners told the miners that, beginning on 1st May, they would have to work longer hours for less pay. Arthur (A.J.) Cook, the Secretary of the Miners' Federation, told them 'Not a penny off the pay, not a minute on the day'.

The owners replied by shutting down the pits. By 1st May 1926 a million miners were locked out of their jobs.

The TUC and the National/General Strike, 1926

The miners' leaders appealed for help to the Trades Union Congress. The TUC called three million other key workers out on strike to support them.

The strike began on 3rd May 1926. Conservative newspapers which supported the government called it the 'General Strike'. 'A general strike is not an industrial dispute', wrote the *Daily Mail*. 'It is a revolutionary movement, intended to inflict suffering upon the great mass of innocent persons in the community and thereby to put [pressure] on the government.'

The TUC leaders, like Ernest Bevin of the Transport Workers, denied this. They always called the strike a 'national strike'. Their aim was not revolution; it was just to get the miners a better deal.

Support for the TUC was solid. Railwaymen, transport workers,

The government and the strike

builders, steelworkers, printers – all came out on strike. Public transport and big industries almost everywhere stopped working.

Baldwin's government swung into action with the plans made in the nine months of the subsidy. Baldwin signed up 200,000 special constables, ready to help the police. He sent sailors to shovel coal to keep power stations working and soldiers to unload ships.

A government news-sheet called *The British Gazette* (edited by the ex-Liberal reformer Winston Churchill) repeated again and again that the strike was an attempt at revolution, an attack on Parliament's right to run the country.

The strikers' paper, *The British Worker*, denied the accusation. But many of the upper and middle classes believed the government. Some volunteered to drive buses and trains, and to do other jobs hit by the strike.

The work done by these amateur strike breakers has sometimes been exaggerated. In London only 40 out of 4400 buses were on the road by the end of the strike.

The TUC gives in

Even so, on 12th May 1926, after only nine days, the TUC leaders called off the 'National Strike' and told members to go back to work.

They had not won a better deal for the miners. Baldwin promised nothing. But many TUC leaders were convinced the government was going to win. Others feared that the strike to help the miners might really turn into a strike to start a revolution in Britain. 'Some of the TUC were afraid of the power they had created', wrote Arthur Cook.

Some workers were not ready to give in and felt betrayed by the TUC. Others felt relieved. Most of them drifted back to work.

All except the miners. They struggled on alone for another six months. Cold and hunger finally drove them back down the pits in the winter – on the mine-owners' conditions.

The effects of the strike

The 'General Strike' was a disaster for the trade unions. They lost prestige, money and members. Individual workers suffered, too. Employers such as the railway companies cut wages before taking workers on again. Many strikers lost their jobs for good when bosses sacked them.

The following year the government brought in the Trade Disputes Act (1927). This made 'general' strikes illegal and banned 'sympathetic' strikes in support of workers in another industry.

The Trade Disputes Act also made it more difficult for trade unions to give money to the Labour Party. It abolished the 1913 'contracting out' rule (see Unit 40). In future the unions had to ask each member to sign a form 'contracting in' – that is, agreeing to pay part of their subscription to the Labour Party.

Many voters now felt that if strikes could not win improvements, a Labour majority in the House of Commons was even more necessary. In the 1929 general election, the first after the 1926 strike, Labour won more seats than any other party. Its leader, Ramsay MacDonald, took over from Baldwin as Prime Minister.

National or General Strike?

A statement about the strikers' aims in The British Worker, *8th May 1926.*

'There is so far as the Trade Union Movement is concerned no 'attack on the community'. There is no 'challenge to the Constitution'. The workers have exercised their legal . . . right of withholding their labour in order to protect the miners against a degradation [lowering] of their standard of life.'

This cartoon, which first appeared in Punch, *was reprinted on the front page of* The British Gazette, *12th May 1926.*

UNDER WHICH FLAG?

John Bull. "ONE OF THESE TWO FLAGS HAS GOT TO COME DOWN—AND IT WON'T BE MINE."

1 a) Why do you think the government decided to reprint the cartoon on the front page of *The British Gazette?*

b) You are a parent in 1926 and against the strike. Explain to your son or daughter how the cartoon supports your point of view.

c) *The British Worker* statement is replying to two anti-strike points of view: 1) that it was an 'attack on the community',   2) that it was a 'challenge to the Constitution'. Write a sentence on each of these phrases to show what it means.

d) In your own words, explain *The British Worker*'s reply to these points.

In the 1960s a Salford-born writer remembered how a miner, Jack Lashford, felt about people who volunteered to do strikers' jobs.

"Enthusiastic young men of the middle classes came forward to man footplates, drive trains and buses. 'Bastards', Jack Lashford said bitterly, 'I know what I'd like to do with 'em.'
'It's a game for 'em, Jack.'
'Game?', he retorted with pop-eyed indignation. 'Six loaves of bread a week, that's what a two shillin's [10p] wage cut means to me. Kids goin' short o' grub. It's a fine bloody game.' "

Walter Greenwood, *There Was a Time,* 1969

2 Older people in your area may have taken part in the General Strike. Ask them about it. Look up copies of your local newspaper for April and May 1926. Use this oral and printed information to write an account of the strike in your area.

There were really two Britains in the 1920s and 1930s. There was the Britain which depended for its living on the old, staple industries such as coal and shipbuilding. The other Britain was built on new industries making new products – motor vehicles, electrical goods, man-made fibres.

New industries, new jobs

Most of the new industries grew up in the Midlands and South-East of England. In London in 1934 fewer than one worker in twelve was unemployed. In Birmingham the figure was barely one in twenty. A huge difference from Jarrow's eight out of ten and Merthyr's seven! (see Unit 42).

The Midlands prospered because of the motor industry. In the 1920s William Morris and Herbert Austin built big mass-production factories at Oxford and Birmingham. By 1939 they produced between them 60 per cent of all vehicles made in Britain. In that year Britain's roads had two million cars on them, compared with only 132,000 in 1914.

The big car-assembly factories gave work to hundreds of smaller firms who supplied them with component parts. That meant tens of thousands of jobs. Regular jobs and wages meant more work for builders putting up new houses – council and private – and factories, stores and cinemas. They also meant more customers for the factories turning out new products such as the first plastics, rayon clothing, radio sets and other electrical goods.

Electricity played a big part in developing the prosperous areas of Britain. Before the 1920s most electricity was supplied by separate local companies. Then new bigger power stations were built.

In 1926 the power stations were linked together in a National Grid, whose tall steel pylons carried power to factories and homes all over Britain. In 1920 only 730 households had mains electricity. By 1938 the figure had rocketed to nine million.

Factory owners no longer had to bother about building their factories near to coal for steam power. They could plug in to electricity almost anywhere. Many chose to open works in the Midlands and South-East, often alongside new roads. Lorries rather than railway trains supplied them with raw materials and carried away their products.

Some people from the north of England, Wales and Scotland migrated to the busy Midlands and South-East to find jobs. But most stayed on in their home areas – the 'depressed areas'.

The unemployed and the dole

The human face of the depression was long-term unemployment. The first fifteen weeks out of a job were covered by unemployment insurance. This had started for workers in a few industries in 1911 (see Unit 41). In 1920 Parliament extended the cover to all workers on wages of less than £5 a week.

But months and years of unemployment, not weeks, often

stretched in front of workers such as miners and shipbuilders. To deal with these cases the government paid 'extended benefit'. This handout was kept as low as possible and was soon known by everyone as the 'dole'.

The dole was the cause of the collapse of the Labour government elected in 1929.

The Labour government, 1929–31

This was the second Labour government in Britain. The first had lasted for ten months in 1923–4, after Labour had won 191 seats in the 1923 general election. That was fewer than the Conservatives, but the Labour leader, Ramsay MacDonald, had been able to become Prime Minister with the support of Liberal MPs.

In 1929 MacDonald was back in power with a Labour majority in the House of Commons. That was in June. In October came the Wall Street Crash, when share prices slumped on the New York Stock Exchange.

The Wall Street Crash signalled the start of a massive American slump (see Unit 26). Its shockwaves were soon felt all round the world.

Ever since the First World War most European countries, including Britain, had depended on the USA to buy their goods and to lend them money. Now the Americans stopped buying. Instead of lending they began to ask for their loans to be repaid. A world slump started.

For Britain the world slump meant that between 1929 and 1931 its export earnings dropped by almost half. In the same years unemployment shot up to almost three million, or about one in every five workers. In the depressed areas the figures were even worse.

MacDonald's Labour government saw its biggest difficulty as 'balancing the budget', so that it collected in as much in taxes as it paid out. On the one hand, idle companies and unemployed workers could not pay taxes. On the other, the government was paying out more and more on the dole. To advise on the problem MacDonald set up a committee led by Sir George May.

Forming the National government, 1931

In June, 1931, the May Committee said that the budget could only be balanced if the government spent less, especially on the dole. MacDonald accepted the advice.

But most Labour ministers and MPs could not stomach the idea of their party making things even harder for the unemployed. The government broke up in August, and MacDonald announced he was going to form a new 'National' government with backing from Conservative and Liberal MPs.

Most Labour Party members saw MacDonald as a traitor. The voters did not.

In October 1931 MacDonald called an election. The voters returned only 46 Labour MPs to Parliament, compared with 556 supporters of the National government – most of them Conservatives. When MacDonald retired in 1936 the Conservative

Life on the dole

The Means Test

Making jobs

The Jarrow Crusade, 1936

The lifting depression

Stanley Baldwin came back as Prime Minister.

What was life like on the dole? For most of the 1930s an unemployed man was given 17s. (85p) a week, with 9s. (45p) for his wife and 3s. (15p) for each child. It was enough to keep families from starving, but little more, especially after the National government brought in the 'Means Test' in 1931.

The Means Test was a set of questions. To get any money, the unemployed had to prove by their answers that they were completely broke, with no money saved, no goods they could turn into cash and no relatives who could support them. If a son or daughter had a regular job, their parents would fail the Means Test and be expected to live off their children's wages.

Other government policies were less miserly. Some aimed to create jobs in the depressed areas. In 1932 Parliament passed the Import Duties Act, which placed taxes on manufactured goods coming into Britain. The idea was to boost home industries by making their products cheaper than foreign ones.

In 1934 the Special Areas Act said that government grants could be given to depressed area such as South Wales and Tyneside. The grants were used to open industrial estates and new factories.

One outcome of the Special Areas Act was the 'Jarrow Crusade'. Hunger marches – unemployed people marching to London to bring attention to their problems – had begun in the 1920s. But the Jarrow Crusade in 1936 became the best known.

The Crusade took place after the local shipbuilding firm, Palmers, closed down. This raised the total of Jarrow men out of work to eight out of ten.

Led by Ellen Wilkinson, the town's Labour MP, the Jarrow Crusaders marched to London to demand help under the Special Areas Act. They wanted a new steelworks, but they didn't get it. It was built in another Special Area, South Wales, instead.

There were a few other examples of government help for the depressed areas. Scottish shipyards received money to build two new ocean liners, the *Queen Mary* and *Queen Elizabeth*. Some cotton spinning firms were paid to close factories so others stayed in work.

In the later 1930s unemployment began to fall. In 1931 the number of jobless had been 2,800,000; roughly one worker in ten. By 1937 it was down to 1,670,000; roughly one worker in twenty.

The government's policies had created some jobs. But the new industries had created more. The number of customers wanting coal or ships might be falling, but the number wanting products like cars and electrical goods was increasing every year. This meant more jobs, and these jobs gave people the money to begin spending again.

Hitler played his part, too. By 1937 Britain was beginning to re-arm in case of war. Re-armament meant more jobs for workers everywhere – especially for the steelworkers, miners and shipbuilders of the depressed areas.

Prosperity and poverty

The map on page 163 shows all the places mentioned in these tables.

A Occupations – men only

	Number of workers in every thousand unemployed for a year or more, summer 1936
Coal miners	123
Shipbuilders and repairers	95
Cotton workers	67
Builders and building labourers	24
Furniture workers	21
Workers in motor vehicles, cycles etc.	10

The Pilgrim Trust, *Men without work*, 1938

B Unemployment figures, 1934

Place	Percentage of workers without jobs
Jarrow	68
Merthyr Tydfil	62
Coventry	5
High Wycombe	3.3

D. Nicholl, *The Hungry Years*, 1974

C Infantile mortality, 1935

Place	Deaths of babies per thousand live births
Jarrow	114
Sunderland	92
Scotland	77
Home counties	42

D. Nicholl, *The Hungry Years*, 1974

1 a) Referring to table A, give two reasons why unemployment was 1) so high in the top three occupations, 2) so much lower in the others.

b) Referring to table B, list all the reasons you can think of for the differences between unemployment in Jarrow and Merthyr Tydfil, compared with Coventry and High Wycombe (a furniture making centre).

c) Can you see any connection between the facts in table B and those in table C? Explain what the connection was.

d) From the map on page 163 choose *three* areas of staple industry and show how table A explains why each suffered very high unemployment.

Walter Greenwood wrote Love on the Dole *when he was thirty. The story was based on his own experiences of unemployment in the northern industrial town of Salford.*

"You fell into the habit of slouching, of putting your hands into your pockets and keeping them there; of glancing at people, furtively, ashamed of your secret, until you fancied that everybody eyed you with suspicion. You knew that your shabbiness betrayed you; it was apparent for all to see. You prayed for the winter evenings and the kindly darkness. Darkness, poverty's cloak. Breeches backside patched and re-patched; patches on knees, on elbows. Jesus! All bloody patches.

Nothing to do with time; nothing to spend; nothing to do tomorrow nor the day after; nothing to wear; can't get married. A living corpse; a unit of the spectral [ghostly] army of three million lost men."

Walter Greenwood, *Love on the Dole*, 1933

An interview with an unemployed Midlands man.

"Everybody does some work in this world . . . That's one thing that makes us human; we don't wait for things to happen to us, we work for them. And if you can't find any work to do you have the feeling that you're not human. You're out of place. You're so different from all the rest of the people around that you think something is wrong with you."

E. Bakke, *The Unemployed Man*, 1933

Another unemployed man describes the effect of the Means Test on his life.

" . . . my wife . . . obtained a job as house-to-house saleswoman, and was able to earn a few shillings to supplement our dole income. It was from this time that the feeling of strain . . . became more marked. I felt a burden on her . . . There were constant bickerings over money matters, usually culminating in threats to leave from both of us. The final blow came when the Means Test was put into operation . . . Eventually, after the most heartbreaking period of my life, both my wife and my son, who had just commenced to earn a few shillings, told me to get out, as I was living on them and taking the food they needed."

H. L. Beales and R. S. Lambert, *Memoirs of the Unemployed*, 1934

2 a) From these two extracts and the one on the previous page, identify the main problems facing unemployed people in the 1930s.
  b) Which of these problems would you personally have found most difficult to cope with?
  c) Why would the Midlands man in the second extract have more reason to feel 'out of place' than an unemployed northerner?
  d) Write a letter from either the man or the wife in the third extract which shows what effect the Means Test had on their lives.

Inside the Savoy Cinema, Hayes, Middlesex, 1937

In 1931–2 unemployed men were asked, 'What attracts you to the cinema?'

"The pictures help you to live in another world for a little while."
" . . . it really makes you think that things will go all right for you, too, because you put yourself in the place of the actors."

E. Bakke, *The Unemployed Man*, 1933

3 A pint of beer, five cigarettes, fish and chips and a cinema seat all cost between 2 and 4 old pennies in the 1930s. Imagine you are out of work with 4d. in your pocket. What would you spend them on and why?

The Jarrow Crusade

A cartoon from the Daily Express *in 1936.*

'Work at last'

Nearly forty years later a writer interviewed people involved in the Jarrow Crusade.

Paddy Scullion, a Jarrow councillor in 1933 and one of the organisers:

"We were more or less missionaries of the distressed areas of the country, let alone Jarrow. We had distressed towns as well as Jarrow . . . and we took the poverty to the people that didn't know poverty existed and didn't know what it meant."

Ritchie Calder, who covered the march for a newspaper:

"In one family there were four volunteers from whom only one could go. And the brothers gave the trousers and the jacket and the father gave the boots and the uncle gave the raincoat . . . the family marched with one man."

Guy Waller, who was also a journalist in 1936:

"The march produced no immediate startling upsurge in employment to the town; it took the war to do that."

J. Pickard, *Jarrow March*, 1982

4 a) In the cartoon what do 1) the man and 2) the object he is looking at represent?

b) What is the message of the cartoon?

c) The interviews are about an event many years before. Do you think this makes them less valuable as evidence? Explain your answer.

d) Imagine it is 1936 and you are organising a hunger march. Make notes for a talk to the marchers explaining what you plan to do about 1) food, 2) shelter, 3) bad weather, 4) medical care, 5) publicity.

e) Explain whether you agree with this statement: 'Falling unemployment in the late 1930s proves that hunger marches were effective'.

Britain declares war, September 1939

Sunday, 3rd September 1939, 11.00 a.m. The Prime Minister, Neville Chamberlain, came on the radio to tell the country that Britain was at war with Germany (see Unit 8).

'May God bless you all', he ended his broadcast. 'May He defend the right, for it is evil things we shall fight against.'

No cheering crowds greeted the war as they had done in August 1914. One woman rushed to her window, poked out her head and shouted, 'It's war – war – we shall all be bombed to death within a few hours.' Another told an interviewer for a poll, ' I leant against my husband and went quite dead for a minute or two'.

In fact, Germany did not strike at Britain for nine months. Then, in May 1940, Hitler's troops drove into France, defeating the French and British armies (see Unit 9).

Churchill's Coalition government

Chamberlain resigned as Prime Minister and his place was taken by Winston Churchill. Churchill formed a Coalition government – one which included Labour leaders, such as Clement Attlee and Ernest Bevin, as well as Conservatives.

Preparing for war

Before this, in 1939, the government had already made many preparations for war. Plans had been made to start conscripting (calling up) men for the armed forces and to evacuate women and children from the cities in case of bombing raids. Millions of gas masks had been given out. Ration books were already printed.

Food rationing

Food rationing began for sugar, butter and bacon in January 1940. Later most basic foods, except bread, were rationed. The government set up a Ministry of Food, under Lord Woolton. His job was to see that the nation's supplies of food were fairly shared out and that everyone had a healthy diet.

Woolton did a good job. Millions of poorer people ate better during the war than they had done before it. The result was a great improvement in health. One sign of this was a drop of almost half in the number of women dying in childbirth between 1939 and 1946.

Evacuation

Evacuation began even before Chamberlain declared war. Evacuation meant moving children, and sometimes their mothers, out of cities such as London, Birmingham and Liverpool, that were likely to be bombed. Altogether, some three million people were evacuated into small towns and the countryside.

Thousands of the evacuees came from Britain's worst slums. They were often underfed, badly clothed, dirty. Some came from homes so poor that they didn't know how to use a knife and fork, a lavatory, or even how to sleep in a bed.

People who took in such evacuees were horrified at this evidence of the poverty of the 'other' Britain of slums and depressed areas. Many decided that something ought to be done about it.

National Assistance Board

Apart from evacuees, many others came to need help because of the war – families bombed out of their homes, widows of dead servicemen, old people separated from their families. In 1940 the government set up a National Assistance Board to assist anyone who needed emergency help. This idea of the government providing help for those who needed it was an important step towards the post-war Welfare State (see Unit 45).

Employment

The war brought an enormous demand for ships, aircraft, tanks, guns. Coal-mines, steelworks, shipyards, factories, needed every worker they could find. By 1940 unemployment was already lower than at any time since the First World War. Soon, it had practically disappeared.

As with rationing, the people who benefited most were the ones who had been worst off before the war. In the depressed areas men who had existed on the dole for years now found themselves with regular jobs again.

Women at work

The war also gave women more job opportunities. In December 1941 the government made women, as well as men, liable to conscription.

Women conscripts were given a choice – either they could enrol in the women's branch of one of the fighting services or they could take a civilian job the government ordered them to do. Even more than in the First World War, women took over men's peacetime jobs, from forking muck on farms to operating cranes in steelworks.

In ways like these the war meant job opportunities, better food, improved care. But for people in the cities it could also mean death and destruction.

The Blitz, 1940–1

After the Battle of Britain in 1940 (see Unit 9) Hitler ordered his *Luftwaffe* (air force) to bomb London and other cities – Liverpool, Glasgow, Manchester, Birmingham, Coventry, Plymouth. This was the Blitz.

Beginning on 7th September, an average of 200 German aircraft bombed London every night for 57 nights running. Incendiary (fire) bombs did even more damage than high explosive ones. On the night of 29th December so much of London was burning that the glow in the sky could be seen in Oxford, 90 kilometres away.

In London and other cities people set up night-time homes in cellars and basements, in corrugated metal 'Anderson' shelters in their gardens, or on the platforms of London's tube stations. In the day they went about their ordinary jobs.

Civil defence

They found time to volunteer for extra jobs, too. They fought fires in the AFS (Auxiliary Fire Service), dug out bodies and survivors from the ruins of bombed buildings as members of the ARP (Air Raid Precautions), dealt with fire-bombs as volunteer fire-watchers.

Thousands of men, too old or unfit to be called up for the armed forces, joined the Local Defence Volunteers (LDV), ready to fight off any German invaders. They were later renamed the Home Guard.

After the spring of 1941 Hitler called off his bombers. He needed them for his attack on the USSR (see Unit 9). German air attacks were never as heavy again. The worst came in the last year of the

V1s and V2s

Effects of the war

The Beveridge Report, 1942

war, when Hitler launched two 'secret weapons' against Britain.

The V1 was a flying bomb with its own jet engine that people nicknamed the 'Doodlebug'. The Germans fired 10,000 of these against London between June 1944 and the end of the war. The Doodlebugs were unreliable and fairly slow-moving, and three-quarters of them were shot down before they reached their targets.

The V2 was more dangerous. The most revolutionary weapon of the war, it was the ancestor of later inter-continental and space rockets. It had a range of 320 kilometres and was very fast and difficult to stop. Fortunately for Britain's cities, the Allied armies in Europe captured the V2 launching sites in the spring of 1945.

The German bomber and rocket attacks on Britain killed more than 60,000 civilians. Yet the shared dangers and hardships and the feeling that everyone was working for the same goal – victory – brought the people of Britain closer together than ever before.

People grew used to being treated more equally. They also became used to having important parts of their lives organised by the government. If government planning was the way to win the war against Hitler, many people asked, why not use it afterwards to win a war against poverty and hardship?

Politicians of all parties shared these feelings, and the government asked a civil servant named Sir William Beveridge to prepare a report on the future of 'social security'.

The Beveridge Report came out in 1942. It suggested that all the existing schemes for pensions, unemployment benefits, health insurance and so on should be brought together and improved.

Beveridge suggested that workers and employers should each pay a weekly 'national insurance' contribution. In return, workers would be entitled to various cash benefits in times of need – sickness, unemployment, old age, bereavement.

The benefits would be based on a minimum standard of living 'below which no one should be allowed to fall' and there would be no Means Test. Beveridge also suggested that the government should pay weekly family allowances for each child still at school.

Those were Beveridge's suggestions for attacking want. But want, he said, was only one of 'five giants' blocking Britain's path to a better future.

The other giants were disease, which would need a new approach to health care; ignorance, which could be dealt with only by a better education system; squalor (filthy living conditions), which called for more and better houses; and idleness, which called for efforts to make sure that everyone had a job.

People snapped up the Beveridge Report as soon as it was printed. Tens of thousands of copies were flown out to soldiers fighting overseas. Practically everyone supported its ideas. 'There has been possibly more widespread discussion on this than on any single event since the outbreak of the war', said a government report in March 1943.

Life in wartime

A government poster issued before the Blitz.

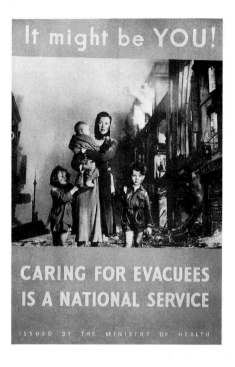

It might be YOU!

CARING FOR EVACUEES
IS A NATIONAL SERVICE

ISSUED BY THE MINISTRY OF HEALTH

The entry for 20th April 1941 in a diary kept by a woman living in London.

". . . last Wednesday's casualties. . . will probably make a new and tragic record when the tired rescue squads finally finish getting the bodies out of the wreckage.

. . . In many cases, well-built shelters deep down beneath expensive brick and concrete proved little better than the kitchen tables under which humble families. . .crouched and listened to hell breaking loose around. . .

The only inspiring thing about the whole ghastly business was to see how people took up life again next day. . . struggling to work by buses that had to go on endless detours around torn-up streets, and buying spring flowers from hawkers who set up their. . . barrows on pitches glittering with powdered glass."

Mollie Panter-Downes in *London War Notes, 1939-45,* ed. W. Shawn, 1972

1 a) Was Mollie Panter-Downes writing near the beginning or the end of the Blitz?
  b) What does the passage tell you about the different precautions that people took against air raids?
  c) What does the writer find 'inspiring' about the way people behaved after the raids?
  d) In your own words try to explain why she found their behaviour inspiring.
  e) What effect was the poster intended to have?
  f) How do the two slogans try to persuade people who would see the poster?
  g) What is imaginary about the picture in the poster?
  h) If you had been a civil servant in the Ministry of Information, where would you have ordered the poster to be displayed?

In January 1941 an opinion-testing organisation, 'Mass Observation', asked people about the six changes they thought were most likely after the war.

	Percentage expecting this to be a major post-war trend (in January 1941)
Less class distinction	29
More state control	21
Education reforms	19
Levelling of incomes	15
Increased social services	14
Dictatorship, fascism	13

T. Harrison, *Living Through the Blitz*, 1975

2 Choose any two changes and say   1) What people meant by them,   2) Why they expected them to take place,   3) Whether, in your view, they did take place.

Starting on the Beveridge plan

The wartime government knew that Beveridge's plans were very popular, both with civilians and the armed forces. In 1943 and 1944 politicians began to think hard about post-war 'reconstruction'.

In 1944 the Coalition government set up a Ministry of Insurance to work out a scheme of social welfare on the lines suggested by Beveridge. In 1945 Parliament passed a law to pay a family allowance of 5s. (25p) a week for every child after the first.

The Butler Education Act, 1944

Parliament had already passed an Education Act in 1944. The Act's details had been worked out by the Coalition government's Education Minister, a Conservative named R. A. Butler.

Up to now, only children who were clever enough to win scholarships, or whose parents could afford to pay for them, had been able to go to secondary schools. The rest had stayed on in the senior classes of elementary schools until they left at fourteen.

The 1944 Education Act ordered local authorities to provide free secondary education for all children. It promised government money to set up suitable schools for children of every 'age, ability and aptitude' up to a new leaving age of fifteen (introduced in 1947).

For secondary education this meant a 'tripartite' system, with three types of schools – 'grammar' for children good at book learning, 'technical' for those good at applied science, and 'modern' for the remaining 75 per cent who were thought best suited to learning practical skills. An examination at age eleven, the 'eleven plus', decided which type of school a child went to.

All three types were supposed to provide education of equal value. But most parents wanted their children to attend a grammar or a technical school, because they provided the surest way to a good job. Children who were sent to modern schools were often thought of as failures. This was one reason why, from the 1950s onwards, local authorities started to replace the tripartite system with comprehensive schools.

General election, 1945

By July 1945 Germany had been defeated and Britain voted in a general election. Conservatives had controlled Britain's government for most of the 1930s. Many voters now blamed them for the depression of those years. This was the main reason why Labour won a landslide victory in 1945, with 393 MPs out of 640.

Labour government, 1945–51

Clement Attlee became Prime Minister. His new Labour government faced huge problems. Vast stretches of London and other cities lay in ruins. Food, clothing and fuel were still in short supply and had to go on being rationed. Britain was deeply in debt because of the huge cost of the war.

Yet the voters expected no delay in turning Britain into a 'welfare state'. This meant a country where the government made sure that everyone had the minimum requirements for a decent life – jobs, homes and care for the sick, the old and children.

National Insurance

The Labour government's National Insurance Act of 1946 turned many of the Beveridge Report's most important ideas into the law of the land. In return for a 4s. 11d. (24½p) a week contribution from all workers except married women, it gave everyone the right to sickness and unemployment benefits and to retirement and widows' pensions. There was no Means Test. Rich or poor, everyone paid the same contributions and drew the same benefits.

The National Health Service

The other main foundation stone of Labour's welfare state was the National Health Service (NHS). The man in charge of organising this was Aneurin Bevan, the Minister of Health. Bevan's idea was to provide everyone with free medical treatment of all kinds. It was to be paid for partly out of taxes and partly out of National Insurance contributions.

Both the National Insurance Scheme and the National Health Service went into operation on the 'Appointed Day' – 5th July 1948.

The NHS immediately proved immensely popular. Doctors' surgeries were packed. Dentists and opticians were booked up for months ahead. In the NHS's first year, dentists treated 8.5 million patients and doctors wrote out 187 million prescriptions. By 1950 the service was costing £350 million a year, instead of the £140 million that the government had allowed for.

Critics claimed that a lot of this money was being wasted on unnecessary treatment. In fact, the rush to use the NHS was due more to the poverty of the 1930s, when people on the dole had managed without spectacles or let their teeth go rotten because they could not afford treatment.

Nationalisation

The post-war Labour government also made changes in industry. The biggest was 'nationalisation'. This meant the government setting up public corporations – groups of managers and experts – to take over important industries and run them on behalf of the people of Britain as a whole.

The industries that were nationalised included coal mining (1947), transport – railways, canals, London's buses and tube trains, and long-distance road haulage – (1948), and the steel industry (1951). The electricity (1948) and gas (1949) industries, many parts of which had been owned by local authorities, were also nationalised.

One reason for nationalisation was that such industries as coal mining and the railways were badly run down. They needed the sort of spending that only the government could possibly afford.

Labour leaders also believed that nationalising an industry would make sure that it was run for the country's benefit instead of mainly to make profits for its shareholders. They also hoped that most people would work harder if they were part-owners of the industries in which they worked.

Many Conservatives disagreed. They didn't much mind the government nationalising run-down industries such as coal-mining, especially when it paid the previous owners generous compensation. But they argued that the country benefited when most industrial firms were privately owned. Then firms had to compete to give customers the best value.

The arguments raged most fiercely about nationalising steel. When the Conservatives were back in power they returned steel to private ownership (1953).

In 1950 an election was due. One major issue for the voters to decide about was nationalisation. The other was the dreariness of life in Britain in the later 1940s.

Hardships in post-war Britain

One of the worst times was the icy winter of 1946–7. For week after week people had to shiver in queues for coal, and the electricity in their homes was often cut off for hours.

If they had homes, that is. During the war four million houses had been blown to pieces or damaged. From 1941 to 1945 no new ones had been built. In the late 1940s houses were still so scarce that thousands of families had to set up home in empty army huts.

Food went on being rationed, including bread, something that had not been necessary even during the war. Clothes, too, were still rationed until 1949.

Taxes were high. The government had big bills for building houses, schools and hospitals, re-equipping Britain's run-down industries and supporting the National Health Service. Defence spending ate up a lot of money, too. The tense conditions in Europe (see Unit 10) meant that Britain still needed strong armed forces.

General elections, 1950 and 1951

In the 1950 general election the Conservatives appealed to the voters to vote for freedom – from rationing, high taxation and government controls. Labour's slogan was 'fair shares for all'.

Labour won the election, but its majority was cut to only six MPs. In 1951 another general election took place. The Conservatives won and Winston Churchill took over once more as Prime Minister.

The achievements of the 1940s

What had been achieved in the six years since the fighting ended?

Neither jobs nor wage rates fell off after the Second World War as they had done after the First. This was mainly because world trade grew steadily after 1945 instead of slumping as it had done after 1918.

Britain was able to find buyers for her exports, and this meant plenty of jobs. So did all the government spending on modernising industry and on new building. In the late 1940s, and all through the 1950s, there were never more than two workers in every hundred without jobs. This compared with something like eleven in every hundred in the 1930s.   Family incomes rose, too, especially with more jobs open to women. Before the war they had often not had the chance to work.

These changes, and the coming of the welfare state, meant that by the start of the 1950s people were enjoying lives which were more comfortable, and more secure, than anything their grandparents had dreamed of.

The general election, June 1945

In May 1945 the Daily Mirror *printed a discussion between a housewife and Sir William Beveridge.*

"The first thing I asked was: 'Do you think your plan will really go through?'...

'That depends on you', he said. 'If you and your friends see that the people you put in Parliament want these proposals you'll get them. If you put in people who are against them – well, you won't.'

'Well, I've read about people who say they think social security is a fine thing, but who say we can't have it because "the country can't afford it".'

'It just isn't true', he answered. 'What is true is that we can't afford to do without it . . . A healthy, happy human being puts back into his country his own value. An unhealthy, half-fed person takes out from the community all the time.'"

Daily Mirror, 7th May 1945

1 a) What did people mean by 'social security'? What did Beveridge's plan say about it?

b) What reasons does Beveridge give for having a social security system?

c) How does he suggest that people could make sure social security would come?

d) Does the result of the 1945 general election suggest that his advice was followed? Explain your answer.

e) Do you think the *Daily Mirror* printed this interview to influence the election result? Explain your answer.

A cartoon in the News Chronicle, *23rd May 1945.*

LOVE ME, LOVE MY DOG

2 a) Who is the man?

b) How had he shown himself to be a 'national leader' in recent years?

c) Put into words three statements that the artist is making about the Tory (Conservative) Party.

d) Is the cartoonist trying to persuade people to vote Tory or Labour in the coming general election?

The beginnings of the Welfare State

Leaders of the British Medical Association (BMA) were opposed to the National Health Service. But the BMA Secretary, Dr Charles Hill, held a ballot of doctors and found that most were strongly in favour. This cartoon appeared in the Daily Mirror *after the ballot.*

Newspaper comments on the 'Appointed Day'.

"A New Britain, a State which takes over its citizens six months before they are born, providing care and free services for their birth, for their early years, their schooling, sickness, workless days, widowhood and retirement. Finally, it helps defray [pay] the cost of their departure. All this with free doctoring, dentistry and medicine, free bathchairs too if needed, for 4s. 11d. out of your weekly pay packet."

Daily Mail, 5th July 1948

"Can the next generation reap the benefits of a social service state while avoiding the perils of a Santa Claus state?"

The Times, 5th July 1948

3 a) Did many doctors object to the NHS? What reasons might they have had?

b) Suggest reasons why most doctors favoured the scheme.

c) What does the cartoon say was the attitude of the public to the NHS?

d) Which two social service schemes started on the 'Appointed Day'?

e) List the benefits and services which came into force, according to the *Daily Mail*.

f) Do you think *The Times* is for or against the new 'social service state'? Give reasons for your opinion.

g) Do you think Britain *did* go on to become a 'Santa Claus state'?

4 Test your understanding of Units 44 and 45 by writing a couple of sentences to explain each of the following:

evacuation	rationing	Coalition government
Blitz	ARP	V2
Beveridge Report	Welfare State	nationalisation.

Labour's difficulties

A cartoon from the Daily Mail, *1946. The artist has added to it posters used in the 1945 election.*

5 a) Who do the two figures with the pram represent?

b) What three promises did the election posters make in 1945?

c) What does the cartoonist say has happened to each of these promises?

d) Imagine you are a supporter of the Labour government. How would you explain its difficulties over housing and food supply to the couple with the pram?

e) What connection might there be between the situation shown in this cartoon and the result of the 1951 election?

A writer summarises the changes that took place in Britain in the years after the Labour government had created the Welfare State.

"In the quarter of a century between 1950 and 1974 real incomes doubled . . . After the war most people still rented their homes from private owners. Yet now more than half own their own homes, and most of the others are in council estates and tower blocks . . . Our possessions have multiplied. After the war only one-third of families had a car; now [1981] the figure is approaching two-thirds. And more than a tenth of families has more than one. Homes with television sets rose from almost none to almost all in twenty years; well over half the sets are now colour . . Nearly all homes have a refrigerator; three-quarters of them have a washing machine; two-fifths have a deep freeze . . . even at times of high and rising unemployment, it means Britain is another country from the one that survived the 1930s."

A. Burnet and W. Landels, *The Time of Our Lives*, 1981

6 a) What does the writer mean by 'real incomes doubled'?

b) Which change do you think has most improved the quality of life?

c) Which change do you think has brought most disadvantages?

d) What do you think the author means by saying that present-day Britain is 'another country' from the Britain of the 1930s?

e) Which facts do you think would most support the idea that it is 'another country'?

f) What factors do you think have helped to cause the change?

BRITAIN SINCE 1945: EMPIRE, COMMONWEALTH AND IRELAND

A weakened Britain, 1945

In 1945 the British people still thought of their country as a great power. But Britain could no longer match the USSR and the USA.

Like Europe's other war-damaged countries, Britain had to accept Marshall Aid to feed its people and get its industries going again (see Unit 10). It also had to rely upon American leadership in NATO to guard against possible attack by the Russians.

The end of the British Empire

In the next twenty years the British broke up their once world-wide Empire. In a few places – Palestine, Cyprus, Malaya – there was fighting before the change took place. But more often the independence movements were political and power was handed over peacefully. In place of the Empire appeared such new independent countries as India (1947), Pakistan (1947), Ghana (1957), Nigeria (1960), Jamaica (1962) and Kenya (1963) (see Units 68, 57 and 39).

The Suez War, 1956

Yet many people still thought that Britain was strong enough to 'go it alone' in international affairs. Most of them saw the truth in 1956 when British and French forces attacked Egypt to win back control of the Suez Canal (see Unit 54).

The Suez attack raised a storm of protest from other countries. The invaders had to withdraw. What happened at Suez made it clear to everyone that Britain no longer had enough influence in the world to treat countries like Egypt in the high-handed kind of way that it might have done earlier.

Slowly, the British people accepted Britain's less powerful position. Some believed that with fewer responsibilities overseas Britain would now be able to look after its own people better.

Others doubted this. They believed that the Empire had helped to keep Britain safe and prosperous. Now it would need other friends. This was one reason why Britain eventually became a member of the European Community in 1973 (see Unit 11).

The Commonwealth

Britain tried to keep on friendly terms with its old colonies through the Commonwealth, the group of independent nations who had once been part of the British Empire. The Queen is head of the Commonwealth, but neither she nor the British government has any power over its member nations' affairs.

Commonwealth immigration

Many people from Commonwealth countries came to live in Britain after 1945.

In the 1950s Britain was short of workers for buses, hospitals and the London Underground. Transport and health bosses ran recruiting campaigns in the Caribbean. In the 1950s West Indian workers were arriving in Britain at a rate of about 20,000 a year.

By the 1960s the West Indians had been joined by people from India, Pakistan and Africa. Like the West Indians, they usually came looking for work or to join family members already here.

By 1981 four out of every hundred people in Britain were of African or Asian descent. Most lived in the places where the jobs had been when they or their parents first came.

Commonwealth Immigration Acts

Until 1962 Commonwealth citizens were allowed to enter Britain freely. But by then the government was getting worried – partly about housing and job shortages, and partly about the trouble caused by the hostile attitude of some whites towards blacks.

In 1962 the government brought in the Commonwealth Immigration Act, limiting the number of Commonwealth citizens allowed to settle in Britain. In 1968 and 1971 Parliament passed other acts on similar lines.

Some people claimed that the Immigration Acts were racist. They pointed out that they were directed only at blacks, Afro-Caribbeans and Asians, not at white Commonwealth citizens.

Blacks already living in Britain were not always treated fairly. Often they were barred from buying certain houses or getting jobs because of their colour.

Race Relations Acts

Parliament passed laws to try to stop this sort of thing. The first of these Race Relations Acts was passed in 1965. Others followed in 1968 and 1976.

The Race Relations Acts made it an offence to discriminate against people because of their colour and to say in public anything intended to stir up racial hatred. They also set up first a Race Relations Board (1965) and then a Commission for Racial Equality (1976) to help Britain's black citizens to obtain fair treatment.

In the 1980s, however, many blacks still believed that they were not treated as fairly as they would have been with white skins.

Britain and Ireland

Meanwhile, a big problem had grown up for Britain in Northern Ireland. To understand it we have to go back to the start of the century, when all of Ireland was under British rule. At that time the people of Ireland had no elected government of their own. Instead they sent members to the British Parliament.

Irish Nationalists objected to this. They said that the Irish were a separate people from the British. They wanted Ireland to have 'Home Rule' so that the Irish could run their own affairs.

Nationalists and Unionists

In Northern Ireland, called Ulster, many people were Unionists – so called because they wanted to go on being united with Britain. Most were the descendants of colonists from Britain who had settled in Ireland centuries before. Whereas Nationalists were usually Catholics, most Unionists were Protestants.

The Easter Rising, 1916

In Easter Week 1916 a group of Irish Nationalists organised an armed rising in the Irish capital, Dublin. After a week of street fighting this 'Easter Rising' was crushed by British soldiers.

The British executed the leaders of the Easter Rising as traitors. But to Irish Nationalists they became heroes.

Sinn Fein and the IRA

A Nationalist group calling themselves Sinn Fein organised a guerilla army – the Irish Republic Army (IRA). In 1919 fighting broke out in Ireland between the IRA and the British army. After

Ireland divided, 1922

Unrest in Ulster

British soldiers go to Ulster, 1969

Violence spreads

Anglo-Irish Agreement, 1985

three years of bitter warfare the British and the Nationalists signed a peace treaty in London in 1922.

The British government agreed that Southern Ireland should become an independent country, the Irish Free State. In return, the Irish agreed that the people of Ulster should be allowed to vote on whether to become part of the Free State or remain part of Britain.

The IRA opposed this. As it expected, the majority of Ulster's people voted to stay linked with Britain.

The new province of Northern Ireland had its own elected government for local affairs in Belfast. Catholics made up a third of the total population, but they had little say in Ulster's government. They were unfairly treated by the Protestant majority in matters like housing and job opportunities, too.

In the 1950s the Catholics started a peaceful Civil Rights movement, holding meetings and making protest marches. By the middle 1960s the movement was winning more and more support.

The IRA was now a secret organisation of armed men, sworn to unite the whole of Ireland by force. Members of its 'Provisional' wing set themselves up as the protectors of the Ulster Catholics.

In 1969 IRA 'Provos' started to make bomb attacks on Ulster police-stations and power-stations. The Unionists organised a secret armed force of their own, the Ulster Defence Association (UDA), to strike back at them.

In 1969 the British government sent soldiers to Northern Ireland to try to keep order. Many Catholics welcomed them at first. But their attitude changed when the soldiers began raiding Catholic districts in search of IRA weapons and suspects. They came to believe that the British government had sent the soldiers to make sure that the Protestants stayed in control.

In the early 1970s shootings and bombings increased. On 'Bloody Sunday', in Londonderry in January 1972, British troops shot dead thirteen Catholic demonstrators.

Northern Ireland was close to civil war. In 1972 the British government suspended the Ulster Parliament and took complete control of the government there. British soldiers rounded up IRA supporters and threw them into prison without trial.

But the fighting went on and became more savage. IRA men imprisoned by the British went on hunger strike. Hundreds of innocent people were killed or terribly injured by IRA bomb attacks. Many others suffered or died in revenge attacks by the UDA and other extreme Protestant organisations.

People were killed when IRA bombs exploded in English cities such as London and Birmingham. In 1984 an IRA bomb killed five people at a hotel in Brighton, and narrowly missed killing the British Prime Minister, Margaret Thatcher.

In 1985 Britain's and Ireland's political leaders signed an Anglo-Irish Agreement to try to bring peace to Ulster. But a lasting solution to Northern Ireland's problems still seemed far away.

Living in multi-racial Britain

The birthplaces of black and Asian residents in Britain in 1981.

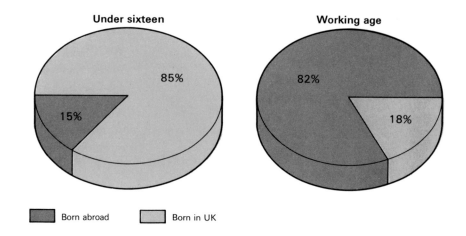

Under sixteen

85%

15%

Working age

82%

18%

Born abroad   Born in UK

S. Fothergill and J. Vincent, *The State of the Nation*, 1985

1 a) Suggest reasons why so many black and Asian people of working age in 1981 were born abroad.

b) Which changes in the law were bound to mean that most of the younger people in black and Asian communities were born in Britain?

c) In the future, would you expect the figure of 15 per cent in the under-16 chart to grow or shrink?

Extracts from interviews with young adult black people carried out by Peter Gillman for The Sunday Times Magazine, *30th September 1973.*

Paul, aged 18:
"When I was small I used to go around saying that I'm English and I'm proud of being English. But then it suddenly hit me that the English didn't want me to be an Englishman so then I thought I'll never be an Englishman. It's difficult. You're always a bit confused. . ."

Trevor, aged 22:
"You can go further here. Though it wasn't nice when I first came. You get called things like black bastard. I wasn't really used to those things . . .

But I'm more cool now. Here is nice. The weather is horrible. But you're more free. You can do a lot of things . . ."

Tamara, aged 22:
"I think that people who are prejudiced are very unintelligent, very stupid, even if they're well educated.

I'm not uptight about being black. I never think about it. It doesn't matter.

There are opportunities for black people . . . If you think everyone's against you because you're black it's not going to work."

2 a) Have any of the experiences and ideas of these people become out of date since 1973?

b) Do you agree with Tamara that prejudice is stupid?

c) Do you think that studying history makes people less prejudiced, or might it make them more so? Give reasons for your opinion.

Northern Ireland

A cartoon by an Irishman.

Cormac, *Republican News*

British opinions

"The English have every reason to feel proud of their country's recent record in Northern Ireland, since it sets the whole world a uniquely impressive example of . . . service in the cause of peace. Nothing done by any other country in recent times so richly deserves the Nobel prize."

Peregrine Worsthorne, *Sunday Telegraph*, 3rd May, 1981

"The total withdrawal of the British Army . . . would be of no benefit to the hundreds who would inevitably be killed in the sectarian civil strife which would follow such a short-sighted move . . . Withdrawal now would, in effect, be the signal for chaos."

John Horgan, *The Listener*, 1971

An Irish opinion

" . . . the British authorities, aided by the media, . . . played down the atrocities committed by the British forces, minimised loyalist responsibility for violence, and depicted the situation as one long succession of violent acts committed by republicans. They portrayed the IRA as the cause . . . of the conflict . . . They refused to acknowledge that partition and the continuing British presence were the root of the problem."

Liz Curtis, *Nothing But the Same Old Story*, 1985

A British cartoon

Cummings, *Daily Express, August 1970*

3 a) For each source decide whether you think it is biased in favour of the British or the IRA and give the reasons for your decision.

b) Does the bias in the sources make them useless as historical evidence?

c) What further evidence might help you to decide which of these sources comes closest to the truth?

PART SIX
THE WORLD AND THE SUPERPOWERS

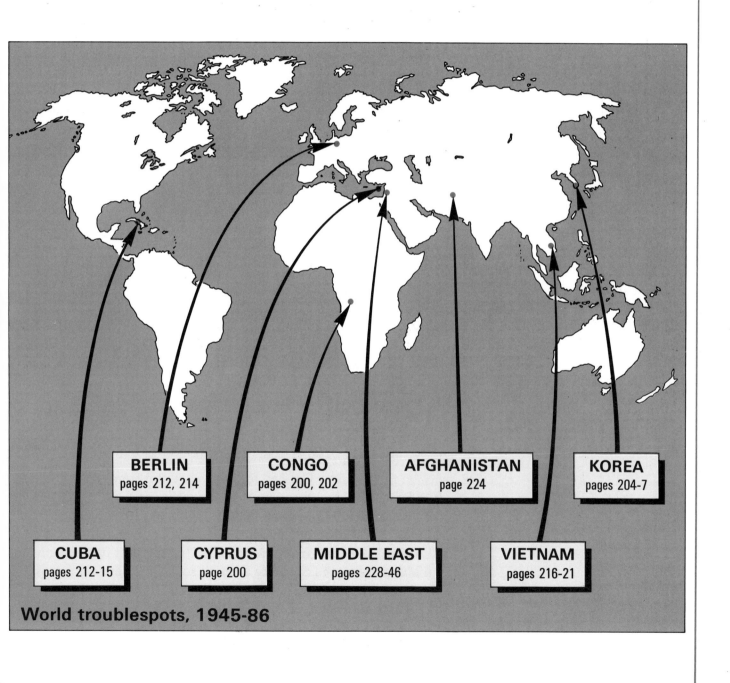

BERLIN
pages 212, 214

CONGO
pages 200, 202

AFGHANISTAN
page 224

KOREA
pages 204-7

CUBA
pages 212-15

CYPRUS
page 200

MIDDLE EAST
pages 228-46

VIETNAM
pages 216-21

World troublespots, 1945-86

The end of Hitler's war

A shot rang out in the shelter beneath the burning ruins of Berlin. The man's body slumped across a sofa. Adolf Hitler had shot himself through the mouth and blown his brains out.

It was the afternoon of Monday 30th April 1945. In the week which followed the last of Hitler's soldiers surrendered. The Second World War in Europe was over.

The birth of the United Nations

While all this was going on in Europe, an important meeting was taking place far away on the other side of the world. In the American city of San Francisco representatives from fifty nations were meeting to talk about the future of the world. On 26th June 1945 they signed an agreement called the Charter of the United Nations.

The United Nations Organisation (UN) took the place of the pre-war League of Nations (see Unit 7). Its main aim was to do what the League had failed to do – to see that the world stayed at peace.

The UN's founders also wanted to encourage the people of the world to work together in other ways – against disease, hunger and all mankind's other problems.

The UN is organised in four main sections – the General Assembly, the Security Council, the Secretariat and the Specialised Agencies. The money to pay for the UN's work comes from contributions by its members. The better off a member is, the more it is expected to pay. Over the years this has meant that a big part of the UN's expenses has been paid by the USA, its richest member.

The UN General Assembly

The UN General Assembly meets once a year. Every autumn each member sends a political leader to the UN headquarters in New York to join in discussions about international problems.

In the General Assembly every UN member has one vote. But from the beginning the strong nations did not want small countries to have too much say in world affairs. For this reason they gave the real power in the UN to the Security Council.

The UN Security Council

The Security Council has five permanent members – the USA, the USSR, and three of their main allies in the Second World War – Britain, France and China. Ten other members (six up to 1966) serve on the Security Council for two years at a time.

The Security Council can be called together at a moment's notice to deal with serious disagreements between countries, especially if they look like leading to war. It can call upon other members of the UN to lend it soldiers from their armies to carry out its decisions.

This may make the Security Council sound very strong, but in fact it has a big weakness.

The veto

The original Security Council rules said that it could only order action when all five of its permanent members agreed. This meant that any one of them could stop the UN from acting by using its 'right of veto' – by saying no.

When the UN was founded, both the USSR and the USA insisted upon this right of veto. This was because neither of them wanted the United Nations voting to take actions which might be against their interests.

In the years after 1945 the USA and the USSR were by far the strongest countries in the world – 'superpowers', as they came to be called. They also became enemies in the 'Cold War'.

Sometimes quarrels between the superpowers nearly brought war. This happened over Berlin in 1948, for example (see Unit 10), and Cuba in 1962 (see Unit 50).

Over both Berlin and Cuba the UN was bypassed, like the League of Nations had been over Czechoslovakia in 1938. Officially it could do little more than look on and hope that the superpowers would settle their differences peacefully. But unofficially it helped to keep them in touch and talking to one another.

The UN Secretariat

All the work of the UN is supervised and linked together by the Secretariat. The Secretariat is a team of thousands of secretaries, clerks, translators and other officials. Its job is to organise the day-to-day work of the UN and to see that its decisions are carried out.

The head of the Secretariat is the Secretary-General. He gets the job when the General Assembly agrees to a name put forward by the Security Council. So far, the person appointed to this job has always come from a small country.

The UN Specialised Agencies

The job of the UN's Specialised Agencies is to help the people of the world improve their lives. Each agency tackles human problems of a particular kind. The World Health Organisation (WHO), for example, fights disease. The Food and Agriculture Organisation (FAO) works out and teaches better ways of farming.

In the 1970s the FAO led a so-called 'Green Revolution' in the world's poorer countries. It developed better kinds of seeds and new ways to tackle pests and disease.

Yet people continued to go hungry. Sometimes, as in Ethiopia in 1985, they starved. Without the work of the FAO there would have been more Ethiopias. Even so, it was clear that more than seeds and pesticides were needed to solve the world's food problems.

Wars and peace-keeping

What about the peace-keeping work of the UN?

Soldiers from many different countries have seen action as members of UN forces since 1945.

Korea

In 1950 South Korea was attacked by its neighbour, North Korea (see Unit 48). The UN sent armies, under American commanders, to defend it. The fighting in Korea went on until a cease-fire was arranged in 1953.

The Middle East

In 1956 Israel, France and Britain attacked Egypt in a quarrel about the Suez Canal (see Unit 54). When the fighting ended, UN soldiers flew in to patrol the border between Israel and Egypt and make sure that fighting did not flare up again. In the next thirty years UN soldiers were called upon to keep the peace between

The Congo

quarrelling groups in the Middle East many times.

In 1960 an African colony, the Congo (later called Zaire), became independent. It had previously belonged to Belgium.

The Belgians had done nothing to prepare the Congo's people for independence. The government broke down almost at once. Its soldiers mutinied. The Belgians encouraged the richest part of the country, called Katanga, to break away so that they could still control its rich copper mines.

The Security Council rushed UN soldiers to the Congo. Dag Hammarskjold, the UN Secretary-General, flew out himself to try to help. He was killed in an aeroplane crash there in 1961.

The UN soldiers had two jobs in the Congo – to protect people's lives and to try to hold the country together. But the Congo's problems were too complicated, and there was too much interference from other countries, for the UN forces to solve them. In 1964 UN forces withdrew and left the Congolese to try to sort out the difficulties for themselves.

Cyprus

From 1964 onwards UN soldiers also tried to keep peace on the Mediterranean island of Cyprus. The problem here was the suspicion and dislike between Greeks and Turks, the two groups of people who live on the island.

The UN soldiers kept the Greeks and the Turks apart, and saved Cyprus from a full-scale civil war in the 1960s. But in 1974 soldiers from Turkey took over the north of the island for the Turks and set up a separate government there.

The Changing UN

By the 1970s the UN had changed a lot. When it started in 1945 50 countries were members. By 1976 the number of members had grown to 176. Most of the new members were newly independent countries in Africa and Asia. Usually they were very poor.

These new members wanted the UN to do more to end worldwide evils like poverty and racial prejudice. They also wanted it to stop strong countries from taking advantage of weak ones. They claimed that the greed of the rich white countries was one reason that the world's poor nations were so badly off.

Attacks like this turned many people in the better-off countries against the UN. Why should we go on picking up its bills when all that it does is criticise us? they asked. The whole organisation is just a useless talking shop, they said scornfully.

They were wrong. The UN was far from perfect. But it had done a lot of good in the world.

Its Specialised Agencies, like the WHO and the FAO, had saved millions of lives. Its blue-helmeted soldiers had helped to keep the peace in danger spots all over the world.

And it had given the world a meeting place where hostile countries could talk over their differences. As the British statesman Winston Churchill once said – 'Jaw, jaw is better than war, war'.

The UN in 1945

Two cartoonists look at the new UN in 1945.

1 a) What clues can you find which help to give the date of the top cartoon?

   b) The cartoonist called it 'Hope dawning'. Explain what he meant.

   c) In the bottom cartoon what is Low saying about the weaknesses of the UN?

   d) Do you think Low was right? Give two examples to support your opinion.

   e) If you could use only one of these cartoons to illustrate some notes on the UN, which would you choose and why?

The UN at work

A doctor working for the World Health Organisation with hospital patients in the Congo in 1960.

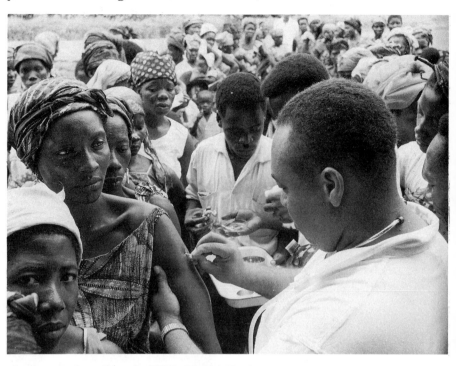

A reporter describes the UN's World Health Organisation (WHO) in action in the Congo in 1960.

"Take a tropical country four times the size of France, with a population of 14 million, strip it of doctors, stop purifying drinking water and stop collecting refuse – and you have the makings of disaster. That was the Congo in the summer of 1960.

The public health service that had been maintained by the Belgians collapsed after the Congo became independent. Some 2000 doctors and sanitary engineers had gone home, and this land of steaming jungle was faced with a desperate shortage of doctors. Smallpox, typhoid, sleeping sickness and meningitis raged. . . . Uncollected refuse in a dozen towns was piled to the roofs, and rats with bubonic fleas ran wild.

At a few hours' notice, 150 doctors and sanitary engineers from 40 countries packed their kit and took off for the jungle. . . .

They . . . ran short of catgut for sutures, and of antibiotics. When delicate work with scalpel and syringe was finished, they washed babies, scrubbed floors and cleaned latrines. But the group survived, . . . and they stopped epidemics, cured thousands and laid the foundation for a permanent public health service.

The organization responsible for this . . . is the World Health Organization, an agency of the United Nations and perhaps the most effective of all our international groups . . . It went into the Congo when Dr Ralph Bunche, in Leopoldville as a representative of the UN, became alarmed at the mass exodus of Belgian doctors. He sent a cable, and the Congo became a job for Dr M. G. Candau, director-general of WHO in Geneva.

. . . The morning the assignment came to him, Dr Candau sat down at the telephone in his office . . . His calls took him round the world – to a hospital in Haiti, to a government building in New Delhi, . . . and to... dozen other countries – a successful effort to assemble quickly a group o... experts to handle the Congo emergency . . .

With the help of the International Red Cross, 26 teams were soon ready to take off; 48 hours later Dr Candau himself was in Leopoldville.

The teams fanned out into the jungle, by boat, jeep and helicopter. Engineers repaired DDT sprayers which had been rusting in garages . . . They explained to the Congolese the need for chlorinating the water. They played records and showed films, and in time the people began to co-operate. Tons of refuse were removed and pure water flowed once more in the villages.

A French doctor arriving in the village of Bunia found 30 cases of bubonic plague. When the inhabitants refused vaccination, he talked for two hours; finally, in desperation, he vaccinated himself. There was a chatter of discussion, and suddenly the mob of villagers dissolved into a line of men, women and children meekly awaiting their turn . . .

In town after town, village after village, as the long days of work succeeded each other, the danger of epidemics receded."

George Kent in *The Rotarian*, 1961

2 a) Explain why WHO doctors were needed in the Congo in 1960.

b) How would you have solved the problem facing the doctor in the last but one paragraph of the extract?

c) Write two sentences about the work of one UN Agency other than the WHO.

A UN peace-keeping force's watch-tower between Egyptian and Israeli armies in Sinai in 1973.

3 a) Which UN body was responsible for sending to the Middle East the soldiers shown in the photograph above?

b) Write two or three sentences to explain why they were sent there.

c) Choose one other part of the world to which UN soldiers have been sent. Write two or three sentences to explain why they were sent and what they did there.

4 a) *Either* draw a picture *or* design a poster to show the useful work done by the UN since it was founded.

b) Look through recent copies of newspapers and magazines to see what news items about the UN you can find. What sort of problems has it been dealing with recently?

e Cold War

The USA was the world's richest and strongest country in 1945. Its factories turned out half of all the world's manufactured goods. It had the world's biggest air force and navy. It had millions of the best armed fighting men. And only the USA had atomic bombs.

After the USA came the USSR. Its industries were not as strong, but it had a bigger army. Soviet soldiers were the masters of all Europe from the middle of Germany eastwards (see Unit 14).

No other European nation could match the USSR's strength. Germany and France lay in ruins. Britain was worn out, its strength used up in beating Hitler.

It was Europe's weakness that brought the Americans into the picture. They had fought with the Russians as allies against Hitler. But friendship between them barely lasted the war out.

President Truman of the USA accused the Russians of using their soldiers to force their communist way of life on to the other countries of Europe. Stalin, the ruler of the USSR, believed that many Americans hated communism so much that the USA might attack the USSR with atomic bombs at any time.

Only a year after the end of the Second World War people were starting to speak of a 'Cold War' between the USA and the USSR. Although the two powers were not actually fighting one another, they were always quarrelling.

Truman and containment

President Truman decided to use American power and money to 'contain' Soviet influence – that is, to stop it from spreading. This idea of containment is sometimes called the Truman Doctrine. From 1946 containing communism became the main aim of the USA in its dealings with the rest of the world.

Containment was tried out first in Europe. The Marshall Plan, the Berlin Airlift and NATO were all examples (see Unit 10).

War in Korea

In 1950 containment was tested out in Asia, too. The place where this happened was Korea, a small eastern land bordering on China.

Before the Second World War Korea had been ruled by Japan. When Japan surrendered in 1945 Korea was occupied in the north by Soviet forces and in the south by Americans. The boundary between them was the earth's 38th parallel of latitude.

In 1948 the occupation ended. The Soviet army left behind a communist government in the north and the Americans set up a government friendly to themselves in the south.

Both Korean governments claimed the right to rule all of the country. In June 1950 the North Koreans decided to settle the matter. Their soldiers crossed the 38th parallel in a full-scale invasion of South Korea.

The USA and the Korean War

President Truman acted quickly. He sent American soldiers and war planes, mostly from nearby Japan, to fight for the South Koreans. Then he persuaded the UN Security Council to back him.

The Russians missed their chance to veto UN support for Truman. They were absent from the Security Council when the vote was taken. So the Korean War became a UN operation.

Sixteen nations, including Britain, sent troops to fight for the UN. But the war was really an American affair. Nine out of every ten UN soldiers in Korea were American. So, too, was their Commander, General Douglas MacArthur.

At first the communist armies swept all before them. But after three months of hard fighting the Americans pushed them back across the 38th parallel, deep into North Korea.

By this time the American aim was no longer just to protect South Korea. They were out to unite all of Korea under a government friendly towards the USA.

China and the Korean War

The map on page 197 shows that Korea has a long border with China. Only a year before Mao Zedong had won the struggle to rule China by driving out Chiang Kaishek (see Unit 62).

The Americans had backed Chiang in the struggle and still recognised him as China's rightful ruler. Mao believed that, if all Korea came under American control, they might let Chiang use it as a base. And China's main factories and power-stations were only a short distance from the border with Korea along the Yalu River.

Mao warned the Americans to stay back from China's borders. When his warning was ignored, he sent thousands of experienced Chinese soldiers across the Yalu to help the North Koreans.

The Chinese drove back the advancing Americans. A new and fiercer war began in Korea. It was really between the USA and China, although neither country officially admitted this.

MacArthur said that the only way for the Americans to win was to attack China itself. But President Truman turned down the idea. He feared that an American attack on China might start another world war. When MacArthur criticised the President's decision in the newspapers, Truman sacked him.

The Korean War dragged on for another two and a half years. It ended at last in July 1953.

The Korean War ends

The death of Stalin was one reason the Korean War ended. He had been encouraging the Chinese to fight on. The new American leader, President Eisenhower, also hinted that he might use atomic weapons if the Chinese did not sign a cease-fire.

The cease-fire left Korea still divided more or less along the line of the 38th parallel. Yet both sides claimed that they had won a kind of victory.

The Chinese said that they had proved that nobody need be afraid of standing up to the Americans. The Americans said that they had shown communists everywhere that it did not pay to try to spread their rule by force.

33,000 Americans had died. Over 100,000 more had been wounded. Containment in Korea had been expensive. But the Americans felt that it had worked.

War in Korea

1 a) Look back at the unit on the
   League of Nations (Unit 7)
   and explain what is meant by
   the words on the gravestone.

 b) The two figures represent the
   UN and President Truman of
   the USA. Why do you think
   that   1) the UN is shown
   carrying a gun,   2) Truman
   is shown leading the UN by
   the hand?

 c) What does the cartoon
   suggest that the two figures
   are doing?

 d) What comparison is Low
   making between the League
   and the UN?

 e) Is Low for or against what the
   UN and the USA are doing?

*Refugees retreating south during
the Korean War, 1950.*

2 Imagine that you are reporting
   this scene for a radio audience.
   Describe the behaviour and
   feelings of the refugees, the
   soldiers and yourself. To make
   the account more lifelike, add
   details which the photograph
   cannot give, such as sounds,
   movements and smells.

A cartoon by Low in the Evening Standard *at the start of the Korean War.*

HISTORY DOESN'T REPEAT ITSELF

China and the Korean War

American views on how to deal with China after Mao sent troops to Korea.

General MacArthur:

"My views . . . follow the conventional [usual] pattern of meeting force with maximum counterforce . . .

. . . here in Asia is where the Communist conspirators have elected [chosen] to make their play for global conquest . . . if we lose this war to Communism in Asia the fall of Europe is inevitable . . ."

In M. Miller, *Plain Speaking*, 1976

General Omar Bradley:

". . . our military mission is to support a policy preventing Communism from gaining . . . the military power to rule the world . . . Red China is not the powerful nation seeking to dominate the world. Frankly . . . the [MacArthur] strategy would involve us in the wrong war, at the wrong place . . . and with the wrong enemy."

In D. Rees, *The Age of Containment*, 1967

President Harry S. Truman:

"If we do have another world war, it will be an atomic war. We could expect many atomic bombs to be dropped on American cities. And a single one of them could cause many more times the casualties that we have suffered in all the fighting in Korea. I do not want to be responsible for bringing that about."

In J. Murray Brown (ed.), *Portraits of Power*, 1979

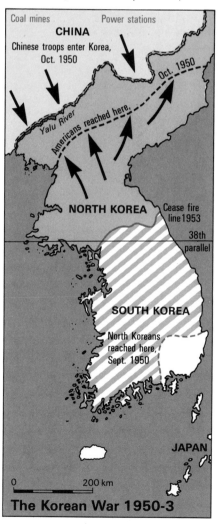

The Korean War 1950–3

3 a) How does the map help you to understand 1) why the Chinese joined in the Korean War, 2) the importance of the fact that Japan was occupied by US troops at the time?

b) What does MacArthur believe is the reason for China sending troops into Korea?

c) How does Omar Bradley disagree with him?

d) Is MacArthur's view fact or opinion?

e) Is Bradley's view fact or opinion?

f) Which general's view do you think Truman would have agreed with? What makes you think this?

g) Which general's view agrees more with the policy that the Americans actually followed?

The H-bomb

The bomb exploded in a blinding burst of green-white light. The fireball at its centre grew into a towering pillar of flame. A huge coloured mushroom of poisonous cloud boiled high into the sky.

It was November 1952. American scientists had blasted a whole island out of the Pacific Ocean. They had exploded their first hydrogen, or H-bomb.

The H-bomb was many times more destructive that the atomic, or A-bomb that destroyed Hiroshima (see Unit 65). By 1953 the Russians had made one, too. By 1957 so had the British. But only the Americans and the Russians could afford to go on making them.

H-bombs made the superpowers stronger than ever. Just how strong was spelled out by a Russian general. 'There are optimists and pessimists in Britain', he told a British visitor. 'The pessimists think that five H-bombs will wipe out everyone in Britain, the optimists think it would take eight. We have two hundred.'

The fact that both the USA and the USSR had H-bombs decided how they behaved towards one another for years to come.

Eisenhower and Dulles

The American people elected Dwight D. Eisenhower as President in 1952. Eisenhower, or 'Ike', had been the general in charge of the D Day invasion of Hitler's Europe. Later he had become the first Commander-in-Chief of NATO.

American Presidents appoint a person called the Secretary of State to take charge of dealings with foreign countries. Eisenhower gave this job to John Foster Dulles. Dulles believed that the communists were plotting to conquer the world and he was determined to stop them.

SEATO, 1954

In 1954 Dulles persuaded a number of nations to join the United States in the South East Asia Treaty Organisation (SEATO). His idea was for SEATO to contain the spread of communist power in Asia like NATO had done in Europe (see Unit 10).

But Dulles wanted to do more than contain communism. He spoke about 'liberating' people who were already under communist rule.

The Hungarian Rising, 1956

The people of Hungary put Dulles' words to the test. They had been under Soviet control since 1946. In 1956 they rebelled against their Hungarian communist rulers (see Unit 14). When Russian tanks rolled in to crush them, the rebels sent out desperate appeals for help to the Americans.

The help never came. For one thing, Dulles had another problem at that time – the British and French attack on Egypt (see Unit 54). He also decided that risking an H-bomb war with the USSR was too high a price to pay for 'liberating' Eastern Europe.

Brinkmanship and massive retaliation

After the Hungarian Rising Dulles went back to strengthening American plans to contain communism. His policy became known as 'brinkmanship' because of the way he seemed ready to take the USA to the brink of war with the USSR to get his way.

Dulles made up for the Russians' bigger army with warnings to the USSR that if Soviet forces attacked the USA, or any of its allies, there would be 'massive retaliation' by the Americans with H-bombs.

Most Americans supported Dulles' massive retaliation policy. They knew that the Russians did not have the war planes to drop as many bombs on the USA as the Americans could drop on them.

The Sputnik, 1957

Then, on 4th October 1957, the USSR sent the world's first earth satellite, the Sputnik, roaring into space.

Sputnik did not worry the Americans. But the rocket that blasted it into space did. A rocket powerful enough to do that could also carry an H-bomb to its target.

Nuclear missiles

The Americans began to speed up work on rockets of their own. Soon they had a whole range of them. These bomb-carrying rockets were called 'nuclear missiles'.

The biggest were the Inter-Continental Ballistic Missiles – ICBMs. They were kept in underground forts all over the United States, ready to hurl their deadly warheads at a moment's notice. The Polaris, another missile, was carried by nuclear-powered submarines cruising deep beneath the oceans.

By the end of the 1950s the Americans and the Russians had enough nuclear missiles to kill everybody on earth. Little wonder that people spoke of a 'balance of terror'. Both Russian and American leaders came to see that in a full-scale war their two countries would just destroy one another.

Nikita Khrushchev, the man who took Stalin's place as leader of the USSR, realised this. He once said that capitalist and communist countries would only really agree 'when shrimps learned to whistle'. But, in a world of H-bombs, he believed that they had to try to live peacefully, side by side.

Khrushchev and peaceful co-existence

In place of Cold War threats, Khrushchev suggested 'peaceful co-existence'. Like all communists, he believed that the capitalist way of life of countries like the USA would break down of its own accord one day. So why risk a nuclear war? It made more sense to wait.

President Eisenhower welcomed Khrushchev's talk of peaceful co-existence. He invited the Soviet leader to visit the USA. Afterwards the two men agreed to hold a summit meeting in Paris in May 1960 to work out solutions to some of their differences.

The U-2 incident, 1960

The Paris summit never even started. As the leaders were on their way, a Russian missile shot down an American aircraft over the USSR. The aircraft was a U-2 spy plane, specially designed to take photographs of military targets from the edge of space.

Khrushchev angrily accused Eisenhower of planning for war while talking peace. He stormed off back to the USSR. He seemed to be furious. Secretly, however, Khrushchev was perhaps rather pleased at having made the Americans look like hypocrites.

Either way, the Paris summit meeting was over before it even started.

The nuclear age

In May 1956 a reporter watched an American H-bomb test over the Pacific.

". . . it was like experiencing a nightmare in broad daylight. Through high-density goggles I saw a super-sun rise over the vastness of the blue-black Pacific, with a dazzling burst of green-white light estimated to equal, for a brief instant, the light of 500 suns at high noon. I watched the enormous fireball expand in a matter of seconds to a diameter of about three miles, more than seventeen times that of the fireball of the atomic. . . bomb that had devastated Hiroshima and Nagasaki.

. . . I was staggered by the thought of what this fireball and the mushroom would do to any of the world's great cities.

But as I kept on watching, a second, more reassuring thought became uppermost in my mind:

This great. . . cloud it seemed to me, is actually a protective 'umbrella' that will for ever shield mankind. . . this rising super-sun is really a symbol of the dawn of a new era in which any major war has become impossible; no aggressor will ever dare to start a war because of the certainty of absolute and swift self-annihilation."

William Laurence, in *American Weekly*, 1956

A Campaign for Nuclear Disarmament (CND) poster published in Britain in the 1950s. Its caption reads 'Stop Nuclear Suicide'.

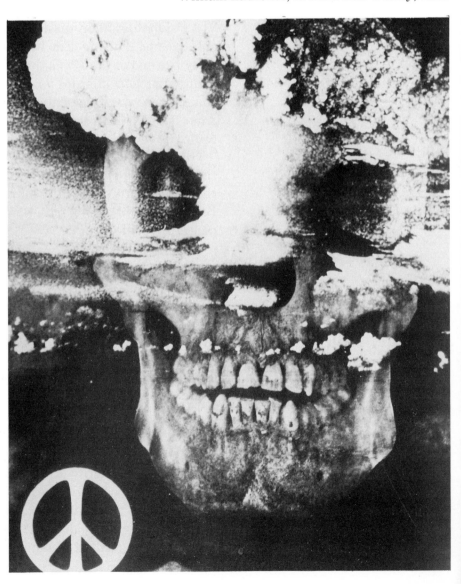

1 **a)** What reason does the writer give for believing that the H-bomb will help to keep the world at peace?

b) Do you think that the artist who designed the poster would agree or disagree with him? Give reasons for your opinion.

c) More than thirty years have passed since the first H-bomb tests. Does this make the opinion of either the writer or the poster more right or more wrong?

d) Do you think that the existence of nuclear weapons makes peace or war more likely today? Give reasons to support your opinion.

The Sputnik age

A cartoon from an American newspaper, October 1957.

2 a) What event is the cartoon commenting on?

b) Which country does the man represent?

c) What object has knocked off his hat?

d) Explain why the man looks
1) surprised,
2) worried.

e) Explain how this event affected the balance of military power between the superpowers.

Part of 'Your Attention Please' by Peter Porter. The poem was written in 1962 after the USA set up the Distant Early Warning (DEW) system to detect approaching Soviet missiles. DEW gave the American President ten minutes to order US missiles to be fired in reply.

3 a) What does this poem tell you about the fears caused by the nuclear arms race in the 1950s and 1960s?

b) How does it illustrate
1) the idea of Massive Retaliation,   2) the dangers of relying on it for defence?

c) Do you think the poem deals fairly with the problems of defending western countries?

d) Do you think the poem has any relevance today? Explain your opinion.

"The Polar DEW has just warned that
A nuclear rocket strike of
At least one thousand megatons
Has just been launched by the enemy
Directly at our major cities.
This announcement will take
Two and a quarter minutes to make,
You have therefore a further
Eight and a quarter minutes
To comply with the shelter
Requirements published in the Civil
Defence Code – section Atomic Attack.
A specially shortened Mass
Will be broadcast at the end
Of this announcement –
Protestant and Jewish services
Will begin simultaneously –
Select your wavelength immediately
According to instructions
In the Defence Code. Do not
Take well-loved pets (including birds)
Into your shelter – they will consume
Fresh air. Leave the old and
bedridden, you can do nothing for them.
. . . .
This announcement is ending. Our President
Has already given orders for
Massive retaliation. . ."

P. Porter, *Collected Poems*, 1983

The Berlin Wall, 1961

Just after midnight on Sunday 13th August 1961 trucks rolled through the silent streets of East Berlin.

At the border with West Berlin soldiers jumped out and blocked the streets with coils of barbed wire.

By morning they had closed off all but twelve of the eighty crossing points to West Berlin. Within days workmen were replacing the barbed wire with a lasting barrier of concrete.

The division of Germany

To understand why the Berlin Wall was built we have to go back to 1945, when the countries that had beaten Hitler divided Berlin and the rest of Germany between them (see Unit 12). This was supposed to be a temporary arrangement, but the wartime allies could not agree on how Germany should be ruled.

All hope of uniting Germany as one country again vanished when the Russians blockaded West Berlin in 1948 and 1949 (see Unit 10). In 1949 the Western Powers (the USA, Britain and France) joined their zones together to form the Federal German Republic (West Germany). The Russians replied by turning their zone into the German Democratic Republic (East Germany).

West Germany prospered. By 1961 her people were amongst the best off in the world (see Unit 12).

Escapers from East Germany

The East German people were not so well off. Their wages were lower. They had less to buy in the shops, less chance to speak their minds. Millions fled to the West. The easiest way to escape was to catch a train from East to West Berlin and not bother to come back.

By July 1961 the number of East Germans making these one-way trips had risen to 10,000 a week. Many of the escapers were highly skilled workers – engineers, doctors, scientists. East Germany's rulers knew that their country could never prosper without such people. They built the Wall to stop any more of them from leaving.

The Berlin Wall's effects

From the viewpoint of East Germany's prosperity, the Berlin Wall was a success. The bleeding away of skilled manpower was stopped overnight. East Germany's industries began to grow stronger. Living standards started to improve.

The West angrily criticised the East Germans and the Russians for building the Wall. But for them, too, it was not altogether a bad thing. By turning Berlin into two separate cities the Wall cut down the risk of it becoming a cause of war between the superpowers.

Cuba and Castro

Cuba is far away from Berlin. It is an island only 145 kilometres from the coast of the USA. In 1959 a revolutionary reformer named Fidel Castro took over its government.

Cuba's banks and railways and many businesses were American-owned. So, too, were a lot of its big sugar plantations.

Castro decided that he needed more money to make changes in Cuba. To get it he started to take over sugar plantations and other American-owned businesses.

The USA and Cuba

In the American government's eyes Castro was stealing American property. Not only this, he seemed to be founding a communist state right on the United States' doorstep.

President Eisenhower agreed to give weapons and ships to refugees from Cuba who wanted to overthrow Castro. When Eisenhower retired in January 1961 his plan was given the go-ahead by the new President, John F. Kennedy.

The Bay of Pigs, 1961

On 17th April 1961 a force of 1400 anti-Castro Cubans landed at the Bay of Pigs on Cuba's south coast. Castro had tanks and 20,000 men waiting. Within days the invaders were all captured or killed.

But Castro believed that Kennedy would attack again, so he asked the Russian leader, Khrushchev, for help. Khrushchev sent him shiploads of rifles, tanks, aircraft. Kennedy grew worried. He ordered a close watch to be kept on Cuba.

The Cuban Crisis, 1962

On Sunday 14th October 1962 an American U-2 spy plane flew high over the island taking photographs. They showed Russian missile launching sites being built.

What had happened was this.

Ever since the U-2 incident of 1960 (see Unit 49) Khrushchev had been making threats against the USA. These had worried Kennedy. Although the Americans already had more long-range missiles than the Russians, Kennedy ordered nearly a thousand more.

Russian missile bases

When Castro asked for help, Khrushchev saw a chance to level up the 'balance of terror'. He would threaten the USA from missile bases in her own backyard – Cuba. These would put the Russians in a position to wipe out practically every big city in the USA.

When Kennedy saw the U-2 photographs he said grimly, 'This is the week I better earn my salary'. Some advisers wanted him to send bombers to destroy the missile bases. He also thought about sending American soldiers to capture them.

American blockade

Instead, Kennedy ordered American ships and aircraft to set up a quarantine, or blockade. They were to stop any Russian ships carrying more missile equipment to Cuba. Kennedy then told Khrushchev to take away his missiles and destroy the bases. He warned that any missile fired from Cuba would be treated as a direct Russian attack on the USA and ordered 156 long-range missiles aimed at the USSR to be made ready to fire.

For ten terrifying days in October 1962 the world trembled on the edge of nuclear war. People waited in fear for the next news flash on their radios and televisions.

'Eyeball to eyeball'

The first sign of hope came at 10.32 a.m. on 24th October 1962. News reached Kennedy that twenty Russian ships heading for Cuba had stopped and turned round. 'We're eyeball to eyeball and I think the other fellow just blinked', murmured one adviser.

Finally Khrushchev ordered his soldiers in Cuba to destroy the launching sites and return the missiles to the USSR. In return, Kennedy called off the blockade and promised to leave Cuba alone.

The most dangerous crisis of the Cold War was over.

The Berlin Wall

A description of the Berlin Wall written by a British historian in 1974.

" . . . the East German . . . government decided to . . . prevent their people escaping from their particular 'workers' paradise' by walling them in.

Unfortunately, they would keep trying to escape. There were awful scenes when the Wall was erected in Berlin, with people flinging themselves out of high windows and crashing to their deaths, one of them an eighty-year-old woman who jumped from five storeys up. All in all, the Wall and the frontier fence have now [1974] claimed over 170 known victims, whose memorials stand beside the hateful barrier. As recently as 1972 its effectiveness was 'improved' by the installation of a . . . booby-trap and automatic shrapnel-firing system, designed to give the refugee no chance of survival, while relieving the guards of the necessity of shooting him in full view. Within six weeks . . . this had proved its worth."

John Terraine, *The Mighty Continent*, 1974

1 a) Who ordered the Berlin Wall to be built? Say when and explain why.
b) Do you think the people who ordered it to be built would be pleased with the result? Give reasons for your answer.
c) Suggest ways in which the Wall might have had drawbacks for these people.
d) Do you think that John Terraine approves or disapproves of the Wall? Give examples of his choice of words and incidents to explain your view.
e) Does Terraine's attitude mean that we should not trust his account?

Kennedy and Khrushchev

In June 1961 President Kennedy and Mr Khrushchev met in Vienna to talk about disagreements between their countries. Khrushchev was very unfriendly to Kennedy. Afterwards Kennedy said this to a reporter.

"I've got two problems. First, to figure out why he [acted] . . . in such a hostile way. And second, to figure out what we can do about it. I think the first part is pretty easy to explain. I think he did it because of the Bay of Pigs. I think he thought that anyone who was so young and inexperienced as to get into a mess like that could be taken, and anyone who got into it, and didn't see it through, had no guts. So he just beat hell out of me. So I've got a terrible problem. If he thinks I'm inexperienced and have no guts, until we remove those ideas we won't get anywhere with him."

In William Manchester, *The Glory and the Dream*, 1975

2 a) How long after the Bay of Pigs invasion did the Vienna meeting take place?
b) Why might Khrushchev have thought at this time that Kennedy was 'young and inexperienced' and 'had no guts'?
c) What effect did the Bay of Pigs have on relations between Cuba and the USSR?
d) Imagine that you are Kennedy, faced with the Cuba missile crisis sixteen months after this meeting. How might your beliefs about Khrushchev's opinion of you affect how you deal with the crisis?
e) Do you think that Kennedy's behaviour over the Cuba crisis of 1962 would change Khrushchev's opinion of him? Give reasons for your view.

Cuba, 1962

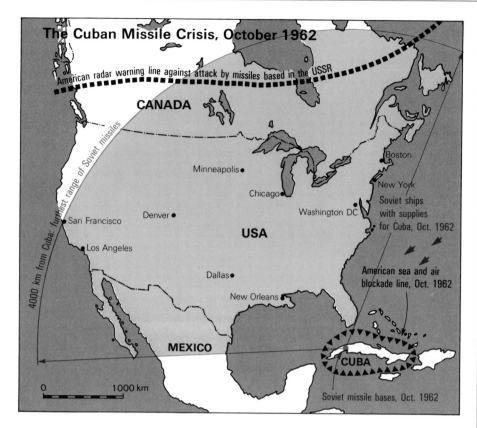

The Cuban Missile Crisis, October 1962

A cartoon in The Guardian, *25th October 1962.*

"And then I said, 'To hell with you'"

3 a) Use the map to explain how the USSR hoped to gain from having missile bases in Cuba.

b) Suggest why a blockade was a good way of dealing with the crisis for the USA.

c) In the cartoon, what has the artist imagined has happened?

d) What does the cartoon tell you about problems of dealing with a crisis in the nuclear age?

e) After the crisis, Khrushchev said that 'Mankind won'. How does the cartoon help to explain what he meant?

Vietnam lies to the south of China, in South-East Asia. Most of its people live in villages, growing rice on flat and fertile fields surrounded by jungle.

French soldiers conquered Vietnam in the 1880s. The French ruled there for the next sixty years. Then, during the Second World War, Japanese soldiers marched in and took over. Many Vietnamese hated foreign rule. They set up nationalist groups to win back their independence.

Ho Chi Minh and the French

One of the Vietnamese nationalist groups was called the Viet Minh. Its leader was a revolutionary communist named Ho Chi Minh. Ho Chi Minh wanted two things. First, an independent Vietnam. Second, a communist Vietnam.

In 1945 the Second World War ended. The Viet Minh took over the government of North Vietnam from the Japanese. But soon the French came back, wanting to rule Vietnam again. In 1946 war broke out between them and the Viet Minh.

At first the Americans were sympathetic towards Ho Chi Minh. He kept quiet about being a communist. He made the Americans believe that all he wanted was to free Vietnam from foreign rule.

But in 1949, after the victory of Mao Zedong's communists in nearby China (see Unit 62), Ho stopped pretending. The Americans saw that he was a communist. Their attitude changed. They decided that he was just a puppet for his next-door neighbour, Mao Zedong.

By 1954 the Americans were paying the French 500 million dollars a year – most of the cost of their war against the Viet Minh.

The Americans also helped the French to set up a rival government in the south of the country. Many southern Vietnamese welcomed the new government, especially when the Americans persuaded the French to promise them full independence.

The war between Ho Chi Minh's forces and the French army dragged on for eight years. It ended only when the Viet Minh trapped and crushed the French at the Battle of Dien Bien Phu in 19

North and South Vietnam

A peace conference was held in Geneva. The French agreed to leave and Vietnam was divided in two, rather like Korea (see Unit 48). Communists ruled the North and non-communists the South.

The next step was supposed to be the election of one government for the whole country. But the elections never took place – mainly because the government of South Vietnam and the Americans feared that Ho Chi Minh would win them.

So Ho Chi Minh set out to unite Vietnam by war. He ordered sabotage and terrorism against the government of South Vietnam.

As part of their worldwide plan to contain communism, the Americans sent weapons and advisers to help South Vietnam.

The domino theory

Containment was especially important to the Americans in Vietnam because of an idea that their leader from 1953 to 1961,

President Eisenhower, called the 'domino theory'.

The domino theory went like this. Asia had a lot of unsettled countries. If one of them – Vietnam, say – fell under communist rule, the Americans believed that others would follow. They would be knocked over one by one, like a line of toppling dominoes.

The Americans were especially afraid that communist China might try to take over in South-East Asia – rather like the Russians had done in Eastern Europe. So, in the 1950s and early 1960s, first President Eisenhower and then President Kennedy poured American money and weapons into South Vietnam. Kennedy sent soldiers, too – not to fight themselves, but to advise and train the South Vietnamese forces.

It was all a waste of time. By the early 1960s it was clear that the government of South Vietnam was losing the war.

The Vietcong

Ho Chi Minh had a guerilla army of 100,000 men fighting in South Vietnam by then. These guerillas were called the Vietcong. Many were communists from the North who had marched into the South along secret jungle trails.

By 1965 the Vietcong controlled large areas of South Vietnam. The country's American-backed government was close to collapse.

President Johnson and Vietnam

By now the United States had a new leader, President Lyndon B. Johnson. Johnson faced a difficult choice. He could cut his losses and let the communists take over, or he could send in American soldiers to try to stop them.

Johnson was too worried about the domino theory – and about losing face – to make the first choice. He had already ordered American aircraft to bomb railways and bridges in North Vietnam. Now he sent in American soldiers. By 1968 over 500,000 of these 'grunts', as they called themselves, were fighting in South Vietnam.

The Russians and the Chinese sent more weapons and supplies to Ho Chi Minh. Thousands more communist troops marched south along secret jungle trails to do battle with the Americans.

Warfare in Vietnam

All through the late 1960s war raged in Vietnam. It was a war of ambushes and of sudden attacks. After an attack the Vietcong would melt away into the jungle, or turn into peaceful villagers.

Ordinary villagers helped and protected the Vietcong. Sometimes they did this out of fear, sometimes out of sympathy. 'The people are the water, our armies are the fish', one Vietcong leader said.

A guerilla war like this meant that the Americans often had no enemy to strike back at. As one soldier put it, finding the Vietcong was 'like trying to identify tears in a bucket of water'.

The American fighting men grew angry and frustrated.

They sprayed vast areas of countryside with deadly chemicals to destroy the Vietcong's supply trails. They killed or maimed thousands of innocent villagers with terrible weapons like napalm fire bombs. Napalm was a burning jelly, which stuck to its victims and burned away their living flesh.

Such actions were cruel and inhuman. And they were useless.

The Vietnam War and public opinion

President Nixon and Vietnamisation

The Americans leave Vietnam, 1973

The fighting went on, even when Johnson stepped up, or 'escalated', the war by bombing cities in North Vietnam to try to force the communists to give in and make peace.

Film reports of the suffering in Vietnam were shown all over the world on television. For the first time in history, people far away from any fighting were able to see in their own homes the horror and cruelty of modern war. Millions of them came to see the Americans as cruel and bullying monsters.

The war caused bitter disagreements in the USA. Countless families mourned sons, brothers, husbands, dead in Vietnam.

By the end of the 1960s many Americans were sick and ashamed of the killing and the destruction. 'L.B.J., L.B.J., how many kids you killed today?', chanted angry demonstrators.

President Johnson saw at last that by sending American soldiers to fight in Vietnam he had led the USA into a trap. The war was destroying his country's good name in the world and setting its people against one another.

In 1968 Johnson stopped the bombing of North Vietnam and started to look for ways of making peace. But he knew that the war had made many Americans hate him so much that it was hopeless to try to get re-elected as President. He decided to retire.

Richard Nixon took over as President in 1969. Like Johnson, he wanted to end the Vietnam War. But he, too, wanted to do it without the Americans looking as if they had been beaten.

Nixon worked out a plan. He called it the 'Vietnamisation' of the war.

He set out to strengthen the South Vietnamese army. He wanted to make it seem strong enough to defend South Vietnam on its own. This would give him an excuse to withdraw all the American fighting men from Vietnam.

Nixon sent Henry Kissinger, his adviser on foreign affairs, to secret talks with North Vietnamese and Russian leaders in Moscow.

He offered to withdraw all American troops from Vietnam within six months in return for a cease-fire. When the North Vietnamese were slow to agree he started bombing their cities again in order to 'persuade' them.

A sort of agreement was finally patched together in January 1973. By March 1973 the last American soldiers had left Vietnam.

But the fighting between North and South never really stopped.

The real end of the Vietnam War came in May 1975. As frightened Vietnamese supporters of the Americans scrambled for the last places on rescue helicopters, victorious communist tanks rolled into Saigon, the capital city of South Vietnam.

The communists marked their victory by giving Saigon a new name. They called it Ho Chi Minh City.

In Korea, twenty years earlier, the Americans had claimed that they had made containment work. In Vietnam they knew, and so did everyone else, that they had failed.

American aid to Vietnam

The Vietnam War

0   200 km

CHINA

Dien Bien Phu

Hanoi

NORTH VIETNAM

LAOS

THAILAND

PHILIPPINES

American bombing raids on N. Vietnam and Vietcong-controlled areas of S. Vietnam

SOUTH VIETNAM

CAMBODIA

To Malaysia, Indonesia and rest of South-East Asia

Saigon

Area controlled by Vietcong c. 1973

★ Main American bases

American men and money sent to South Vietnam 1966–72.

Year	Military aid (thousands of millions of dollars)	Armed forces (thousands)
1966	6.1	280
1968	21.0	545
1970	16.7	330
1972	9.3	40

1 a) How does the map help you to understand why the USA feared Chinese interference in Vietnam?

b) Use the map to explain what is meant by the 'domino theory'.

c) List three different ways in which the USA tried to 'contain' communism in Vietnam.

d) How does the map suggest that American policies failed?

e) Draw two bar graphs to show: 1) the amount of US military aid to South Vietnam, and 2) the changing size of US armed forces in Vietnam.

f) Give *two* reasons why US aid increased between 1966 and 1968.

g) Give *three* reasons why it fell after 1970.

h) Why does the number of fighting men fall by a bigger percentage than the amount of aid from 1970–2?

US soldiers in Vietnam

In March 1968 US soldiers attacked the village of Son My and massacred most of the people. This poster is built up from a photograph taken just afterwards, with added words from the US government enquiry into the massacre.

A letter sent home by a young American soldier fighting in Vietnam.

"Dear Mom and Dad:

Today we went on a mission and I am not very proud of myself, my friends, or my country. We burned every hut in sight!

It was a small rural network of villages and the people were incredibly poor. My unit burned and plundered their meager possessions. Let me try to explain the situation to you.

The huts here are thatched palm leaves. Each one has a dried mud bunker inside. These bunkers are to protect the families. Kind of like air raid shelters.

My unit commanders, however, chose to think that these bunkers are offensive. So every hut we find that has a bunker we are ordered to burn to the ground.

When the ten helicopters landed this morning, in the middle of these huts, six men jumped out of each 'chopper'. We were firing the moment we hit the ground. We fired into all the huts that we could.

It is then that we burned the huts. Everyone is crying, begging and praying that we don't separate them and take husbands and fathers, sons and grandfathers. The women wail and moan.

Then they watch in terror as we burn their homes, personal possessions and food. Yes, we burn all rice and shoot all livestock."

In S. Hersch, *My Lai 4: A Report on the Massacre*, 1970

2 a) Look at the first sentence in the soldier's letter. After reading the rest of the letter do you think it is justified?

b) Can you suggest any reasons which might explain the commanders' view about houses with bunkers? Would these reasons be enough to justify the orders they gave?

c) What is the poster saying about the Vietnam War? It is trying to 1) inform, or 2) influence the person looking at it?

d) Does the evidence in the letter support the evidence in the poster?

e) Do you think 1) the letter, or 2) the poster is more reliable as evidence?

A cartoon from July 1967, when President Johnson sent the first American troops to fight in Vietnam.

'JUST GIVE US THE TOOLS AND WE'LL GET THE JOB DONE'

This cartoon of the early 1970s comments on President Nixon's policy at that time.

3 a) What does the 1967 cartoon suggest were 'the tools'?

b) What is it saying about the cost of US involvement?

c) In your own words explain the 1970s cartoon.

d) How did Nixon try to 'save face' at this time?

'He's trying to save face.'

After Cuba

'They talk about who lost and who won. Human reason won. Mankind won.'

The words are Khrushchev's, speaking after the Cuban Missile Crisis of 1962 (see Unit 50).

Kennedy felt the same. Both leaders knew that for ten days they had been close to bringing death to millions of people. They began to work harder to make such dangerous situations less likely.

It was fear that made them do this. Fear of what might happen if their countries did not learn to get on better together.

The Test Ban Treaty and the hot line, 1963

In August 1963 the USA and the USSR signed the Test Ban Treaty, agreeing to stop testing new nuclear weapons in the atmosphere or under water. They also set up a special telephone link between Washington and Moscow. On this 'hot line' their leaders could talk directly to one another. In the future, any dangerous crisis would be dealt with more quickly and with less risk of misunderstanding.

The hot line proved its value in 1967. War broke out between Israel and Egypt (see Unit 54). The USA was friendly with Israel, and the USSR with Egypt. But both took great care not to let these friendships drag them into fighting one another.

By then Kennedy was dead and Khrushchev had been sacked. But new American and Russian leaders went on trying to reduce tension. Even the long and bloody war in Vietnam (see Unit 51) was not allowed to interfere with 'détente', as these moves were called.

The Chinese leader, Mao Zedong, attacked détente. He disagreed with the Russians on other matters, too.

China and the USSR

Quarrels between the USSR and China had begun during the 1950s. Mao was angry when Khrushchev criticised Stalin (see Unit 22). And when Russian leaders started talking about peaceful co-existence and détente, he accused them of 'revisionism' – that is, of altering some of communism's most important ideas.

Secretly, Mao was worried that the USA and the USSR might one day gang up on China. So he declared that the only way to deal with American capitalism was to fight it to the death.

This kind of talk seemed like the ravings of a madman to Khrushchev. When Mao asked him to supply China with nuclear weapons, Khrushchev refused. In 1960 he cut off all Soviet aid to China and brought home the experts who had been helping the Chinese to modernise their industries.

The quarrel continued after Khrushchev was sacked. In the 1960s and 1970s Russian and Chinese leaders went on attacking each other's brands of communism.

But a lot of this arguing about whether Russians or Chinese were the best communists was just a smoke-screen. The real quarrel was about land.

The Chinese claimed that 1.5 million square kilometres of the USSR were rightfully theirs. Big armies watched and sometimes clashed on the long frontier between the two countries.

The Chinese came to fear a Russian nuclear attack. They dug hundreds of shelters deep underground – 'in case the Bear comes', as one Chinese told a reporter.

The Russians for their part feared an invasion by Chinese soldiers. China had so many people – a thousand million by the 1980s. This was three times the population of the USSR.

The enmity between China and the USSR had important effects on both countries' relations with the USA in the early 1970s.

None of the three countries wanted the other two to gang up on it, so détente between the USSR and the United States went on. And détente between the United States and China began.

American-Russian détente

A landmark in American-Russian détente came in 1972 when President Nixon flew to Moscow to sign the Strategic Arms Limitation Treaty (SALT) with the Russians.

The idea of SALT was to slow down the arms race. Each country agreed how many missiles of various types the other should have, how many submarines to fire them from, and so on. This 1972 SALT agreement was to last until 1978, when both sides agreed they would look again at the position.

The Helsinki Agreement, 1975

Another result of détente was an agreement signed in Helsinki, Finland, in 1975.

In the Helsinki Agreement Western leaders officially recognised the existing boundaries between the communist and non-communist parts of Europe. In return the Russian leader, Brezhnev, signed a Declaration of Human Rights – rights which all the governments at Helsinki said that they would allow their people. These human rights included freedom of speech and freedom from unjust arrest.

Some in the West criticised the Helsinki Agreement. They said it gave recognition to Stalin's conquests in eastern Europe in return for worthless promises. Supporters of the agreement disagreed. They hoped it might lead to communist rule becoming less harsh.

American-Chinese détente

The first sign that China was interested in détente came in 1970.

For years the Chinese government had made it very difficult for anyone from western countries to visit China. But in 1970 they invited an American table-tennis team to play there. The American government, correctly, took this as a hint that the Chinese wanted to settle some of their differences with the USA.

The man behind the Chinese move was Zhou Enlai, China's Prime Minister and Mao Zedong's right hand man. Zhou believed that China needed friends on the international scene, especially while the Russians were so unfriendly.

President Nixon's adviser, Henry Kissinger, flew to China for secret meetings with Zhou. Late in 1971 the USA agreed to communist China joining the United Nations, something it had vetoed for years. In February 1972 Nixon flew to China to meet Mao.

By the 1980s China and the USA had made important agreements on trade and other matters.

Cold War again?

But, as China and the USA became more friendly, suspicion grew again between the USSR and the USA. Russians still feared that the Americans wanted to wipe out communism, and them with it. Americans still feared that the Russians wanted to conquer the world for communism.

In December 1979 Russian soldiers marched into a small neighbour of the USSR called Afghanistan. The American Congress refused to renew the SALT agreement because of this.

The arms race in the 1980s

Both sides went on developing deadly new missiles. By the end of the 1970s the Russians had the SS-20. Its three nuclear warheads could destroy targets anywhere in Europe within fifteen minutes of being launched.

The Americans had the Cruise. The Cruise was a pilotless air-craft with a nuclear warhead fifteen times more destructive than the bomb that had wiped out Hiroshima. It could deliver its warhead to within 100 metres of a target more than 3000 kilometres away.

By the middle 1980s Cruise missiles were threatening the USSR from bases in Britain and other NATO countries, while Russian SS-20s and other missiles were targeted onto both the USA and West Europe.

START and Star Wars

Attempts were made to slow down the arms race. In June 1982 American and Russian representatives began Strategic Arms Reduction Talks (START) at Geneva in Switzerland. START was to carry on where the earlier SALT agreements had left off.

The trouble was that neither side would stop while it felt that the other was ahead. Americans didn't feel safe without more, and deadlier, nuclear weapons than the Russians. Equally, the Russians didn't feel safe without more, and deadlier, nuclear weapons than the Americans. START made little progress. Détente looked dead.

In 1983 President Reagan of the United States ordered American scientists to start work on a Strategic Defence Initiative – his 'Star Wars' plan, as people were soon calling it. The idea of Star Wars was to set up a sort of giant shield in space and use weapons like lasers to shoot down Russian missiles before they could reach the USA.

In 1985 tiny signs of hope for a safer world appeared. Reagan had increased American military strength so much that he seemed ready to start talking seriously about slowing down the arms race.

The Russians seemed ready, too. In 1985 their new leader, Mikhail Gorbachev, gave the go-ahead for more talks with the Americans. In November he travelled to Geneva to meet Reagan.

Reagan and Gorbachev met again at Reykjavik in Iceland in 1986. There they quarrelled over Star Wars. Even so, they agreed to let their advisers carry on with talks on cutting arms.

Only the future would show whether such talks could really help to slow down the arms race and so make the world a safer place.

The USSR and China

1 a) What can you learn from the map about reasons for hostility between China and the USSR?

b) What other reasons were there for this hostility?

c) Copy the map and add some notes to show the differences between the two countries in population, weapons and industrial strength.

d) What reasons can you think of for China's policy of détente with the USA?

The USSR and China in the 1980s

Areas of the USSR claimed by China

0   500   1000 km

USSR

MONGOLIA

Vladivostok

KOREA

Beijing

JAPAN

CHINA

New weapons in Europe

A photograph taken in Amsterdam in 1984.

A cartoon published in 1982.

PHEW, THAT WAS CLOSE

BRICK

2 a) Which weapon are the demonstrators particularly protesting about?

b) What idea are they trying to get over by lying on the ground?

c) Which two countries are speaking in the cartoon?

d) Which continent has been turned into a large hole?

e) How does the cartoon help to explain the action of the demonstrators?

Détente

A cartoon in the Sunday Times, *29th November 1981.*

From speeches by world leaders:

President Reagan, 1980

"We know only too well that war comes not when the forces of freedom are strong, but when they are weak. It is then that tyrants are tempted."

Mr Brezhnev, 1981

"Any dreams of achieving military superiority over the USSR would better be abandoned. If necessary, the Soviet people will be able to make further efforts to ensure the reliable defence of their country."

3 a) In the cartoon which country is represented by 1) the bear, 2) the man in the top hat?

b) What point is the cartoon making in the picture on the left? Choose two of the places named and explain why the bear and the man were interested in them.

c) Explain the point of the picture on the right. For two of the places, say why they were important to the man and the bear.

d) Would you say that the cartoon is pro-USSR, pro-USA, or neutral?

e) Do the extracts support or conflict with the cartoon's viewpoint?

f) Draw a diagonal graph to show the ups and downs in détente between the USA and the USSR. Start with the low point of the Cuban Crisis of 1962 and add: West Berlin, Test Ban Treaty, hot line, SALT, the Helsinki Agreement, Chinese-Soviet rivalry, Afghanistan, SS-20s and Cruise, START, the Strategic Defence Initiative, missile control talks, and any more recent events.

g) Does your graph show that détente has gone on at a steady rate, or has its growth been interrupted?

h) How do the cartoon and the speeches help you to understand the difficulties in the way of détente between the USSR and the USA in the 1980s?

PART SEVEN
THE MIDDLE EAST

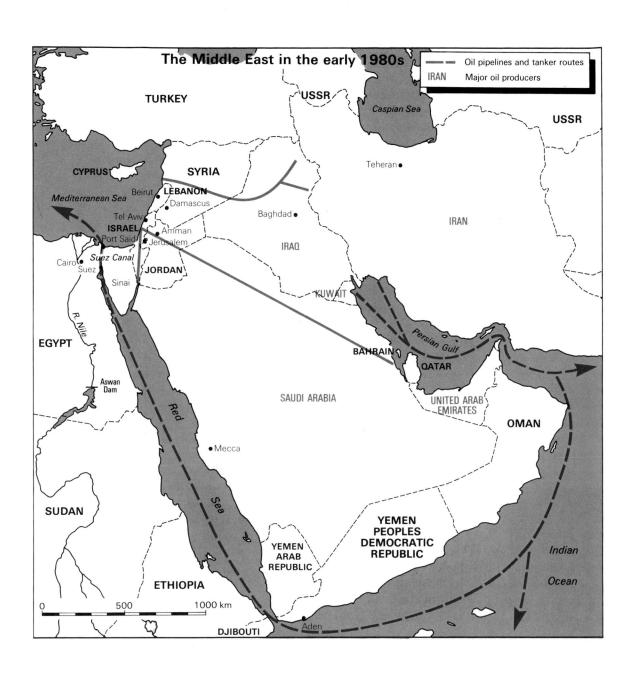

The Middle East in the early 1980s

- - - Oil pipelines and tanker routes

IRAN — Major oil producers

TURKEY

USSR

Caspian Sea

USSR

CYPRUS

SYRIA

Teheran

Mediterranean Sea

Beirut

LEBANON

Damascus

Tel Aviv

Baghdad

IRAN

ISRAEL

Amman

Port Said

Jerusalem

Cairo

Suez Canal

IRAQ

Suez

JORDAN

Sinai

KUWAIT

EGYPT

R. Nile

Persian Gulf

BAHRAIN

QATAR

Aswan
Dam

Red

SAUDI ARABIA

UNITED ARAB
EMIRATES

OMAN

SUDAN

Sea

Mecca

YEMEN
PEOPLES
DEMOCRATIC
REPUBLIC

Indian

Ocean

YEMEN
ARAB
REPUBLIC

ETHIOPIA

0   500   1000 km

DJIBOUTI   Aden

The Jews

Hundreds of years before the birth of Christ a wandering people called the Jews settled in Palestine, on the eastern shores of the Mediterranean. In 63 BC their land was overrun by the Romans.

In 66 AD the Jews rose in rebellion. The Romans defeated them and took a terrible revenge. Jews were killed, sold into slavery or sent into exile. Jews called this the Diaspora – the Scattering.

Over the next 1800 years most of the people in Palestine came to be Arabs. By 1900 only one person in ten there was a Jew.

The Jews who left Palestine scattered over Europe and the Middle East. No matter where they lived, or for how long, other peoples looked upon these Jews of the Diaspora as outsiders. Often they were persecuted. This was especially true in Europe.

The Jews kept alive their religion, their customs, their language. But their lives were often hard. And short. In the late nineteenth century thousands of Russian and Polish Jews – men, women and children – were killed in bloody massacres called *pogroms*.

The Zionist Movement

In 1897 an Austrian Jew named Theodor Herzl started the Zionist Movement. The Zionists' aim was to set up homes in Palestine for Jewish settlers. 'Why should we be aliens (outsiders) in foreign lands', wrote one Zionist, 'when the land of our forefathers is. . . still capable of receiving our people?'

At this time Palestine was ruled by Turkey. So were most of the other lands between the Mediterranean Sea and the Persian Gulf.

The people of all these lands were Arabs, speaking the same language and following the same Islamic religion.

The Middle East and the First World War

When the First World War began in 1914, Turkey became an ally of Germany and so found herself at war with Britain.

The British already controlled Egypt. British officers rode out from there to persuade the Arab peoples to rise in rebellion against the Turks. In return they promised that the Arabs would be helped to set up independent countries after the war.

The promise was broken. After the war, Britain and her ally, France, carved up between them the Arab lands they valued most. The British persuaded the League of Nations to grant them the right to rule Palestine and Mesopotamia (now Iraq), and the French took over Syria and Lebanon.

All these lands were called 'mandates'. A mandate was a sort of colony. The difference between a mandate and an ordinary colony was that the ruler of a mandate promised the League of Nations that it would prepare its people to govern themselves.

The British and Palestine

So far as Palestine was concerned, this gave the British a problem. Just two years earlier they had made another promise about Palestine to the Zionists.

The Balfour Declaration, 1917

In 1917 Arthur Balfour, the British Foreign Secretary, had sent a letter to a British Zionist leader. It said that the British government 'view with favour the establishment in Palestine of a national home for the Jewish people, and will use their best endeavours to facilitate (help) the achievement of this. . .'.

This Balfour Declaration meant that the Zionists could send more and more Jewish settlers to Palestine. In the 1920s they bought land there, set up farms, built settlements.

Zionist settlers

In the 1930s the number of Jewish immigrants rose even more, especially after the Jew-hating dictator Adolf Hitler became the ruler of Germany (see Unit 6). In 1917 there had been about 57,000 Jews in Palestine, making up 9.7 per cent of the population. Nineteen years later, in 1936, their number had risen to 384,000, or almost 34 per cent of the population.

The Arab people of Palestine were alarmed by all these newcomers pouring in and buying up their homes and farms. They struck back by attacking the Jewish settlers.

The Arab rebellion, 1936-9

In 1936 rumours spread that the British were planning to divide Palestine between Jews and Arabs. The Palestinian Arabs started a desperate full-scale revolt against British rule. They attacked British bases and ambushed military convoys. They shot down Jewish settlers as they worked in the fields.

The British used soldiers to crush the Arabs and armed 14,000 Jewish settlers to help them. Officially, the members of this force were special police. Unofficially, they were the first soldiers of an undercover Zionist army called the *Haganah*.

By 1939 the Arab rebels were beaten. But war clouds were now gathering in Europe.

The British government could not afford the money and men needed to deal with more trouble from the Arabs in Palestine, or from other Arabs who sympathised with them. So, in May 1939, it announced that it would stop immigration after five years.

Zionist leaders raged that the British had betrayed them. But they hated Hitler's Nazis even more than they now hated the British. Until they were sure that the British and their allies were going to win the Second World War, they held their fire.

Palestine after the Second World War

The Second World War ended in 1945. Very soon, tens of thousands more Jews from Europe were crowding on to leaky old ships in order to get to Palestine. Most were refugees, survivors of Hitler's concentration camps (see Unit 9). Zionist leaders like David Ben Gurion convinced them that they would be safe only in a land whose people and rulers were Jews like themselves.

Both Jews and Arabs now believed that they had to fight to survive. To the Jews survival meant getting into Palestine; to the Palestinian Arabs survival meant keeping them out. Soon they were ambushing, bombing and killing one another.

To reduce the trouble in Palestine the British tried to keep out the Jewish newcomers, stopping their ships and turning them back. This triggered off ruthless anti-British attacks by groups of Zionist terrorists like the Irgun.

The USA and the Zionists

The United Nations' partition plan, 1947

The founding of Israel, 1948, and the First Arab-Israeli War

The Palestinians

Zionist saboteurs blew up bridges and power stations. Gunmen raided military camps and killed British soldiers. In July 1946 the Irgun dynamited the King David Hotel, the British headquarters in Jerusalem, killing ninety-one people.

Despite such actions, the Zionists won a lot of international sympathy, especially in the USA. Many Jews lived there and politicians hoped to win their support by backing Zionism. President Truman urged the British government to allow into Palestine every Jewish immigrant who wanted to go there.

In 1947 Truman persuaded the United Nations Organisation to vote in favour of a plan to partition, or divide, Palestine. The UN plan meant that the Jewish people would at last have an independent homeland of their own. It gave them just over half of Palestine, including much of the most fertile land.

Zionists accepted the United Nations' plan. But the Arabs of Palestine turned it down. Why should we hand over half our homeland to foreigners? they asked angrily.

The British tried to keep the peace between warring Jews and Arabs. But they came under attack by both sides. In May 1948 they pulled out their soldiers and officials and left.

Ben Gurion immediately said that the Zionists were taking over a large part of Palestine and setting up their own country called Israel. Ben Gurion became its first Prime Minister.

Arab countries such as Egypt and Jordan sent armies to destroy Israel at birth. There was fierce fighting. But Israel beat off the Arab attacks. A cease-fire was arranged early in 1949.

The Israelis, as the Jews in Palestine now called themselves, finished up with more land than the United Nations' plan had offered them. It included part of Jerusalem, a holy city to Jews and Arabs alike. The non-Israeli part of Jerusalem was controlled by the Arab government of Jordan.

The people who suffered most in this 1948-9 war were the Arab peoples of Palestine – the Palestinians, as they now began to call themselves. The war made more than a million homeless.

Some Palestinians fled from their homes so that they would be safe during the expected battles between the invading Arab armies and the Haganah. Others were driven out by the Israelis.

When the war ended the Israeli government refused to let the Palestinian refugees return to their old homes. Instead, the refugees squatted in miserable camps just outside Israel's borders, in the neighbouring Arab countries of Egypt, Jordan and Lebanon.

Across the barbed wire fences that marked Israel's border, the refugees could see Israeli farmers working land they believed was rightfully theirs. In a few years, a third of Israel's Jewish population was living on land once owned by Arabs.

The Palestinian refugee camps became breeding grounds of hatred. Their people clung to the hope that one day Israel would be destroyed so that they could go back to their old homes.

Zionism

The cover of a Zionist publication, 1938. It shows a Zionist's idea of Palestine.

David Ben Gurion later described how he felt, at the age of twenty, on his first night in Palestine, in 1906.

"I did not sleep. I was among the rich smell of corn. I heard the baying of donkeys and the rustling of leaves in the orchard. Above were the massed clusters of stars clear against the deep blue firmament [sky]. My heart overflowed with happiness as if I had entered the realm of joy. . . A dream was celebrating its victory. I am in Eretz [the land of] Israel, in a Hebrew village called Ptach Tikva – 'Gate of Hope'."

David Ben Gurion in Amos Elon, *The Israelis: Founders and Sons*, 1971

1 a) What was the aim of the Zionist movement?

  b) Explain why David Ben Gurion felt so happy and excited.

  c) Why do you think the settlers had named their village 'Gate of Hope'?

  d) Who do the people at the bottom of the picture represent?

  e) How does the artist try to arouse sympathy for them?

  f) Is he showing Palestine as it was, or as Zionists believed it could be?

  g) What important fact about Palestine does the artist *not* show? Can you suggest why?

  h) What do you think is the picture's message? Put it into words that might be used as a radio 'commercial'.

  i) What would be the feelings of a Palestinian Arab about the picture? Put these into words that might be used as a radio 'commercial'.

Jews and Arabs

A ship arriving at Haifa in Palestine in 1946 with 1300 passengers on board.

2 a) Copy out the banner. Try to fill in the words that are blocked out by the mast.
   b) Where have the people on the ship come from?
   c) What do they want to do?
   d) The men in white shirts in the foreground are British port officials. Why are the people on the ship looking at them anxiously?
   e) Imagine you are one of the passengers. The others choose you to speak on their behalf. What would you say to the port officials?

Population of Palestine and Israel.

Year	Arabs	Jews
(Palestine)		
1922	590,000	84,000
1932	770,000	180,000
1937	850,000	400,000
1940	950,000	460,000
(Israel)		
1952	250,000	720,000
1962	170,000	1,950,000
1967	220,000	2,350,000

3 a) Draw bar graphs to show changes in 1) the Arab population,
2) the Jewish population, of Palestine-Israel.
   b) Explain the fall in Arab population by 1952, and its fall later.
   c) Explain the rise in the number of Jews, 1) before, and 2) after
1940.

Arab and Jewish views of British rule in Palestine.

An old Palestinian living in a refugee camp in Lebanon.
"Put this in your book. The British cheated us. They promised us freedom
and instead we had the Mandate. And do you know what the policy of the
Mandate was? It said that we, the people of Palestine, were not mature
enough to govern ourselves. . . And worse than that even, they brought
ruin to our land and made us homeless. You, the British, brought
foreigners to Palestine and made us exiles."

In J. Dimbleby, *The Palestinians*, 1979

Ben Hecht, a leading American Zionist.
"The Jews of America are with you [Zionists in Palestine]. . . You are the
grin they wear. . . Every time you. . . send a British railroad sky-high. . . or
let go with your guns and bombs at the British betrayers and invaders of
your homeland, the Jews of America make a little holiday in their hearts."

New York Herald Tribune, May 1947

4 a) Explain what the Palestinian means by 'the Mandate'.
   b) Who are the 'foreigners' he speaks of?
   c) Do you agree or disagree that the British 'cheated' the Palestinians?
Give reasons for your answer.
   d) What was happening in Palestine at the time Ben Hecht wrote this?
   e) What facts could you use to 1) support, and 2) contradict his view
that the British were 'betrayers and invaders of our homeland'?
   f) Why were American Jews important to Palestine's future, both at
this time and later?

5 Choose any three of the following and write a short paragraph about
each to show its importance in the history of Palestine since 1900.

The Zionist Movement	The Arab rebellion
The Balfour Declaration	The Irgun
The British Mandate	David Ben Gurion
Zionist immigration	The founding of Israel

Egypt

Egypt is the strongest of Israel's Arab neighbours. She is much bigger, with more land and more people – thirty million in the 1970s compared with Israel's three million.

Most Egyptians live along the fertile, well-watered banks of the River Nile. The other nine-tenths of their country is desert.

The British in Egypt

Up to the 1940s the British ruled Egypt. Many Egyptians hated this. They often rioted and marched through the streets in angry demonstrations.

After the Second World War the British left the Egyptians to run their own affairs. But they left troops in part of Egypt called the Canal Zone. The troops were there to guard the Suez Canal, an important waterway linking the Mediterranean to the Red Sea. The canal was owned by the British and French. To many Egyptians this was a sign that colonial rule was by no means ended.

In 1952 a group of army officers drove out Egypt's idle and pleasure-loving King, Farouk, and took over the government. Soon after, in 1954, the British government agreed to withdraw its troops from the Canal Zone.

President Nasser

One of the leaders of the officers was Gamal Abdel Nasser. In 1956 Nasser became Egypt's President.

Nasser made many improvements. He gave farmers more land and sent experts to advise them on better ways of using it.

Nasser also built a great new dam across the River Nile at a place called Aswan. The dam was completed in 1970 with help from the USSR. It brought water to areas which had been too dry to farm and gave Egypt another 800,000 hectares of crop-growing land. It also produced over five times more electric power than the whole of Egypt had used before.

Nasser and Israel

But Nasser wanted to do more than make life better for Egypt's people. He thought that it was Egypt's duty as a leading Arab country to help the Palestinians to get back their land from the Israelis. So he helped to train and arm Palestinian guerillas, called *fedayeen*, to carry out hit-and-run raids into Israel.

By 1956 the Israelis had had enough of this. They hatched a plot to bring about Nasser's downfall. The Israelis' fellow plotters were the British and the French, who had their own reasons for wanting to get rid of Nasser.

The Suez Affair, 1956

The British and French quarrel with Nasser was over the Suez Canal. Although the British had taken away their troops, they and the French still owned the Canal. Then, on 26th July 1956, Nasser announced that he was taking it over to get money to pay for the Aswan Dam.

The British and the French governments were furious. They decided to get rid of Nasser. The final details of their plot with Israel were settled at a secret meeting in France between the Israeli

The Suez War, 1956

Prime Minister, Ben Gurion, and the British and French Foreign Ministers. The meeting took place on 24th October 1956.

Five days later, on 29th October, Israeli troops invaded Egypt, driving forward across the Sinai Desert towards the Suez Canal.

The day after, 30th October, the French and British claimed that they were worried about damage to the Suez Canal. To protect it, they ordered both the Israeli and the Egyptian armies to keep at least ten miles away.

As had been planned, Israel said that she would obey. Why not? Her soldiers were still nowhere near the Canal anyway.

But Nasser refused. Why should he? To do so would mean voluntarily giving up an important part of his own country – which his soldiers already controlled.

On 31st October British and French aircraft began to bomb Egyptian airfields. They destroyed practically the whole Egyptian air force on the ground.

On 5th November British and French soldiers landed near the Egyptian city of Port Said. They captured the city, but the Egyptians struck back by sinking scores of ships to block the Canal.

Rows, protests and demonstrations broke out all over the world over this Suez War. Arab sympathisers with the Egyptians blew up desert pipelines carrying oil to ports for shipping to Western Europe. The USSR threatened to use nuclear missiles to help the Egyptians. Most important of all, the Americans stopped financial help to Britain until the attack was called off.

Because of all this opposition the attackers had to withdraw from Egypt. A United Nations Emergency Force (UNEF) was set up. Its blue-helmeted soldiers moved into the area to keep the peace along the border between Egypt and Israel.

Nasser after Suez

The Suez War was a disaster for the plotters. Far from bringing about the overthrow of Nasser, it made him a hero. His picture could be seen in shops, cafés, homes and workplaces all over the Arab world, from North Africa to the Persian Gulf.

Nasser came to see himself as the leader not just of the Egyptian people, but of all Arabs. He now felt even more strongly that it was his duty to destroy Israel and make Palestine an Arab land once more. He also wanted to make sure that Egypt suffered no more Israeli attacks.

Nasser built up Egypt's army and air force with weapons from the USSR. He made military alliances with Syria and Jordan, two of Israel's other Arab neighbours.

By 1967 Nasser was ready for a final showdown. His soldiers marched through Cairo carrying blood-red death's head banners with the slogan 'Death to Israel'. 'All Egypt is now prepared to plunge into total war which will put an end to Israel', Cairo Radio told the world on 17th May.

Nasser was sure that Egypt and her allies would win the coming war and that Israel would be destroyed. So were other Arabs. Their newspapers printed cartoons showing a scared and tiny Israeli being crushed by a gigantic Arab soldier.

The Israelis knew they had to fight or die. So they struck first.

The Six Day War, 1967

On 5th June 1967 Israeli war planes wiped out the powerful Egyptian air force on the ground while its pilots were eating breakfast. Israeli tanks then smashed the Egyptian army in Sinai and raced across the desert to the banks of the Suez Canal.

The Israelis then turned against Jordan, who had joined in the war to support Egypt. They drove the Jordanians out of their part of Jerusalem and overran the rest of Palestine up to the banks of the River Jordan. This gave them the area known as the 'West Bank'.

Finally, Israel dealt with Syria. Israeli soldiers seized the Golan Heights, a part of Syria overlooking Israel. In just six days they had defeated all their enemies and won the war.

The development of Israel

Israel's crushing victory in the Six Day War of 1967 was one sign of how strong it had grown since 1948. Its population was approaching three million people. Many were more immigrants from abroad. Some were European and American Jews who came to Israel eager to play a part in building the new Jewish homeland. Others were refugees who had been driven from their homes in Arab countries as a result of the Arab-Israeli wars.

The hard work of such newcomers helped to make Israel strong. They planted a hundred million trees. Many joined farming settlements called *kibbutzim*, where they sweated to turn desert into fertile land. On a *kibbutz* the workers grew crops of vegetables and fruit to sell for high prices in Europe.

The Israelis also built roads, houses, schools, hospitals, whole new towns. They set up nuclear power stations and modern factories to make a wide range of valuable goods for export – skilfully cut diamonds, fashionable clothes, chemical products. Israel became a prosperous, modern country, with ways of life more like those of the USA and Europe than those of its Arab neighbours.

But the changes cost a lot of money.

The USA and Israel

A great deal of it came in gifts from Jews in the USA. American Jews also made sure that their government went on helping Israel. In particular, they saw to it that Israel's army and air force were never short of the latest weapons.

Such equipment was vital to Israel. Every young Israeli, man or woman, had to spend time in the army – three years in the case of a man, twenty months for a woman. When their training was completed they kept their uniforms at home, ready to become fighting soldiers at a moment's notice.

The help given by the USA made many Arabs look upon Israel as an American colony in disguise.

The Americans had good reasons for being interested in the Middle East. The main one was oil. In 1980 alone the USA imported 261 million tonnes to power its industries – and 34 per cent of it came from the Arab countries of the Middle East.

Israel and its neighbours

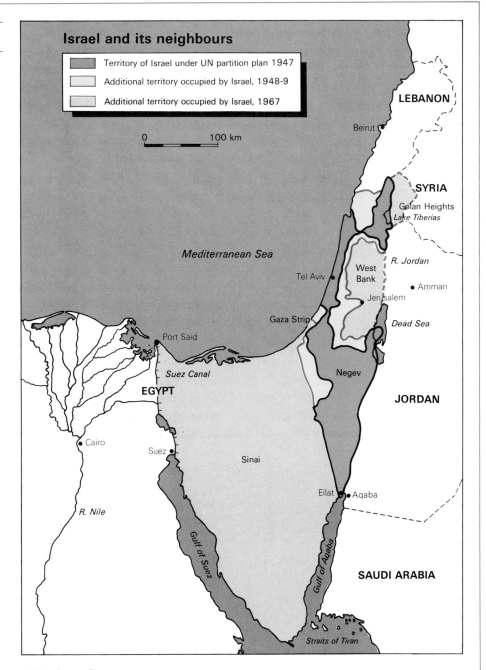

Israel and its neighbours

- Territory of Israel under UN partition plan 1947
- Additional territory occupied by Israel, 1948-9
- Additional territory occupied by Israel, 1967

0   100 km

LEBANON

Beirut

SYRIA

Golan Heights
Lake Tiberias

Mediterranean Sea

R. Jordan

Tel Aviv

West Bank

Amman

Jerusalem

Gaza Strip

Dead Sea

Port Said

Negev

Suez Canal

EGYPT

JORDAN

Cairo

Suez

Sinai

Eilat   Aqaba

R. Nile

Gulf of Suez

Gulf of Aqaba

SAUDI ARABIA

Straits of Tiran

1 Look at the map.

a) Measuring along the Mediterranean coast, how long in kilometres was the territory controlled by Israel in   1947,   1949,   1967?

b) East from Tel Aviv, how wide was Israel in   1947,   1949,   1967?

c) Do these distances suggest any reasons why the Israelis   1) struck first when they thought they were about to be attacked in 1967,   2) refused to give up the Left Bank to the Palestinians after 1967?

d) What reasons do you think the Israelis had for keeping   1) the Egyptian desert areas of Sinai,   2) the Syrian Golan Heights?

e) How does the map help to explain   1) why there is a Palestinian refugee problem,   2) why this problem has been difficult to solve?

f) How might an Israeli use the map to justify Israel's actions since 1947?

g) How might an Arab use it to condemn Israel's actions since 1947?

Before the Suez War

Part of President Nasser's speech on 26th July 1956, announcing that he was nationalising the Suez Canal.

"In 1856 the Suez Canal Company was formed... Egypt undertook to provide... workers for digging the Canal... One hundred and twenty thousand workers died digging the Canal for nothing; they dug the canal with our lives, our skeletons, our bones and our blood...

The Canal Company annually takes £35,000,000. Why shouldn't we take it ourselves?

... They sucked our blood... and stole our rights. Today... we retrieve those rights...

At this moment as I talk to you some of your Egyptian brethren... have started to take over the Canal Company and its property and to control shipping in the Canal — the Canal... which goes through Egyptian territory, which is part of Egypt and which is owned by Egypt."

In H. Browne, *Suez and Sinai, 1971*

Part of a confidential letter sent by the British Prime Minister, Sir Anthony Eden, to President Eisenhower of the USA on 6th September 1956.

"In the 1930s Hitler established his position by... acts of aggression... His actions were tolerated and excused by the majority of the population of Western Europe. It was argued... that Hitler... was entitled to do what he liked in his own territory...

Similarly, the seizure of the Suez Canal is, we are convinced, the opening gambit... by Nasser to expel all Western influences and interests from Arab countries. He believes that if he can get away with this... he will be able to mount revolutions... in Saudi Arabia, Jordan, Syria and Iraq... These new governments will in effect be Egyptian satellites, if not Russian ones. They will have to place their united oil resources under the control of... Egypt and under Russian influence. When that moment comes Nasser can deny oil to Western Europe and we... shall all be at his mercy."

In H. Browne, *Suez and Sinai, 1971*

2 a) Who owned the Suez Canal Company up to 1956?
  b) Give two reasons why Nasser believed that Egypt had the right to take over ownership of the Suez Canal.
  c) If you were an Egyptian listening to this speech, which two phrases would most stick in your mind?
  d) In what way did Eden claim that Nasser was like Hitler?
  e) What did Eden claim would happen to other governments in the Middle East if Nasser 'can get away with this'?
  f) Which point made by Eden would be most likely to worry an American President?
  g) Using the text and these two pages of sources, make a list of the main events of the Suez crisis, from Nasser's nationalisation of the Canal to the sending of UNEF. Wherever possible, give the dates of the events.

The Suez War and after

The Times 2nd November 1956.

ANGRY COMMENT IN U.S.

'TRICKERY AND DECEIT'

From Our Own Correspondent

WASHINGTON, Nov. 1

President Eisenhower's restrained declaration of a policy of non-involvement in the Middle East crisis is hardly reflected in the bitter denunciation and anger vented by most American commentators on Britain and France for intervening in the hostilities—and by now the impression has been fostered that it is they rather than Israel who resorted to force of arms.

The Daily Mirror 25th November 1956.

U.N. TELLS BRITAIN QUIT SUEZ

THE United Nations last night demanded the immediate withdrawal of British, French and Israeli forces from Egypt.

The demand came in a resolution put before the General Assembly by the 17-nation Asian-Africa Group—WITH THE SUPPORT OF AMERICA.

The vote in favour was 65 to 1.

Earlier, in the Commons, Sir Anthony Eden told M.P.s that British troops would not leave Egypt until a United Nations force took over.

A United Nations resolution calling for the setting up of such a force was passed last night by sixty-five votes to nil.

3 a) What information about 1) American opinion, 2) American action is there in these extracts?

b) Look back at Sir Anthony Eden's letter to President Eisenhower. With the help of the newspaper extracts, write a reply from Eisenhower to Eden, explaining why he cannot support him in the Suez War.

c) Why do you think it was the Asian-Africa Group which put forward the resolution at the UN?

Part of a speech by President Nasser in 1960.

"Israel does not merely imply those who raped Palestine and entrenched themselves there. . . after having massacred its lawful population. Israel also means the force of evil and treachery, and a colonialist conspiracy to stamp out Arabism. . .as. . .in 1956."

In H. Browne, *Suez and Sinai, 1971*

4 a) Who does Nasser mean by 1) 'those who raped Palestine', and 2) Palestine's 'lawful population'?

b) What event in 1956 is Nasser referring to?

c) What does he mean by calling this event a 'colonialist conspiracy'? Does the evidence suggest that his claim is true or false?

The PLO

After their crushing victory in the Six Day War of 1967, the Israelis refused to give back the lands that they had conquered. The Palestinians became worse off than ever. Even more were driven from their homes.

The defeat of the Arab armies made the Palestinians give up hope of Egypt, or any other Arab state, winning back their homeland for them. They would have to regain it by their own efforts.

The Palestinians had already organised themselves into separate *fedayeen* guerilla groups. Now these groups joined to form the Palestine Liberation Organisation – the PLO. Its best known leader was a bearded engineer turned guerilla leader, Yasser Arafat.

The PLO set up military camps in Jordan and Lebanon to train young Palestinians for war against Israel. 'I have learned to handle a rifle and many other weapons', one thirteen-year-old boy recruit told a visitor. 'You cannot fight Israel with words.'

The PLO attacks

The PLO also used other kinds of violence to draw world attention to the Palestinian cause.

In 1968 PLO guerillas made a bomb attack on an Israeli jet at Athens airport. In 1970 they hi-jacked three western airliners and blew them up in the Jordanian desert. In 1972 a breakaway Palestinian terrorist group shot dead eleven members of Israel's athletics team at the Munich Olympic Games.

The PLO attitude was that any action that harmed Israel or its supporters was justified. If innocent civilians suffered that was sad, but it could not be helped.

Israel strikes back

Israeli troops hit back fiercely. They raided Jordan and Lebanon. These raids often killed far more innocent people than had died in the Palestinian attacks to which they were replying. The Israelis' idea was to force Jordan and Lebanon to clamp down on the PLO.

The plan succeeded in Jordan. In September 1970 the soldiers of Jordan's King Hussein drove the PLO out of their country in a short but bloody war. The PLO called this 'Black September'. They moved to set up new bases in Lebanon.

In November 1974 Yasser Arafat was invited to put the Palestinian point of view to the United Nations General Assembly.

Yasser Arafat

With a pistol strapped to his hip, Arafat told the Assembly, 'I have come bearing an olive branch and a freedom fighter's gun. Do not let the olive branch fall from my hand.'

Arafat's 'olive branch' was a scheme to replace Israel with a new state in which Arabs and Jews would be equal citizens. There was one problem. Before such a state could be set up, Jewish-run Israel would have to be destroyed.

Arafat knew that this was just a dream. He soon became more concerned with gaining land where the Palestinians could set up a country of their own.

The Palestinians and the Left Bank

The favourite choice for such a country was the Israeli-occupied West Bank. In 1976 Arafat persuaded the United Nations General Assembly to vote its support for setting up a Palestinian state there.

But the Israelis showed no sign of being willing to give up the Left Bank. From the moment they occupied it in 1967 they had built fortified settlements there as fast as they could.

What about Egypt during these years after the 1967 war?

President Sadat of Egypt

The Arab defeat had been a terrible blow to Nasser. He continued to scheme against Israel, but in October 1970 he died from a heart attack. Anwar Sadat took his place as President.

Compared with Nasser, Sadat was little known. He was keen to make the Arab peoples respect him. So he built up Egypt's armed forces again and made another military agreement with Syria.

The Yom Kippur War, 1973

On 6th October 1973 both countries suddenly attacked Israel. The date was carefully chosen. It was the day of a Jewish religious festival called *Yom Kippur*. The Israelis were in a holiday mood and many soldiers were on leave. The last thing they expected was to have to start fighting for their lives.

In this October, or Yom Kippur, War of 1973 the Arab armies were more successful than ever before. Egyptian soldiers smashed through Israeli defences along the Suez Canal and advanced into Sinai. Syrian helicopters and tanks recaptured the Golan Heights.

Once they recovered from the shock, the Israelis fought back fiercely. The Americans rushed war planes and other weapons to them to replace ones destroyed in the first fighting. The Israelis drove back their Egyptian and Syrian attackers. After three weeks the fighting was ended by yet another uneasy cease-fire.

After Yom Kippur

The Yom Kippur War worried both the USA and the USSR. The Americans supported Israel, while the Russians backed Israel's Arab neighbours. Yet neither wanted to be dragged into war over the Middle East.

The Yom Kippur War gave the Americans another worry, too. After it, the oil-producing Arab countries, led by the USA's main supplier, Saudi Arabia, refused to sell them any more oil unless they gave less help to Israel.

For both reasons American governments worked hard to persuade Israel and the Arab countries to become more friendly.

President Nixon sent his Secretary of State, Henry Kissinger, jetting between Israel, Egypt and Syria to thrash out a peace agreement. In late 1973 Kissinger persuaded Sadat and Mrs Golda Meir, the Prime Minister of Israel, to agree on certain points.

As a first step, the troops of the two sides – still angrily face to face – separated to let UN soldiers move into position between them. Arrangements were made for meetings between Arab and Israeli leaders to try to work out 'a final, just and lasting peace'.

The cost of keeping Egypt's armed forces always ready for war with Israel was helping to keep the Egyptian people poor. When Sadat quarrelled with the Russians in 1974, Kissinger saw to it that the American government loaned him a lot of money to strengthen Egypt's industries.

Sadat and Begin

In 1977 Sadat surprised everyone by flying to Israel to try to make peace. He said that Egypt was ready to recognise Israel and live in friendship with her – something which no Arab country had ever said before. In return he wanted Israel to give back some of the Arab lands she had overrun.

Menachem Begin was now the Prime Minister of Israel. Begin was a hard-line Zionist who had led the Irgun terrorist group in the last days of the British mandate. His only concern was the safety and strength of Israel. The last thing he seemed likely to do was to hand back any land to the Arabs.

But Begin had reasons of his own for needing to make a deal with Sadat.

Israel's internal problems

The main one was that 2800 Israelis had been killed and 8000 wounded in the Yom Kippur War. This was many more casualties than Israel had suffered in any previous war. Out of a population of barely three million, the country could not afford such losses.

Another reason was that Israel, too, was being slowly crippled by the need to be always ready for war. In 1974 it had spent 40 per cent of its Gross National Product – the value of all the goods and services it produced – on its armed forces. Such massive spending led to steep price rises and ever-increasing taxes.

Another problem for Begin was growing disunity among Israel's people. One of the main divisions was between Israelis of European origin and the growing number who had come from eastern lands.

These eastern, or Sephardic, Israelis were usually poorer than the European Israelis. They were less well housed and less well educated. And they had less influence. By the middle of the 1970s they made up over half the country's population. Yet in Israel's Parliament, the *Knesset*, only two out of every ten members were Sephardic.

Problems such as these helped to cause strikes and demonstrations in Israel. So when the Americans made it clear to Begin that they wanted him to make a deal with Sadat, he agreed.

The Camp David Agreement, 1978

President Carter of the USA played a leading part in working out the agreement. Its main outline was drawn up in September 1978, at a meeting between Carter, Sadat and Begin at Camp David in the USA.

The Camp David Agreement led to the signing of a full peace treaty between Egypt and Israel in 1979. But the peace was a very shaky one.

Begin agreed to hand back land in Sinai to Egypt. But he made no move to give the Left Bank to the Palestinians or the Golan Heights to Syria.

The death of Sadat, 1981

Other Arabs attacked Sadat as a traitor for signing the treaty with Israel. In 1981 he was shot dead by some of his own soldiers while he was taking the salute at an army parade.

The Palestinians

From a book by a British journalist who worked in Israel in the 1960s.

" . . . it is still possible to come upon a deserted Arab village wrapped into the hills, its walls gaping, the roofs long vanished . . . Tractors drive past. The neighbouring kibbutz is likely to be farming the village's land . . . To the Israelis that kibbutz requires no more vindication [justifying] than the annual harvest or the blue sky overhead. To the Palestinians, the ruined walls of the village provide the only history they care to remember – a nightmare of the past which is also a prophecy for the future."

D. Pryce-Jones, *The Face of Defeat*, 1974

About the same time a fourteen-year-old Palestinian boy in a refugee camp spoke to a French reporter.

"My parents live in the camp over the road. They lost their home in 1948 and then had to get out again in 1967. Nobody can take that kind of life. Life is very hard in the tents. When it rains all the blankets get wet, and you have to huddle up together to keep warm. I want to join the fedayeen to liberate our country, and I think everybody ought to join the commandos, so as to change this terrible way of living."

G. Chaliland, *The Palestinian Resistance*, 1969

1 a) How do you think the village in the first source came to be ruined?
b) Explain what is meant by a *kibbutz*.
c) Imagine you are one of the Jewish settlers on this *kibbutz* and are showing a visitor the ruined Arab village. How would you explain it?
d) Which details in the boy's statement would you use to explain why the first author describes the village as 'a nightmare of the past'?
e) How does the Palestinian boy help to explain what the first writer means when he describes the village as 'a prophecy for the future'?

Peace moves

A cartoon from The Guardian *in November 1977.*

2 a) Which country is the man coming from and where is he going?
b) What is his name?
c) Why is he visiting the other country?
d) Explain why the sharks on 1) the right, and 2) the left, object to his visit.
e) Describe one result of his visit.
f) Test your knowledge of the *Old Testament*. Where did the cartoonist get the idea for his picture from?

Palestinians in Lebanon

In the 1980s many obstacles still stood on the road to lasting peace between Israel and the Arab peoples. The biggest had been there ever since Israel was born – how to give the Palestinian Arab refugees a real homeland again.

The Palestinians' main base was still in Lebanon. Here they ran their camps in their own way, independent of the Lebanese government. Many Lebanese hated the Palestinians as troublesome intruders. But their government was in no condition to deal with the problem.

About half of Lebanon's three million people were Muslims and half were Christians. For years the two religious groups had lived in peace, sharing the powers of government between them. But the Muslims began to believe that the Christians were treating them unfairly. In 1975 this belief, plus disagreements about how to deal with the Palestinians, helped to start a civil war.

War in Lebanon

Outsiders soon joined in the fighting. Apart from the Palestinians there were soldiers from Syria, whose government hoped to turn Lebanon into a puppet state. By 1977 Syrian troops controlled roughly half of the country. The fighting in Lebanon went on, however, becoming more confused with every month that passed.

Israel and Lebanon

In the summer of 1982, Israeli tanks rolled across Lebanon's border with Israel. The Israeli Prime Minister, Menachem Begin, said that his government's aim was to destroy PLO guerilla bases near Israel's borders.

In fact, Begin planned to impose peace in Lebanon at the point of Israeli guns. Then he intended to set up a government, led by Lebanese Christian politicians, which would do what Israel wanted. His idea was that a friendly Lebanon would act as a buffer to protect Israel against future attacks.

The Israeli plan failed. For a time they did drive most of Arafat's PLO fighters out of Lebanon and they pushed back the Syrians. But no friendly and obedient government took over the country. Instead the fighting grew even more confused and bloody.

Soon it became difficult to know who was fighting whom. Israelis fought Palestinians, Palestinians fought Lebanese, Lebanese fought other Lebanese, Syrians fought Palestinians, Palestinians fought other Palestinians – the permutations seemed endless.

So did the fighting. Weeks turned into months, months into years, and still it went on. In Beirut, Lebanon's capital, the shell-cratered streets echoed endlessly with the thud of explosions and the rattle of gunfire. Every day the list of dead – Lebanese, Palestinians, Israelis – grew longer.

In 1985 growing criticism of the war in Israel forced the Israeli government to withdraw its soldiers. But war-torn Lebanon went on being battered by bombings, shellings and massacres.

Iran and the Shah

Life was no more peaceful on the eastern edge of the Middle East. Here the Arab lands meet those of a people called the Iranians.

Iran, the Iranians' country, is rich in oil. Before 1979 it was ruled by an emperor called the Shah. The Shah used the money from Iran's many oil wells to try to make the country more modern and western in its ways. Because he was a strong anti-communist, the Americans gave him a lot of support.

Many Iranians hated the Shah. For one thing, most of them were desperately poor. For another, he ruled as a dictator, throwing into prison or driving from the country anyone who criticised him. Worse still, many of his policies went against their religious beliefs.

The Iranian Revolution, 1979

Most Iranians are Muslim followers of the religion of Islam. When the Shah's modernising changes came into conflict with traditional Islamic beliefs, bitter quarrels began. On one side were supporters of change and new ways. On the other were supporters of old ways and customs – Islamic fundamentalists.

In December 1978 half a million of the Shah's opponents took to the streets of Iran's capital, Teheran, waving banners with slogans like 'Death to the Shah' and 'Hang the American Puppet'. A month later, in January 1979, the Shah fled from the country.

The Ayotollah Khomeini

An elderly Islamic religious leader called the Ayatollah Khomeini became Iran's real ruler. 'Do not allow the Westerners and their lackeys [servants] to dominate you', Khomeini told the Iranian people.

In November 1979 400 of Khomeini's student followers took him at his word. They stormed into the United States' Embassy in Teheran and took fifty Americans as hostages. It was more than a year before the American government managed to persuade Khomeini to set them free.

Khomeini stopped the Shah's westernising policies and started running Iran strictly according to the ancient laws and teachings of Islam. He forbade people to drink alcohol. He said women should only appear in public with their heads and bodies fully covered.

Despite such strict rules about personal behaviour – and severe punishments for breaking them – Khomeini's ideas appealed strongly to many Iranians. They were sick of being told to copy the West. Khomeini made them proud of their own background.

The Gulf War, 1980

Khomeini fiercely criticised other leaders of Islamic countries who did not share his fundamentalist views. This helped to start a war between Iran and a neighbouring Arab country called Iraq. In 1980 Iraq's soldiers invaded Iran in order to overthrow Khomeini and grab some of Iran's richest oil wells.

They failed to do either. In 1987 Khomeini was still in power and the Gulf War between Iraq and Iran was still going on. Despite many thousands of deaths – an estimated 100,000 Iraquis and 250,000 Iranians by 1986 – neither side had gained from it.

It seemed that peace was just as much a dream in this part of the Middle East as it was in the Lebanon.

The 'Palestine problem'

In 1967 an American writer described how he saw the 'Palestine problem'.

"Stripped of propaganda and sentiment the Palestine problem is, simply, the struggle of two different peoples for the same strip of land. For the Jews, the establishment of Israel was a Return, with all the mystical significance the capital R implies. For the Arabs it was another invasion. This had led to three wars between them in twenty years. Each has been a victory for the Jews. With each victory the size of Israel has grown. So has the number of Arab homeless . . . to find a solution which will satisfy both peoples is like trying to square a circle."

I. F. Stone, *New York Review of Books*, 3rd August 1967

Also in 1967, a British historian suggested ways to solve the problem.

"The Palestinian Arabs could (a) be given monetary compensation for the loss of their property situated in Israel; (b) be given an extra indemnity for having been forced, as innocent victims of the conflict between Israel and the Arab states, to spend twenty years as refugees; (c) be given the option of either returning to their former homes, on condition of becoming loyal citizens of Israel . . . or else being settled on good land *outside* Israel; but for Israel to offer the choice of returning home . . . is psychologically very important for producing a change of heart among the refugees. If Israel appealed to the world to help her raise a fund for these four purposes, money would pour in."

Arnold Toynbee, *Encounter*, October 1967

1 a) What did I. F. Stone see as the basic 'Palestine problem' in 1967?

b) From what you have read in the units on the Middle East, do you agree with him?

c) Why do you think that neither 1) the Israelis, nor 2) the Palestinian Arabs, showed any interest in Arnold Toynbee's suggestions for solving the problem?

d) Take three events since 1967 and for each explain how it has made the problems of the Palestinian Arabs *either* easier *or* more difficult to solve.

e) Suggest reasons why finding a solution to the problem is important for the rest of the world, as well as for Arabs and Israelis.

2 The following people have all played parts in the recent history of the Middle East: President Nasser; Yasser Arafat; President Sadat; Golda Meir; President Carter; Menachem Begin; The Ayatollah Khomeini.
Choose any *two* whose activities you think were especially important. For each of them, write a short factual paragraph about the events in which they were involved.

3 a) Write short paragraphs to describe, and account for, events in: 1) The Lebanon, 1975–86; 2) Iran, 1979–86.

b) Look through recent copies of newspapers and magazines to see what information you can find about what is happening in the Middle East at the present time. Write a few sentences summarising any up-to-date information you find concerning the countries or events that you have read about in this unit.

PART EIGHT
AFRICA

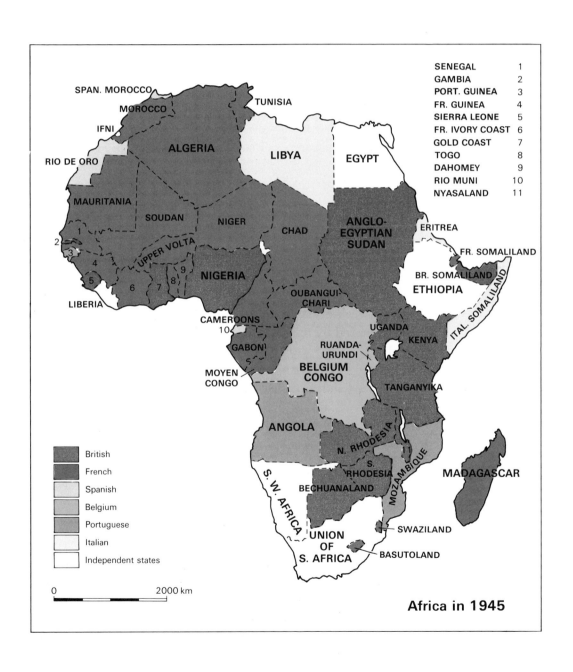

SENEGAL 1
GAMBIA 2
PORT. GUINEA 3
FR. GUINEA 4
SIERRA LEONE 5
FR. IVORY COAST 6
GOLD COAST 7
TOGO 8
DAHOMEY 9
RIO MUNI 10
NYASALAND 11

SPAN. MOROCCO
MOROCCO
TUNISIA
IFNI
RIO DE ORO
ALGERIA
LIBYA
EGYPT
MAURITANIA
SOUDAN
NIGER
CHAD
ANGLO-
EGYPTIAN
SUDAN
ERITREA
FR. SOMALILAND
UPPER VOLTA
NIGERIA
BR. SOMALILAND
ETHIOPIA
ITAL. SOMALILAND
LIBERIA
OUBANGUI-
CHARI
CAMEROONS
UGANDA
KENYA
GABON
RUANDA-
URUNDI
MOYEN
CONGO
BELGIUM
CONGO
TANGANYIKA
ANGOLA
N. RHODESIA
S.
RHODESIA
MOZAMBIQUE
MADAGASCAR
S. W. AFRICA
BECHUANALAND
UNION
OF
S. AFRICA
SWAZILAND
BASUTOLAND

British
French
Spanish
Belgium
Portuguese
Italian
Independent states

0   2000 km

Africa in 1945

In 1945 most of Africa was divided into colonies, lands ruled by European nations who had conquered them in the nineteenth century. By the 1980s this was no longer so. Only the southern tip was still ruled by white men. Africa had become 'decolonised'.

The decolonisation of Africa

Decolonisation began soon after the end of the Second World War. It started partly because the war had greatly weakened colony-owning countries such as Britain and France. The war also strengthened African nationalism – the demand by Africans to run their own affairs.

African soldiers had fought in the armies of their colonial masters. Some had seen white soldiers defeated in battle by the Japanese. The idea that white men were unbeatable was destroyed.

The ex-soldiers expected more say in their countries when they came home. So, too, did the growing number of educated Africans – lawyers, businessmen, teachers – in the towns.

The 'wind of change'

Nationalism was boosted when the people of India won their independence in 1947 (See Unit 68). African leaders, too, began to call for independence. In 1960 the British Prime Minister, Harold Macmillan, spoke of a 'wind of change' blowing across Africa. By then, that wind had already begun to blow away colonial rule.

One of the first countries where this happened was Ghana, in West Africa. Before Ghana became independent in 1957 it was a British colony called the Gold Coast.

Nkrumah and Ghana

The best known leader of the Gold Coast nationalist movement was Kwame Nkrumah. He had been born in a mud hut village and educated by missionaries. Later he studied in Britain and the USA. In 1947 he returned to work for the Gold Coast's independence.

In 1949 Nkrumah set up a new political party called the Convention People's Party – CPP – demanding 'self-government now'

Nkrumah travelled around the country, telling workers and villagers that independence was the key to a better life – schools, hospitals, higher prices for their crops. He called on them to oppose British rule by striking and refusing to buy British-made goods.

Nkrumah caused the British so much trouble that in 1950 they threw him into prison. This only made him more popular. In 1951 his CPP swept to victory in the Gold Coast general election, winning thirty-four of the thirty-eight seats which ordinary people were allowed to vote for.

The British saw that Nkrumah had the people behind him. They set him free and asked him to organise an African government.

Ghana's independence, 1957

At first Nkrumah's new government controlled only parts of the Gold Coast's affairs. Six years later it took complete control. On 5th March 1957 the colony was reborn as Ghana.

To begin with Nkrumah ruled through an elected Parliament modelled on Britain's, with himself as Prime Minister. But he soon decided that this type of government was unsuitable for Ghana. By the 1960s the CPP was the only political party he allowed. People who opposed his leadership fled abroad or were thrown into prison.

Nkrumah claimed that this was necessary to turn Ghana into a prosperous, modern country. He said that it was the only way to stop rival politicians wasting time in squabbling and to make the different peoples of Ghana see themselves as part of one nation.

Nkrumah did some good things. He built schools, hospitals, roads. But he also wasted a lot of money. He put up expensive new government buildings, mainly for show. Taxes and prices rose sharply. They rose even higher when Ghana earned less from her main export, cocoa, because its world price fell.

By 1966 many people in Ghana were sick of Nkrumah's broken promises. There was dancing in the streets when a group of army officers overthrew him. He died in exile six years later.

Nigeria's independence, 1960

In 1960 Nigeria, another British colony in West Africa, won its independence. But many Nigerians soon lost their faith in the politicians who were running the country. In 1966 the army took over the government there, too.

When the British first drew up Nigeria's boundaries they put together separate African peoples who had always been very different from one another – in language, in religion, in ways of life.

After independence many of the best educated Nigerians belonged to a people called the Igbo. Igbo worked all over Nigeria and held many of the country's best paid jobs. Other Nigerians were jealous of their success. In 1966 vicious riots broke out and 30,000 Igbo were massacred.

Igbo from all over Nigeria fled back to their homeland in the country's eastern region. Here, in 1967, they set up an independent country. They named it Biafra.

The Biafra War, 1967–70

Biafra had rich oil wells which the Nigerian generals did not want to lose. The result was a bitter civil war, with the rest of Nigeria united against Biafra. The Igbo were bombed and starved into surrender and in 1970 Biafra again became part of Nigeria.

White Africans

In Ghana and Nigeria almost everyone is black. In other parts of Africa many white people had settled. In some cases their families had lived there for several generations. In these places the whites ran things to benefit themselves and de-colonisation came more slowly.

Colonial Kenya

Kenya was a British colony in East Africa. From about 1900 onwards white farmers settled there. So did lots of Indians, who became traders and shopkeepers. But both were outnumbered by the black Africans who already lived in Kenya.

The white settlers took land from the Africans. Instead of growing food for their families, as the African farmers did, they grew crops such as coffee to sell abroad. To get cheap labour they made the Africans pay taxes on their huts. The only way the Africans could pay was by working on the white men's farms.

The biggest group of Africans in Kenya belonged to a farming people called the Kikuyu. They resented the whites grabbing most of Kenya's best land. 'What is misery?' asked one of their songs. 'It is a man without land.'

Kenyatta

Jomo Kenyatta became the main Kikuyu leader. In 1946 he set up a political party called the Kenya African Union. Kenyatta wanted two things for the Kikuyu and other African peoples of Kenya – more land and more say in the government.

Mau Mau

In the early 1950s some of the Kikuyu became impatient. They organised themselves into the Mau Mau. Mau Mau was part secret society, part guerilla army. Its aim was to drive white farmers and their workers off the Kikuyu lands.

In 1952 Mau Mau began attacking farms and villages. The white rulers of Kenya accused Kenyatta of organising Mau Mau. He denied this, but they put him in prison. Then they sent soldiers to hunt down the Mau Mau. Four years later the army had crushed the movement. Mau Mau fighters were dead or in prison camps.

Yet Mau Mau signalled the end of white rule in Kenya. The British government of Macmillan saw that many African grievances were justified. It acted before they exploded again.

Macmillan started by giving Africans more say in the way Kenya was ruled. By 1961 elected African members were in a majority on the Legislative (law making) Council. They demanded the release of Kenyatta to take over as the country's leader.

Independent Kenya, 1963

Kenyatta was released from prison in 1961. In 1963 Kenya gained its independence and he became President. He held this position until his death in 1978.

Kenyatta persuaded the different African peoples of Kenya to work together with one another. He asked the whites, too, to stay on and use their skills to help to build the new Kenya. Many did.

Kenya remained united and peaceful under Kenyatta's rule. Many people became better off. But at a price.

An 'Africanisation' policy in the later 1960s robbed many Kenya Asians of jobs and businesses. Many took refuge in Britain.

Kenyatta allowed only one political party in Kenya – his own Kenya African National Union (KANU). Parliament became little more than a rubber stamp, doing what a small group of powerful men close to Kenyatta told it to do.

And although business and industrial firms prospered, they were often owned and controlled by foreigners. A lot of their profits finished up abroad, instead of being spent to benefit Kenya's people.

Neo-colonialism

Some people asked whether Kenya had stopped being a political colony only to become an economic one. White foreigners no longer ruled, but it seemed that they still got most of the benefit from the riches of the land and the work of the people.

This kind of situation was called 'neo' (new)-colonialism'. In the years that followed independence, neo-colonialism was an obstacle facing many independent African countries.

Colonial Africa

Africa chained, a cartoon by Ronald Searle, 1959.

1 a) What point is Ronald Searle making about the condition of Africa in 1959?

b) Who, or what, did he believe was chaining Africa at this time?

c) If you had seen this drawing in 1959, would you have thought that it was a fair or an exaggerated picture? Give facts in support of your answer.

d) Name one country that had freed itself from the chains by 1959.

e) Name two countries that freed themselves after 1959.

f) Choose any one African country and write a paragraph about how it changed from a colony into an independent state.

Ghana

A group of students celebrating in 1966.

2 a) Which country and which event are shown in this photograph?

b) Explain whether you think it is a snapshot or a staged picture.

c) How useful is the photograph as evidence that the man named on the placards really was unpopular? Explain your answer.

Kenya

Incomes and education in Kenya in the early 1950s.

	Africans	**Indians**	**Europeans**
Average annual incomes, 1953	£27	£280	£660
Government money spent per child on primary education, 1954	0.15p	0.9p	£49.30p

3 Make up a discussion between a colonial official and a Kenyan African nationalist. One defends the figures above and the other criticises them.

Jomo Kenyatta, who was born not long after the British arrived in Kenya, made this comment about the work of missionaries in his country.

"When the missionaries arrived, the Africans had the land and the missionaries had the Bible. They taught us to pray with our eyes closed. When we opened them, they had the land and we had the Bible."

In D. Lamb, *The Africans*, 1985

One of the Mau Mau leaders was Waruhiu Itote, known as 'General China'. This is an extract from his life story, written after Kenya became independent.

"In 1939, seventeen years old, . . . I decided to leave home and try my fortune in Nairobi . . .

. . . three of us decided to start a vegetable business . . . It was very profitable . . . We bought potatoes at five shillings a bag in Karatina and sold them for twelve shillings in Nairobi, with two shillings transport costs as the only operating expenses.

When we came up with the idea of starting a shop and tried to get a licence . . . I had my first experience of racial discrimination. Indians apparently had little difficulty, but for Africans it was nearly impossible . . . Nairobi was full of such pinpricks in those days: the Railway Station lavatories . . . marked EUROPEANS, ASIANS, and NATIVES; hotels we could not enter except as servants, and even certain kinds of beer that we could not drink.

Sometimes we would talk quietly about these problems . . .

Gakingu . . . showed me how his farm was sandwiched in between two European estates with their hundreds of acres of coffee, yet he was not allowed to grow any. More bitter was the knowledge that some members of his clan were still living who could remember when they had themselves farmed the land belonging to the Europeans."

W. Itote, *Mau Mau General*, 1967

4 a) What do Kenyatta and Itote agree was the major Kenyan grievance?
   b) Look back at the table at the top of the page. Does it support the view that there was racial discrimination in Kenya as a colony?
   c) For each of the sources on this page, say how it could be used to explain the support given to Mau Mau.

1 GUINEA 1958
2 SENEGAL 1960
3 GAMBIA 1965
4 GUINEA-BISSAU 1974
5 SIERRA LEONE 1961
6 LIBERIA 1847
7 IVORY COAST 1960
8 MOZAMBIQUE 1975
9 BURKINA FASO 1960
10 BENIN 1960
11 SWAZILAND 1968
12 LESOTHO 1966
13 TOGO 1960
14 GHANA 1957
15 MALAWI 1964
16 BURUNDI 1962
17 UGANDA 1962
18 CENTRAL AFRICAN REPUBLIC 1960
19 EQUATORIAL GUINEA 1968
20 RWANDA 1962
21 ZIMBABWE 1980
22 BOTSWANA 1966
23 DJIBOUTI 1977

Africa in 1986
(with dates of independence)

5 a) Compare this map with the one on page 247. What do they tell you about a major difference between the citizenship of most Africans aged fifteen or sixteen in 1986 and the citizenship of most of their parents at that age?

b) Which two countries owned most African colonies in 1945?

c) What do you understand by the 'wind of change'?

d) How does the map show that it was blowing strongly in the 1960s?

e) Why do you think that it was blowing so strongly then?

f) Write down three ways in which a colony and an independent country are different.

g) Using the information in this unit and the next, list *five* African countries which have won independence. For each one, give the name of the state which ruled it as a colony and the year of independence.

h) Choose *one* of your five countries and write an account which shows   1) how it won independence,   2) who its best known leaders have been,   3) any important events that have taken place there since independence.

i) Why do you think so many countries changed their names at independence?

Rhodesia

White soldiers and settlers marched into the lands between Central Africa's Limpopo and Zambesi Rivers in the 1890s. They overran the black nations who lived there, destroyed their governments and forced them to hand over most of their land.

The whites called their new colony Rhodesia, after Cecil Rhodes, the British empire-builder who had organised the take-over. They made profitable use of it. Coal and copper mines were dug. Roads and railways were built. Thousands of acres were planted with tobacco, sugar and tea.

In 1922 the British government made the area into the self-governing colony of Southern Rhodesia. This meant that the Rhodesian whites could elect their own Parliament. This Parliament ran most things inside Rhodesia the way they wanted.

In the 1950s four out of every hundred Southern Rhodesians were white. North of Southern Rhodesia were two more British colonies, where nearly all the people were black. One was Northern Rhodesia, the other Nyasaland.

The Federation of Rhodesia and Nyasaland, 1953

In 1953 the whites of Southern Rhodesia persuaded the British government to put the two Rhodesias, together with Nyasaland, into a single Federation of Rhodesia and Nyasaland. They claimed that the Federation would make it easier for the people of the three colonies to work together, in ways that would benefit all of them.

Most of the seats in the Federation's Parliament were given to the whites of Southern Rhodesia. This made the blacks believe that its real aim was to keep the whole area under the control of the whites.

Basic facts of life like wages seemed to prove that they were right. In 1961, the average white wage-earner was taking home £1200 a year, compared with the average African's £87. 'For the African, the partnership is a sham', reported a British official.

African leaders organised strikes and protests. In some places rioting broke out and demonstrators were killed.

Independence for Malawi and Zambia, 1964

In 1963, after meetings with both black and white leaders, the British did away with the Federation. The next year they gave independence to Nyasaland and Northern Rhodesia. Nyasaland took the African name Malawi and Northern Rhodesia became Zambia. Both had black leaders – Hastings Banda in Malawi and Kenneth Kaunda in Zambia.

The Rhodesian whites made it clear that they expected Britain to give them independence, too. But the British government refused. We'll talk about giving you independence, they said, when you give the Africans more say in governing Rhodesia.

Ian Smith and Rhodesian UDI, 1965

The Prime Minister of Rhodesia was Ian Smith. Smith and his white Rhodesian Front Party were determined to keep the whites in control. If Britain would not give Rhodesia independence, said Smith, they would simply take it.

They did just that. Smith made a Unilateral Declaration of Independence (UDI) on 11th November 1965.

The British Labour Government of Prime Minister Harold Wilson accused Smith of rebellion. But it refused to send in British soldiers to overthrow him. Instead it relied upon sanctions. Britain asked other countries to stop trading with Rhodesia. The idea was to force Smith to call off UDI by starving Rhodesia of vital supplies.

Sanctions were a failure. Rhodesia got oil and the other goods she needed through white-ruled neighbouring countries such as South Africa and Mozambique, a Portuguese colony.

The Patriotic Front

But by the middle 1970s Smith was facing a more serious threat. Rival African nationalist groups in Rhodesia put their quarrels aside and formed a joint organisation called the Patriotic Front. Its leaders were Robert Mugabe and Joshua Nkomo. Their aim was to end white rule in Rhodesia by force.

The Patriotic Front set up bases and training camps in Zambia and Mozambique, which had won its independence in 1975. Armed guerillas filtered across Rhodesia's borders to attack bridges, railway lines and farms.

Smith's South African allies became afraid that the guerilla war might spread to their land. They put pressure on him to call off UDI. British officials came back to Rhodesia to organise a free election.

Rhodesia becomes Zimbabwe, 1980

For the first time everybody, black as well as white, had a vote. The result was that in 1980 Rhodesia elected a black government. It also obtained its independence from Britain, and an African name, Zimbabwe. The Patriotic Front leader, Robert Mugabe, became Zimbabwe's first Prime Minister.

By the time Zimbabwe was born most of the countries of black Africa had won independence. But they faced many problems.

Problems of independent Africa. 1: Poverty

One was that they were so poor. In colonial times their rulers had made them concentrate on turning out raw materials. Sometimes the raw materials were minerals like copper. More often they were farm crops, such as cocoa or cotton. White traders shipped out these raw materials and turned them into manufactured goods in the factories of Europe.

One result was that independent African countries had few factories of their own. Millions of their people still lived by growing 'cash crops', such as cocoa, cotton, coffee or ground nuts.

The more land farmers used for cash crops, the less they had for growing food. Every year it became more difficult to feed Africa's increasing number of people.

The prices farmers were paid for their cash crops were very unreliable, too. In 1975 Africans could buy 148 barrels of oil with the money that foreign buyers paid for one tonne of cocoa. But in 1980 a tonne of cocoa would buy them only 63 barrels of oil.

Such big changes in what traders call 'commodity prices' made it very difficult to plan for the future. From year to year African countries never knew how much money they would have.

2: Conflicts

Another problem for black Africa has been conflict between different groups of people inside the same country.

National boundaries had been fixed by Europeans in colonial times. Peoples with very little in common were often jumbled together in one country. In Zaire, once a Belgian colony called the Congo, there were 200 separate peoples speaking 75 languages.

Such differences in language, religion and ways of life often led to dislike. In some places the dislike grew into hatred. In the Congo at the start of the 1960s, and in Nigeria at the end (see Unit 57), hundred of thousands died in fierce civil wars. In the former British colony of Uganda a bloodthirsty dictator named Idi Amin slaughtered thousands more.

Sometimes such conflicts were made worse by outside interference. African countries became pawns in a Cold War power game. This was so in the former Portuguese colony of Angola. In the 1980s Angola was torn by civil war. One side was backed by men and weapons from the communist government of Cuba, acting on behalf of the USSR. The other was backed by men and weapons from South Africa, secretly encouraged by the USA.

3: Ways of government

Under the strain of such problems most African countries gave up the European-style political systems they started off with. By 1984 only seven of the continent's forty-one main independent nations allowed any opposition political parties.

Seventeen of the rest were countries where the rulers allowed people to vote only for candidates belonging to one political party.

Kenya, Malawi and Zambia were all 'single party states' of this kind. Their rulers claimed that this was the best way to unite the different groups and peoples in their countries.

The remaining seventeen African countries, including Ghana and Nigeria, were ruled by soldiers. These soldier rulers usually claimed that they had seized power to work out more honest and efficient ways of running their countries.

Some Africans had doubts about the soldiers doing any better than the politicians. When the army took over the government of Nigeria, a Nigerian lawyer told a reporter, 'Far better to have a shabby democracy in which people have some say in running things than a shabby military régime [rule] in which they have none.'

Yet there were still signs of hope. In Kenya, Jomo Kenyatta's idea of encouraging different peoples and races to work together seemed still to be working. The same was true in Zambia under the leadership of Kenneth Kaunda and in Tanzania under Julius Nyerere.

Even in these more fortunate countries, however, most people were poor. In less fortunate ones, such as Ethiopia and Sudan, many thousands were killed in vicious civil wars or starved to death as famine swept across their parched and dusty plains.

In the middle of the 1980s one thing was clear. Independence had been an important step for Africa, but its peoples still had great problems to overcome before their hopes of a better life became real.

Rhodesia

A cartoon from Punch, *1966.*

"You're getting nowhere, man—let us *try."*

1 a) What is the present-day name of the country shown as a mine?

b) Who was its leader at the time of the cartoon?

c) Which country does the man lying down represent?

d) How were the tools in his case supposed to defuse the bomb?

e) Which group of people does the man with the hammer represent?

f) What methods did they use to deal with the bomb?

Commodities

Two figures to show the importance of the commodity market.

2 a) From the point of view of international trade, which of the six countries in the diagram do you think is in the healthiest position?

b) Suggest reasons why African countries depend on so few products for their export earnings.

c) What effect does this have on their standards of living?

d) Suggest why it is useful to know the amount of oil that a commodity can buy.

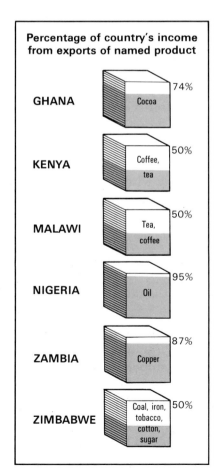

Percentage of country's income from exports of named product

GHANA — Cocoa 74%

KENYA — Coffee, tea 50%

MALAWI — Tea, coffee 50%

NIGERIA — Oil 95%

ZAMBIA — Copper 87%

ZIMBABWE — Coal, iron, tobacco, cotton, sugar 50%

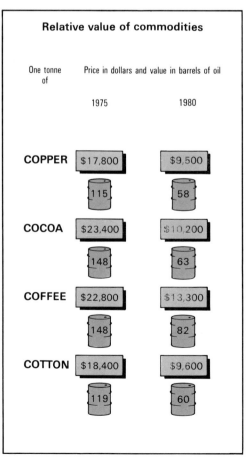

Relative value of commodities

One tonne of	Price in dollars and value in barrels of oil	
	1975	1980
COPPER	$17,800	$9,500
	115	58
COCOA	$23,400	$10,200
	148	63
COFFEE	$22,800	$13,300
	148	82
COTTON	$18,400	$9,600
	119	60

Sharpeville, 1960

The crowd in the South African town of Sharpeville on 21st March 1960 was noisy but cheerful. Until the police started shooting. Then people screamed and started to run.

Soon the dusty space in front of the police headquarters was empty. Except for the bodies of the dead. There were sixty-seven of them. They were all black. Half of them had been shot in the back.

The incident came to be called the Sharpeville Massacre. It came about because of a way of running things in South Africa called 'apartheid'.

Peoples of South Africa

To understand apartheid we need to look at South Africa's people. Most are black. But most of the country's wealth and all of its powers of government are in the hands of white people.

In the early 1980s there were about 4.5 million white South Africans and about 23 million blacks and other non-whites – Indians, for example, and people of mixed race called 'coloureds'.

Many of the white South Africans are the descendants of settlers from Europe who went there more than 300 years ago, long before whites settled in other parts of Africa. For such South African whites, Africa is home.

Their ancestors led the way in making South Africa rich. It has fertile farmlands, modern factories, gold and diamond mines, fine modern cities. It is the richest nation in all Africa. It also has the biggest, best trained and best equipped armed forces.

South Africa is what we have made it, say the whites. It is our land, not the black man's. That is the way we are going to keep it.

Afrikaners

Most white South Africans are descended from settlers from either Holland or Britain. Those of Dutch descent speak a language called Afrikaans, a sort of Dutch. They are called Afrikaners.

In 1948 the Afrikaner Nationalist Party won a general election in which only whites could vote. In the 1980s it still controlled the country's government.

The Nationalists had one main aim – to keep South Africa a country where whites ruled. They started the apartheid policy to make sure of this.

Malan and apartheid

'Apartheid' is an Afrikaner word that means 'apartness'. It is based on the idea that people of different races should be kept apart as much as possible. The foundations of apartheid were laid by Dr Daniel Malan, the Nationalist Prime Minister from 1948 to 1954.

In 1950 Malan brought in the Group Areas Act, one of the first and most important apartheid laws. The Group Areas Act set aside most of South Africa for use by the whites.

Verwoerd and the Bantustans

In 1959 a Nationalist Prime Minister named Hendrik Verwoerd set aside smaller areas for the blacks. In these 'Bantustans' blacks were supposed to be free to run their own affairs. Verwoerd told them that they must look upon the areas as their 'homelands'.

But the Bantustans had the country's poorest farming land and hardly any industries. Over half of the black South Africans lived not in these homelands, but in the European areas of the country. That was where the whites needed them to be, too, working for low wages in their mines, factories and homes. The prosperous white way of life depended upon this.

Enforcing apartheid

So the Nationalist Government worked out ways to keep the blacks in the European areas under control. It forbade them to live in the same districts as whites, to attend the same schools as whites, to marry whites. It also forbade them to vote, to go on strike, to take skilled jobs.

Pass Laws

Then there were the Pass Laws. The government made blacks carry a pass, or identity card, everywhere they went. The police could demand to see the pass at any time. Anyone picked up without one could be thrown straight into prison. This happened to hundreds of thousands of blacks every year.

All the laws were part of apartheid. Some white MPs belonging to other parties protested about them. They believed that South Africa's future lay in giving blacks a share in running the country. They wanted to start allowing them more rights, not fewer.

South Africa leaves the Commonwealth, 1961

The Nationalist Government ignored such protests. It also ignored protests from abroad. In 1961 a conference of Commonwealth Prime Ministers condemned apartheid. Verwoerd's reply was to take South Africa out of the Commonwealth rather than make any changes.

Opposition to apartheid

In the years which followed, international protests about apartheid continued. In many countries people boycotted South African goods. South African teams were kept out of the Olympic Games. Other countries refused to play them at cricket, rugby and other sports. Such actions made little difference. Apartheid went on.

Black leaders in South Africa itself protested against apartheid. In the 1950s one of the best known black spokesmen was Albert Luthuli, a chief of the Zulu people.

Albert Luthuli and the ANC

Luthuli was the leader of a black political party called the African National Congress (ANC). He was a strong believer in the peaceful protest methods that Gandhi had used to oppose British rule in India (see Unit 66).

Luthuli told his followers to refuse to obey the apartheid laws, but not to use violence. In 1960 he was awarded the Nobel Peace Prize for his non-violent struggle for the rights of his people. The police still arrested him. He was sent to a lonely farm and forced to stay there until he died in 1967.

The Sharpeville shootings, 1960

In 1960 black leaders decided to hold a big demonstration against the Pass Laws. They told people to go to their local police stations and hand in their passes. The idea was that if enough people did this the whole system would break down.

On the morning of 21st March 1960 a crowd of several thousand people gathered outside the police headquarters in Sharpeville.

Nelson Mandela and the ANC

Economic growth

Soweto, 1976

Steve Biko

The police were afraid and angry. You know what happened next.

The Sharpeville killings made many blacks give up Luthuli's idea of peaceful protest. They started making plans to use force.

The government's reply was to make the apartheid system even stricter. Verwoerd banned the ANC and other black political parties and threw their leaders into prison.

The best known of these leaders was Nelson Mandela, who was caught and imprisoned in 1962. In 1987 Mandela was still in prison. Despite this, most blacks still looked upon him as their leader.

In the 1960s and 1970s South Africa went on becoming richer. Its gold and other valuable raw materials meant big profits for businessmen. So did the cheap labour of its millions of black workers. Money from abroad poured in to set up new, modern industries.

By 1970 South African whites were enjoying the highest standard of living of any people in the world.

Some blacks also benefited from the growing prosperity. The growth of industry meant more skilled jobs. By the 1970s there were not enough white South Africans to do them. The government started to allow blacks into jobs once reserved for whites. Wages rose. By 1978 black mine-workers, for example, were earning four times as much as they had done in 1970.

But many blacks did not share in this prosperity. One in five had no job. And all of them still had to obey the hated apartheid laws.

So unrest ticked on like a time-bomb. In 1976 it exploded again.

An hour's journey away from Johannesburg, South Africa's biggest industrial city, is a vast, sprawling shanty town of corrugated iron shacks. This is Soweto. Here live a million of Johannesburg's black workers. They have to, because even though they work in Johannesburg, apartheid forbids them to have homes there.

In 1976 the government ordered that at least half the teaching in black schools must be done in Afrikaans. Many teachers and pupils did not speak Afrikaans, so they objected.

In Soweto hundreds of black students gathered for a protest meeting. The police opened fire on them. Twenty-five of the students were killed and another 200 were injured.

News of the Soweto killings triggered off demonstrations and riots all over South Africa. The riots were against apartheid generally, not just the killings. By the time they died down, over 500 more blacks and coloureds had been killed by the police.

The following year Steve Biko, a young black leader, was beaten to death while in prison.

Despite incidents like the Soweto killings and the death of Biko, some black leaders still hoped for peaceful change in South Africa. They tried to persuade the government to start dismantling the apartheid laws. Then, they said, the country could begin to move towards a system of government in which all its people, blacks and whites, coloureds and Indians, had a fair say.

Apartheid

"Apartheid is better described as a policy of good neighbours."

Dr Verwoerd, March 1961.

This cartoon about Verwoerd's statement was printed in the Daily Mirror, *6th March 1961.*

1 a) What points does the cartoonist make to answer Dr Verwoerd?

b) What other point is he making by showing the man's gun?

Dollie Fourie, an Afrikaner, talks to an English visitor about her maid.

"She's been working nine years for me now. She came to me when she came out of school . . . I never used to have a maid. I did everything myself. Then when Erina – she's the youngest – was five months old, I broke my arm.

About three days after, this girl came by the back door. She was so black . . . I said to her, 'Listen, can you put a nappie on?' She says she doesn't know. I said 'You'll have to learn if you don't'.

She couldn't speak a word of Afrikaans. She couldn't speak English. And now, if I go out in the afternoon, I can ask her to help the kids with their homework. She studies all the time with them. She couldn't do a bit of cooking when she came to me and now, if I've got visitors, I've just got to tell her, 'Look, we'll do this and this and this'. It's finished. I don't need to worry about food again.

. . . their morality can never, ever come up to the Europeans . . . Their standard of living is much lower. They can't think what's going to happen tomorrow . . . Like we're worried about our kids . . . Have they got food? Are they doing OK in school? They never worry about that – that I've seen. . . . I suppose I'm old-fashioned . . . but I see some of my English neighbours – their maids with them at the table, having a cup of tea. That's one thing I'll never allow. Mine knows where her place is and I know where mine is . . . And, I must say she's very honest . . . If a cent falls she'll pick it up and give it back to me.

. . . She knows too with the television . . . If we're watching she's welcome. But she comes in and sits at the door. I won't allow her to sit on my things. As far as I'm concerned, we're still not on the same level. I suppose that's just the way I grew up."

In B. Hutmacher, *In Black and White: Voices of Apartheid,* 1980

2 a) Would you expect Dollie Fourier to support or to disagree with apartheid?

b) In which ways does Dollie believe that she is superior to black people?

c) Are her beliefs supported or contradicted by what she tells you about her maid, Vera? Explain your answer.

d) Imagine you are Vera. From this source, and the text of the unit, tell a friend how you feel about Dollie and white people generally.

Desmond Tutu

One of the leaders of the movement for peaceful change in South Africa was a black priest named Desmond Tutu. In 1984 Tutu was awarded the Nobel Peace Prize for his efforts to end apartheid. In 1986 he became the first black Anglican Archbishop of South Africa.

Tutu called upon rich foreign countries to stop trading with South Africa and to withdraw the money they had invested in its industries. He believed that this would help to force the South African government to change its ways.

Most blacks admired Tutu's courage in standing up to the government. But many believed that his hope of achieving real change without fighting for it was just a dream.

ANC guerillas

After the Soweto killings the banned ANC said that the only way to end apartheid was to overthrow white rule by force. Thousands of its young supporters left South Africa to train in nearby African states as guerilla fighters. In the 1980s they began to return.

The first targets for the ANC's bombs and rockets were police stations and oil refineries. Then they began to strike at civilian targets. In May 1983 a booby-trapped car exploded on a busy street in the city of Pretoria. It killed nineteen innocent people and wounded two hundred others.

P.W. Botha and apartheid

By this time the Nationalist Government had a new leader, P. W. Botha. Botha had taken over as Prime Minister in 1978. In 1984, under a new constitution, he became the country's President.

By Afrikaner nationalist standards Botha was a reformer. In some ways he was ready to give the blacks a better deal – over jobs, wages, living conditions. But he still intended to keep the real power to run the country in the hands of the whites.

Botha believed that he could do this in two ways. First, by dividing the non-white peoples against one another – coloureds against blacks, middle-class blacks against working-class blacks, and so on. Second, by defusing the political discontent of non-whites by giving them extra rights of other kinds.

Botha's reforms

So in 1979 Botha allowed black workers to form trade unions. In 1984 he set up separate, though largely powerless, Houses of Parliament for South Africa's coloured and Indian peoples. In 1985 he scrapped the apartheid law forbidding mixed marriages and sexual relations between whites and non-whites. He even spoke of releasing the imprisoned ANC leader, Nelson Mandela.

But Botha's changes satisfied nobody. Some whites thought that he was going too far. Most non-whites thought that he was not going far enough.

1985 was South Africa's worst ever year of riots, shootings, burnings and killings. By the end of the year almost nine hundred people had died, most of them black.

Some Afrikaner Nationalists blamed the trouble on Botha. They said that his reforms were encouraging blacks to believe that they might one day get a share of political power.

To die-hard Nationalists any such idea was madness. They turned down flat any talk of 'one man, one vote'. What this would mean, they said, was not democracy, but 'one man, one vote, one time' – and then black dictatorship for ever after.

They believed that the only way for South Africa to avoid the civil wars and the other troubles that had followed the coming of black rule to the rest of Africa was for the whites to hang on to power at all costs.

And the whites could do it, they said – if only they showed enough determination. Hadn't they got the richest industries, the best organised government and the strongest armed forces in Africa?

South Africa faces the future

But in the 1980s signs were growing that more and more whites, even ones who had once supported apartheid, no longer believed that it was possible to hang on to power for much longer.

For one thing, international boycotts of the products of South Africa's industries and farms were beginning to threaten their prosperity. So was a widespread boycott of white-owned shops by black customers inside South Africa. In some places rioting black youths made people who ignored this boycott drink detergent and eat flour they had just bought.

Partly because of these troubles South Africa's currency, the rand, started losing value against other world currencies like the dollar and the pound. In January 1985 one South African rand was worth over 80 British pence. By January 1986 its value had dropped to only 39 British pence.

What worried the whites most, however, was the growing black anger, the riots and the killings. These – and a matter of arithmetic.

Experts worked out that by the year 2000 the white population would increase only slightly, from 4.7 million to 5.2 million. But South Africa's black population would jump from 23 million to 50 million – and 20 million of them would live in or around the white industrial areas.

Facts like this convinced more and more whites that there was only one way to solve South Africa's problems and safeguard their own futures. A new way of running the country acceptable to the black majority had to be worked out. The problem was – how?

The Uitenhage shootings, 1985

On 21st March 1985, twenty-five years to the day after the Sharpeville shootings, South African police gunned down nineteen blacks in a shanty town called Uitenhage. The blacks were demonstrating against rent increases.

'This country is tearing itself apart', wrote one South African newspaper. 'We are writing our history in blood.'

Another newspaper expresed its fears in a cartoon. The cartoon showed three gravestones. The first said 'Sharpeville 1960'. The second said 'Uitenhage 1985'. The third said 'Watch this space'.

Winnie Mandela speaks

Extracts from an interview in 1986 with Winnie Mandela. Her husband, ANC leader Nelson Mandela, had been in prison for twenty-four years.

"I did not know that a human being could hate as much as the Afrikaner does. . .

They have destroyed the traditional way of life we have known throughout the ages.

We have had to seek permission from the white 'baas' to come and work in white South Africa. We have had to put up with the hated pass laws. . .

I cannot own land. I have no political rights, I am just the same as my grandfather who has never seen the door of a classroom.

My educational qualifications. . . are of no consequence. . . Because I am a black woman I am not even the guardian of my children. I am a minor. I remain that minor until the day I die. . .

I cannot choose a home in the residential area of my liking because the white man, my white ruler, determines that I live in the black ghetto of Soweto. . .

We have had to take up arms. . . because it was the only answer. . .

There was no other course open to us. . . We have been speaking to deaf ears for generations. The Afrikaner did not even pretend to listen. The Afrikaner knows only one language. . . violence. And that is why we are seeing the violence in the townships today. . .

We are fighting for a share of the power, late as it is in the day. We are so generous that we are still talking in terms of sharing power because the country belongs to all of us, black and white. . . We shall not drive the white men into the sea. . . They will have a part in the South Africa of tomorrow."

Winnie Mandela in *Woman*, 8th February 1986

1 a) Name three ways in which Winnie Mandela is discriminated against.
  b) If you were Winnie Mandela, which of these forms of discrimination would hurt and anger you most? Explain your answer.
  c) Who does she blame for the violence of the mid-1980s?
  d) What changes does she believe necessary to make a better future possible for the people of South Africa?
  e) From reading Units 59 and 60 and their sources, how do you think an Afrikaner supporter of apartheid would justify *not* giving blacks a share of political power?

2 Match each name with a description from the second column. Copy out the correct sentences and add to each one a sentence of your own to explain it more fully.

Apartheid	are the official homelands of black Africans.
Afrikaners	is a town where many of Johannesburg's black workers live.
Sharpeville	is a black African leader imprisoned in 1963.
Luthuli	is a system of laws to separate blacks and whites.
Mandela	are the descendants of Dutch settlers in South Africa.
Soweto	was a Prime Minister who strengthened apartheid.
Bantustans	is a town where African demonstrators were shot in 196
Verwoerd	was an African leader who believed in non-violent resistance.

PART NINE
EAST ASIA

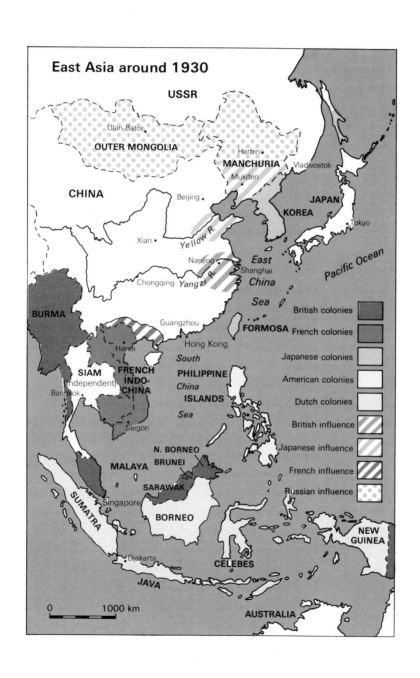

East Asia around 1930

USSR

Ulan Bator

OUTER MONGOLIA

Harbin

MANCHURIA   Vladivostok

Mukden

CHINA   Beijing   JAPAN

KOREA

Xian   Yellow R.   Tokyo

Nanjing   East

Shanghai   China

Chongqing Yangzi R.

Sea

BURMA   Guangzhou

FORMOSA

Hong Kong

Hanoi   South

SIAM   FRENCH   PHILIPPINE

(Independent) INDO-   China

Bangkok   CHINA   ISLANDS

Saigon   Sea

N. BORNEO

BRUNEI

MALAYA

SARAWAK

Singapore

BORNEO

SUMATRA   NEW
                          GUINEA

Djakarta   CELEBES

JAVA

0   1000 km   AUSTRALIA

Pacific Ocean

British colonies
French colonies
Japanese colonies
American colonies
Dutch colonies
British influence
Japanese influence
French influence
Russian influence

The peasants

'You know, we have a saying that peasants are nothing more than a foot of mud and a pile of shit. In the spring, when the land turns to oozing mud and it's raining, windy and cold right through to your skin, it's easy to feel that way. Life is hard in the villages and life really is full of mud and shit. But you need mud and shit to grow the crops, and where would China be without the grain we deliver to the state each year?'*

The speaker was a sixty-five-year-old Chinese peasant farmer. He was speaking in the year 1975. But his words would have been just as true about the foundations of life in China a hundred, a thousand, or even three thousand years earlier.

To understand why, let us look at a few facts about China.

Land, people and government

First, it is a very big country – the biggest in the world apart from the USSR. It covers ten million square kilometres. This makes it about forty times the size of Great Britain.

Second, it is a country with lots of people – an estimated 1000 million in the 1980s. This means that something like a quarter of mankind is Chinese.

Eight out of ten of China's people are peasant farmers. China has rich land for growing food – rice in the valleys and on the hillsides of the hot south, grain on the plains of the colder north.

But China also has areas where the land is too high, or too hot, or too cold to grow reliable crops. So peasants in the best lands have always had to grow more than they themselves need in order to feed the rest of China, including the townspeople.

Food supplies depended on whether China had rulers strong enough to protect the peasants from bandits and civil wars, to see that roads and canals were in good order to move the crops, and to arrange for storing food against times of flood or drought.

China's rulers were its emperors. They ran the country through a system of civil servants or 'scholar officials'. From 1646 onwards the emperors were foreigners from Manchuria. To many Chinese Manchu rule was an insult to their pride.

At the end of the nineteenth century good government in China had almost completely broken down. One reason for this was growing peasant poverty. The population was growing fast. Villagers had less land to grow food and earn money to pay their rents and taxes. Often they became so desperate that they rebelled.

Foreigners in China

The other reason for the breakdown of good government was the influence of powerful foreign nations. Such nations controlled China's trade and some of its most important cities. A notice in a park in China's great seaport city of Shanghai summed up the situation. 'Dogs and Chinese not allowed' it said.

*In B. M. Frolic, *Mao's People*, Harvard University Press 1980

This was terribly humiliating for the Chinese. In earlier times they had made many of mankind's important scientific breakthroughs. They had discovered paper making, for example, printing, gunpowder, the magnetic compass.

But such discoveries helped to make them over-confident. They saw no need to learn from the West. The first Europeans to go to China were either sent away or forced to run their trading businesses from a tiny part of one port, Guangzhon in south China.

Then, in the middle of the nineteenth century, empire-building industrial countries like Britain began to see China, with its millions of people, as a huge new market for the goods from their factories and for the crops grown in their empires.

The British sent armoured steamships to force the Chinese to buy opium grown in India. Soon British, French, German and Russian ships and troops were busy 'opening' China to the West.

The foreigners forced the emperors to sign treaties giving them control over China's ports and all sorts of other rights. They agreed between themselves about the parts of China in which each country could build railways and silk factories, open new docks and set up trading companies.

Foreigners owned these businesses, foreigners ran them, foreigners took the profits from them.

'The rest of the world is the carving knife and the serving dish, while we are the fish and the meat', wrote a young Chinese named Sun Yatsen.

Sun Yatsen

Sun had been educated abroad. He travelled widely, visiting western countries such as the United States and Britain. He also lived for a time in Japan.

In the 1860s the Japanese people, too, had been faced with the threat of a western take-over. They had dealt with it by taking up western ways themselves, setting up modern industries and organising an up-to-date army and navy (see Unit 65).

Sun's travels helped to convince him that China, too, had to copy foreign ways. Only then would it have a chance of becoming a strong, modern country where people would have better lives.

So Sun became a revolutionary. He organised a political party which later came to be called the Guomindang – the National People's Party. In 1895 Sun organised a plot to overthrow the emperor's government, but it failed. He had to flee abroad.

But Sun went on working to replace the out-dated rule of the emperors. He set out his plans in 'Three Principles of the People'.

The Three Principles of the People

The first Principle was to get rid of poverty in China by giving the land to the peasants who farmed it. Sun called this the Principle of the People's Livelihood.

The second Principle was to get rid of foreign control over China and to persuade all Chinese to work together as one people. This was the Principle of the People's Nationalism.

The third Principle was to train all the people of China to have a

The Double Tenth

The warlords

Sun and the Russians

Communism in China

Chiang Kaishek and the communists

Mao Zedong

say in running the country's affairs. Sun called this the Principle of the People's Democracy.

It was 1911 before Sun returned to China. This was a bad year of floods, famines and growing unrest. On 10th October – the 'Double Tenth' – the army mutinied. The soldiers forced the emperor, a five-year-old boy at this time, to abdicate (give up his position).

Revolutionaries took advantage of all the confusion to set up a new government in south China. They chose Sun, who had hurried back to China from the USA, to be its leader.

But Sun's new government did not have the money or the soldiers to hang on to power. He had to hand over as President to a general called Yuan Shikai, who had both.

In 1915 Yuan died. China broke up into areas ruled by warlords, generals with their own private armies. They were often in the pay of the foreigners who controlled China's trade. The warlords were always fighting each other.

Sun knew that to win control of China he had to defeat the warlords. He turned for help to Russia and to the newly formed Chinese Communist Party.

In 1917 the government of Russia had been taken over by the Bolsheviks, led by Lenin (see Unit 16). The foreign countries who were trying to hang on to their privileges in China had sent armies to try to crush the Bolsheviks. Sun's China and Lenin's Russia had the same enemies. This is one reason why Sun asked Lenin for help.

In 1921 a group of Chinese followers of Lenin set up the Chinese Communist Party, based on his ideas. They soon had a lot of support, especially among badly paid workers in ports like Shanghai.

In 1923 Sun formed an alliance with the Chinese communists and the Russians. Both agreed to help him to beat the warlords. The Russians sent Sun weapons and advisers to help him to set up his own army. The Chinese communists organised strikes and risings by workers in towns controlled by the warlords.

The leader of Sun's army was Chiang Kaishek. When Sun died in 1925, Chiang took his place as the leader of the Guomindang.

Helped by the communists, Chiang began bringing the warlords to heel. By 1927 most of south China was under his control.

But Chiang's alliance with the communists worried the business-men and landowners who were giving him money for his armies.

In the countryside the communists were taking land away from its owners and giving it to the peasants. In some cities workers were taking over factories. Chiang's rich supporters did not want ideas like these to spread.

Nor did Chiang. He decided to stamp them out.

In 1927 Chiang ordered his soldiers to kill all the communists they could lay hands on. In the great ports of Guangzhon and Shanghai his men slaughtered communists in thousands.

The communists who escaped fled to the countryside. One group was led by a young teacher named Mao Zedong.

Foreign intervention

A Chinese woodcut from around 1910 showing starving peasants attacking a landlord.

A French cartoon from 1898 comments on foreign intervention in China.

A modern American writer who lived in China in the 1940s suggests reasons for the poverty of its people.

"The trading and investment concessions . . . enabled foreigners to transfer substantial quantities of real wealth from the 'under-developed East' to the advanced industrial West and Japan . . .

Large-scale importation of cheap, machine-made goods undermined one sector of the economy after another. This was especially true of the textile trades. Millions of weavers, unable to compete with the power-driven looms . . . lost their main means of livelihood . . .

The rising tide of landless and destitute people enabled landowners to raise rents and jack-up interest rates. It enabled grain dealers to force harvest-time prices lower in winter and spring prices higher . . . Not only the labourers and tenants but also the landowning middle peasants felt the squeeze more and more. . . . They had to go ever more frequently to the money lender, and once saddled with debt found it impossible to break free . . .

. . . many landowning peasants went bankrupt, sold out their holdings strip by strip, and ended up with the yoke of rent around their necks, or left for the city hoping to find some work . . . Others became soldiers in the armies of the warlords or joined local bandit gangs."

William Hinton, *Fanshen*, 1966

1 a) Which nations are represented by the figures in the cartoon?
  b) What has the artist shown them doing?
  c) What do you think the Chinese artist is trying to show about the mood of the peasants in the picture?
  d) In your own words, say how William Hinton sees the connection between foreign influence in China and peasant hardship.
  e) How does he suggest that foreign influence added to disorder?

Russian communists such as Lenin said that the key to winning a revolution was the support of town workers. Some Chinese communists thought this would be true for their country – even after Chiang had massacred many of them in the towns.

Mao Zedong thought differently. He believed that the 1927 massacres proved that communist power in China would grow from the nine out of ten Chinese who were peasants. The important issues were ones to do with their lives, such as the rents they paid to landlords and the way they were treated by the government.

Communists at Jiangxi

Backed by other Chinese communists who agreed with him, Mao won the support of the peasants of Jiangxi, a mountain area in south China. They took land away from rich landowners and gave it to the peasants. They reduced the taxes the peasants had to pay and cancelled their debts to money-lenders.

Mao Zedong encouraged the peasants to elect committees to run their own affairs. Years later a peasant told a reporter:

'We arranged a mass meeting and elected a revolutionary committee. That then was our new government. There were various departments in the committee: a defence and a land department, and a grain department, and a department for women's affairs, and a department for young communists . . .'*

An American visitor gave an example of the result:

'There was a peasant lad who had joined the Reds and I asked him why he had done so. He told me that his parents were poor farmers, with only four mou of land [under an acre] which wasn't enough to feed him and his two sisters. When the Reds came to his village, he said, all the peasants welcomed them, brought them hot tea . . . Only the landlords ran. When the land was redistributed his parents received their share. So they were not sorry but very glad when he joined the "poor people's army".'**

The Red Army

It was Mao and another communist named Zhu De who organised the peasants into this 'Poor People's', or Red, army. They trained it to fight a hard-hitting, fast-moving guerilla type of war. The Red Army's fighting tactics were summed up in four slogans:

'When the enemy advances, we retreat!
When the enemy halts, we trouble them!
When the enemy tries to avoid a battle, we attack!
When the enemy retreats, we pursue!'

By the end of 1931 Mao had organised a communist government, or soviet, in Jiangxi.

* In Jan Myrdal, *Report from a Chinese Village*, 1967
** In Edgar Snow, *Red Star Over China*, 1938

Chiang's attack on Jiangxi, 1934

Chiang Kaishek was quick to see that the Jiangxi Soviet would, in the end, be a more serious threat to his Guomindang government than the warlords were. He set out to crush it.

In 1934 the Guomindang army surrounded the Jiangxi Soviet with over half a million well-armed soldiers, supported by 400 war planes. Against them stood a Red Army of 100,000 men, armed only with rifles and home-made spears and bombs.

Day after day Chiang's air force bombed and machine-gunned the Red Army and its peasant supporters. A million were killed or starved to death as Chiang slowly tightened his grip around Jiangxi.

The Long March, 1934–5

But, in October 1934, 90,000 men of the Red Army smashed their way through Chiang's armies. They set out with thousands of their peasant followers on an amazing fighting retreat – the Long March.

The Long March lasted for over a year. It took Mao and his followers across 9000 kilometres of wild rivers, frozen mountains and treacherous swamps. Constantly under attack, half-starved, the marchers overcame incredible difficulties.

When the Long March ended, the survivors were safe in the mountains of a northern province called Yanan. But out of 120,000 marchers who had left Jiangxi, only 20,000 reached Yanan.

The importance of the Long March

The Long March came to be seen as one of the most important events in China's history. Why was this?

First, it kept communism alive in China. Despite all Chiang's attempts to crush them, the communists survived to start building up their strength again.

Second, the Long March carried communist ideas to new peasant supporters over half of China's vast countryside.

Third, the success of the Long March made Mao the main leader of the Chinese Communist Party. From now on it was his ideas about how to gain power that counted. And the most important of these ideas was still this – that whoever wanted to control China had to start by winning the support of the peasants.

Japan and Manchuria, 1931

China faced another problem in the 1930s, as well as the struggle between Chiang and the communists.

In 1931 Japanese soldiers grabbed an outlying part of the country called Manchuria. They did this to get their hands on its farmlands and its rich supplies of coal and iron. The following year they also attacked China's greatest trading city, Shanghai.

Chiang refused to fight back. He was still more concerned with using his armies to destroy the communists. He called this policy 'internal pacification before resistance to external attack'.

The Xian Incident, 1936

Chiang's refusal to fight the Japanese made him more and more unpopular. Even his own generals disagreed with him. In December 1936, one of them called the Young Marshal kidnapped Chiang while he was visiting an army base in a northern city named Xian.

This kidnapping was known as the Xian Incident. The Young Marshal only let Chiang go when he agreed to put aside his differences with the communists and start fighting the Japanese.

The Japanese Invasion, 1937

China in the Second World War, 1941–5

The Civil War, 1946–9

Reluctantly, Chiang agreed to join with the communists in a 'United Front' against the Japanese. In return, the communists agreed to accept him as China's official leader.

In 1937 the Japanese began a full-scale invasion. By 1938 they had overrun most of eastern China. Chiang retreated with his Guomindang government to a mountain city called Chongqing.

The main communist armies retreated, too. But Red Army soldiers still carried on a fierce guerilla war in the areas occupied by the Japanese.

In 1941 the Japanese attacked the American naval base at Pearl Harbor (see Unit 65). This attack made the fighting in China part of the Second World War. The USA now poured weapons into China.

Chiang made little attempt to use the American supplies to beat the Japanese. He waited for the Americans fighting in the Pacific to do that, while he built up armies for war against the communists.

Meanwhile, the Red Army and its peasant supporters were still fighting a fierce resistance war. They carved out vast 'liberated areas' which the Japanese could rule only when they had large forces there. Whenever the Japanese forces went away, the Red Army and peasant committees took over again.

In August 1945 the USA dropped atomic bombs on Japan and the Japanese government surrendered (see Unit 65). The Japanese armies in China surrendered, too.

Chiang and Mao began talks about governing China between them. But soon they were quarrelling again.

The Americans backed Chiang. At the end of the Second World War the government of President Truman was very worried by the spread of communist power in Europe (see Unit 32). The last thing Truman wanted was a communist take-over of China, too.

So the Americans sent Chiang more money, weapons, supplies of all kinds. They air-lifted his troops to take over cities in northern China from the Japanese. By 1946 a civil war had begun.

Most people expected Chiang to win. But although Chiang held most of the cities, the communists held the country areas they had liberated from the Japanese. And they had strong support from peasants in the rest of the country.

The peasants were determined to seize the chance to get rid of landlords once and for all. As Mao's 'Poor People's Armies' marched across China, peasants everywhere welcomed them as liberators.

City people, too, had had enough of Chiang. Factories were at a standstill because of power cuts and shortages of raw materials. Hungry crowds began looting food and coal shops.

Even Chiang's soldiers deserted him. Whole armies went over to Mao, taking their American weapons and equipment with them.

By 1949 Chiang knew that he was beaten. He fled across the sea to the island of Taiwan, then usually called Formosa.

Mao and the communists were the masters of China. As Mao had once foretold, 'the countryside had conquered the city'.

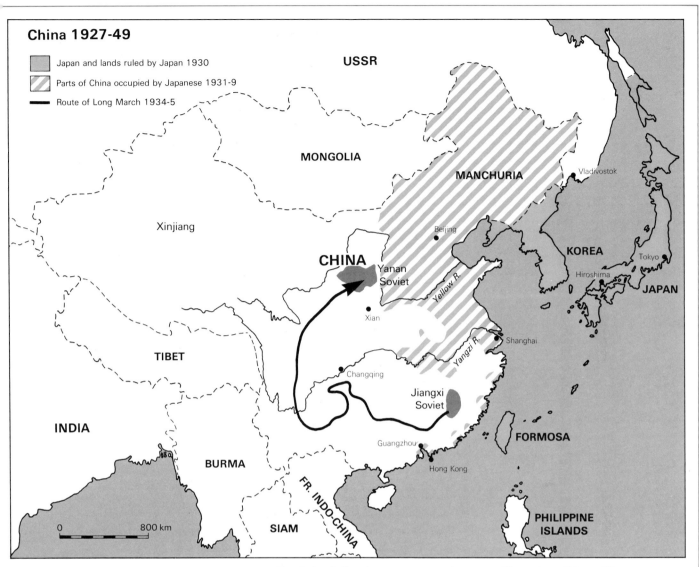

China 1927-49

Japan and lands ruled by Japan 1930

Parts of China occupied by Japanese 1931-9

Route of Long March 1934-5

USSR

MONGOLIA

MANCHURIA

Vladivostok

Xinjiang

CHINA

Beijing

KOREA

Yanan Soviet

Xian

Yellow R.

Hiroshima

Tokyo

JAPAN

TIBET

Changqing

Yangzi R.

Shanghai

Jiangxi Soviet

INDIA

Guangzhou

FORMOSA

0   800 km

BURMA

Hong Kong

SIAM

FR. INDO-CHINA

PHILIPPINE ISLANDS

The beginnings of modern China

1 a) Find the following towns on the map: Shanghai, Xian, Chongqing, Beijing. Choose any *two* and write two or three sentences about each to explain the part it has played in Chinese history in the twentieth century.

b) Find the following areas: Manchuria, Jiangxi, Yanan, Taiwan. Choose *two* and write two or three sentences about the importance of each in the history of twentieth-century China.

c) Which was the first part of China to be attacked by Japan in the 1930s?

d) What reason does the map suggest for this being the first part to suffer attack? What other reason is given in the unit?

e) Find the route of the Long March. Using the text and the map, suggest reasons why the marchers took such a roundabout route.

2 Each of the following years was important in the history of China: 1911, 1921, 1923, 1925, 1927, 1931, 1934, 1936, 1941, 1945, 1949.

a) Draw a time line which shows each of these dates. At the side of the date write the key event of that year.

b) Choose any *four* events that you think were especially important. Write two or three sentences about each to explain its importance.

The Long March

A survivor recalled one day in the mountains of western China.

"One day we camped at the foot of a steep cliff, so high that the summit was out of sight. We were in such bad shape that we could not climb this cliff without first having something to eat . . . I collected some dry twigs to make a fire and resolutely started roasting my shoes . . . after we had baked the shoes for some time we washed and scraped them clean, then boiled them in a basin. Boiling turned the leather yellow and soft and its appetising smell made us hungrier than ever . . . when the shoes were cooked our squad leader cut them in to small bits and distributed them among the men to eat before climbing the cliff the next day."

In *Long March: Eye-witness Accounts*, 1963

In 1935 Mao Zedong made a speech about the importance of the Long March.

"For twelve months we were under daily . . . bombing from the air by scores of planes. We were . . . pursued . . . on the ground by a big force of several hundred thousand men. We encountered untold difficulties and great obstacles on the way; but by using our two legs we swept across a distance of more than 6000 miles through the length and breadth of eleven provinces.

. . . The Long March . . . proclaims to the world that the Red Army is an army of heroes and that . . . Chiang Kaishek and his like are nobodies.

. . . Without the Long March, how could the broad masses have known so quickly that there are such great ideas in the world as are upheld by the Red Army? The Long March is a . . . seeding machine. It has sown many seeds in eleven provinces which will sprout, blossom into flowers, bear fruit and yield a crop in future."

Mao Zedong, *Selected Works*, 1963

3 a) What does the first extract tell you about   1) the difficulties of the Long March,   2) the discipline of the Red Army?

b) Give two reasons why the Long March was important, according to Mao.

c) Was either of these reasons more important than the other to China's future? Explain your view.

d) After Mao became ruler of China he continually reminded people of the Long March. Why do you think he did this?

A painting about the Long March. 'Storming the Liuting Bridge over the Tatu River', by Li Tsung Tsin, May 1935. Communist soldiers risk their lives to capture machine guns on the bank on the right.

4 a) What idea is the artist trying to give of the action at the bridge?

b) Would Mao approve or disapprove of the picture? Explain your answer.

All these people were involved in China between 1944 and 1949 and had views on the reasons for the Chinese Communist Party (CCP) victory. (KMT is short for Kuomintang, the old way of writing Guomindang.)

General Stilwell, US military adviser to Chiang Kaishek in 1944
"KMT: Corruption, chaos, neglect, taxes, words not deeds. Hoarding, black market, trading with the enemy.
CCP: Reduce taxes, rents and interests; raise production and standard of living. Practise what they preach."

In F. Green, A Curtain of Ignorance, 1965

A French observer writing in 1947
"The easy success of the communists can only be explained by their superior morale."

American reporter based in Shanghai, writing for Business Week, *1948*
"Over the years Chiang has alienated almost every economic group in China, peasants, workers, businessmen, even his own soldiers. He has refused to undertake land reform, has been unable to establish a sound currency and is the leader of an incompetent and graft ridden [corrupt] civil administration and army."

In F. Green, A Curtain of Ignorance, 1965

A Chinese university teacher at Tsing Hua University near Beijing, 1948
"We have become so completely convinced of the hopelessness of the existing government that we feel the sooner it is removed the better. Since the communists are obviously the only force capable of making this change, we are willing to support them as the lesser of two evils."

In D. Bodder, Peking Diary 1948–9: A Year of Revolution

General Barr, US adviser to Chiang Kaishek 1947–8, writing in 1949
"The government . . . found its armies scattered along thousands of miles of railroad . . . In order to hold the railroads it was also necessary to hold the large cities through which they passed . . . the troops degenerated from field armies capable of offensive combat, to garrison and lines of communication troops, with an inevitable loss of offensive spirit."

In L. Chaffin, The Communist Conquest of China, 1967

Chiang Kaishek, explaining his defeat
"[The communists] did everything to nullify reconstruction projects . . . to disrupt the nation's economic life and to upset its social order . . . Finally the people became so confused and bewildered that all they asked was peace at any price."
Chiang Kaishek, *Soviet Russia in China: A Summing Up at Seventy*, 1967

Mao quoted by a British historian, Stuart Schram, in History Today, *1981*
"Mao told Japanese delegations that it was thanks to the intervention of the Japanese imperial army that the CCP had been able to win victory."

5 a) List reasons for the CCP victory which appear in two or more of the above extracts.
  b) Do you think that any of these writers would have preferred communist rule to an honest and efficient Guomindang government?
  c) What did Mao mean by saying the Japanese had helped the CCP?
  d) Which of the extracts do you think gives the most important reasons for the CCP victory? Explain your choice.

On 1st October 1949 Mao Zedong stood with other communist leaders on top of the Gate of Heavenly Peace in the great square of China's capital city, Beijing. Before him paraded thousands of the victorious peasant soldiers of the People's Liberation Army.

Mao's official position was Chairman of the Chinese Communist Party (CCP), which now ruled 'People's China'.

Changes for the peasants

The support of China's peasants had given the communists their victory. Wherever the People's Liberation Army had won control, its soldiers had encouraged the peasants to take land away from landlords and divide it amongst themselves.

In 1950 Mao's new government followed this with a Land Reform Law. All over China landlords were put on trial, accused of mistreating peasants or of working with the Japanese. Thousands were put to death. Their lands passed to the peasants. China became a land of peasants farming their own fields.

But not for long. Like Soviet leaders in the 1930s, China's communist rulers needed cheap farm products to pay for developing the country's industries. They also needed cheap peasant labour.

In 1952 the communist leaders drove all western businessmen from the country. In 1953, with Russian advice, they drew up a Five Year Plan for industry. Like Stalin's plans (see Unit 20) this concentrated on building up heavy industry.

The collectives

Communist officials persuaded and bullied the peasants to put their private lands together into 'collectives', roughly one for each of China's villages. In these collectives some peasants joined teams to work the land. Others joined gangs to wheel earth or carry rocks to build roads, dams and houses.

Social changes

Along with these changes went important social reforms. The communist leaders made massive efforts to provide more teachers and classes for the nine out of ten Chinese who could not read. They trained doctors and health workers to tackle sickness and teach people how to prevent disease, by keeping water supplies pure and getting rid of flies. In a law of 1950 they gave women equal rights.

By the later 1950s everyday life was improving in China. New industries were growing, with Russian help. The collectives were farming more land than ever before. Food production had increased and famine seemed a thing of the past.

The Great Leap Forward

Many communist leaders were satisfied with the rate of progress. But for Mao Zedong the pace was too slow. In 1958 he launched the 'Great Leap Forward'.

The Great Leap combined a drive for faster industrialisation with more massive changes in the countryside. Here Mao brought together the collectives to form communes.

Communes

Communes were groupings of all the villages in one district. They had an average population of 30,000 people. This was enough for them to organise their workers into brigades – some to work on the land, some in workshops or mines, still more to labour building roads and dams, new schools and clinics.

Industry

Mao had come to dislike the Soviet way of industrialising by putting heavy industry and big factories first. He now decided that China would do without high technology factories which depended on foreign money and help from foreign experts. China's industrial growth would start instead from small workshops and 'backyard' furnaces in the communes. Mao meant to show that there was a Chinese way of industrialising which was better for China than either the Soviet or the Capitalist way.

For Mao the communes were also a way of involving all the people in China's future. That is why communes were made responsible for their own schools, nurseries for the children of working parents, health clinics, rest homes for the elderly and canteens to feed people who were labouring long hours every day.

The Russians go home, 1960

The Great Leap Forward led to an open row with the Russians. Mao was already quarrelling with them about other things, such as the fact that they would not share their nuclear weapons with him. Soon, in 1960, the USSR called home its experts working in China.

The Great Leap fails

Economically, the Great Leap Forward proved a disaster. The 'backyard' furnaces turned out iron of such poor quality that it could not be used. Some factories had to close down because the people running them did not understand how to plan supplies of materials or fuels. In others, eager but unskilled workers ruined valuable machines by running them at two and three times their maximum permitted speeds.

The result was that industrial production in 1960 was lower than it had been in the year before the Great Leap started.

On top of these industrial failures, in 1959 and 1960 the crops failed. In some parts of the country there was drought; in others, heavy rain and floods. There was famine again in China. Reports claimed that ten million people had starved to death.

The challenge to Mao

Other communist leaders blamed Mao for the disaster. One of them, Liu Shaoqi, said it was 'seventy per cent man made' – and everyone knew that the man he meant was Mao. Another leader who criticised Mao was a veteran of the Long March named Deng Xiaoping. You will read more about him later.

Liu and the others undid many of Mao's schemes. They gave peasants in the communes small plots of land of their own. They paid factory workers higher wages. The aim was to encourage people to work harder by rewarding them for doing so.

Mao believed that such changes would make people more concerned about their personal interests and affairs than about the good of all. He also hated the power that his rivals' policies gave to bosses and experts – factory managers, doctors, teachers, university scientists. He said that such people were robbing the peasants and workers of their right to share in running the country.

By the mid-1960s Mao had added Communist Party officials to his black list. He believed that many of these 'bureaucrats' had become more concerned with keeping their power as local bosses, and the good life that went with it, than with building the new China.

The Cultural Revolution

To turn the tables on his opponents Mao organised China's young people to begin the 'Cultural Revolution'. Mao wanted them to force their elders back on to what he believed was the true communist path. 'Learn revolution by making revolution', he told them. He hoped that while doing this they would also help him to get rid of rival leaders like Liu Shaoqi.

Red Guards

From 1966 millions of teenage 'Red Guards' roamed about China. They marched through the streets waving their copies of the 'Little Red Book' – a collection of Mao's sayings. Everywhere they plastered up slogans and pictures of Mao. To them he was the 'Great Helmsman' and 'The Red Sun in Our Hearts'.

The Red Guards attacked anyone they claimed was not living according to Mao's teachings. People could get into serious trouble during the Cultural Revolution for wearing a little lipstick or slightly out of the ordinary clothes, for collecting stamps, playing chess or keeping pets. All these things were branded as 'anti-revolutionary'.

More seriously, the Red Guards beat up teachers, experts in industry, government officials – anyone they could say was not a full-blooded revolutionary. All over China thousands were killed, thrown into prison or driven from their jobs. In places, the Red Guards themselves split into rival gangs, who fought over which was the most truly revolutionary.

The People's Liberation Army could have stopped the beatings and killings. But it supported Mao during the Cultural Revolution and let the violence go on.

With the army's support Mao was also able to deal with his rivals in the Communist Party leadership – 'the capitalist roaders', as he called them. The lucky ones, like Deng Xiaoping, Mao packed off to work as labourers in factories or on farms. Unlucky ones, like Liu Shaoqi, disappeared. Mao had Liu arrested in 1967. He died from beatings and lack of medical care in a secret prison two years later.

Liu was one victim among many. In 1980 the General Secretary of the Chinese Communist Party claimed that the Cultural Revolution had led to a million deaths and thirty million cases of beatings and ill-treatment.

By the end of the 1960s China's leaders – even Mao himself – could see that the Red Guards were destroying much of the progress made since 1949. The government was disorganised. The education system had just about collapsed. Production of all kinds of goods had fallen steeply.

Only the army remained intact. The Party leaders used it to disband the Red Guards. They ordered them back to school or off to work in the countryside. Life began a slow return to normal.

Peasants and landlords

The trial of a landlord before a People's Court in the province of Guangdong, 1953. He was found guilty and shot.

A Chinese peasant describes how Ching-ho, a landlord in his village, was treated in 1948, when the Red Army took over the district.

". . . the people went to Ching-ho's courtyard to help take over his property. . . then we began to beat him. Finally he said, 'I have forty silver dollars under the k'ang [sleeping platform]. We went in and dug it up. The money stirred up everyone. We beat him again. He told us where to find another hundred after that. But no one believed that this was the end of his hoard. We beat him again and several militiamen began to heat an iron bar in one of the fires.

Altogether we got $500 from Ching-ho that night. . . we decided to eat all the things that Ching-ho had prepared to pass the New Year – a whole crock of dumplings stuffed with pork and peppers and other delicacies. . .

. . . In the past we never lived through a happy New Year because he always asked for his rent and interest and then cleaned our houses bare."

In William Hinton, *Fanshen*, 1966

In 1927 peasants in parts of south China had dealt with landlords in much the same way. Mao had defended their actions at the time.

"This is what some people call 'going too far'. . . Such talk. . . is wrong. The local tyrants, evil gentry and lawless landlords have themselves driven the peasants to do this. For ages they have used their power to tyrannise over the peasants and trample them underfoot.

. . . The peasants are clear-sighted. Who is bad and who is not, who is the worst. . . who deserves severe punishment and who deserves to be let off lightly – the peasants keep clear accounts and very seldom has the punishment exceeded the crime."

Mao Zedong, *Selected Works*, 1963

1 a) In the picture, who are 1) the people sitting at the tables, 2) the person kneeling in front of them? Which law led to scenes such as this?

b) Write a discussion between someone who believes that the peasants in the first extract were 'going too far' and a supporter of Mao who believes that peasants are 'clear-sighted' in dealing with landlords.

Life in Mao's China

A poster from the campaign to persuade peasants to join collective farms. It shows peasants of Tachai village building walls to stop floods washing the fields away.

2 What would be your thoughts about this poster if you were 1) a leader of the Communist Party in your village, 2) a peasant who had just obtained land of your own?

An American writer described a visit to China in the early 1970s.

" 'What is the principal difference', I asked a Chinese friend, 'between this street in Wuhan today, and this street before the Revolution?'

He thought for a moment and answered: 'The flies. You can't imagine what it was like to walk down the streets of a Chinese city in the old days. You could hear a humming in the air, strong, like the sound of violins in an orchestra. It was the flies. If you looked down you could hardly see the pavement for flies. . .'

I asked an American who had been in China before the Revolution what the principal difference he noticed today was. 'The smell', he said. . . 'You can't imagine the variety of smells in the old Chinese city' . . . Another friend said the thing he noticed most was the absence of beggars . . . the horrible cripples and mutilated persons, the men without noses . . . mothers who thrust their babies at you – babies with watery-blind eyes and open sores at the mouth. . .

'And' said my friend, 'there was that other sight of old China – the coolie [labourer] who fell in his traces. Perhaps he was pulling a heavy load. Perhaps he was just standing, waiting for work. . . The crowd passed on, walking round him, no one stopping. . . Finally a refuse cart would come and the body would be hurled in among the dung and the ashes.'

I looked again at Wuhan. . . There were no beggars. There were no mutilated children. . . Coolies still hauled carts but, thin and wiry as they were, none collapsed, none looked ill-fed or diseased."

Harrison Salisbury, *To Peking and Beyond*, 1973

3 a) What does Harrison Salisbury mean by the 'Revolution'?
  b) Does his account suggest any reasons why the Revolution succeeded?
  c) List four ways in which the people he questioned thought life was better in Wuhan in the 1970s. If you had lived there, which improvement would have been most important to you?

Mao speaking to Red Guards, 6th April 1967.

"Have no fear of chaos. . . The more chaos you dish up and the longer it goes on, the better. Disorder and chaos are always a good thing. . . They clarify things. . . But never use weapons. It is never a good thing to open fire."

In Dick Wilson, Mao: The People's Emperor, 1979

A former Red Guard gave this account in 1975 of the Cultural Revolution.

"Between June and November 1966 we locked up almost every university head, deputy department head, professor and lecturer. Every day we rounded them up and read them quotations from the works of Chairman Mao. . . Every day they had to clean the lavatories and carry out the night soil. . .

Most of them deserved their fate. Chairman Mao was right when he warned us always to be on guard against intellectuals (brain-workers). You can't trust intellectuals. . . They resist the Party line, become arrogant, develop a bourgeois way of thinking, and worship foreign things.

Take old Wang [a university professor], for example. When the Red Guards went to his place and took it apart, it was full of fancy scrolls and feudal Chinese art. Must have been worth a fortune. We dug out foreign coins and books, and you should have seen the furniture! He had closets full of leather shoes, fancy clothes and junk like that. . .

How can a socialist society tolerate people like that teaching the young? True, he was a leading specialist in physics and we needed his skills, but was it worth the cost, to keep this stinking bourgeois remnant alive to infect students with his rotten way of life?"

In B. M. Frolic, Mao's People, 1980

Another former Red Guard speaking in 1980.

"I spent eight years fanning the flames of revolution. . . it was like losing a big chunk of your life. Now I would like to contribute to the motherland, but what do I have? I never finished high school."

In F. Butterfield, China: Alive in a Bitter Sea, 1982

4 a) What did Mao mean when he advised the Red Guards to make chaos?

b) Why did he want them to behave like this?

c) Do you think Mao would have approved or disapproved of the students' treatment of old Wang and other university teachers? Explain your view.

d) How does the speaker in the second extract justify the students' actions? What arguments could be used to answer him?

e) If you had been the student in the third extract, would you have regretted being a Red Guard, or would you have thought that it had been worthwhile? Explain your answer.

f) Compare the account of the Cultural Revolution in this Unit with the story of Stalin's purges in the USSR in Unit 21. How many 1) similarities, 2) differences, can you see between them?

g) Can you suggest reasons for *either* the similarities *or* differences?

The Gang of Four

In 1976 Mao died. His widow and three others tried to take control of the government and re-open the Cultural Revolution.

For a short while this 'Gang of Four' seemed set to bring back the Red Guard terror. But other communist leaders united to have them arrested in 1976. It was the end of the road for Mao's way of doing things in China.

Deng takes over

The Chinese Communist Party's new leader was Deng Xiaoping, the 'capitalist roader' Mao had sacked in the Cultural Revolution. Alongside him was Zhao Ziyang, who was made Prime Minister in 1980. Their first aim was to repair the damage done by the Cultural Revolution and the Gang of Four. Then they wanted to make China a leading industrial nation.

Deng and Zhao decided that the quickest way to do this was to buy equipment and technical knowledge from abroad. As Deng said:

'No country can now develop by closing its door . . . We suffered from this and our forefathers suffered from this. Isolation landed China in poverty, backwardness and ignorance.'

Dengism

Deng's China began to sign agreements with the USA, Britain, Japan and other industrial countries. By the 1980s foreign firms were building new factories in China to make everything from computers to face creams.

Deng and Zhao also offered the Chinese people more personal rewards for hard work.

In the countryside, most of the land was handed back to the peasants as separate family farms. They could decide for themselves which crops to grow. And they could keep the money they earned from selling them, once they had paid rent to the government.

The change brought a dramatic increase in food production. Each year between 1978 and 1985 this grew at *twice* the rate that it had done during the collective and commune years from 1952 to 1978.

Factory workers were rewarded, too. If they produced more, they were given extra money called 'responsibility payments'.

The more the peasants and workers earned, the more they had to spend. Not just on food either, but on the television sets, refrigerators and stylish clothes which now began to appear in the shops.

A few Chinese feared that China was travelling down a road that would lead back to capitalism, to the rich ill-treating the poor and to evils such as unemployment and inflation.

But most ordinary Chinese probably agreed with Deng when he said:

'Whatever system induces the peasants to produce more should be adopted, be it collective or individual . . . It does not matter whether the cat is black or white, so long as it catches mice.'

Life in Deng's China

A picture and article from The Economist, *16th October 1982.*

"The Chinese are discovering the delights of buying now and paying later. These days it is possible, in the luckier parts of China, to acquire a television, a tape recorder, a washing machine or a fridge by putting down a quarter of the price and paying off the rest over a year. For those with even more expensive tastes, gold jewellery is being sold in the shops for the first time since 1962. A recent article in the English-language newspaper *China Daily* remarked that, as bicycles and television 'have become increasingly commonplace, trendy Chinese have started to fix their sights on new status symbols'.

The post-Mao consumerism is evident in the streets of Peking [Beijing]; women trendies prefer bright dresses to baggy shirts and trousers. Trousers have returned with the chills of autumn, but they are better cut than they used to be. Highish heels are commonplace. Cosmetics are being used, discreetly. The Avon Corporation, dreaming of a million Chinese doorbells, is a partner in a Peking cold cream factory.

Home-grown private enterprise is still pretty private, largely confined to tiny businesses. However, Peking now has 780 tailors, who sell all the custom-made clothes they can make. A report by the New China News Agency said that sales of off-the-peg garments by department stores dropped 30% this summer. Uniformity is out, originality is in."

1 a) Using the picture and the text, list *three* ways in which life for the people of China was different under Deng than it had been under Mao.

b) Suggest reasons for the changes that had taken place.

c) Would anyone be unhappy about the changes? Explain your answer.

d) Imagine that you had the chance to be a teenager in China. Which would you choose – to be living there in the 1960s or in the 1980s? Explain your choice.

'Opening' Japan

1854. American warships steamed into Tokyo harbour and forced the Japanese government to sign a treaty. The treaty gave the USA special trading rights in Japan.

Within five years European countries had forced Japan to sign similar agreements. Japan had to let in foreign traders and allow them to be exempt from the need to obey Japanese laws.

Japanese shame at the treaties led to rebellions against the court officials who had ruled Japan in the Emperor's name for centuries. In 1868 the Emperor Meiji took over the government himself.

The Meiji's modernisation

The Meiji gave the Japanese people a slogan – 'a prosperous nation, strongly armed'. Then he began turning the slogan into fact.

He sent young men to study the industries and science of Britain, Germany and the United States. He hired foreign experts and technicians to teach the Japanese people modern skills.

The Japanese used their new knowledge and skills to build railways, steelworks, shipyards, factories. To give the new industries a skilled workforce, the Meiji's government built 54,000 new schools. In 1872 it made education compulsory for everyone.

The Meiji also gave Japan a modern, well trained army and navy. By the start of the twentieth century Japan was the one Asian country strong enough to deal on equal terms with the great powers of Europe and the USA. The rest of the world first realised this in 1905 when Japan defeated Russia in war, completely destroying a Russian war fleet at the Battle of Tsushima.

But Japan still had problems. Most of the country is covered by high mountains and Japan was short of farmland to grow food. It was also short of raw materials such as coal and iron ore.

Japan the trader

Up to the 1920s Japan coped with these problems by selling the products of its industries to other countries. This earned it money to buy foreign food and raw materials.

By the end of the 1920s Japanese businessmen were finding this more difficult. After the American Wall Street Crash of 1929 (see Unit 25) the situation grew worse still. The USA was Japan's best customer, especially for its silk. But now all kinds of trade between nations fell drastically.

Japanese army leaders, backed by some politicians, decided that if Japan could not get the goods it needed by trade, it should take them by war.

Japan and China

This was the reason Japanese soldiers attacked first Manchuria in 1931, and then the rest of China in 1937 – to get their hands on Chinese land, coal and iron ore (see Unit 62).

In 1932 the Japanese gave Manchuria a new name, Manchukuo, and a puppet Emperor called Pu-yi – the boy Emperor the Chinese had overthrown in 1911. Manchukuo was supposed to be independent, but everyone knew that it was a Japanese colony.

In both 1931 and 1937 the Japanese generals struck without the permission of either the Emperor, Hirohito, or the Japanese government. Some government leaders believed that Japan should try to win prosperity by building up its international trade again. But so many politicians supported the generals that the government had to go along with them.

Japan and South-East Asia

Beyond China lay other lands the Japanese generals had their eyes on – Indo-China (now called Vietnam), Malaya (now Malaysia) and the East Indies (now Indonesia). These lands were rich in valuable raw materials like oil and rubber. And their rice could be used to feed the people of Japan's cities.

The problem was that these lands of South-East Asia were already colonies of Britain, France or Holland.

When Hitler's armies overran Europe in 1940 (see Unit 9) Japan's leaders grabbed their chance. They started by sending their soldiers to take Indo-China from the French.

Japan and the USA

This worried the Americans. They earned a lot of money from trade with Asia. They now feared that Japan might seize this trade.

Ever since the start of the Japanese attack on China in 1937, the USA had been cutting down exports of goods that the Japanese might use to make war – aircraft and chemicals, for example. Now, in July 1941, they stopped all shipments of oil.

Japan faced disaster. It imported 80 per cent of her oil from the United States. Without oil its industries would shudder to a stop.

'Japan is like a fish in a pond from which the water is being gradually drained away', a top naval officer told Emperor Hirohito.

The question was, how to stop the drain?

Konoye and Tojo

Japanese leaders like the Prime Minister, Prince Konoye, wanted to talk and make a deal with the Americans. But talking failed to bring an agreement. In October 1941 Konoye resigned and General Tojo took over as Japan's Prime Minister.

Tojo was well known for his belief that a sharp use of force was often the best way to solve disagreements. This had earned him a nickname – the Razor.

There was plenty of oil in South-East Asia. Tojo decided that Japan must grab it – and make it impossible for the Americans to use their Pacific battle fleet to stop them.

The Pearl Harbor attack, 1941

On 7th December 1941 Japanese warplanes roared in over Pearl Harbor, the American navy's main base in the Pacific Ocean. Their bombs and torpedoes sank or badly damaged eight American battleships, blew up hundreds of aircraft and killed over 2000 men.

When the Pearl Harbor attack took place the USA and Japan were still at peace. But on 8th December 1941 the USA declared war on Japan.

Since Germany was Japan's ally (see Unit 7) Hitler declared war on the USA. Hitler's war in Europe and Japan's war in Asia became one war – the Second World War.

Japan's conquests, 1941–2

In the months which followed, Japanese forces swept like a flood over South-East Asia and the islands of the western Pacific. On 25th December 1941 they captured the British colony of Hong Kong, off the coast of China. Two months later they marched into Singapore, Britain's chief stronghold in the East. In March 1942 they forced the American defenders of the Philippine Islands to surrender.

By the summer of 1942 the Japanese had conquered over 2.5 million square kilometres of land, rich in raw materials and inhabited by more than a hundred million people.

Many of these people welcomed the Japanese at first. They saw them as fellow Asians who had come to free them from European rule. They were impressed, too, by how easily the Japanese defeated the Europeans. In years to come this would be very important. Never again would the peoples of South-East Asia respect and fear their old masters as they had done in the past.

The Greater East Asia Co-Prosperity Sphere

One South-East Asian newspaper at the time described Japan as 'the light of Asia, the guide and teacher of her peoples'. The Japanese encouraged this impression. They talked about organising the newly conquered lands into 'The Greater East Asia Co-Prosperity Sphere', a trading area that would benefit everyone – but especially the Japanese, who would control it.

Japanese rule

The real meaning of Japanese rule soon became clear to the people of South-East Asia. Japanese soldiers ordered them about and treated them as inferiors. Their leaders were expected to become puppets. Any who objected were thrown into prison or killed

Behaviour like this quickly turned admiration for the Japanese into hatred. Anti-Japanese guerilla bands formed in the jungles.

Japan's failure to keep the support of the people of its newly conquered empire helped to bring about eventual Japanese defeat.

The Pacific War, 1942–5

But Japan's first setback in war came at sea. In May 1942, in the Battle of the Coral Sea, planes from American aircraft carriers beat back a big Japanese invasion force threatening Australia.

In June 1942, the Japanese suffered an even worse defeat. Their navy attacked an important American base called Midway Island. Again, carrier-borne warplanes beat them off with heavy losses.

In the next three years Allied fighting men slowly and bloodily pushed the Japanese out of the lands Japan had conquered. By 1945 they were ready to invade Japan itself.

But the invasion never came.

On 16th July 1945 Allied scientists tested the world's first atomic bomb. Even they were shocked by the result. They had invented the most destructive weapon mankind had ever known.

Hiroshima, 1945

On 6th August 1945 an American bomber dropped an atomic bomb over the Japanese city of Hiroshima. It wiped out most of Hiroshima and killed almost 10,000 of its people.

A few days later a second atomic bomb was dropped on the city of Nagasaki. The horrified Japanese government surrendered.

The Second World War was over.

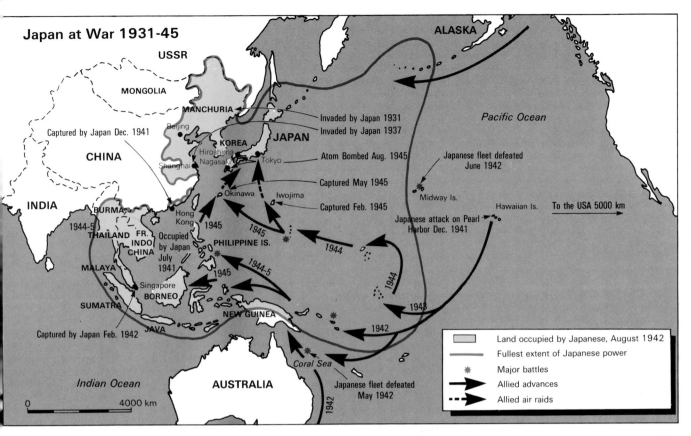

Japan at War 1931-45

USSR

MONGOLIA

MANCHURIA

Captured by Japan Dec. 1941

CHINA

Beijing

Shanghai

KOREA

JAPAN

Hiroshima
Nagasaki

Tokyo

Okinawa

Iwojima

ALASKA

Pacific Ocean

Invaded by Japan 1931

Invaded by Japan 1937

Atom Bombed Aug. 1945

Captured May 1945

Captured Feb. 1945

Japanese fleet defeated
June 1942

Midway Is.

Hawaiian Is.   To the USA 5000 km

Japanese attack on Pearl
Harbor Dec. 1941

INDIA

BURMA

1944-5

THAILAND   FR.
INDO
CHINA

Occupied
by Japan
July
1941

Hong
Kong   1945

PHILIPPINE IS.

1945

1945

1944

1944-5

1944

1943

MALAYA

Singapore

BORNEO

SUMATRA

JAVA

NEW GUINEA

Captured by Japan Feb. 1942

1942

Coral Sea

1942

Indian Ocean   AUSTRALIA

0   4000 km

Japanese fleet defeated
May 1942

	Land occupied by Japanese, August 1942
	Fullest extent of Japanese power
*	Major battles
→	Allied advances
⇢	Allied air raids

Japan at war, 1931–45

1 a) Use the map and the text to make a pyramid time line of the fighting in Asia and the Pacific, 1931–45, with February 1942 at the peak.

b) Choose *four* events from this period which you think were particularly important. Write two or three sentences about each.

c) With the help of the map, explain how the following were so important to both sides in the Pacific War: sea power, air power, islands.

Attack on Shanghai, 1937

'Dawn over Asia.' This cartoon appeared in Punch *after the Japanese attack on China in 1937.*

2 a) Why has the cartoonist used the idea of a rising sun for his picture?

b) Is he making a prediction about future events in Asia and the Pacific? If so, what is it?

c) Did events prove him right or wrong? Explain your answer.

The atomic bombs

A sixteen-year-old boy recalls the bombing of Hiroshima when he was ten.

"Everything in sight which can be called a building is crushed to the ground and sending out flames. People who are burned so badly that the skin of their bodies is peeling off in red strips are raising shrieking cries that sound as though the victims would die in the next minute. The street is so covered with dead people and burned people stretched out and groaning, and the fallen houses and things, that we can't get through.

No matter how much I might exaggerate the stories of the burned people who died shrieking, and of how the city of Hiroshima was burned to the ground, the facts would still be clearly more terrible and I could never really express the truth on this piece of paper; on this point I ask for pardon."

In Arata Osada, *Children of the A-Bomb*, 1959

A photograph taken in Nagasaki after it was bombed on 9th August 1945.

4 a) Why does the boy say he 'can never really express the truth'?
  b) Which of these two sources gives you the more vivid impression of an atomic attack? Explain your answer.
  c) More people were killed by high explosive bombs dropped on the German city of Dresden in February 1945 than by atomic bombs in Hiroshima or Nagasaki. Do you think that this fact makes dropping the atomic bombs any less important as an event in world history?

Why the A-bombs were used

A letter to his son from one of the US airmen who bombed Hiroshima.

" . . . Today the lead plane of our little formation dropped a single bomb which probably exploded with the force of 15,000 tons of high explosive. That means that the days of large bombing raids, with several hundred planes, are really finished. A single plane disguised as a friendly transport can now wipe out a city. That means to me that nations will have to get along in a friendly fashion, or suffer the consequences of sudden sneak attacks which can cripple them overnight.

What regrets I have about being a party to killing and maiming thousands of Japanese this morning are tempered with the hope that this terrible weapon we have created may bring the countries of the world together and prevent further wars."

In F. Knebel and C. W. Bailey, *No High Ground*, 1960

5 a) Do you think that the writer of the letter is   1) sorry,   2) hopeful, about what has just happened? Explain your opinion.

  b) Do you think that events since 1945 show that he was right in his beliefs about the bomb's effects on relations between countries?

These sources express views about why the atomic bombs were dropped.

Harry S. Truman, the US President in 1945
"The final decision of where and when to use the atomic bomb was up to me. Let there be no mistake about it. I regarded the bomb as a military weapon and never had any doubt that it should be used."

H. S. Truman, *Memoirs Vol. 1*, 1958

Admiral William D. Leahy, President Truman's adviser in 1945
" . . . the use of this barbarous weapon at Hiroshima and Nagasaki was of no material assistance to our war against Japan. The Japanese were already defeated and ready to surrender because of the effective sea blockade and the successful bombing with conventional weapons."

W. D. Leahy, *I Was There*, 1950

General Curtis Le May, US air force commander in 1945
"I think President Truman made the proper decision because I firmly believe that it saved lives in the long run by doing it and shortened the war and that was what we were after."

In L. Giovannitte and F. Freed, *The Decision to Drop the Bomb*, 1965

Clement Attlee, British Prime Minister when the bombs were dropped
"In the light of what we knew at the time, which was that the military were in command in Japan and that the Japanese would fight to the last man . . . In the light of that I believe the decision was right."

In L. Giovanitti and F. Freed, *The Decision to Drop the Bomb*, 1965

6 a) Which of the other writers disagrees with President Truman's decision?

  b) Explain why the writer disagrees.

  c) What is the main reason that the other two agree with Truman?

  d) Imagine you were a British or American prisoner of war in Japan in 1945. Would you be for or against dropping the atomic bomb? Why?

  e) Imagine that you, not President Truman, have to decide whether or not to drop atomic bombs on Japan. What do you decide – and why?

289

Defeated Japan, 1945

Japan lay in ruins at the end of the Second World War. 'Devastated, hopeless, flat broke and leaderless', wrote a visitor in 1945.

Its biggest cities were 'a vast sea of ashes', wrote another visitor. 'No bits of walls, no cellars even, just ashes.' Its people were almost starving. It had no raw materials for its factories.

Yet only five or six years later Japan was on the way to becoming the richest country in Asia. Twenty years later it was the second richest in the world. How did it happen?

Revival

The revival was started off by help from the USA. American food, equipment and money poured into Japan, especially after 1949.

The main reason the Americans were so generous was the victory of Mao Zedong's communists in China (see Unit 62).

After the Second World War the Americans based their foreign policy on the idea of 'containing' communism, or stopping it from spreading (see Unit 32). With China under communist rule, the USA wanted a strong and friendly ally nearby.

In 1950 American soldiers became involved in a war to prevent communists from taking over Korea (see Unit 48). Japan became their main supply base.

Orders for supplies poured into Japan. The Japanese people grabbed the chance this gave them to get back on their feet.

The growth of industry

Most of Japan's factories had turned out cheap textiles and low quality household goods before the Second World War. Now its firms concentrated on more profitable products – steel, machinery and high quality goods needing lots of scientific 'know-how'.

By 1956 Japan had taken the place of Britain as the world's biggest ship-building nation. By 1961 it was the world's third largest steel producer, after the USA and the USSR.

Japan went on to become one of the world's biggest producers of cars, high quality cameras, television sets and electronic equipment of all kinds. It exported many of these goods to other countries.

One reason for Japan's success in industry and trade was an ability to spot products that people all over the world would be keen to buy. A second was its ability to make these products better and more cheaply than anyone else.

Exports

Exporting goods for sale to other countries was very important to Japan. Food and raw materials had to be imported to feed people and keep them at work. Exports paid for these imports.

Japan's success as an exporter sometimes caused problems with other industrial countries. With so many people buying Japanese products, foreign manufacturers grew afraid that their own industries might be destroyed.

Their fears were understandable. Take two examples. In the 1950s Britain was a world leader in motor-cycle making, as was Germany in camera making. By the 1970s both these industries had been wiped out because so many buyers preferred to buy rival Japanese products.

In the 1980s rival manufacturers all over the world called upon their governments to do something to reduce imports from Japan.

offered to make it easier for them to sell their goods in Japan. They set up factories in countries such as Britain to assemble Japanese products such as cars, so providing jobs for British workers.

Not only industry changed in Japan after the Second World War. So did the way in which the country was governed.

Government

Before the war only some of the people had the vote. Japan was really ruled by admirals, generals and a few right-wing politicians. They used the Emperor, Hirohito, as a figurehead for their plans.

From 1945 to 1952 the USA occupied Japan. For the first five of these years the American general, MacArthur, ran the country almost like a new Emperor.

The Treaty of San Francisco, 1951

American rule was ended by an agreement called the Treaty of San Francisco, signed in 1951. But the two countries continued to work closely with one another.

Before the Americans ended their rule in Japan they set up a democratic system of government. They gave all adults the vote to elect a national Parliament called the Diet. The Diet was given full power to run the country. The Emperor, Hirohito, kept his title, but he had little real power.

On the whole, this new system of government worked well. So did other reforms brought in by the Americans.

Farmers

In 1946 MacArthur's government brought in the Owner Farmer Establishment Law. This said that nobody could own more than three hectares of land. Anyone who owned more had to sell it to the government, which then re-sold it to peasants at low prices.

By 1950 over two million hectares had been re-distributed. Four millon peasant farmers became the owners of their own land. The government encouraged them to farm it in the most up-to-date ways. By the 1960s, five million fewer Japanese farmers were producing one third more food than before the war.

Armed forces

Memories of their wartime sufferings made many Japanese strongly anti-war. Japan's armed forces were far smaller than in the 1930s. Their name, the Self Defence Forces, was chosen because Japan declared it would never again try to get its way by war.

Japan in the 1980s

In the 1980s the people of Japan were among the best off in the world. Nobody was short of food. Most people lived in comfortable, if small, homes filled with televisions and other modern equipment.

Yet, despite Japan's prosperity, not all Japanese were happy about what was happening to their country.

Some said that business bosses were running Japan for their own benefit. They complained about the endlessly growing factories polluting the cities and the countryside. Many feared that the changes were threatening their country's traditional ways of life.

Progress in Japan

Part of an article on modern Japan by a British writer (g.n.p. is gross national product – the value of all goods produced in a country).

"When I first went to Japan in 1962, it was an Asian country with an income less than half of Britain's. It is nearly twice as rich as Britain now and more than twice as much a society that works.

The thirteenfold increase in Japan's real g.n.p. in the past 30 years has not only been the fastest economic growth by any country ever . . . it is growth that has gone to the right places . . .

Japan has raised its citizens' average age of death from under 55 in 1949 to top Scandinavian rates of over 78 for a woman, over 73 for a man, now. It has brought infant mortality down from 115 per 1,000 in 1933–37 to under 9 per 1,000 now . . . the Americans have nearly twice as many physicians per head, but (with infant mortality at 18 per 1,000) lose twice as many babies.

. . . the Japanese have just carried through the first big industrial revolution in world history during which crime rates have gone down. In 1948–73 Japanese crime rates halved. All crimes are now 5 times higher . . . in America . . . although Japan has one third fewer policemen per head . . .

Japanese crime rates are low because arrest rates per crime are high . . . If you and I decide to mug an old lady in Tokyo tonight, we face a 78 per cent chance of being arrested, against around a 2 per cent risk if we mug her in parts of New York. Japanese policemen . . . have a target time for arrival on the spot after any emergency telephone call anywhere; the national average is now just over 3 minutes, going down. The police are helped because so many Japanese live in groups which notice . . . any member's deviant [out of line] behaviour, but that is another Japanese triumph. They have created an urban society in which fewer people are lonely."

Norman Macrae, 'Must Japan Slow?', *The Economist* 23rd February 1980

'Stars' by the Japanese poet Takenaka Iku.

"Over Japan there are stars.
Stars that stink like petrol
Stars that speak with foreign accents
Stars that rattle like old Fords
Stars the colour of Coca Cola
Stars that hum like a fridge
Stars as coarse as tinned food
Stars cleaned with cotton wool and tweezers
And sterilised with formalin
Stars charged with radioactivity."

In *The Penguin Book of Japanese Verse,* 1970

1 a) How does Norman Macrae support his statement that, compared with Britain, Japan is 'more than twice as much a society that works'?

b) Does he give enough evidence to make you agree with him? Explain your answer.

c) Is the poem praising or criticising life in Japan? Explain your answer.

d) Why do you think that the British writer and the Japanese poet have different attitudes to life in Japan?

PART TEN

THE INDIAN SUB-CONTINENT

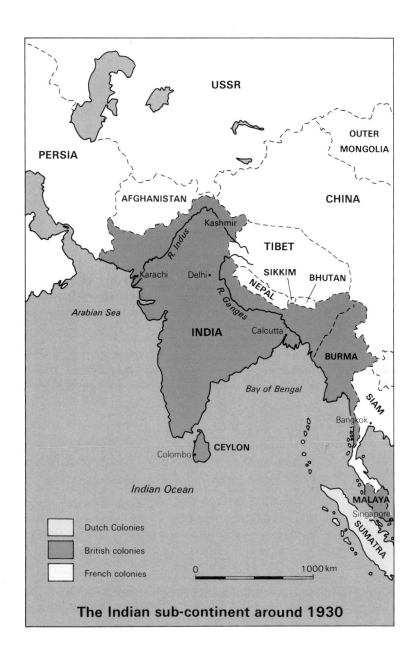

The Indian sub-continent around 1930

USSR

PERSIA

AFGHANISTAN

OUTER MONGOLIA

CHINA

Kashmir

R. Indus

TIBET

Karachi

Delhi

SIKKIM

BHUTAN

NEPAL

R. Ganges

Arabian Sea

INDIA

Calcutta

BURMA

Bay of Bengal

SIAM

Bangkok

CEYLON

Colombo

Indian Ocean

MALAYA

Singapore

SUMATRA

Dutch Colonies

British colonies

French colonies

0   1000 km

Amritsar, 1919

In the great dusty square of Amritsar, the holy city of the Sikhs, a crowd had been gathering for hours. Some had come to protest about the arrest of two of their leaders by the British. Others had come just because the day was a holiday.

Then the soldiers came. They blocked the only exit from the enclosed square with armoured cars. Suddenly, without warning, they started firing into the tightly packed mass of unarmed people.

When the soldiers finished shooting, 379 Indians lay dead and 1200 were wounded.

The Amritsar Massacre, as people came to call it, took place on 13th April 1919. General Reginald Dyer ordered the shooting.

Dyer was the British military commander in Amritsar. Three days earlier, Indians in the city had rioted in protest at the arrest of two of their leaders. A mob had beaten up an English woman doctor and set fire to a Christian church. The rioters also burned down two banks and killed their English managers.

Dyer intended to teach the people of Amritsar a lesson – and to show anyone else who might think of rioting against British rule what was likely to happen to them. 'My idea was to make a wide impression', he said later.

Dyer did make a wide impression. But it was not the one he intended. After the killings in Amritsar many Indians saw their British rulers as brutal tyrants. They never trusted them again.

British India

Today, something like one in every six of the world's people live in the sub-continent which was known as British India in the 1920s. They are divided between three separate countries – India, Pakistan and Bangladesh.

These people differ from one another in how they live, what they look like, how well off they are. Language is one example of this variety. The people of the sub-continent speak 15 quite different main languages – as well as more than 1500 less popular ones!

At the time of the Amritsar Massacre the British had ruled India for almost 200 years. They had originally conquered it for one main reason – to make money. And making money continued to be one of their main reasons for being there.

But not the only one. Many British people believed that they had duties in India, too. One was to give its people firm and honest government. Another was to modernise India.

So, in the nineteenth century, the British built dams and irrigation canals to help farmers to increase food production. They built roads and railways to make travel and trade easier. They opened schools and colleges which trained Indians to become doctors, lawyers and teachers.

All these changes helped the British as well as the Indians. They made India an easier and more profitable country to run.

Ruling India brought the British enormous benefits. Indian customers bought millions of pounds' worth of goods from their factories – mile upon mile of cotton cloth from the mills of Lancashire, for example. Indian soldiers fought in their wars – 800,000 of them in the First World War alone.

By the end of the nineteenth century some educated Indians were beginning to think it was time that India was run more for the benefit of the Indians. A political group called the Indian National Congress was set up in the 1880s to try to bring this about.

The Indian National Congress

For years Congress worked to persuade the British to let Indians become partners in running the country. But the Amritsar Massacre helped to change the Congress leaders' attitude. They began working to overthrow the British. 'From now on', said one, 'co–operation in any shape or form with this satanic [devilish] government is sinful.'

The man who spoke these words was Mohandas Gandhi. So far, Congress had been a sort of pressure group of a few thousand rich and well educated men. In the 1920s Gandhi turned it into a mass political movement, with millions of supporters amongst India's poor. Even the smallest villages had Congress branches, run by elected committees. For a few pence a year anyone could join.

Gandhi

Gandhi himself was well educated and came from a rich family. But to show his sympathy for the poor he dressed in simple cotton robes and ate only vegetables and fruit. Indians worshipped him like a saint. They called him Mahatma – the 'Great Spirit'.

Gandhi was particularly concerned about the poorest of the poor, a group that people called the 'untouchables'.

Gandhi and the untouchables

The biggest number of people in Gandhi's India followed the teachings of the Hindu religion. An important part of Hinduism is belief in the 'caste' system. This says that every Hindu is born into a special group in society called a caste.

There are four main castes. The highest is made up of Brahmins, whose ancestors were once priests. The lowest are the Shudra, whose ancestors were peasants.

Untouchables were people outside the caste system. They lived by doing unpleasant jobs that caste Hindus looked upon as unclean – sweeping up rubbish and cleaning out lavatories, for example.

Untouchables got their name because caste Hindus believed that to be touched, or even approached, by one of them was a kind of pollution. In some places untouchables had to shout a warning before walking down a street so that caste Hindus could avoid being touched by their shadows.

Gandhi himself was a caste Hindu. But he fiercely attacked the unjust way in which untouchables were treated. He gave them a new name – the *Harijans*, which meant 'Children of God'.

He persuaded Congress to work to improve their position. He set a

Gandhi, the village and industry

Satyagraha

The Salt March, 1930

personal example, too. He ate with *Harijans*. He took a *Harijan* child into his home. He cleaned out lavatories and did other work considered suitable only for *Harijans*.

In economic affairs Gandhi turned his back on the idea of making people happier by using machines and building factories. He called upon people to follow simple lives in villages, producing themselves all that they needed for food, clothing, shelter. This, he believed, was the way to a more satisfying life.

To set an example, wherever Gandhi was he spent an hour every day spinning cotton yarn to make cloth – *khadi* – for his own clothes.

In 1929 Gandhi helped an English–educated younger man named Jawaharlal Nehru to become the President of Congress. Between them, he believed, they could unite all the people of India behind Congress. Nehru would attract the rich and educated, while Gandhi himself continued to attract the support of the poor.

To win independence for India, Gandhi told his followers to do everything they could to make life difficult for their British rulers. But, he said, they must never use violence.

Violence was evil, said Gandhi. And it was not necessary. There were only a few hundred thousand Britons in India. There were hundreds of millions of Indian peoples. The British could only rule India if the Indian peoples helped them.

Gandhi believed that the Indian peoples could make the British leave by 'civil disobedience' or 'passive resistance' – simply refusing to obey their laws, pay their taxes or buy their goods. Gandhi called this *satyagraha* – an Indian word which means 'soul force'.

Gandhi led many campaigns of civil disobedience in the 1920s and 1930s. The most famous was his 'Salt March' in 1930.

Most of the people of India laboured and sweated for long hours in the fields in blistering heat. Salt in their food was as essential to them as air and water.

Yet British 'salt laws' said that anyone buying salt had to pay a tax which doubled the price. And making your own salt was illegal.

To Gandhi the salt laws symbolised everything that was wrong about British rule in India. They were a tax on the sweat of the Indian poor. To show this to the world, he decided to break them.

In April 1930 Gandhi led thousands of followers on a 380 kilometre march to the sea. On a beach near the city of Bombay he picked up a piece of natural salt. It was a signal for Indians all over the country to break the law. They defied their British rulers by drying out sea water in the sun to make their own salt.

The Salt March was also a signal for other *satyagraha* demonstrations all over India. Sometimes Gandhi's followers demonstrated peacefully, as he wanted them to. At other times there was fighting and people were killed.

When this happened Gandhi did the one thing that he knew would frighten his followers. He fasted. He refused to eat or drink until they were shamed into stopping fighting for fear that he would die.

The spinning wheel

Gandhi photographed with his spinning wheel at a demonstration in Mirzapore Park, Calcutta, June 1925.

A follower of Gandhi explained the importance of spinning.

"Through spinning, Bapu [Gandhi] hoped to instil in us something of his own reverence for manual labour. He wanted us all to do some physical labour, so that we could identify with the workers who earn their bread by the sweat of their brow. He wanted to teach us the dignity of 'bread' labour, as he called it."

In Ved Mehta, *Mahatma Gandhi and His Apostles*, 1977

Nehru explained Gandhi's views about village industry.

"Gandhi had an unrivalled knowledge of the Indian villages and the conditions of life that prevailed there. It was out of that personal experience that he evolved his programme of the spinning wheel and village industry.

If immediate relief was to be given to the vast numbers of the unemployed and the partially employed. . . if the villagers' standards were to be raised, however little. . . if they were to be taught self–reliance instead of waiting helplessly. . . for relief from others, if all this was to be done without much capital, then there seemed no other way. . . the problem of India was one of scarcity of capital and abundance of labour – how to utilise that wasted labour, that manpower that was producing nothing."

J. Nehru, *Mahatma Gandhi*, 1949

1a) Imagine you are an educated Congress leader, like the writer in the first source. Why might you have agreed to follow Gandhi's example by taking up spinning?

b) What difference is there between the explanations of Gandhi's belief in spinning given in the two extracts? Do the two explanations contradict one another?

c) Explain what Nehru meant by saying India's problem was 'scarcity of capital and abundance of labour'.

d) Where do you think that Gandhi's ideas might usefully be followed today?

Round Table Conference, 1931

Gandhi's *satyagraha* campaigns helped to persuade the British to hold meetings with Indian leaders about India's future.

In 1931 Gandhi and others travelled to England for a Round Table Conference with the British Prime Minister. The idea was to find a way of ruling India that would satisfy everybody.

But the Round Table Conference failed, just as earlier meetings had done. Why? Partly because the British were not ready to hand over as much power as the Indians wanted. Partly, also, because different groups of Indians could not agree among themselves.

Hindus and Muslims

The big problem was religion. Most of the people of India belonged to either the Hindu or the Muslim communities. Although in many parts of India the two communities lived peacefully side by side, in others they disliked one another.

So far as the future was concerned, the trouble was that India had a lot more Hindus than Muslims. And many Muslims did not trust the Hindus to treat them fairly once India became self-governing.

The Muslim League

Congress did have some Muslim members, and it claimed to speak for all the peoples of India. But most of its supporters and leaders were Hindus. So as early as 1906 some Muslims had set up a separate Muslim League to look after their interests.

The Government of India Act, 1935

In 1935 the British Parliament passed a law called the Government of India Act. This law said that a new system of government for India must start in 1937.

British India was already divided into areas called provinces. Many of them, like Bengal in the north-east and the Punjab in the north-west, had more people than most countries in Europe. Each had its own provincial government to run its affairs.

In 1937 the British handed over control of these provincial governments to parliaments elected by the people who lived there. For the time being, though, the British themselves kept control of the all-India government with its headquarters in New Delhi.

This meant that the British still controlled both the Indian armed forces and India's relations with other countries. To many people it seemed that the British were still India's real masters.

Even so, most Indian political leaders agreed to help to work the new system. It was a step in the right direction, they decided.

India and the Second World War

The Second World War changed this. In 1939 the British government declared that India was at war with Germany without asking the Indian leaders or people.

The Congress governments in all the provinces immediately resigned in protest. Demonstrations and riots broke out. To quieten the unrest the British put Nehru and other Congress leaders into prison.

Subhas Chandra Bose

One man escaped – Subhas Chandra Bose. Bose had never believed in Gandhi's and Nehru's non-violent methods. To him there was only one way to get the British out of India – to kick them out. He tried to do this by helping their enemies.

By 1942 Bose was in Malaya, which the Japanese had just conquered from the British (see map, page 287). He persuaded Indian soldiers who had been captured while fighting for the British to join his Indian National Army (INA). The INA's aim was to help the Japanese to drive the British out of India.

The Cripps Mission, 1942

Winston Churchill, Britain's wartime Prime Minister, feared that a Japanese invasion of India was now very close. He ordered the release of Nehru and the other Congress leaders. In March 1942 he sent a member of his government, Sir Stafford Cripps, to India.

Cripps' job was to persuade Congress leaders to support the British against the Japanese. In return, he promised that Britain would give India full independence the moment the war ended.

The Quit India Campaign, 1942

Gandhi persuaded the Congress leaders to turn down the offer. He demanded independence now, war or no war. When the British refused he called upon his followers to start the biggest campaign of non-violent protest India had ever seen. He gave them a new slogan to hurl at the British – 'Quit India!'.

The British threw Gandhi and the Congress leaders back into prison. The news turned the Quit India campaign into a rebellion.

Crowds set fire to police stations and post offices. They beat up and killed Indians who worked for the government. They burned down 250 railway stations.

The British used soldiers and aircraft with machine guns against the rebels. By the time they had crushed them, over 1000 people had been killed and another 60,000 put into prison.

The end of the Second World War, 1945

In the next two years British and Indian soldiers slowly drove the Japanese army back from India's frontiers. By 1944 it was clear that the Japanese were going down to defeat.

Bose and his INA went down with them. In August 1945 Japan surrendered. Bose died the same month, killed in a plane crash.

By now the British had set free the Congress leaders they had imprisoned in 1942. But unrest in India was getting worse by the day. The British decided that the business of ruling India was more trouble than it was worth. They began planning to leave.

Jinnah and Pakistan

What followed was a tragedy. Congress, led by Gandhi and Nehru, wanted India to go on being one country when the British left. But the leader of the Muslim League, Mohammed Ali Jinnah, thought differently.

'How can you even dream of Hindu-Muslim unity?', he asked a visiting French woman.

'Everything pulls us apart. We have no inter-marriages. We have not the same calendar. . . . No Hindu will take food from a Muslim. No orthodox Hindu will even touch Hindu food if the shadow of a Hindu of a lower caste has polluted the bowl.'*

*In Eve Curie, *Journey Among Warriors*, 1943

By the time he spoke these words in 1942, Jinnah had persuaded the Muslim League to demand a separate country of its own when the British left. He said that it should be made up of the parts of northern India where most Muslims lived. He called it Pakistan.

Congress and the British were against dividing India like this. India was one country, said Gandhi. What Jinnah was demanding was not division, but vivisection – cutting a living body in two.

Meetings to try to keep India united went on. But the British Viceroy (Governor), Lord Mountbatten, could not find an arrangement that both Congress and the Muslim League would accept.

The Partition of India, 1947

Hindus and Muslims had grown to fear one another. In many places fear turned to hatred. Soon people were killing one another in cities and villages all over India. Mountbatten decided that only the partition of India could stop a bloody civil war.

In April 1947 Mountbatten told the government in Britain that India would have to be divided, as Jinnah was demanding. Sadly, Gandhi and Nehru agreed.

Boundaries were hurriedly drawn up before the killings grew worse. It was a difficult job, especially in the many places where Hindus and Muslims lived as neighbours in the same towns or villages.

Most difficult of all was the position in the Punjab province. Right in the middle of the Punjab, sandwiched between a Muslim majority in the west and a Hindu majority in the east, lived a third religious group, the Sikhs.

The Sikhs wanted to become part of the new India. But any attempt to divide the Punjab fairly between Hindus and Muslims was bound to slice the Sikh homeland in half.

Independence, 1947

On 15th August 1947 British rule in India came to an end. Two new, independent countries were born – India for the Hindus and Pakistan for the Muslims.

It was a bloody birth. Out for revenge for earlier killings, Hindus and Sikhs slaughtered Muslims in the new India, and Muslims slaughtered Hindus and Sikhs in the new Pakistan.

Millions of refugees flooded across the new frontiers. Hindus and Sikhs from Pakistan crowded on to trains and lorries heading for India. Muslims from India fled towards Pakistan.

About a quarter of a million refugees never made it. They were ambushed and killed on the way.

Gandhi, frail and now seventy-eight years old, travelled from place to place trying to stop the killings. He saved many lives. 'A one man boundary force', Mountbatten called him.

The death of Gandhi, 1948

It was Gandhi's last service to India. On 30th January 1948 he was shot dead. His killer was one of his own people, a young Hindu who thought him a traitor for agreeing to let India be divided.

'The light has gone out of our lives and there is darkness everywhere', said Nehru in a radio broadcast to the Indian people. 'Our beloved leader, the father of the nation, is no more.'

India and the Second World War

A cartoon by David Low in a British newspaper, 1942.

ALTERNATIVE

1 a) Name the leaders of the two groups represented by the men in the middle of the picture.

b) How did their ideas about India's future differ?

c) Who is the man on the left of the picture? Why is he going to India?

d) Who does the man on the right represent? What is the cartoonist suggesting about his intentions towards India?

e) Why is the time on the clock shown as five minutes to midnight?

f) Explain the title of the cartoon.

g) Is the cartoon biased towards   1) the man with the briefcase,   2) the men in the centre,   3) the man with the gun? Explain your answer.

2 Test your knowledge about India and Pakistan's steps to independence by writing one or two sentences to explain the meaning and importance of each of the following:

The Amritsar Massacre

Satyagraha

The Salt March

The Cripps Mission

The Muslim League

Congress

Untouchables

The Government of India Act

The Quit India Campaign

The Indian National Army

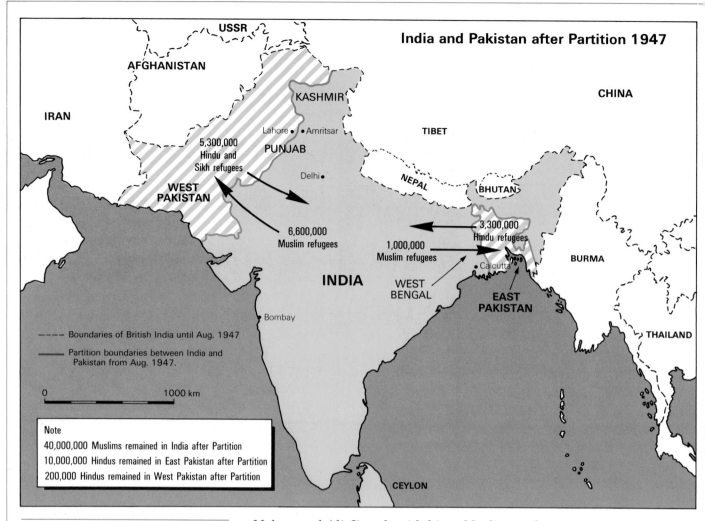

India and Pakistan after Partition 1947

--- Boundaries of British India until Aug. 1947

— Partition boundaries between India and
Pakistan from Aug. 1947.

0   1000 km

Note
40,000,000 Muslims remained in India after Partition
10,000,000 Hindus remained in East Pakistan after Partition
200,000 Hindus remained in West Pakistan after Partition

Partition

Mohammed Ali Jinnah said this to Muslim students in 1941:

> "It is as clear as daylight that we are a nation. And a nation must have
> territory. A nation does not live in the air. It lives on the land, it must
> govern land . . . that is what you want to get."

Jamil-ud-din Ahmad (ed.) *Some recent speeches of Mr Jinnah*, 1943

3 a) What do you understand by the word 'partition', as it is used in this
Unit?

  b) Use the text and the source to explain why   1) Jinnah believed that
     the partition of British India was necessary,   2) Gandhi was opposed
     to the idea.

  c) Give reasons for the refugee movements shown on the map.

  d) What is the distance which separated East from West Pakistan?

  e) Why do you think these two parts of Pakistan in 1947 were so far
     apart?

  f) Of which province of British India was East Pakistan a part before
     1947?

  g) Before 1947 the people of East Bengal grew jute which they sold to
     mills in West Bengal to make into ropes and sacks. The money they
     were paid for the jute was used to buy rice grown by farmers in West
     Bengal. Explain why this stopped after 1947.

  h) How would the changed situation affect   1) the livelihood of a
     farmer in East Bengal,   2) a mill worker in West Bengal?

Violence

Some of the many thousands of victims of the riots in the Punjab which followed the news of India's partition, September 1947.

A British historian recalled what he saw in India in 1947 just before partition was decided upon.

"In April and May, 1947, the author of this book saw not only the actual trouble spots of northern India but also some of those places which were as yet untouched by the disease of communal violence. He listened to men who were not only talking of war but actively preparing for it. He saw armouries of weapons, some stolen, some bought, some manufactured in secret workshops. In one place he even saw light artillery, mortars and a small tank . . .

. . . there was no doubt that partition meant that fewer might die. There was no alternative which could have guaranteed peace . . . Mountbatten made his choice and history will remember him for the speed and decision with which he pursued its fulfilment. He made mistakes . . . but few men could have done better and most would have done worse. India had already entered the valley of the shadow, and her only hope was to be hurried through it as quickly as possible."

Michael Edwardes, *The Last Years of British India*, 1963

4 a) Find the Punjab on the map opposite.

b) Use the text to explain why there was a lot of trouble in the Punjab when India was partitioned in 1947.

c) 'Partitioning India was not a good idea'. Would Michael Edwardes have agreed or disagreed with this view? What arguments does he give in support of his judgement about partition?

d) Does the fact that Edwardes visited India in 1947 make his judgement more likely to be correct? Explain your answer.

Nehru

Jawaharlal Nehru was the first Prime Minister of independent India.

One of his biggest challenges was to hold India together. Not easy, with 360 million people in 1951 belonging to several different races, following many religions and speaking 15 main languages.

The government of India

Nehru also had to decide on a workable system of government. He wanted India to be a parliamentary democracy, ruled by a parliament elected by the people. Again not easy, particularly since four out of every five Indians then could not read.

In 1950 Nehru brought in a new constitution. It was based on the idea tried out in the late 1930s, of running India as a federation.

Federation meant that India was divided into regions. Each had a provincial government to control such matters as health and education. A national government ran the country as a whole.

Both the national and the provincial governments were chosen by parliaments elected by the people. Rich and poor, men and women, caste and *harijan* – all had votes.

India became the world's biggest parliamentary democracy. Forty years after independence it was still united and still ruled by leaders chosen in free elections.

But the right to vote guaranteed nobody the right to eat. Four out of five of India's people were poor villagers, struggling to scrape a bare living from farming.

Nehru's Five Year Plans

In 1951 Nehru introduced the first of a series of Five Year Plans. One of its main aims was to make farming more up-to-date. Under the Plan Nehru's government took electricity to thousands of villages and built many kilometres of new irrigation canals.

By the 1960s India's farmers were beginning to grow more food than ever before. New strains of rice and corn, fertilisers and pesticides, tractors and electric water pumps – all played a part.

Nehru's Five Year Plans gave India more modern industries, too. Gandhi had taught that modern industry was evil. Nehru disagreed. He wanted to move India into the machine age.

By the 1960s India's industries were producing large amounts of steel, cement, chemicals and manufactured goods. It became, for example, the world's largest producer of railway wagons.

Yet most Indians were still very poor. In 1958 the average person's income was £25 a year – well under a tenth of the level in Britain at the time.

Population growth

One reason for the poverty was the growing number of people. Every year in the 1950s the country had 5 million more. By 1969 India's total population was 515 million – and still rising.

These millions of extra mouths ate up all the extra food from the farms. If bad weather made the harvest fail, millions of people faced death from famine. This happened several times in the 1960s.

Kashmir and Pakistan

Another problem was that India never became friendly with Pakistan. One reason for this was Kashmir.

In 1947 Kashmir was one of the largest of the many areas in India ruled by their own princes, under British guidance. In 1947 these 'princely states' had to decide whether to join India or Pakistan. Most joined the state whose lands surrounded them.

But Kashmir has a border with both India and Pakistan. And while most of its people are Muslim, its ruler was Hindu.

In 1948 Kashmir's ruler decided to join India. Many of the people rebelled. They wanted Kashmir to become part of Pakistan. Both India and Pakistan sent in troops to swing the decision their way.

For a time the fighting seemed likely to grow into a full-scale war. But the United Nations arranged a cease-fire. Kashmir was divided down the middle. It continued to cause bad feeling between India and Pakistan, and brought more fighting between them in 1965.

Mrs Gandhi takes over, 1966

Nehru died in 1964, after ruling India for seventeen years. Congress was still India's most popular political party and in 1966 its leaders chose his daughter, Mrs Indira Gandhi (no relation to Mahatma Gandhi), to become Prime Minister.

Mrs Gandhi made more improvements to industry and to farming, building power stations and starting schemes to irrigate more land. She also tried to persuade people to have fewer children.

Some of Mrs Gandhi's changes made the more old-fashioned Congress leaders turn against her. In 1969 the Congress Party split.

In a general election in 1971 Mrs Gandhi's Congress I (for Indira) won most of the seats in Parliament. It nearly wiped out the opposition wing of Congress.

But Mrs Gandhi's opponents claimed that she had behaved dishonestly in the election. They said that, for example, she had used government aircraft and cars to carry her supporters round the country. In 1975 a judge found her guilty and said that she should be disqualified from holding any elected position for five years.

Mrs Gandhi's emergency, 1975–7

Mrs Gandhi replied by declaring a 'state of emergency' and throwing thousands of her opponents into prison. She went on ruling without asking for Parliament's agreement to her actions. She closed down newspapers and magazines which criticised her.

Mrs Gandhi's high-handed behaviour cost her a lot of support. In 1977 she lost an election and resigned. But in 1980 the voters brought her back to power.

Progress in India

By the middle 1980s India had made good progress towards solving some of its old problems. The average Indian was living twice as long as his or her grandfather had. By 1985 food output was increasing faster than the population was growing. In the same year Indian factories turned out enough goods to make India the world's seventh largest industrial nation. Their products ranged from cotton cloth to silicon microchips.

Yet, like any other country, India had problems. One was the old one of how best to hold together its many different peoples.

The death of Mrs Gandhi, 1984

East and West Pakistan

Independent Bangladesh, 1972

Rulers of Pakistan, 1947–85

This problem was highlighted on the morning of 31st October 1984. Two soldiers of Indira Gandhi's own bodyguard shot her dead.

The killers were Sikhs. In the 1980s some Sikhs believed that Mrs Gandhi was out to destroy their religion. They wanted to break away from India and set up their own country.

Indira Gandhi was replaced as India's Prime Minister by her forty-year-old son, Rajiv. The future would show how he would cope with the challenges of ruling this vast and varied land.

Pakistan's problems after independence were similar to India's. In particular, it was short of food and work for its people.

On top of these problems, Pakistan was divided into two parts. One lay to the west of India. The other was 1500 kilometres away, to the east of India. Their people even spoke different languages, Urdu in West Pakistan and Bengali in East Pakistan.

East Pakistan had more people and produced most of the country's wealth. But the government was controlled by leaders from West Pakistan.

The people of East Pakistan felt that they were not getting a fair deal. In 1971 they rebelled. When the Pakistani army moved in to crush the rebellion, millions of refugees fled into India.

Faced with the problem of how to feed all these extra mouths – and perhaps glad of a chance to humiliate Pakistan – Mrs Gandhi sent the Indian army into East Pakistan.

In less than two weeks the Pakistani army there was beaten. The rebels took over the government. East Pakistan now became an independent country called Bangladesh – Land of Bengal.

Pakistan also had problems over government. Jinnah died barely a year after winning independence. Between 1951 and 1958 the country had eleven different Prime Ministers. The politicians quarrelled so much that in 1958 the army took over.

Army leaders like Ayub Khan (President from 1958 to 1969) and Yahya Khan (1969 to 1971) made various improvements. They had irrigation canals dug, to increase the amount of farming land. They had power stations and textile factories built to provide more jobs.

But most Pakistanis were still desperately poor. And the defeat in the 1971 war with India and the loss of East Pakistan made the army and its leaders very unpopular. Yahya Khan had to resign.

Pakistan's new leader was a civilian politician named Zulfikar Ali Bhutto. But Bhutto also made himself unpopular. In 1977 he was accused of cheating in an election and the army overthrew him.

His place was taken by General Mohammad Zia ul-Haq. In 1978 General Zia had Bhutto tried for plotting to murder a political opponent. The following year he had him hanged.

Bhutto's execution summed up the stern nature of General Zia's rule. Zia was a supporter of strict Islamic ideas. He promised the people of Pakistan elections, but not until he had stamped out law-breaking and corruption.

In 1987 the people were still waiting.

Independent India

Two faces of independent India. The first picture shows one of the steelworks built under Nehru's Five Year Plans.

This photograph, of Looni, shows an example of the kind of village the reporter below is describing.

Life in India

Part of a report by a writer in The Guardian, *describing life in an Indian village where he lived for four years in the 1970s.*

"Village life is the backbone of India. While four out of every five Englishmen live in cities, four out of every five Indians are villagers. And even those Indians who have gone to work in the towns still look on the village as home.

Bhagyanagar is just one of half a million villages in India . . .

. . . there is no electric light, no running water. . . A handful of high-caste . . . families possess bicycles, but the harijans have to make do with their own two feet. There is one radio in the village . . .

. . . The land around Bhagyanagar is among the most fertile in India. Farmers can count on two harvests a year and need do little more than plant seed to see crops shoot up before their eyes. But the people have remained poor due to a succession of natural disasters and the sub-division of land into tiny plots with each new generation."

Andrew Bulmer, *Inside the Soul of India*, 13th September 1976

1 a) Why are both steelworks and villages important in India today?

  b) How does Andrew Bulmer explain the fact that the villagers are poor, despite their fertile soil?

  c) What steps have Indian governments taken to deal with the causes of poverty he describes?

WHO WAS WHO?

On the next four pages you will find photographs of leading figures in the history of the twentieth century, together with one or two clues as to who they are. You should be able to identify each of these men and women and call to mind some of the events in which they were involved. As you work through the book, test your knowledge every now and then by writing a few sentences about some of these people. You can also use these pages to help with revision for tests and examinations at the end of your course.

A photograph taken at a peace conference in 1919. The men in top hats are (left to right) the French Prime Minister, the President of the USA and the British Prime Minister (Unit 3).

The founders of the Rome-Berlin Axis. *Il Duce* (left) and *Der Fuehrer* (right), photographed in the late 1930s (Unit 7).

The British Prime Minister who believed that appeasement would prevent war in Europe. Photographed in 1938, returning from an important meeting in Munich (Unit 8).

Allied leaders of the Second World War – Britain's on the left, the USA's in the centre, the USSR's on the right. Photographed at the Yalta Conference in February, 1945 (Unit 9).

Two men who helped to end almost a hundred years of enmity between their countries. The President of France (left) and the Chancellor of West Germany (right) in the 1960s (Units 12 and 13).

The leaders of Egypt (left), India (centre) and Yugoslavia (right), photographed together in 1961 (Units 14, 54 and 69).

The USSR's leader in the 1970s (right) on a visit to West Germany in 1973. Behind him is his host, the man responsible for Ostpolitik (Units 12 and 22).

He won the Russian people's support in 1917 by promising them 'peace, bread and land'. Photographed in the early 1920s (Unit 16).

The American President who introduced the containment policy and gave economic aid to Europe after the Second World War. Photographed in 1945 (Unit 10).

The American President (left) who in 1960 found himself in trouble over a high-flying aeroplane. On the right, his 'brinkmanship'-supporting foreign affairs adviser (Unit 49).

Two 1960s Presidents of the United States. The one on the left told Americans they were facing a 'new frontier'; the one on the right promised them a 'great society' (Unit 32).

In 1955 this man began to change American society by persuading people not to catch buses. Photographed in 1964 with his wife and co-worker, Coretta (Unit 31).

An early 1960s photograph of the leaders of Cuba (left) and the USSR (right). A 1962 disagreement between their countries and the USA grew into a dangerous international crisis (Unit 50).

The founder of the Independent Labour Party, he warned Britain's workers not to let themselves be kicked around. Photographed at an anti-war rally in London in 1915 (Unit 40).

The expert on social security whose 1942 report provided the foundations for Britain's welfare state. Photographed at work in 1944 (Unit 44).

A husband and wife political team in 1951. He was Argentina's President, but many people saw her as the driving force of the partnership (Unit 31).

A South-East Asian nationalist leader in 1954. His armies had just defeated their French colonial rulers at the battle of Dien Bien Phu (Unit 51).

A nationalist leader from the Middle East in 1974. He is seen demanding United Nations' support to win a homeland for his people (Unit 55).

The 'wind of change' blew away British colonial rule in his country in 1957. Prime Minister, then President, in 1964 he was overthrown (Unit 57).

Her husband was imprisoned in 1962 for opposing apartheid. By the 1980s she, too, was an important leader in the same struggle (Unit 60).

Imprisoned by the British in 1952, he was released to become his country's President when it won independence in 1963. A 1977 photograph (Unit 57).

In the 1930s he led the Long March. In the 1960s he launched the Cultural Revolution. Photographed in 1967 (Units 62 and 63).

He liked cats which caught mice, and by the 1980s had reversed many of the policies of the man in the previous picture (Unit 64).

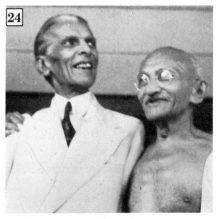

A Muslim (left) who wanted to divide India when the British departed, and a Hindu (right) who wanted it to remain united (Unit 68).

India's Prime Minister, apart from a short break, from 1966 until her death in 1984. She had the same surname as one of the men above, but was not related to him (Unit 69).

Acknowledgements

Short extracts taken from:

Purnell, *History of the Twentieth Century*, BPC Publishing Ltd 1969; Frank Richards, *Old Soldiers Never Die*, Faber and Faber 1933; W.L. Shirer, *The Rise and Fall of the Third Reich*, Secker and Warburg 1960; K. Ludecke, *I Knew Hitler*, Hutchinson 1938; Richard Collier, *Duce*, Collins 1971; Christopher Isherwood, *Mr Norris Changes Trains*, The Hogarth Press 1935; A. Hitler, *Mein Kampf*, 1924 trans. R. Manheim, Sentry Paperbacks 1943; Richard Mayne, *Post War*, Thames and Hudson 1983; Merle Miller, *Plain Speaking*, Coronet Books 1976; Howard Zinn, *A People's History of the United States*, Longman 1980; Joan Hasler, *The Making of Russia*, Longman 1969; M. Florinsky, *The End of the Russian Empire*, Collier 1976; G Vernadsky, *A Source Book of Russian History Vol.3*, Yale University Press 1972; A. Rothstein, *History of the USSR*, Penguin 1950; M. McCauley, *The Russian Revolution and the Soviet State 1917–21: Documents*, Macmillan 1975; Fedor Belov, *The History of a Soviet Collective Farm*, Routledge 1956; Mikhail Sholokhov, *Virgin Soil Upturned*, Putnam 1931; John Scott, *Behind the Urals*, Riverside Press 1942; Eleanor Lipper, *Eleven Years in Soviet Prison Camps*, Hollis and Carter 1951; Wright Miller, *Russians as People*, Phoenix House 1960; D. Wilcox, *Americans*, Delacorte Press 1978; S. Winslow, *Brother Can You Spare A Dime?* Paddington Press 1976; F. L. Allen, *Since Yesterday*, Hamish Hamilton 1940; Irving Bernstein, *The Lean Years*, Houghton-Mifflin 1960; *The Public Papers and Addresses of Franklin D. Roosevelt*, Random House 1938; N.G. Toler and J.R. Aswell, *These Are Our Lives*, N. Carolina University Press 1939; Arthur Schlesinger, *The Coming of the New Deal*, Houghton-Mifflin, 1959; D. Congdon (ed.) *The Thirties*, Simon and Schuster 1962; Frances Perkins, *The Roosevelt I Knew*, Hammond 1947; S. Terkel, *American Dreams Lost and Found*, Hodder and Stoughton 1980; Geoffrey Hodgson, *In Our Time*, Macmillan 1976; R.D. Heffner, *A Documentary History of the United States*, Mentor 1952; F.L Allen, *Only Yesterday*, Pelican 1938; P. Jacobs and S. Landau, *To Serve the Devil*, Vintage Books 1971; James Baldwin, *The Fire Next Time*, Dial 1963; Keesing's Research Report, *Race Relations in the USA*, Charles Scribner 1970; T.H. White, *Breach of Faith: The Fall of Richard Nixon*, Jonathan Cape 1970; Eric Williams, *From Columbus to Castro*, Deutsch 1970; W. Claypole and J. Robottom, *Caribbean Story Book 2*, Longman 1981; F. R. Augier and S Gordon, *Sources of West Indian History*, Longman 1965; C. Stella Davies, *North Country Bred*, Routledge 1963; Walter Greenwood, *There Was a Time*, Penguin 1969; Walter Greenwood, *Love on the Dole*, Jonathan Cape 1933; E. Bakke, *The Unemployed Man*, Nisbet 1933; H.L. Beales and R.S. Lambert, *Memoirs of the Unemployed*, Gollancz 1934; J. Pickard, *Jarrow March*, Allison and Busby 1982; W. Shawn (ed.), *London War Notes 1939–45*, Longman 1972; T. Harrison, *Living Through the Blitz*, Collins 1975; A. Burnet and W. Landels, *The Time of Our Lives*, Elm Tree Books 1981; Liz Curtis, *Nothing But the Same Old Story*, Information on Ireland 1985; D. Rees, *The Age of Containment*, Macmillan 1967; J. Murray Brown (ed.), *Portraits of Power*, Octopus 1979; P. Porter, *Collected Poems*, Oxford University Press 1983; John Terraine, *The Mighty Continent*, Futura 1974; William Manchester, *The Glory and The Dream*, Michael Joseph 1975; S. Hersch, *My Lai 4: A Report on the Massacre*, Random House 1970; Amos Elon, *The Israelis: Founders and Sons*, Weidenfeld and Nicolson 1971; J. Dimbleby, *The Palestinians*, Quartet Books 1979; H. Browne, *Suez and Sinai*, Longman 1971; D. Pryce–Jones, *The Face of Defeat*, Quartet Books 1974; G. Chaliland, *The Palestinian Resistance*, Penguin 1969; D. Lamb, *The Africans*, Methuen 1985; W. Itote, *Mau Mau General*, East African Publishing House 1967; B. Hutmacher, *In Black and White: Voices of Apartheid*, Junction Books 1980; William Hinton, *Fanshen*, Penguin 1966; Jan Myrdal, *Report from a Chinese Village*, Penguin 1967; Edgar Snow, *Red Star Over China*, Gollancz 1938; *Long March : Eye-witness Accounts*, Foreign Language Press 1963; Mao Zedong, *Selected Works*, Foreign Language Press 1963; F. Green, *A Curtain of Ignorance*, Jonathan Cape 1965; D. Bodder, *Peking Diary 1948–9: Year of Revolution*, Fawcett Publications Inc.; L. Chaffin, *The Communist Conquest of China*, Weidenfeld and Nicolson 1967; Chiang Kaishek, *Soviet Russia in China: A Summing Up at Seventy* Harrap 1967; Harrison Salisbury, *To Peking and Beyond*, Arrow Books 1973; Dick Wilson, *Mao: The People's Emperor*, Futura 1979; B. M. Frolic, *Mao's People*, Harvard University Press 1980; F. Butterfield, *China : Alive in a Bitter Sea*, Coronet 1982; Arata Osada *Children of the A-Bomb*, G.P. Putnam's Sons 1959; F. Knebel and C.W. Bailey, *No High Ground*, Harper and Row 1960; H.S. Truman *Memoirs Vol.1*, Doubleday and Co. 1958; W.D. Leahy, *I Was There*, McGraw Hill 1950; L. Giovannitti and F. Freed, *The Decision to Drop the Bomb*, Coward McCann 1965; *The Penguin Book of Japanese Verse*, Penguin 1970; Ved Mehta, *Mahatma Gandhi and His Apostles*, Penguin 1977; J. Nehru, *Mahatma Gandhi*, Asia Publishing House 1949; Eve Curie, *Journey Among Warriors*, Doubleday 1943; Michael Edwardes, *The Last Years of British India* New English Library 1963.

We are grateful to the following for permission to reproduce copyright material:

Atheneum Publishers Inc. for an abridged extract from *Breads of Faith: The Fall of Richard Nixon* by T.H. White; TRO Essex Music Ltd and Ludlow Music Inc. for twelve lines of lyrics from 'End of My Line', words and new music adaption by Woody Guthrie, © 1963 TRO Essex Music Ltd. International Copyright Secured. All Rights Reserved; Chappell Music Ltd and Warner Bros Music for part lyric of 'Brother Can you Spare a Dime?' from *Americana*, music by Jay Gornay, words by E.Y. Harburg, © 1932 (Renewed) Warner Bros Inc. All Rights Reserved; Authors' agents for an abridged extract from *DUCE!* by Richard Collier, © Richard Collier 1971; Economist Newspapers Ltd for extracts from articles by *The Economist*'s Peking correspondent, *The Economist* 4/10/84, and 'Must Japan Slow' by M McCrae *The Economist* 23/2/80; Guardian Newspapers Ltd for article 'Inside the soul of India' by Andrew Bulmer *The Guardian* 13/9/76; Harper and Row Inc. for poem 'Incident' by Comtee Cullen from *Black Voices* 1968; Oxford University Press Ltd for extracts from poem 'Your Attention Please' by Peter Porter from *Collected Poems* © 1983 by Peter Porter; Penguin Books Ltd for poem 'Stars' by Takenaka Iku from *The Penguin Book of Japanese Verse* trans. with an intro. by Geoffrey Bownas and Anthony Thwaite (Penguin Books 1964), Copyright © Geoffrey Bownas and Anthony Thwaite, 1964 pp. 219–20; Syndication International for extract from article by Bev. Gilligan *Woman* Magazine 8/2/86; Times Newspapers Ltd for extracts from article by Peter Gillman *Sunday Times Magazine* 30/73, extract from article *The Times* 30/9/48.